W9-AEO-095

THE UNTOLD STORY

Berry, Me, and Motown

Raynoma Gordy Singleton

With Bryan Brown and Mim Eichler

CB
CONTEMPORARY
BOOKS
CHICAGO

Library of Congress Cataloging-in-Publication Data

Singleton, Raynoma Gordy, 1937–
    Berry, me, and Motown: the untold story / Raynoma Gordy
Singleton.
        p.   cm.
    ISBN 0-8092-4340-7 : $19.95
        1. Singleton, Raynoma Gordy, 1937–   . 2. Sound recording
executives and producers—United States—Biography.   3. Gordy,
Berry.   4. Motown Record Corporation.   I. Title.
ML429.S6A3   1990
782.42166'092—dc20
    [B]   90-32819
                                                                          CIP
                                                                          MN

*This book is dedicated to my children, Cliff Warren Liles, Kerry
Ashby Gordy, William Edward Singleton, Jr., and Rya Noel
Singleton; and to my mother and father, Lucille and Ashby
Mayberry; and to my beloved brother, Stanley "Mike" Ossman.*

Published by Contemporary Books, Inc.
180 North Michigan Avenue, Chicago, Illinois 60601
Manufactured in the United States of America
International Standard Book Number: 0-8092-4340-7

AUTHOR'S NOTE

The conversations presented in this book have been re-created from my memory of events and conversations that took place; they are not intended to represent word-for-word documentations, but they have been written to evoke the real feeling and meaning of what was actually said and I am confident they are faithful to the essence of what was said and to the spirit and mood of the occasions. Likewise, certain names and circumstances have been slightly changed to protect the integrity of every individual who has played a part in this story. All efforts have been made on my part and the part of my cowriters to verify accuracy in spelling and dates and to acknowledge as many people as possible in the scope of the book. To anyone who failed to gain mention, or who was not available for verification of name spelling, the author hereby makes all due apologies.

CONTENTS

ACKNOWLEDGMENTS

With special thanks to my agent, Sherry Robb, who believed in me and breathed life into this timely presentation.

To my brilliant cowriters Bryan Brown, for his sensitivity, perseverance, and precision; and Mim Eichler, for her poetic style, intuition, and creativity.

To Shari Lesser Wenk, the original procurer of this project; Nancy Coffey and Rachel Henderson, who worked untiringly to make this book the best that it could be; and Kathy Willhoite, who put the icing on the cake. My hat's off to Holly George for doing an unbelievable copyediting job and Clare La Plante, my production editor. And thanks, Harvey, for your invaluable assistance.

On the personal side, I'd like to acknowledge my families—the Mayberrys, the Ossmans, the Lileses, the Gordys, and the Singletarys—and my nieces and nephews, Dale, Craig, Stassa, and Albert Warren; Asa, Bruce, and Brian Murray; Shelly and Chris Ossman; Blair Bradfield; and Timothy André Wilson. I love you all.

And a very special "hoorah" to everyone who participated in the phenomenal Motown story.

PROLOGUE
CAN I GET A WITNESS?
1983

As I stepped onto the red-carpeted ramp of the Pasadena Civic Auditorium the night of Motown's twenty-fifth-anniversary celebration, "Motown 25," May 16, 1983, memories overwhelmed me. And what memories they were. Nineteen fifty-eight seemed so long ago, and so much had happened since then.

Simply told, this is a love story. My love for Berry Gordy, my love for the dream we made together, and my eternal love of music. I witnessed one of the greatest triumphs in the history of music recording; I also suffered incredible heartbreak. I experienced the ultimate joy of motherhood, having, together with Berry, given birth to the miracle of Motown. And in the course of twenty-five years, it all faded from my grasp. I was ostracized, terrorized, thrown in jail, pushed to the brink of murder.

It is a harrowing saga, starring a cast of geniuses and fools, heroes and heroines, villains, victims, and casualties. And the hand of fate plays a role as well.

Come on, Ray, you can do it, I said to myself on the way up the ramp. I was already swallowing hard, forcing back the memories and the tears. In my mind I heard Berry's voice: "This gal can do everything!" My senses were flooded with the music of laughter from our first days together, when I would be introduced to a newcomer: "This is Miss Ray, our diamond in the rough. You got a problem, she'll take care of it."

I smiled. Miss Ray, or Mother Motown, they used to call me. And now I could hardly get it together to walk up a damn ramp.

I can't even tell you how many times I'd rehearsed for this trip down memory lane. To say that I'd been having mixed emotions about attending the twenty-fifth-anniversary special would be putting it mildly. I must have changed my dress a hundred times. And as I stood in front of the mirror, checking my appearance for the umpteenth time, I couldn't help but glance at the photograph, taken in 1960, that sat in a silver frame on the bureau. In this now yellowing picture is a young family. A husband and wife and a diapered, smiling baby.

Who was Berry Gordy back then? A human being. Very gifted, also flawed, and very hopeful. And who was that young woman clinging to her husband's side, looking at him and at our son with adoring eyes?

Well, I was many things. Just twenty-three years old, I was living and breathing—sometimes sleeping and eating—all for music, for what would become the Motown sound. I was song-writer, backup vocalist, arranger, involved in every aspect of the business I owned and ran jointly with Berry. I was, according to him, the brains behind the operation, the one with formal musical training. I was mother confessor, troubleshooter, and friend to all the artists who became a part of the family.

Now I was being shown to a seat up in the middle of the balcony. Down below, front row center, sat Mr. Berry Gordy, and beside him, behind him, up on the stage getting ready, was every-body who was anybody. Mary Wells, Martha and the Vandellas, Diana Ross, Smokey Robinson, Marvin Gaye, Stevie Wonder, Mary Wilson. Anna Gaye, Berry's sister and Marvin's ex-wife, who looked as stunningly gorgeous as ever, turned from her seat in the row just ahead of me and gave me a high sign.

I was an outsider looking in, an outcast of the family, stand-ing in the shadows. It was a feeling that I imagined I shared with other family members who were absent—those who weren't invited and those who chose not to attend. We were the men and women who helped build the careers of everyone on that stage; our labors of love had built the house of Motown.

Act after act, star after star, paraded across the stage. Everyone spoke, and everyone paid homage to the King, to Berry. It was his night. Miss Ray was not mentioned. The refrain of Marvin Gaye's "Can I Get a Witness?" came to mind. Who would be my witness?

Suddenly a hush came over the crowd as we watched Marvin walk gracefully to the piano. No matter how well you knew him, the moment Marvin Gaye stepped onto a stage, he was awesome. He sat down at the piano and began to play simple chord changes, soft, moody, almost mystical. I leaned forward in my seat, tapped Anna on the shoulder, and whispered, "How can you live the rest of your life without your man?"

She looked down at Marvin, thinking for a moment, and we both watched as he left the stage and as Berry Gordy strolled up to the microphone, a quiet, controlled, smallish man. Every person in the crowd leapt to his or her feet, the roar drowning out Berry's first words. Anna turned back to me, answering the question I'd asked her with the same one, "How can you live the rest of your life without your man?"

I couldn't answer her at the moment. But out of the outrageous hurricane of memories, in that stunned second, something miraculous happened. As I watched the man who was once my husband, I, the ex-wife and mother of his son and of his fortune, knew what I was going to do, even though it would take me seven more years to truly do it. I was just beginning to see that while a heart can be crushed, a career destroyed, and material wealth depleted, a spirit could not be broken. I would make my peace with fate, or destiny, or the greater power of the universe.

That power, that force, whispered in my ear that night and gave me a plan. I would do it for my parents, my sisters and brothers, my children, my children's children, the millions of people around the world whose lives were touched by the music of Motown. I would do it for history. For myself and by myself. I was going to come out of the shadows and tell my story. As God is my witness, every word of it is true.

CHAPTER 1
DETROIT
1937–1958

I can hear us at home as if it were yesterday. The front porch of my family's house on Blaine Street, a summer's eve in 1947. I was ten years old, a scrappy little thing, dangling my legs off the side, tapping my fingers on the wooden boards of the porch. Brother Tommy is telling ghost stories. His hushed, bloodcurdling voice paints the most gruesome images, and even in that sweltering heat we've got goose bumps all over.

Mama and Daddy are side by side on the porch swing, watching over their brood: eight of us all told, not to mention all the other kids from the neighborhood. As the suspense of Tommy's story builds, you can almost hear our hearts pounding. Then the warm night air becomes thick with the sound of laughter at the end of the tale. Shrieks of delight and surprise. Hooting and hollering. Voices from conversations down the street on other front stoops waft over, hums and honks from the cars that roll on by. If you ask me what really got me started in music, inspired me and filled me, I'd tell you it was these sounds—the music of the family.

Detroit in those days was what I call a big little town. It was all about family—a place of togetherness, familiarity, and safety. So safe in fact that late evenings I'd take the bus home alone from ballet class. The unwritten code of the streets was loyalty and kinship, a protective environment in which a sudden knock at the door meant a welcome visit from Mr. Fuller Brush Man. Or, better yet, the hefty lady from down the block would come on in with her treasure box of Avon products, and my sisters and I would ooh and ah over the magical potions she'd lay out for Mama.

Detroit was a city of romance. The Motor City. Pride and hope and possibility. The automotive industry was booming, cranking

4

out big, shiny dream machines. Employment opportunities were wide and varied. For the black men and women who'd migrated from the South, it was the promised land. It was somewhere to settle down, to build a better future for their kids, a place to shake loose the shackles and fears of the past. I was a romantic child, born of the promise of Detroit, with no cause to believe that my dreams wouldn't come true.

My fearlessness I got from Mama; a pride and a confidence that I could make whatever I wanted of myself, from Daddy. In his eyes I had been blessed with such a multitude of talents that I could do anything and succeed. Daddy taught me to dream. And Mama taught me to be a fighter. Like she had learned to be.

My mother, Lucille, was four foot eleven. No bigger than a minute, pale-skinned with pretty and delicate features, green-eyed Mama was as feisty and strong-willed as a prizefighter. She was born September 23, 1903, in Selma, Alabama, of mixed blood from a French grandmother. When Lucille was only an infant, her mother died, and seven months later her daddy passed away. She was suddenly inherited by an aunt who was just fifteen years old, already a mother to two children, and with four brothers and sisters of her own to look after too. All Mama knew was deprivation—not enough to eat, not enough to keep her clothed, not enough love to prevent her surrogate mother from resenting and beating her.

"Growing up with nothin'," Mama would say to me, pulling my sandy hair back into tight, neat braids, "all I knew was someday my children would never want for anything." And she would sigh a worldly sigh that masked what had been her hardships.

At the age of fifteen, Lucille ran off with a boy, fifteen years old himself, whose name she steadfastly refused ever to divulge. They had two sons, James and Bill. After less than two years, the marriage broke up and the boys became the wards of Mama's in-laws in Chicago. In 1923 she moved from Selma to Niagara Falls, where she met a handsome Filipino named Matt Ossman. By 1936 the Ossmans had moved to Detroit with their six children, Ines, Roslyn, Kathy, Juanita, Tommy, and Mike. In that year Mama and Matt split, and soon she met Ashby Mayberry.

Daddy was tall and dashingly handsome with light-brown skin and full and sensitive features. He had come up to Detroit with professional hopes and plans that didn't exactly include Mama and her ready-made family. But he was the true romantic.

He took one look at Lucille and fell instantly and forever in love with her. For Mama, it was the same thing. The moment she set eyes on this strikingly good-looking and love-filled man, she could barely catch her breath. From that day forward, the two assumed that her six children were theirs together.

The oldest four were all girls and, as Daddy would croon, "all pretty as pictures." The eldest was lovely Ines, quiet, thoughtful, with an eternally subtle smile on her face. Next came Roslyn, the beauty. She had the perfect hourglass figure, buxom and narrow-waisted, and a hauntingly lovely face. Kathy, the attractive intellect, followed Roslyn. Bright and ambitious, she tended to be a bit of a highbrow. The rest of us privately poked fun at her haughtiness, yet we also found ourselves vying for her approval.

The fourth child was Juanita, a wild, spunky, gorgeous girl with long, straight hair that reached down to her knees. Like Mama, she was infinitely loving and had a ready ear or a supportive shoulder for anyone else's troubles. Tommy was darker than the four older girls, kinky-haired, and even as a teenager had the physique that could start a cat fight. He was athletic and organized, not very academically inclined but a notorious planner. If that boy wanted something, by God, he'd find a way to get it.

The sixth child and second son of the Ossman lineage was Mike, favorite of every woman in his life, the consummate gentleman. Mike looked pure Filipino, with heart-melting movie-star eyes and a sheer brilliance in everything he did. He had an artist's vision when it came to drawing or painting, an innate musical talent, a knack for numbers and science, all together with a love of hard work. Mike was my mentor and perhaps the only true soul mate of my life.

"Ashby loved them fiercely, all of them," Mama would say often, matter-of-factly. They became as much a part of him as I was, when I was born on March 8, 1937, to Mr. and Mrs. Mayberry. In time, baby Alice came along. Alice, though darker in coloring, was tiny in stature like me. Looking at our sensual features, everyone could tell we were our father's daughters. But where I was full of crazy schemes, Alice grew up to be the careful conservative. Alice looked at me and my aspirations with a mix of awe and disdain.

Mama, too, as much as she adored me, never quite understood the source of my intensity or the faraway look in my eyes. "What are you thinking about now?" she'd ask, tucking me into bed at night, not even expecting an answer.

For the first ten years of my life we lived in the ghetto at the corner of Mullett and Russell, in an area called Black Bottom. Folks around were very poor, but I imagined my family as displaced royalty, just biding our time in Black Bottom until renovations on our palace were completed. Mama was a queen who ruled over her subjects with a firm, just, and loving hand. And Daddy no doubt was the chivalrous, if not henpecked, knight.

We had good reason to have high hopes for Daddy. I must have been seven or eight the time the whole family gathered around the dinner table in a nervous silence while he studied for a test he'd be taking the next day.

Kathy, with her usual concern for social status, leaned over to me. "If Daddy gets this job, he'll be one of the very first black motormen in Detroit."

"Hear that, Alice?" I whispered in her ear, "Daddy's going to drive the streetcar."

Sure enough. Next day he came home, grinning from ear to ear, not saying a word, and we knew. Mama was laughing, heaping extra mounds of mashed potatoes on our plates, and we couldn't sit still in our seats. We danced and sang out and jumped all over him.

Every night for the following years as Daddy navigated the electric streetcar along a route that miraculously stopped right on our corner, I led Alice down to the track to wait for him. We'd catch a glimpse of him, wave and shout, and as the streetcar clattered to a halt, we'd hop up on it and ride with him to the end of the line. We'd sit up there with Daddy, and the sounds of the city would play like a resounding overture before a great movie.

Then in early 1947 we got some even more exciting news.

"Your father's going to work for Cadillac Motors. And . . ." Mama announced, "we are moving to Blaine Street."

Cadillac Motors! Blaine Street! Visions of our glamorous palace danced before my eyes. I imagined Daddy sitting at a massive desk at the helm of Cadillac corporate headquarters with a throng of secretaries and peons gathered around him.

A week later I stood heartsick in front of the new house at 1700 Blaine Street. *Some* palace, I thought, stomping up the steps to what was really a very charming three-bedroom house in a lovely neighborhood. "What's the matter with you?" twelve-year-old Mike asked me, knowing full well that as usual I'd set my sights a little high. But as far as I could tell, Daddy was already an executive at Cadillac. Every day he would leave for work with his briefcase, strutting out the door immaculately attired. His graceful walk and kind, intelligent face commanded instant respect.

Though his official job at Cadillac was as a janitor, all the bona fide executives would defer to him, calling him *Mister* Mayberry. Many times he was offered the opportunity to move up to foreman or supervisor, but he declined. He watched the foremen in the factory, under life-threatening stress, cracking a whip over the workers as if they were galley slaves. These men in higher positions had to make their quotas, at the expense of the underlings, or suffer heart attacks and humiliation. And Daddy said, "No, thanks, I don't want that."

He embellished his janitorial job, made it into an art form almost, and stayed happy and robust for twenty years until he retired. Until that day, every bigwig in the company would step aside each and every time he came through, tipping their hats to him, saying "Good morning, Mister Mayberry."

At home he maintained the same quiet dignity, dressing elegantly even on his days off. Any boyfriend the girls brought home swallowed and gulped in his presence, sensing that this man was hard to please. They were right. After each stammering suitor had left our house, Daddy's comment was typically, "Where did you find that raggedy bum?"

Our move out of the ghetto to Blaine Street distinguished us as the first black family in an all-white neighborhood. An all-white *Jewish* neighborhood. At first no one seemed to know what to make of us. Some of the Jewish kids later admitted to thinking we were from another country. Their habits and customs were equally foreign to us. But as time went on, the ethnic gaps were bridged by friendships that would last lifetimes. Pretty soon, Mama was trading cornbread recipes with the neighbor ladies for ways to cook matzo balls.

The situation at school, however, gave me cause for culture shock. I had just completed fifth grade when we moved to Blaine Street. But upon enrolling in the new school, I was placed in the third grade.

"What do you mean the third grade?" Daddy had asked, alarmed, "I'm going to call them and—"

"Ashby, lower your voice. I'll get this straightened out." As usual, Mama was going to take matters into her own hands.

"I know what happened, Mama. It's because I'm such a

shrimp. They didn't believe that I'm eleven already!" I was incredibly small for my age. I was indignant.

"You're only ten, Raynoma. And I hope you didn't talk back to the principal in that tone of voice." Mama's tone of voice was indignant too. She was about as headstrong as they came.

I was only partially correct. The decision to move me back to third grade was partly because of my size but also because of the school's high academic level. The sixth graders were already doing algebra. In my old school I'd been an all-A student, and I'd actually skipped a grade. But I had no idea how to do algebra. Once my age was accepted and I'd put in some hard work, though, I moved up to the higher grade, but at my new school I would never be more than an average student. As far as regular schoolwork was concerned, that is.

In extracurricular activities, I was determined to become much better than average. A recreational center in the Blaine Street area offered classes in gymnastics, ballet, tap, and jazz dance. Three nights a week I took classical ballet under the tutelage of the very serious Miss Fitzgerald. Twice a year she staged lavish pageants, and I was thrilled about the entire process: the rigorous discipline of rehearsals, those butterfly-in-the-stomach moments before the curtain rose, the smell of stage makeup, the feel of the starched netting of our costumes. And more than anything, I loved the romantic orchestral music of the ballet, the wondrous strains of Tchaikovsky and Stravinsky.

By the time I was six years old, my parents had recognized that I had an innate musical ability. They'd bought me a piano, a beautiful little mahogany spinet with a mirror on it. It was my most prized possession and would remain so, well into the Motown years. It became, in a sense, my dearest friend; in the reflection of its small mirror I saw myself go from child to adolescent to adult. As I grew, so did the music that we made together. From the first song I had learned, "Peg o' My Heart," to Mozart and Debussy, to the songs and arrangements I'd create on it through the years, that piano heard it all.

As soon as they gave it to me, I had started taking lessons, and within a year I was playing for our church, St. James Baptist, for weddings, funerals, holiday functions. When we moved to Blaine Street, I dispensed with the lessons. It was my decision, partly because of the time I spent studying dance and partly because, as I had told my piano teacher, "You don't know what you're talking about." We had argued over my interpretation of my favorite piece, "Clair de Lune." Having a natural gift, and wanting to go out and have fun like any other ten-year-old, made it difficult for me to take instruction.

"Besides," I said at one family dinner early in our Blaine Street residence, "if I'm going to be writing my own music one day, how can somebody else tell me how to play it?"

"You are impossible," Mama scolded with a smile she couldn't hide.

The dinner table in our household was a forum where we expressed our opinions on whatever subject arose. This night, it looked like the subject of my numerous artistic pursuits was on the agenda.

Daddy started in. "So what's it going to be, Raynoma? Movie star? Singer? Dancer?"

"Not a chance," Mike tried to answer for me. "She's going to be a world-famous piano player—and accompany me when I sing."

"Or me," little Alice piped up.

Mama rolled her eyes at Daddy, "Ashby, don't encourage these damn fool ideas."

"Yeah," Tommy, the chronic planner, echoed, "Raynoma should be a businesswoman. Something practical."

Ines, Roslyn, and Juanita, who would all marry young, insisted in unison that when I came of age I should work toward finding an eligible man, settle down, and become a mother.

I grimaced.

Kathy, who was already earning her college degree and mingling with a crowd of upwardly mobile young black college students, proclaimed, "Mama's right. Show business is full of riffraff. You'd best concentrate on your schoolwork. Who knows? The way you love to argue, you could become a lawyer one day."

"Well, maybe . . . ," I'd said, with an undaunted thrust of my chin, "I'll do it all." I grinned knowingly at my true believer, Mike, kicking him under the table as he winked back at me.

I did want to do it all—except for the part about settling down and having children. Not that I wasn't spending hours imagining all the wonderful boyfriends who'd one day be buzzing around. It was no secret that I had a stack of *True Romance* magazines stashed in my bedroom. I had my artistic aspirations, but I also wove intricate fantasies of swashbuckling, debonair suitors who would sweep me off my feet and carry me away. By the time I was a teenager, I was a Saturday matinee junkie, and for twenty-five cents apiece Alice and I could afford to walk over to the Astor Theater and buy movie tickets to see a feature. I was an open receptacle for the magic of the big screen, for the soundtrack music, the images and words and sounds. I was going to dance with my man one day like Ginger danced with Fred. We'd be as passionate as Bogie and Bacall. We'd have a love as devoted as Jimmy Stewart and Donna Reed's in *It's a Wonderful Life.*

It *was* a wonderful life. In the early years of the 1950s, as I came of age, a grand decade was under way. Folks in Detroit were looking good and feeling great. Sensational show-biz movies debuted in those years, from *All About Eve* and *Sunset Boulevard* to *Singin' in the Rain.* My family and some of the other families on the block found ourselves gathered around our first televisions, enthralled by "The Ed Sullivan Show," "Kukla, Fran and Ollie," "Superman," and of course "The Little Rascals."

But it was music that was my heartbeat, and the music of my generation, especially in Detroit, was that wonderful mélange called rhythm & blues. Early on there were Clyde McPhatter and the Drifters. Then came the Five Satins with "In the Still of the Night," "Talk to Me" by Little Willie John, and "Come Go with Me" by the Del-Vikings. Hank Ballard and the Midnighters got all of us heaving with sighs to their suggestive titles—"Work with Me, Annie," "Annie Had a Baby," and "Annie's Aunt Fanny." I was a pushover for the mid-fifties hit "Sincerely," which was done by the Moonglows.

On the flip side of my album of early musical influences was the whole spectrum of pop, jazz, Broadway musicals, and of course the immortal composers of classical music. In high school I was introduced to Rachmaninoff and Chopin; I joined a harp ensemble that performed arrangements of Jerome Kern's "Just the Way You Look Tonight" and "All the Things You Are." Naturally, as a true daughter of mainstream American culture, I followed the hit parade, danced away to Connie Francis tunes, Frankie Laine's "Mule Train," "Cry" by Johnnie Ray, and the 1951 Dinah Washington song "Harbor Lights," which the Platters would redo almost ten years later. I would forever be hard pressed to find a recording that rivaled Mario Lanza's "Be My Love"—or anything else he ever sang. And no songs ever brought tears to my eyes the way the great standards of George Gershwin, Irving Berlin, and especially Cole Porter did then—and do now.

"You want to do *what*, Raynoma?" Mama said about my desire to go downtown to Cass Technical High School and study music. Central High was the neighborhood school that she expected me to attend.

"Have you lost your mind, child?" she asked as she sat paying the monthly bills, a responsibility that was strictly hers. It was a running family joke that the one time Daddy had ever signed a check the bank had called confused over a signature they'd never seen before. Putting the bookkeeping aside, Mama sighed, "You better go and learn some typing or something so you can get yourself a job."

I whirled in pirouette fashion, trying to contain my frustration. At fifteen I was still minuscule, but the years of ballet had given me a strong dancer's body. I was in a fighter's stance. "But Mama!"

"No *buts*, honey. I know how much you want to do this, but Cass has very difficult entrance tests. It's just not a good idea."

I looked at Mama and thought how much she always tried to give us what we wanted. Always asking, "Did you have enough?" "Is there anything I can do for you?" Just that week she had started some mysterious project down in the basement that was to be a big surprise for all of us kids. I couldn't continue to stand there and argue with her. I had another plan.

On the first day of high school I trotted off to Central; on the second day I took the bus over to Cass and enrolled myself, passing the musical aptitude test with flying colors. It was about a month before Mama knew about it, and by then it was too late. She was so impressed I'd been accepted that she forgave me.

In order to graduate from Cass, a student had to have musical expertise in eight areas. Each of us was required to play a wind instrument, a string instrument, the piano, and an elective instrument. We had to participate in choir, the band, the orchestra, and at least one other ensemble. There were intensive mandatory courses in theory, composition, harmony, and arrangement. My main instrument was the flute, and I also learned trombone, cello, bass, and piccolo. I played the viola in the Cass Symphonic Orchestra. I chose the harp, a challenging yet exquisite instrument, as my elective and performed in the harp ensemble. Of course there was the piano, upon which all the other instruments were based. By the time I left Cass Technical High School, my understanding of music theory made it possible for me to pick up almost any instrument and play. And the discipline that came most easily to me was arrangement: I knew instinctively how different sounds blended together; how to achieve all different kinds of feelings just by alternating an instrumental voice; how to select the instrument that spoke most beautifully and clearly for the particular piece.

"I see that you've studied some arrangement before," one teacher surmised.

"No, ma'am," I told her. My facility for music came from something I was only beginning to realize about myself, something that I wasn't yet ready to articulate. It was just a feeling in my bones.

When I was sixteen, Mama unveiled her surprise in the basement. Impossible though it may seem, all that time she had prevented us from sneaking even one glimpse of the project.

Tommy, Mike, Alice, and I were speechless.

With her own hands Mama had designed and constructed a teenage pleasure palace. There was a gray leather couch and matching chairs, a TV, a record player, and a fireplace. She had painted the walls a deep red and the floor a warm blue. All around the room Mama had installed red and blue fluorescent lights. But the *pièce de résistance* was the bar built from scratch. It was a long L-shaped bar lined with red leather, dotted with chrome studs to give it a quilted look. We knew she was skilled at carpentry, yet this was truly a work of art. The ambience was perfected by matching red vinyl barstools, mirrors behind the bar, and a big round lantern hanging over it like a glowing full moon. It had lettering that read THE BAR IS OPEN.

It most certainly was. Every Friday we had our friends over for parties.

"Can I pour you a drink?" fun-loving Tommy would venture, posing behind the bar.

"Why, yes," I'd reply. And sipping my beverage slowly, trying to be ever so sophisticated, I'd say, "This Kool-Aid has a marvelous bouquet. Wherever did you find it?" And the hors d'oeuvres— potato chips—were tasty too.

"Oh, Paul," I'd gesture to my boyfriend, the swellest guy I could imagine. "Come meet my brother Tommy." Oh, I was madly in love, or so I thought, with the very outrageous Paul Humphrey, a gifted drummer. Paul drove a motorcycle like a maniac, wore leather, a head rag, and a bandanna tied tightly around each thigh.

Every time he paid a visit, he'd roar down the streets on his bike, stop one block away, remove all paraphernalia, and walk shyly up to my house. "How do you do, Mr. Mayberry?"

Although I found out later that Paul was a rowdy sort, at our parties the mere thought of beer or any kind of alcohol was ridiculous. Maybe other kids outside our circle were into that, but not us and our friends. We had only one activity in mind—dancing. We'd play our 78s, turn the red and blue lights low, and move to the music in the dark.

Mama knew exactly what she was doing: by fixing up the basement she was keeping us off the streets. I thought we were being terribly risqué with our dancing. Later, given what teenagers got into during the decades that followed, I'd look back at nights spent down in the basement with a yearning for the innocence and sheer fun of it all.

There was also some very serious work going on downstairs. I had started writing songs when I was twelve years old and had begun making rustic recordings on a Webcore Wire machine that Mama and Daddy bought for us. The Webcore was a very primitive 78 rpm disc-cutting recorder that operated along the old Edison cylinder principles. As you played music into the machine, a needle cut grooves into a piece of vinyl. In those days very few people, especially among our peers, owned equipment. So we were mighty proud of that Webcore, regardless of its simplicity.

"Well?" Mike asked Alice and me, as we finished setting up our basement recording studio. My brother and I were more dedicated to music-making than Alice was. But she had a sweet voice and was a quick study at dance steps. I was going to teach her some of my songs and keep Mike close at hand for artistic direction.

"I think we're going to make some hit songs," I said, taking charge as usual. "That is, if Alice can remember the words." I tweaked my sister's cheek affectionately.

We had high expectations. With Mike serving as engineer, we cut one of my doo-woppish tunes with Alice and I singing a cappella and sent it off to RCA Victor in New York.

I ripped open the reply envelope. "We received your platter, but at this time . . .," my very first letter of rejection began. No matter. We continued to rehearse my songs, making up little dance routines for each one, and the musical entity "Alice and Ray" was born. Stardom, I was convinced, was just around the corner for us.

I soon graduated from Cass, and the future spread out ahead of me full of options. And, if those *True Romance* magazines could be believed, my prince was somewhere out there waiting for me. Which was exactly what my sister Roslyn said one day. She was working at the City-County Building downtown and had spotted a young guy she wanted me to meet.

"Ray, just meet him. He is so intelligent, you can bet he's going somewhere. Dresses nice and looks good." Roslyn insisted, "You'll like him."

"That's not the problem," I said. Roslyn was such a knockout with her voluptuous figure and Lena Horne face. Me they were calling Punella. I must have weighed all of sixty pounds, no more, all straight up and down, as if a big burst of wind could blow me away. I pouted, "You can't bring someone home to meet me after he's looked at you."

"I don't know," she said with a prophetic expression in her eyes. "I think he'll like you."

Well, he did like me. So much so that he swore up and down even Sophia Loren couldn't hold a candle to my beauty. And for me, Charles Liles was everything that Roslyn had promised. What's more, I soon discovered that he played alto, baritone, and tenor sax. I had a weakness for musicians.

Charles thought I walked on water. "Your eyes, your mouth, your hair . . .," he'd crow like a proud rooster. He was also a number-one fan of Alice and Ray, going so far as to become our manager. The first thing he did was to have official contracts drawn up for us. Even though we nailed exactly zero gigs during his tenure, we loved the look of those contracts. But after dating less than a year, we had something other than Alice and Ray's singing career to worry about. I was pregnant.

All my older sisters, Tommy, and Alice urged me to pick a wedding day. Only Mike pulled me aside and asked in a low tone, "Do you love him?"

I liked Charles very much; the whole family did. But I heard myself stutter, "S-s-sure. We're in love," as I looked wistfully at my stack of *True Romance*s.

Poor Charles knew as little about the realities of love and marriage as I. After a small ceremony at Mama and Daddy's, the two of us left to spend a honeymoon night at his Mama's. I turned to say good-bye to Alice, only to find her with her overnight bag on her shoulder. Nothing would keep my little sister from wanting to be with me.

"That's OK," Charles shrugged, "I know how close you two are." Within weeks she moved in with us at my mother-in-law's. We weren't starting out in the most conventional way.

In December of 1955 we had a son, Cliff. Though Charles and I were in love with our baby, we hadn't been having an easy time. We eventually left his mom's for our own place on Canfield Street— a brand-new, two-bedroom apartment on the east side of Detroit. Charles had stopped pursuing his music, quit school, and gone to work for Pontiac Motors. He received subsistence pay from the air force that was really more than adequate, but he felt terribly pressured by the impending costs of raising a family.

And with my whole being caught up in the creative process of having a baby, I neglected my dreams. I listened almost forlornly to the soft up-tempo music drifting from the windows of the couple next door. Whoever is writing that music, I thought, is pretty damn talented. It was a departure from R&B, more of a pop sound, with a Four Freshmen or Lettermen feel. When I finally introduced myself to the man next door, I complimented him on the music. He responded, "Thanks, nice to meet you. Name's William Stevenson. But you can call me Mickey."

As it turned out, he had written the music that I had heard and I remember thinking, This is someone who is bound to go far. I don't recall imagining that our lives and careers would ever intersect in dramatic circumstances—which they would, in the disarming, mystifying way that fate works.

As fate, or other extenuating circumstances would have it, Charles and I came to an impasse. Where was romance? Where was that explosive, electrifying passion that was supposed to happen between a man and a woman? The demands of fatherhood frustrated him, and he came home from work exhausted, argumentative, mad at the world. And raising Cliff was a full-time job for me. Really still children ourselves, we were together two years before we separated.

Although Charles and I weren't legally divorced, he agreed to help out with alimony of ten dollars a week. Unfortunately, the payments never began. When I depleted our savings account by putting down a first month's rent and security deposit on a one-bedroom apartment a block away from my family, Cliff and I were truly on our own. With a huge sense of uncertainty about the future, I moved into our new place at 2040 Blaine Street, one of many addresses that later would make Motown history. I was twenty years old and feeling a lot less dreamy than the child who'd boasted she was going to do it all.

"Listen, Alice, we're good and my songs are great," I announced one afternoon. We were sitting on the piano bench, going over a harmony. We looked at each other in the piano's mirror. I could see Alice's wheels turning: Oh no, what's Ray got up her sleeve? It was time to get Alice and Ray happening. Alice was still in high school, multitalented, very smart, turning heads, and already set on achieving some kind of success in the world. She knew no matter how crazy my scheme, sooner or later I'd talk her into tagging along.

For months we'd been practicing, every afternoon, my growing body of songs, and I'd just decided we were ready to hit the big time. "Alice and Ray are going to start doing the clubs," I told her in no uncertain terms.

"We are? Clubs?" Alice gulped. We'd already done shows for school pageants and parties, familiar arenas where friends and family were present. "Wow, do you really think we're ready?"

"Well," I said, smiling my fearless smile, "we'll see, won't we?"

Not many weeks later, on a Monday night, we were standing breathlessly backstage at the Twenty Grand, one of Detroit's most popular nightclubs. It was very plush—wood beams, thick red-velvet cushions, and large antique mirrors everywhere—with a comfortably dark and intimate ambience. It regularly featured big-name R&B entertainers who came to town: Sam Cooke, Ruth Brown, the Drifters, the Coasters. But on Mondays the Twenty Grand sponsored talent night, when anyone could get up and perform along with the house band. The act receiving the most applause at the end of the night won.

Alice and Ray had prepared arduously for this debut and were about to blow everyone away—or so I hoped. We chose to do a couple of doo-wop tunes I'd written that had fairly simple chord structures, "Mambo Baby" and "It's Christmas Time Again." I wasn't so sure the latter would work, since it was actually spring by then.

"Don't be nervous, Alice," I whispered, picking a thread off her costume. After we'd spent hours applying pearl-white polish, she was biting her fingernails. Backstage we both stretched up on

tiptoes to a high mirror, inspecting our makeup job. Hmm. Not
bad. Just a touch of pale lipstick and a little eyebrow pencil and we
liked what we saw.

We'd searched high and low to find a suitable wardrobe until
we struck gold downtown at Lerner's. We'd bought two of the same
dresses: knee-length, tight-fitting, sleeveless sheaths in black-and-
white checks. We had climbed into three-inch-heeled black suede
pumps and made sure our hairdos looked alike. I'd begun bleach-
ing my short hair very blond; Alice's was an ebony black. In our
black-and-white motif, we cut quite the picture of sophistication
and style, I thought.

There were six acts that night: Moonglow-type vocal groups
and a couple of guys trying to emulate Little Willie John by acting
slick. There were a couple of impressive singers, though. Onstage
at last, worrying that our sweet and young sound would be out-
done, I really punched up my bump-and-grind, much to Alice's
chagrin. "You didn't tell me you were going to do that!" she said
after we ran offstage.

"Sssh, Alice. They're going to judge now." The acts over,
Winehead Willie, the emcee, asked the patrons to applaud their
favorite. I heard a strong round of clapping for the guy I thought
would win. And then Willie called out, "Alice and Ray!" Like
magic, the house broke out in thunderous applause. We'd won the
contest, and we couldn't believe it.

I was so giddy that I didn't listen very carefully when Winehead came up after the show and mentioned something about a
guy he knew who was trying to get some acts happening—managing some groups, that sort of thing. Very confident after such a
smashing debut, I called the guy the next day and set up our very
first audition with a real professional in the music business. Nothing would stop us now.

It was the biggest, most brilliant, gold Cadillac I had ever seen
in my life. Alice and I stopped short. Her eyes got big; I bit my lip.

"Now tell me, again, how he sounded on the phone," Alice
demanded, taking hold of my elbow. We had paused, just outside
his house, to gaze at the sparkling automobile. In minutes we
would be late for our audition.

"I told him we won the contest over at the Twenty Grand and
that Winehead Willie suggested we call him." Shrugging impatiently, I said, "C'mon Alice." Still, looking at that gold Cadillac,

I was beginning to lose my cool. Wow, I thought, a show business guy who's rich too. . . . Now I wasn't so calm about the impending audition.

"No, no, I remember that part. Tell me what *he* said again." Alice wasn't moving a muscle.

"He said, 'Fine—come and audition.' He asked me, 'What do you do?' and I said, 'We sing and write songs.' " I rolled my eyes. It was the fourth or fifth time I'd repeated the conversation to her. All he'd said then, in the most casual of tones was, "OK, why don't you come by tomorrow and we'll see what you've got."

Alice and I stuck up our chins and stepped proudly up the sidewalk, in spite of the gold gleaming car. After all, we'd already won first prize at the Twenty Grand. We sang great, my songs weren't bad, and at least my physical enthusiasm had been noticed. C'mon hips, I said to myself, wishing as always that I'd been given curvier dimensions, Don't fail me now.

The front door was wide open and we could hear the vague harmonies of a singing group. Peeking through the open door into the foyer, and beyond it into the living room, we saw a group of five guys rehearsing together.

"Hello?" Alice called out meekly.

"Hello!" I added in what I hoped was an assertive voice.

No answer. We turned to each other, breathed deeply, and walked on in.

The room was swirling with their voices. I could feel my heart beating fast. And with a wash of exhilaration, I had a spooky feeling that something enormous was about to happen. I felt eight years old, a child full of wonder, in the presence of living, breathing music being born right in front of my eyes.

Abruptly, the singing stopped and five heads whipped around at us.

"Hello," I said, trying to be as nonchalant as I'd been on the telephone, "we have an audition."

"Oh," one of the men said. The five guys looked at each other and then back at us.

Alice and I exchanged bemused looks.

"Wait right here," one of the younger guys said warmly and walked out of the room.

The first thing I saw of Berry Gordy, when he entered the living room moments later, was his shirt. I couldn't believe my eyes. It was an ugly brown-striped shirt with both elbows worn completely through. He had one shirttail stuck into his trousers while the other hung out carelessly.

And then there was the almost laughable state of his hair. I could tell he was trying to get it into one of those processed 'dos the black guys were wearing in those days. This was usually done by straightening out kinky hair with a type of lye and combing it back in smooth, easy waves. This 'do wasn't happening on him, though, especially on the sides, where the edges had reverted to an Uncle Remus–type nap.

Alice shot me a look that read, This guy is a raggedy bum with a bad hairdo. But I was enchanted.

"I'm Berry Gordy," he said. His voice was foggy; he spoke with an unusual rhythm.

"You must be Ray and . . . Alice, is it?" He was incredibly cool. We nodded in response.

An older man, at least sixty, tall, thinnish, and balding, entered the room and sat with Berry on the couch. Berry wasn't saying anything, just leaning back impassively, scrutinizing us up and down, with signs of neither interest nor boredom. The old man, thank God, smiled big and wide, looking at Alice and me.

"OK," Berry said, "let me see what you can do."

We dove into a number, performing in the Twenty Grand style, as I took my wild, hip-shaking routine to never-before-experienced heights of energy. The more I pushed, the redder Alice's face turned and the more impenetrable Berry's expression became.

So we launched into a second song, and I stepped up the bump-and-grind. All the while, I stole glances over at Berry, dying for some reaction. None. On the other hand, the old man was tapping his foot, snapping his fingers, saying "Yeah." The attention of both men, I noted, was tending to wander toward my contest-winning hip area. I threw in an extra thrust of the behind, which got a shout, at least from the older man. It also got a shocked look from poor Alice. Thus encouraged, I did it again, and again once more.

Still nothing from the immovable Mr. Gordy. What is it with this guy? I wondered. I'm all up in his face, twitching, shaking, jiving, and singing my little heart out, and he hasn't so much as blinked an eye.

Undaunted, I signaled to Alice to do a third song, the Christmas tune, wishing on a prayer that if anything could melt the iceman it would be this touching yuletide ballad. We made our big finish, our arms extended like Judy Garland at Carnegie Hall. As all motion ceased and our voices trailed off, an oppressive silence filled the room.

I looked over at the raggedy bum with the bad hairdo, whose mouth didn't want to melt butter, and he was not impressed. I was ready to disappear through an imaginary hole in the floor, when I saw the older man grinning from ear to ear. He could barely sit still. "You girls was great!"

But Berry didn't say a word.

At long last, after what felt like a lifetime, Berry scratched his chin, cocked his head at us, and asked, "Well, what else can you do?"

"Oh!" I jumped, "I . . . I write songs, I write music. I do lead sheets, whatever. I do anything. Play the piano. . . ." I went through my litany of accomplishments until finally, praise the Lord, I saw his eyebrows raise and a tiny glimmer of interest pass over his face. He came very close to me and his eyes searched mine.

"OK, I tell you what, I like you. You stick around and we'll see if we can work something out." Then he asked, "Can you come back tomorrow?"

"Oh yeah," I said, as cool as a breeze on Lake Louise. Very businesslike, I added, "Definitely." Definitely *me*, that was. I knew Alice would be in school—a minor detail to be dealt with later. In the meantime, I felt like swinging my sister around the room, hopping up and down, shouting hallelujah.

To make the afternoon perfect, the older man offered to drive us home so we wouldn't have to take the bus. It was during that carpet ride that we found out he was actually Berry's father, Berry Gordy, Sr. "But you can call me Pops, like everybody that knows me," he said.

Pops talked on in his warm, gentle way, asking us polite questions about our act and the songs we sang. From where I sat in the backseat, it appeared that he was especially interested in Alice, who sat up front next to him. He turned his head frequently to look at her, every time he said something. "Love those outfits," Pops chuckled.

Alice, too, was happy to be chatting away. I was quiet, though, as my thoughts lingered on the afternoon's events. Going over every detail, I tried to savor it, to re-create the glorious sound of the music. I thought about the fantastic thing those five guys had going. What was the song they were rehearsing? Something about "magic"?

I looked out the window of the car, seeing Detroit as I'd never seen it before. It wasn't just a place to wish and dream, it was a place where wishes and dreams really could come true. Until that afternoon, I'd been writing songs, obsessing about music, all in isolation. I'd never had the opportunity to join others who were doing anything similar. To run into other people who were writing songs and singing was like meeting up with long-lost relatives. It didn't even matter how intimidating Berry had been. I wanted more than anything else in my life to be a part of what he was doing.

After we arrived at Mama and Daddy's, rushed into the house, and shut the door behind us, I took Alice by the hands, "Isn't he handsome?"

"Who?" she asked me. "That bum in the ugly shirt? How could you say that? He looks like a creep."

"Well, I love that guy," I told her, "and I'm going to marry him."

"You're out of your mind," Alice laughed, running off to tell the folks about the audition.

I wasn't being that crazy. Sure, Berry wasn't what anyone would call a dashing prince. He wasn't good-looking in the classic sense. He was short. He had a pug nose. But it was the cutest nose on the planet, I thought. And those round light-brown eyes seemed to bore holes in mine. He had that endearing, funny 'do. I'd liked his smell, too—a vague, musty aroma. That walk, almost a skip, with that cute behind of his. I even thought his teeth were beautiful. And there was something about his spirit that shone through—a cool freedom, an original flair, a mystery.

I had no way of knowing exactly what it was. I only knew that as the evening wore on, and the memory of the afternoon played in my mind, I began to feel something about him that I'd never felt before. By the time I tucked Cliff into his crib and fell asleep myself, I already knew that Berry Gordy was going to be the great love of my life.

CHAPTER 2
RAYBER
1958

There was a story Berry loved to tell so much that I could almost mouth the words along with him when he told it.

On a blistering hot Detroit day during what had been his short-lived though promising career in boxing, Berry came out of the gym to find himself staring at two posters on a telephone pole. He had become a pro boxer after quitting high school and before long had proved to be one of the best around. But by that particular afternoon he had begun to see what a dead end boxing could be. He was a witness to how the proud, virile fighters became fallen men, their bodies failed and busted up, their battling spirits gone.

So Berry was standing in front of the telephone pole after a brutal workout. His muscles throbbed, the cuts and bruises all over him were barely healed, and sweat was pouring off him and staining his clothes. And, as Berry told it, he saw the two posters on that pole as a sign for him to make a choice that would change the course of his life. On one of the posters was a picture of a once-prominent black boxer who had long since passed his prime; on the other one was Duke Ellington. Berry looked first at the boxer, a battered and inconsequential man who appeared to be twenty years older than he really was. Then he looked at Duke Ellington, suave and brilliant and eternally young. A legend.

It was a crucial moment in his life, for it was then that Berry decided to go into the music business. But that didn't mean that for one second of his life he'd ever stop being a fighter. Just like me, Berry Gordy, Jr., had gotten a good dose of that in his blood.

He was born on November 28, 1929, to Pops (Berry, Sr.) and Bertha (Mother Gordy to everyone). He was the seventh child in

23

what would eventually be a household of eight kids. Pops and Mother Gordy had moved to Detroit from Sandersville, Georgia, in 1922. Though neither was skilled in anything other than farming, Pops soon talked his way into work as a plasterer. In no time, he owned a plastering and carpentry operation, as well as the Booker T. Washington General Store and a printing business. After the kids were old enough, Mother Gordy studied business at Wayne State University and the University of Michigan, graduating finally from Detroit Institute of Commerce and later becoming one of the founders of the Friendship Mutual Life Insurance Company. Mother Gordy was as sharp as a tack; this lady was a business-woman if ever there was one.

Berry was preceded by four sisters and two brothers, Esther, Fuller, George, Loucye, Gwen, and Anna; Robert was born a couple of years after Berry. They all grew up in a house where loyalty to the family name was an implicit law. Everyone started out in the family business, and each of the offspring was as hard-working and tenacious as the next. Berry was no exception. But, like me, he dreamed of making something more out of his life. That was when he started boxing, inspired, as so many other boys were, by Detroit native Joe Louis.

On the day Berry decided to forgo boxing for music, he didn't know exactly what he was going to do. He knew that he loved music and he had already been frequenting many jazz spots around town. His early sensibilities were influenced by all the great indig-enous talents of Detroit, some of the giants of modern jazz, includ-ing the Jones brothers—Elvin, Thad, and Hank—Kenny Burrell, and Yusef Lateef. Just as he sat down to ponder how he was going to make his musical mark, Uncle Sam came a-knockin'.

Well, there was no way that Berry Gordy was going to be told what to do by any other man. He went into the army, but it wasn't for him. Berry later told me that he got a Section Eight discharge; he convinced them he was crazy, they put him in the hospital, and then they discharged him. I have read since that he served his whole hitch, so I don't know what the truth is—whether he was able to double back and get an honorable discharge or not.

After the army, in quick succession, he met and married Thelma Coleman, went to work for his dad, quit to open the unsuccessful 3-D Record Mart, fathered his first two kids, Hazel Joy and Berry IV, and finally, with another on the way, saw no alternative but to get a job on the assembly line at Ford. Around the time his third child, Terry, was born, Berry wasn't the happiest of fathers or husbands. Soon his marriage to Thelma ended.

In this era, Jackie Wilson was ascending as one of popular music's most spectacular singers and performers. With his powerful, nearly operatic voice, his wild dance moves, and dazzling stage wardrobe, he practically wrote the book on showmanship. Jackie had replaced Clyde McPhatter as the lead singer of Billy Ward's Dominoes and had sung some of their later hits. "St. Therese of the Roses" in 1956 was probably the biggest success of the lot. A year later Jackie decided to go solo and along with his manager, Al Greene, was looking for material.

It so happened that Berry decided what he really wanted to do was to write songs. The choice made sense. He was a natural-born storyteller, and it occurred to him that a song was just a story set to music. A quick study, and a candidate for any kind of challenge, he soon developed a small repertoire of tunes, simple though catchy. It also happened that Berry wasn't the only one in his family trying to get a piece of the musical pie. His older sister Gwen had been writing some songs with her beau, Tyran Carlo Davis, who sometimes went by the name Billy Davis. Berry had collaborated with them on several songs, including one that he was really pushing, a little something called "Reet Petite."

Now, it was one thing to be able to write a song, another thing altogether to get it recorded. To that end Berry needed to meet people in the music business, and once again his family members proved helpful. His sisters Gwen, who was a driving force behind Berry's aspirations, and Anna, both beautiful, glamorous, and industrious, were becoming much admired at many of Detroit's night spots. At the Flame Show Bar, the hottest club at the time, the two young women operated a concession stand and a small photography business. As you arrived on the scene all dressed to the nines, Anna or Gwen would snap your picture and then sell it to you. It was the Flame Show Bar where Berry started hanging out and pitching his songs. It was there as well, according to legend, that he ran into Al Greene, the same Al Greene who was putting together Jackie Wilson's solo career.

In a shrewd move, Berry connected with Nat Tarnopol, Al Greene's associate, who then got Jackie to record "Reet Petite." In the fall of 1957, Berry's first recorded song was a big hit. Suddenly, dreams were becoming realities. Jackie Wilson then cut several more of Berry's collaborations with Gwen and Billy—"That's Why (I Love You So)," "I'll Be Satisfied," "To Be Loved," "We Have Love"—and Berry began to think his time had come.

Unfortunately, getting work was easier than getting paid. Nat Tarnopol, a notorious tightwad, took over Wilson's management when Al Greene died, and he negotiated a minuscule royalty to the songwriters. Even with a hit record, Berry pulled out his pockets and saw that he didn't have a dime.

But in standard Gordy style, Berry swallowed hard the disappointments from the rather unsavory practices of the music industry and began to map out a game plan that could ultimately earn him autonomy. Songwriting was just a cog in the wheel; producing records was where the action was controlled—and where the money was to be made. Being a producer meant writing and arranging a song, finding an artist, and cutting the song in a studio. Then, with record in hand, you went to an established company and licensed it—for an advance and a royalty. The company would release your record, using its existing distribution system, and assume all financial risk. Licensing also allowed for an even bigger payoff if the song was a hit.

To implement what seemed to be a nearly flawless strategy, Berry needed certain ammunition. He needed record company contacts, which he began to acquire with End, United Artists, Mercury, and Chess records out of New York and Chicago. He needed songs, which he was writing regularly with Gwen and Billy. He needed artists, which he did not yet have. But he set out to find young talents everywhere and anywhere in Detroit, using all of his senses to gauge whether the talent was worth developing. Soon Berry assembled a small stable of singers. Together they began rehearsing diligently, striving to create a signature sound or formula that would hit for them.

There were still some necessary resources that Berry lacked. Neither he nor any of his artists could claim a solid background in music. They could play rudimentary chords and sometimes imitate song styles they had heard on the radio. But when it came to communicating with professional producers, engineers, or trained musicians, they didn't have the means. Even more of an obstacle was Berry's lack of organization. Outside his tight focus on the groups, all aspects of his life were in pitiful disarray. He had no car, no clothes, no money. Like those frayed edges and threads hanging off his shirts, there were numerous details awry in his

living situation, his marriage, and his finances, none of which
Berry had the first clue as to how to handle.

Of course, when I met him at that first audition, I didn't know
anything about Berry Gordy. I only knew I liked his damn teeth,
among other things. He had said, "I like you," and his eyes had
searched deep within mine, knowing as little about me as I did
about him. What he must have known, instinctively, was that I had
something he needed. That was part of his wizardry—spotting the
right people at the right time. Unbeknownst to myself, I was about
to provide some of the essential, missing ingredients that Berry
had been waiting for.

"Fellows," he said, to the same guys I'd observed there the day
before, "Ray's going to work with us."

I got a unison of nods and a chorus of hellos.

When I'd arrived, again the door was open, but this time I
had sailed right in and announced myself. The guys, whom I
found out were a singing group called the Five Stars, were standing
in the living room discussing something with Berry. He had on
another raggedy shirt. His eyes were very bright.

"Where's Alice?" Berry asked.

"She's in school," I answered, a little unsure whether I should
be there without her. I waited for his reaction. There was none. I
guessed it didn't matter.

"Oh, you met the Five Stars, this is Billy Davis," Berry said,
gesturing to his songwriting partner, a tall, dapper guy with a
pencil-thin mustache.

I smiled at Billy shyly.

"Let's do it," one of the group, Crathman Spencer, suggested.
Even his speaking voice was musical.

They were sorting out harmonies for a song Berry had written
called "Magic." They started running through the number and
almost immediately I heard a harmony part missing, so I found a
note and joined in. We were jamming vocally and harmonically.
Snapping fingers, tapping toes, swaying this way and that. Before
long, full chords rang out in the living room, all five parts. It
sounded good. And then I saw Berry Gordy smile for the first time.
He was beaming at everybody.

"Yeah," he flashed those beautiful teeth. "That's good. That's
it."

Berry broke into another smile, just for me, with his turned-up delightful nose, his cheeks all puffed and jolly. He gave me an indiscernible nod as if to say, "Whoa, where did you come from?" I felt a tingle up my scalp, a wobble in my knees. I lowered my eyes and looked down so he couldn't see me grinning like a fool.

We pressed on, finishing the verse and then working on the chorus.

"Walter needs to go down, it sounds like," Berry said.

"No," I explained, "he's hitting the fifth of the chord so he needs to go here." I sang the next note.

The Five Stars were very sharp, each guy an excellent singer. Within an hour, all the parts were down and the song was flowing, lead and background vocals together. By that time, Berry had stopped asking any of the guys what note to sing next. He was asking me.

"Now, Ray, I need some kind of an intro."

We thought for a minute and then came up with a refrain, "Magic, uh oh oh, magic, uh oh oh . . ."

Berry was scratching his chin, shaking his head, practically standing there with his mouth open. He seemed to be in awe; where did a *girl* come up with that kind of knowledge?

"Do you really write music, too?" Now his voice was softened by an obvious admiration. I guessed correctly that he hadn't believed me when I'd told him so the day before.

"Oh, sure," I responded, not meaning to seem too boastful and not expecting Berry to almost fall on the floor.

We worked all day on "Magic" until finally, when it was nearly five o'clock, we called it quits.

"Listen," Berry said, "can you come back tomorrow at twelve?"

"I'll be here at twelve," I said, giving him a friendly salute.

I chuckled to myself about the last portion of our rehearsal. As the afternoon had waned, Berry convinced us to let him sing lead, and somehow we were all too polite to comment that his vocals were reminiscent of a croaking frog. Luckily, of his own volition, Berry asked Billy Davis to take a shot at the lead, and it was a vast improvement.

As I scrounged in my purse for bus fare, Crathman Spencer offered to give me a lift home. Besides having a wonderful voice, Crathman exuded a gentlemanly charm. In the car, I complimented him on his vocals. And he told me how talented he thought I was. The day had resulted in a mutual respect between me and all the guys. I felt as if I belonged.

That night was one of those aromatic, cool spring Detroit nights. I rocked Cliff to sleep, singing his favorite bedtime song, "Tonight You Belong to Me." My heart had never felt so light. I laid him in his crib and went in to play the piano, to rid myself of the excess energy so I could sleep.

Before turning out the light, I found myself staring in the mirror on the piano. My hair, still in the fifties-style short blond bob with bangs, was all right. My figure, though small in proportion, was pretty good; at least most men seemed to think so. As I assessed my twenty-one-year-old face, I could actually say that I was beautiful.

Gazing out at the night sky, I realized that a new feminine confidence was being born in myself. The scrappy kid who was half fighter and half dreamer was becoming a woman. For the first time I became aware of something deep inside that made it possible for me to walk into a roomful of male musicians and talk their language, with no excuses for my being female. It was something other than my musical training or native artistry—it was called "mother wit." A streetwise kind of smarts; an earthiness, an ability to roll with the punches or take the ball and run with it. A knack for looking into the soul of another and knowing what moves it. To speak like an angel if need be, or shoot the shit like a damn sailor. To be in the moment and sense the next. Old mother wit was telling me that night, "Raynoma Mayberry Liles, walk and talk softly now. Take it all in and make no false moves. Just let it be." I put away the girlish infatuation I had for Berry and made way for a deeper love. A love that he was going to have to earn.

What the hell am I sitting on? I asked myself four days later on a Friday afternoon. Something was poking me in the behind. We had all just piled into the Cadillac on our way to a club called the Royal Blue, where the Five Stars were going to play. There were four Stars up front and I was in the back sandwiched between Berry and Crathman.

I had gone again the third day to Berry's, where we'd rehearsed other songs in the Five Stars' repertoire, preparing for the engagement Berry had arranged on Friday. As the week progressed, I'd watched for signs of whether or not I was invited. There hadn't been any. But as the time of departure arrived, it was assumed that I was part of the operation, and I'd followed the guys out to the car.

I looked to my right at Crathman and then to my left at Berry, realizing then that I'd plopped down on Berry's upturned palm. I lifted up ever so discreetly so he could retract his hand. Berry didn't budge. Well, what was I supposed to do? I settled back down on it and rode all the way to the Royal Blue with my cheek in Berry's hand. Not once did he say a word or look at me during the whole ride. Not even that sideways, out-of-the-corner smile of his.

The Five Stars were killing at the Royal Blue. Henry Dixon and Walter Gaines suddenly transformed into natural showmen, feeding off the pulse of the crowd. All their material was good, but when they peaked the act with a tune called "Miss Ann," I heard myself let out a catcall. Crathman was featured, and his clear tenor voice seemed to wash over the audience. He knew when to hold back and when to give it all. I exhaled a small sigh, then made sure no one had noticed. Damn if I didn't have a weakness for a talented man.

But there was important work to do and the weeks went by in a steady, marching rhythm. After the Five Stars' success at the Royal Blue we were back Monday rehearsing "Magic." Tuesday we headed out to a friend of Berry's who had a primitive recording studio in his basement—a couple of mikes, a piano, and a tape recorder, nothing more than my own. Yet this felt more professional, a product of teamwork. Yeah, I thought, looking around that basement at the guys, this is the real thing.

And it was sounding nice—except for the lead vocal problem. Billy had sung it through the first few times, and I could sense Berry itching to get up to the microphone.

"OK, let me try, let me try," he finally burst forth, pushing Billy aside.

Already I had the feeling that this was one stubborn fellow. Little did I know that Berry, at this juncture, was still intent on being a performer himself. I bit my lip and glanced away to keep from laughing and saw that everyone else was doing the same thing. On the playback I couldn't hold it in anymore. I started to giggle in an infectious rush, then Crathman started hee-hawing, then Billy and Walter and Henry and all the rest of the guys did too. Even poor Berry had to laugh at himself. I wiped the tears of laughter from my eyes and smiled warmly at him. This was our first recording session together. We had known each other one week.

Things were moving swiftly. From "Magic" we tackled other Gordy/Davis collaborations. The Five Stars and I were thick as thieves; I talked to them in a language they understood. "Let's do a major ninth chord here," I'd say, or "Walter, you try the dominant." From time to time, I'd catch Berry watching me with this sweet look of wonder. Puzzlement, almost. Abruptly, he'd smile that now familiar crooked half-smile out of the corner of his mouth. Sometimes I'd ask him a question and he'd pause, thinking, his tongue in his cheek. It was an idiosyncrasy that described him—tongue in cheek—humorous, a little bit of a tease, a lot of mystery, an artist at disguising whatever more serious thoughts he was having.

But some information hidden behind that cool surface began to filter through. I found out that his house didn't belong to him but to his sister Loucye, a fair-skinned, cute gal with a Betty Boop look, whom we saw only on occasion. Loucye was every bit as aggressive as Berry, but her style was to hold back that drive in polite constraint. Although she hadn't yet said anything, she was understandably anxious to get the perpetual parade of people out of her house. I was also dismayed to discover that the seductive gold Cadillac belonged to Nat Tarnopol, Jackie Wilson's manager.

"Oh," I asked, "Berry's car is in the shop?"

"Shit, girl," one of the guys hooted. Berry didn't own a car. Here I'd thought that he drove a Caddy and had raggedy clothes because he was a rich eccentric. Down the drain went that notion. In fact, the writer of the hits "Reet Petite," "To Be Loved," and "That's Why" barely had a dime.

What Berry did have in ample supply was an assortment of talented artists depending on him for guidance. I began to meet them.

Sonny Sanders, Robert Bateman, Freddie Gorman, and Brian Holland were the Satintones. They appeared to be a very promising bunch, working on a sound that would do their name proud. Light-skinned Sonny, impish at five-foot two, a sun-filled smile and a gingerly freckled face, won me over immediately with a laid-back cool, not to mention his silken tenor voice. Sonny alternated lead vocals with Freddie Gorman, a soulful-eyed, smooth-looking fellow. Freddie's chops were good and he had high hopes: "Pretty soon, I can quit my straight job."

"What's that?" I asked.

"He's one of Detroit's finest postmen," Robert Bateman answered on Freddie's behalf, in a voice pitched so low I guessed right off that he sang bass. But where Robert's voice was low, his height seemed to be near double that of Sonny's. Standing next to Robert, Sonny—and I, for that matter—looked almost like midgets. Brian Holland even chuckled when I was first introduced to the giant, dark-skinned Robert: I had to go up on ballet tippytoes and Robert had to fold himself way down.

Brian reeked of creativity, not so much vocally but in his musical intelligence. This guy, with loving exuberance and deep, distinct dimples, was an attention getter. And then, there was his beautiful head of hair—thick, wavy, with a natural shine. The Satintones, in look and sound, immediately proved to me what excellent instincts Berry had for choosing talent.

"Listen, Berry," I said one day when by chance we were momentarily alone. I'd noticed that a certain buxom, wide-eyed girl named Mamie, ostensibly a singer, had been coming around to see him. It didn't appear to me that what they were doing together was developing her career.

"Look," I continued, "I don't think it's a good idea to mix business and pleasure." As soon as the words escaped my mouth I was mortified. Who did I think I was, telling him what to do?

"Oh?" said Berry, taken aback, a frown on his forehead, his eyes squinting. Then he nodded, "OK. You're right." And Mamie was history.

So the marching rhythm of our legion stepped up in tempo, and I seemed to gravitate easily to the front of the ranks. We rehearsed every day with either the Five Stars or the Satintones. Berry was in and out—dashing off to try to stoke the interest of a disc jockey or make a meeting with an A&R guy from this or that record label.

"OK, just keep things going until I get back," he'd holler, tossing me a grateful look.

I was encouraged to assemble my own group, the Teen Queens, to do my material. Alice and Ray became the nucleus of the group, aided by a fledgling singer with strong potential named Marlene Nero. Upon the somewhat sheepish suggestion of Berry, I agreed to the return of the theretofore exiled Mamie as our fourth member. The Teen Queens and the Satintones engaged in a friendly rivalry, each group trying to top the other with better routines or hotter vocal licks. The competitive spirit within both Berry and me was contagious, it seemed.

"What are you doing?" he asked one afternoon, as I finished

off a lead sheet I'd been writing out for a Teen Queens song of mine called "From This Day Forward."

I held it up to him and he gave a classic double take. "You write lead sheets?"

"Of course. I thought you knew that." I was sure I'd told him so before, but not until Berry saw me doing them did he truly react. He looked ecstatic. Lead sheets, the songs written out in rough sheet-music form, with the melody, chords, and lyrics written note for note on music staff paper, are indispensable. They are what the musicians read from and are necessary for copyrighting.

"Great, that's great!" Then quickly, "Ray, can you write these lead sheets out for me?" I consented and took the lot of lyrics out of his hands, carving out another niche for myself. From then on, I would be responsible for writing out all the lead sheets.

Skills that I took for granted Berry almost regarded as tricks of magic. He was constantly stupefied by my perfect pitch, an ability to identify any note without using an instrument to pick it out.

"OK, Ray," Berry would say, trying to test this esteemed power of mine, "hum me an F sharp." The whole crew would place bets.

"She's not going to get it this time," one cynic might murmur.

I'd hum an F sharp. Right on the money, every time. It became a parlor game, an opportunity to break from the rigid routine. Every time a newcomer was on hand, Berry would be sure to suggest, "Hey, man, give her a note. Just hum any note and she'll tell you what it is."

It wasn't just my ear that was in tune; it was my entire being. If I listened to a song and it was right, the music flowed through me like a vital rush of adrenaline. If someone sang flat or the timing went off, I felt a sort of physical revulsion. It was a built-in barometer that worked independently of my conscious awareness, that old thing I'd named in high school as music in my bones.

"Jackie Wilson? You're kidding!" As I'd arrived that morning Berry announced that the celebrated Jackie Wilson was due shortly to grace us with his presence.

"I've got a new song I want to show you. We're going to rehearse it with Jackie," Berry had also said, and he'd asked what I thought of something he'd written called "Lonely Teardrops." It had originally been intended for another one of his artists, Eddie Holland, the brother of the Satintone with the beautiful hair,

Brian. But on Eddie's demo it had been performed as a languorous track, almost a ballad. Jackie's interpretation was certain to kick up the tempo.

The house was buzzing with anticipation. For weeks now, all I'd heard was Jackie Wilson, Jackie Wilson. And it was no wonder that Berry had such high regard for him. For a guy to take your songs and do them the justice that Jackie had done Berry's work, you had to love the man. Truly, other than James Brown, no one could approach the electric, kinetic excitement that Wilson created onstage. He'd spin around and then slide down into a split. Next he'd jump up in the air, drop the mike and grab it just before it hit the stage, finally climaxing the song as he fell to his knees begging. The women went berserk.

After his shows Jackie would wait in his dressing room adorned in a modest towel, and Nat Tarnopol would line up outside as many ladies as could be accommodated. After they were in place, Jackie would come out in the towel and move right down the line, kissing each and every one. Fat ones, skinny ones, young and old. They'd scream and moan and faint, dropping like a line of dominoes as he passed by.

When Jackie strutted into the house that morning, the place stopped. What a sight: His perfected 'do and his shimmering shirt unbuttoned to the navel. Diamond rings and gold chains. Major flash and personality. His mere presence shouted out, "Jackie's here!"

As Berry and the other guys swarmed around him, hand-slapping and calling out a "Hey, man," I stood back to the side. Even from that distance, I could see that the reports I'd heard were true: Jackie never went anywhere without makeup. His was a thick pancake foundation with eyeliner and rouge; maybe a touch of lipstick, I thought. It was a practice, I understood, he shared with many of his peers. There was something both ludicrous and then completely appropriate about it, a way to call attention to themselves as stars.

Beaming over everybody like a sun god, Jackie led the guys into the living room. Sensing a feminine presence, Jackie let fly his searchlight of a smile, zeroing in his attentions like heat-seeking missiles. "Come here, baby!"

All at once, I was drowning in his silk suit and being smothered by wet kisses, my head spinning from an onslaught of his cologne. In a split second of sanity, I pressed a stiff hand between our bodies, freed myself awkwardly from the embrace, and inched subtly back.

"How do you do, Mr. Wilson?" I said, determined to be as businesslike as possible. Giving him my hand, "I'm Raynoma Liles."

"Raynoma?" Jackie asked.

"We call her Raymond," Berry said, coming up beside me. I glanced over to see him grinning. There were those cute teeth and his funny half-'do and those damn holes in the elbows of his sweater. "Raymond," Berry explained, "because she's just one of the guys."

"Yeah, right," I said, laughing and nodding my head in acceptance of the honor. I could sense Berry's pride in me, and my own pride was so strong I blushed. Just like a damn girl.

"One of the guys?" Jackie echoed, his arched eyebrows raising in disbelief, his laugh billowing up and resounding throughout the house. But by the time we had finished the day's work, his skepticism about me had vanished. And although his energy was so demanding as to be draining, much to my surprise he proved to be quite professional. Trying different feels for background vocals, the Five Stars and I had nailed an intro that Jackie loved— "Shooby-do-wop-bop-bow"—with a gospel-style answering vocal on the chorus—"Say you will." We completed the entire arrangement in a single session. The demo that we cut of "Lonely Teardrops" was later taken to New York to serve as a model for arranger Dick Jacobs. Although he would use professional pop background vocalists in his final cut, the arrangement was identical to the one we'd created that day at Loucye's. Suffice it to say, Jackie Wilson was impressed.

So was Berry. As I was leaving, I felt his hand on my shoulder. "See you tomorrow, Raymond." His hand lingered. His touch was one of familiarity.

I paused, my back to him, wanting to turn around and be taken into his arms.

But I didn't. Maybe the gesture had meant nothing, nothing more than a natural fondness arising from a victorious day together. Maybe there was something more, those comments and quick glances, those half-smiles. So I faltered, then caught myself and skipped off, calling back, "Tomorrow," sounding just as casual as you please.

Keep cool, Ray, I was saying to myself, burning hot and

breathing hard, all the way home. One doe-eyed look at Berry and you'll be out on your butt. We were making music together. I refused to allow anybody or anything, even my beating heart, to interfere with a perfect working relationship.

A new development: "Tomorrow morning, we're moving over to Gwen's place." It had come as no surprise when Berry told us one afternoon that Loucye had reached a saturation point. As loyal as she was to baby brother and as personable as she'd been, poor Loucye's cool reserve was turning into hot resentment at our invasion of her premises. But the Gordy family would never leave one of its own in the lurch, and sister Gwen welcomed us into her abode, an apartment on the upper level of a building just hopping with Gordy enterprises. On the first floor, brothers Fuller and George operated a print shop and a cleaners. Next door to that, street level, Gwen and Billy Davis had set up the offices of their venture, Anna Records. Upstairs, Pops and Mother Gordy, residing and presiding over the family's dominion, lived in an apartment next to Gwen's.

Show Business was Gwen Gordy's middle name, and the working environment at her place bustled with a whole new cast of colorful characters. One of the leading players, of course, was Gwen herself. She was exquisite from head to toe, with an assortment of gorgeous black wigs and dyed shoes to match all her outfits. Her face was flawless, and her figure was so stunning that later she would become a fashion model. With her authoritative professional demeanor, it was obvious that Gwen and Berry had been cut from the same cloth.

As a supporting cast member, there was cousin Gwen Joyce Fuller, the very attractive and very articulate constant companion to Gwen Gordy. The daughter of Mother Gordy's brother, cousin Gwen was both college-educated and a natural administrator and would be relied upon heavily in many of the Gordy family enterprises to come.

I didn't think that any other woman could rival the two Gwens' good looks, but sure enough the namesake of Anna Records had all the Gordy physical charms as well. Anna also had a distinct sincerity, a sometimes naive yet eternally positive outlook. That nurturing femininity mixed with an inborn shrewdness about the male species won her more attention from men than a woman could know what to do with—but somehow she managed.

I was wide-eyed every time I caught the two sisters and their cousin heading out together: wigs and eyelashes, feather boas, all made up in tight satin gowns and six-inch, slip-on heels.

I was also impressed with one artist who I first met upon moving to Gwen's. Eddie Holland, Brian's brother, was so handsome and refined, with those adorable Holland dimples, that it was no wonder Berry saw star potential. He was being cultivated to follow in the Jackie Wilson groove. Performance-wise that was a stretch, because Eddie, quiet and intense, didn't really enjoy gobbling up the spotlight. Vocally, he sounded similar to Wilson and had actually sung most of the demos of Gordy/Davis tunes meant for Jackie. Listening to him sing the first time, though, I'd leaned over to Berry, "Can you hear that?"

"What?" Berry frowned.

"He's off. He's a microtone flat." I whispered, hating to be the bearer of bad tidings.

Berry sputtered for a second, then, "Yeah, I knew it was something, I didn't know what it was. Work with him, OK?"

Later on, getting in the car to head home, Crathman Spencer questioned me in confidence, "Berry doesn't intimidate you, does he?"

"No, why should I be intimidated?"

"Nothing does, does it?" he asked, shaking his head. Crathman and I had started seeing one another romantically. After all those evenings when he'd chauffeured me home, I'd come to feel comfortable with him. We were allies in the great cause of making music; it seemed only natural to extend that alliance into a more intimate sphere. Then there was the lure of his gentle touch and superlative voice.

"What are you thinking about?" I heard Crathman say softly.

"I met the Miracles the other day," I lied. I was thinking about Berry. I couldn't help myself. It went beyond a passion; it wasn't even about physical attraction. My preoccupation was with being a part of his dreams, of his being a part of mine. My obsession was with wanting to see the day when we triumphed together.

"What did you think?" Crathman was asking as the car came to a halt.

"About what?"

"The Miracles? Snap to, baby." I needed to get a grip on myself and put a stop to these reveries. Or at least keep them to myself. Crathman was wonderful company; we were even double dating with his buddy from the Five Stars, Walter Gaines, and my sister Alice. Why mess up a good thing? Now, let's see, the Miracles. Along with the Five Stars and the Satintones, they were the third of the vocal groups in Berry's stable. I'd just seen them briefly the first time. What were their names anyway? Ronnie White, a cool and quiet guy. The dark one, the bass singer, that was Pete Moore. And a tall funny fellow in glasses, Bobby Rogers. Now, who was the one with all that energy and those green eyes and reddish hair?

"You're talking about Smokey. Smokey Robinson," Crathman said as I hopped out of the car at Mama's house. "Wait 'til you meet the girl in the group. Claudette Rogers, Smokey's girlfriend. Sweet as molasses and pretty too."

And so it was that one week later Smokey brought Claudette by rehearsal, and she was everything Crathman had said. In the years to come, Claudette and I would become allies and intimate confidantes in the dramas that would unfold.

Money. That's what we needed. The process of matching the right group with the right song was richly creative but it hadn't brought us a steady source of income. Berry was flat broke, with Gwen supporting him and also shelling out child support for his three kids. And when I found out what slick-talking, hotshot Nat Tarnopol was paying Berry for all the Jackie Wilson hits, my fighting spirit was inflamed: "Get a royalty statement. I want to check this out."

Even that was impossible. The best Nat could offer was an intermittent, nominal advance of fifty or seventy-five dollars, or the loan of a car. For any more, Tarnopol would shrug as if to say "so sue me" and point Berry to the door. It seemed to burn me more than it did Berry. We couldn't continue to be a little school of black guppies swimming in a sea of white sharks.

Something had to give. Some organized method of marshaling our talent had to be achieved. I wasn't sure what that form would be, but I made it my business to start thinking about it.

"Ray," Berry said to me as I was pondering those issues at Gwen's one evening, "I don't think it's a good idea to mix business and pleasure." I cringed. He was referring to my dating Crathman. The very words I'd used in reference to Mamie had now come back to haunt me. Berry's light-brown eyes were impassive, holding out for my reaction. For a beat there was a surge of hope—maybe he did have feelings for me. What about the subtle lilt in his voice, in that otherwise choppy and all-business tone of his? No, I thought, it was just my imagination running away with me. He turned and sauntered off. *Touché*, I thought. And I called after him, "You're right. I'll take care of it."

Crathman took the mandate like a true gentleman. It made sense, after all. We shook hands on the mutual understanding, and he said, "You're the finest. I wish . . ."

"What?" I spoke quietly, hearing a tiny wistful note in his voice.

"I wish you the best. That you get everything you're dreaming of," Crathman Spencer said to me.

"You too, Crath," I said.

I'd just had an idea that would forever mark me as either a genius or a damn fool. More and more, my family was beginning to worry that I was becoming the latter.

"You've been at it nonstop for almost two months," Mama had said. "Now those Gordys sound like very fine folks, but this music business is just spinning your wheels." Then, noticing my plate was empty, "You want some more ham?"

I looked to Alice for support, but all she could do was stick a fork in my slice of ham and into her mouth. Thankfully, Daddy came to my rescue: "Lucille, there's no point in telling Raynoma what to do. We should know that by now." He tweaked my nose, which was the spitting image of his. "You've been looking so pretty lately."

The only person in the family who really believed in the validity of my efforts was Mike, who winked across the table at me. I grinned over at my extraordinarily handsome brother. "Follow your heart," he, a romantic like me, always said. "Follow your heart."

And so I had, not stopping to think through clearly the suggestion I was about to offer Berry. It had become apparent to me that we were quickly wearing out our welcome at Gwen's. Our numbers were ever growing; the traffic and volume throughout her apartment continued to increase. Also an underlying tension had resulted from the undefined boundaries between Gwen and Billy's songwriting collaborations with Berry, their independence with Anna Records, and Berry's territory of talent.

"Look," I'd said to Berry, "this working at Loucye's or Gwen's is ridiculous. Your sisters can't get a moment of privacy. And we shouldn't have to call a rehearsal quits if we're starting to cook, or always walk around on eggshells."

"You got a better plan?" he agreed, sighing.

Then I put it to him. "Yeah, my place."

"Your place?" Berry seemed skeptical.

"Sure, I've got a piano and a tape recorder at my apartment. We could do the demos there, then go into the studio and work from the tape. That way we can work as many hours as we need. C'mon, let's get this thing off the ground." I saw his eyebrows raise with interest at the mention of a tape recorder. There really was no need to tell him that it actually belonged to my brother Mike.

"Furthermore, Berry," I added, not even believing my own boldness, "why don't you just move in? You know, give Gwen a break." Was I out of my mind? I'd just asked the man from whom I'd hid my feelings all this time to move in with me.

"Oh," I cautioned, covering myself, "no strings attached. It's purely a business proposition. You need a place to live, we need a place to work. Why not?"

Several interminable seconds later, Berry nodded. "It's a deal."

It was two in the morning and I'd been staring for hours at the cover of the light bulb hanging from the ceiling. What a remarkable week it had been, an even more remarkable day. Bizarre almost in how casually everything had happened.

Gwen had been hugely relieved to hear that our hordes were soon departing, and the news was simply taken in stride by everyone else. On a sunny morning a week later, Berry had come ambling up the sidewalk with a few books, papers, and tapes in his arms. Lord knows he didn't have more than a couple pairs of slacks and ratty shirts—not enough clothes worth packing a suitcase. No moving van, no official acknowledgment of a new residence. No spending any time getting himself settled in. Within half an hour, the guys were there and we'd gone to work at the piano, picking up where we'd left off at Gwen's the day before.

The only difference in the routine occurred when it was time for everyone to leave. Berry, it was understood, would be staying. Both Walter's and Henry's good-byes held a ring of deference, as though the fact that our headquarters were now at my home altered our respective status. Even Brian Holland, who never failed to brighten into a big dimpled smile when he looked at me, seemed uncomfortable. As if Berry's having moved in with me would affect my closeness with all the guys. No one knew exactly what to make of it. Well, hell, neither did I.

The last of the gang filed out, and I closed the front door. Unsure of myself, I turned to see Berry hovering by the piano in an identical state. He was unaware of my observing him, and his expression was one I'd never seen before. He looked like a little lost boy.

"Make yourself at home," I gestured vaguely.

"Thanks," Berry mumbled, looking around at what wasn't quite a palatial estate.

In fact, I had to squeeze by him to get into the bedroom, conscious of not allowing our bodies to touch. It was important that he had his privacy, that he felt at home, that nothing was expected of him. In the bedroom I cleared a shelf for him and hung his few articles of clothing in what was now his space in the closet. I took in a deep breath and emerged cheerfully, saying, "Say, Berry, I've got to go down to my mom's and pick up Cliff. I'd love you to meet my folks. Would you like to come along?"

His hands were in his pockets and he was shuffling his feet, all shy. "Well, sure."

The smell of Mama's fried chicken greeted us at the door.

"Hello!" I called and heard my parents holler back from the dining room. Almost before I could make introductions, Mama was shooing me off to the kitchen. "Fix him a plate, fix him a plate."

As always there was an abundance of food piping hot on the stove: the fried chicken that had led our noses in, corn on the cob, mashed potatoes and gravy. From the kitchen I could hear Daddy's proverbial question, "So, what is it that you do, son?" To be followed no doubt by other inquiries all aimed at the discovery of Berry's intentions.

I'd seen Berry before with men his senior—his own father included—and knew his manner was singularly respectful. But even so, when I returned with his plate and saw him with his hands folded in his lap, talking to Daddy, really trying to make a good impression, I was really touched. And to Mama's delight, Berry asked for seconds on chicken.

We sat and talked with my folks for hours. By the time we left it was dark already. With Cliff in my arms, Berry and I walked together along Blaine Street. We were both quiet, saying very little.

We listened to the commanding voices of mothers up and down the block calling kids to come in. There were the sounds of crickets, of our feet padding along the walk.

It was about ten o'clock when we got back. Berry busied himself at the piano, tinkering. I put Cliff to bed, dusted an undusty cabinet, fluffed the pillows, and pulled back the comforter on my double bed. The only bed I owned. I was sure that Berry was considering that very fact at that very moment. Maybe he was oblivious. Or maybe he was waiting for an opportunity to let me know that the attraction was more than just that of a friend. Maybe he would take advantage of me, make love to me out of proximity and convenience and break my heart. Maybe he wouldn't. I had gone through every maybe in the book, pulling out every frilly negligee I owned in a frenzy, until finally I'd settled on what I always wore to bed—an old, plain pink cotton nightshirt and a frumpy white terrycloth bathrobe, the world's most unsexy bedroom attire. Mother wit had reminded me of my own words, "No strings attached." At least not unless he strung them.

As Berry came out of the bathroom and I was heading in, we practically bumped into one another. "Sorry," I said.

"No, I'm sorry." He insisted.

"No, really, it was me. I'm sorry." I exclaimed. It was a damn comedy routine, but we were playing it like melodrama.

Barely eyeing one another, we went into the bedroom, and he dropped his trousers, laying them absently on a chair. As I took the side of the bed by the wall, I pretended to be enthralled with the ceiling. I did grab a peek, however, at his boxer shorts. They were checkered and baggy, hanging down almost to his knees. And he had these skinny, slightly knock-kneed legs. Frog legs to match his frog voice. But he did have beautiful feet. With me in my nightshirt and Berry in those shorts, we could have been a black version of Lucy and Ricky Ricardo in their later years.

He got in bed on the other side, and we both lay as close to the far edges as we could without falling off. Straight as arrows, on our backs, with our arms flattened at our sides. I focused on the ceiling and studied the rhythm of Berry's breathing. Or was that the beating of my heart again?

"I'm happy you're here, Berry." I said.

"Great, great," he said. "This is . . . this is going to be . . . great."

Then more silence. With nothing else to do, I stared at the light bulb hanging from the ceiling. This was excruciating. Did

Berry feel what I was feeling? Well, I supposed not, when moments later he began to snore. The thing about the light bulb that was so interesting was its cover. It wasn't a proper shade, more a squarish half-cover, white with pink flowers. I shifted my weight from one hip to the other. But it was cute and homey, the light cover. I wasn't used to sleeping in a straight line, maybe that's why I couldn't sleep. I wondered if I ought to paint the ceiling. Berry didn't seem to have any trouble getting comfortable. Well, I could always buy a new light cover, if I was going to be staring at something this long. Berry exhaled a huge snort, like that of a whale surfacing. His nose, the nose of which I was so fond, was nuzzling my shoulder. What I could really do to be creative is paint a mural on the ceiling, then I could be entertained for weeks. He let out another snort and his behind, that rear end that made me smile, was touching my leg. Well, maybe I could get up and read. Or maybe just move my hands to keep them from going numb. And on and on it went for hours, until, just as the sun was coming up, I dozed off. When I opened my eyes again to my new friend—the ceiling— and turned to look at the clock, I saw that it was time to start the day.

Where my living and working experiences with Berry had begun as a television sitcom, after more than a month now they were turning into something akin to a science fiction flick. Here we were, two able-bodied young adults of the opposite sex, sleep- ing in the same bed every night, engaging in the most intimate of verbal intercourse, and yet both doing everything possible to avoid physical contact. Adding to the complexity of the situation, there were certain things I'd found out about Berry—and some things I then did in an effort to understand him—that really bothered me.

"What did you just say?" I asked him. He'd been mumbling one day, during the period not long before we started our music company, Rayber. It was a particularly lean week when the con- stant scrounging for money was yielding nothing.

"I've got to get out of this business," he muttered again.

"What business?"

Berry looked up at me and then back down. Maybe he hadn't meant for me to hear. He paused and let out a helpless groan. "I have a few girls."

"What do you mean a few girls?"

"Down on John R," he said, "but I've got to get out. I can't do this."

It took a minute for the nickel to drop. One strip of John R

Street was Detroit's red-light district, not far from its heavily trafficked hotel and nightclub area. It wasn't anywhere that I'd spent much time, but I got the general picture. The Flame Show Bar was there, lots of fancy dudes with dollars to spare. Glamorous nightlife right alongside parasitic lowlife. Strip joints, small-time guys selling reefer, johns out to score hookers. It hit me—could Berry have meant that he was a . . . ? No, impossible, I thought, not my Berry.

I shrugged casually, as if I'd known all along, "Oh, yeah, well . . ." As I spoke, I watched him guardedly, showing not one sign of the shock I was feeling.

"Oh, yeah, well . . . ," he echoed and paused, silent again. He appeared to be torn over whether or not to continue. Finally he spoke in a distant voice, "I can't do what the motherfuckers down there do. They beat the women up, forcing them out on the street if they're sick or tired or pregnant. Heartless sons of bitches. They don't want to hear no sob stories. It's just 'give me money,' and if a girl gets uppity he kicks her ass. I can't do that shit. I can't make them go out on the street. I feel sorry for my girls. Sorry if, say, she's sick or can't work, or maybe just doesn't want to. But then on the other hand I've got so much riding on these acts, no money coming in, a ton of expenses and. . . ." Berry kicked a nearby chair. And then in a swift change of mood, he smiled and joked, "I'm just not cut out for it."

If my reaction was somewhat ambivalent, so too was my state of mind as I boarded the bus the following afternoon. I stared out the bus window at Detroit's prettier neighborhoods passing by, thinking through what I was feeling, searching for logic like someone grabbing at straws. It had been two months since that fateful audition at which I first met Berry, and I realized, sitting on the bus, that something had happened to me along the way in getting to know him. Some switch had been flipped, a gear shifted. Whatever it was, there were moments when I felt that I had no conscious control. As if I was possessed. Even though the idea of living my life in love with someone involved in this was terrifying, I would live that life if necessary.

So, I'd finally decided that afternoon when Berry had gone out and I'd dropped my paperwork, the bottom line was: I had to know everything there was to know about Berry Gordy. I had rushed Cliff over to Mama's, then boarded the bus.

I stepped off onto John R Street, like Dorothy awakening in

the land of Oz. Girls stood on the corner in skintight dresses, the shortest of shorts, the highest of heels. Net stockings and layers of face paint. Chewing on gum, rocking their hips. Their words and gestures beckoned the guys walking by; some girls ran out to cars and leaned into the windows. I tiptoed through this foreign world, at once fascinated and repelled, pretending to myself that I was mysteriously protected from their tough expressions. Don't make eye contact, Ray, I said to myself. What if one of the girls asked me what I wanted? And worse, it occurred to me as my pace accelerated, what if I ran into Berry?

Even that possibility couldn't stop me. I was moving with someone else's motion, and suddenly I found myself walking up to the porch of a house where several girls were offering their services in loud voices to an array of potential clientele. In a sort of dream state I floated up the steps and stood on the porch with the other girls. The girl closest to me turned and gave me a look of major effrontery—what the hell do you think you're doing?, her look said. Oblivious to any danger, I brushed away my inner reason urging me to hightail it out of there and casually walked over to the other side of the porch. I'd traveled to John R to find out how the other half lives, and come hell or high water I was going to get what I'd come for.

And then I saw them—the pimps, the "motherfuckers" whom Berry had bemoaned. No wonder poor Berry felt out of his league. These cats were classic sleazeballs, jive talking in their hardened voices, stalking up and down John R in their big tall hats and silk suits. And their Cadillacs. Berry, cute as all get-out to me, was just a short, little knock-kneed fellow in raggedy clothes next to these macho men. I almost laughed as I reminded myself that Berry, who didn't own a car, had to take the bus down to John R Street. Now, what kind of pimp was he, taking the bus?

And what kind of spy was I, hopping up on that porch for anyone and everyone to see how clearly I did not belong? My sanity returned as abruptly as it had departed, and I raced to catch the bus. When I reached Blaine Street, I sighed in relief.

Just after I got home, Berry arrived with only a few dollars in his pocket. I assumed his girls on John R hadn't produced much business. But we said nothing. We hadn't discussed what he'd divulged the day before, nor would the subject ever arise again. Several times I tried to bring it up, but I simply couldn't; I'd also decided never to tell him where I'd been or what I'd done. And,

God knows, never did I utter a word to him of what happened next.

It was a week after my visit to John R, and we were flat broke. I was about to do something desperate. My heart hurt; I was nauseated and perspiring heavily. Thoughts reconsidering my awful decision raced through my mind. But then I thought of Berry. If he could separate himself from the lurid scenes he participated in on John R, then stroll in just a regular nice guy, so could I. Was it possible that I wanted so desperately to get under Berry's skin, to know how this man's mind worked, that I was going to accept this sleazy—but money-making—proposition?

On my way out the door, I caught a glimpse of a lead sheet I'd started. It was a new song of Smokey's on which Berry had scrawled some notes. A lump stuck in my throat. That was me, that was my life—a gifted musician, a proud young mother. But my baby wasn't getting enough to eat. The electric bill and water bill and gas bill were all overdue. That was also me—a fighter who'd do whatever she could to take care of herself and her own.

Six o'clock. I'd reached my destination, and my knock resounded through the apartment building. No answer. Thank God, maybe it was called off. Then I heard footsteps. The door opened and she was smiling. "Don't worry, honey. It's as easy as riding a bicycle. Once you do it, it's like you always knew how."

I was mute, shaking and stumbling as she pulled me down the hallway. Only a few days before, this travesty had started innocently enough. I'd been chatting with a neighbor, Roberta, whom I'd surmised traded sexual favors for money. Just after my trek to John R, I'd broached the subject of her money-making venture and had asked delicate questions about her life, all the while comparing her answers to the sad images of the John R girls.

"Honey, those street whores make two dollars a pop and sleep in some pigsty. I make ten bucks in less than an hour and, well," she gestured, "look at my clothes." It was true. Her wardrobe was expensive and stylish. But what about her pimp, Dickens, that scary-looking guy with the black felt hat and flashy red Cadillac? Oh, no, Roberta protested, Dickens didn't beat her. And if he ever did, it wouldn't bother her, she was so in love with him. She was happy to turn over her earnings to him so that he could provide for and protect her. Roberta's attitude made me want to cry in pity for her.

Roberta had noticed my stack of unpaid bills a few days

before, so it wasn't out of the blue that she had suggested a way for me to make some extra money. My first reaction was that it was unthinkable: I was a naive innocent, a girl who used to play for the church choir, who lay awake each night desiring the man sleeping next to me, turning down advances from other men to save myself for him.

This morning Roberta had come by and announced that a high-paying trick was coming at six o'clock. I could take the trick and find out what it was all about. See if it was for me. And it was no big deal, she assured me: "Sugar, it's survival. There's no right or wrong about it. Ask Berry if that's not so—he should know." Shame had infiltrated my senses. Roberta knew about Berry. Thanks but no thanks had been my response.

"He's a nice, clean-cut white man," she'd said. "Six o'clock. Just think about it. Just once won't kill you."

Now here I was, standing in front of a bedroom door with Roberta whispering, "Oh, he's going to love you. I told him all about you."

"No," I gasped for air, "I can't, I'm sorry, this is insane." I wrenched my elbow from her grasp.

"Sure you can do this," she cooed, her hand reaching for the bedroom doorknob. "Think of your child," she added through gritted teeth, then patted my hair and shoved me inside the room.

The man was about forty years old. Flabby, with the whitest, pastiest skin I'd ever seen, covered all over by a dense matting of grimy black hair. He was standing by the bed. Naked. Except for a pair of short black socks. That's what the devil must look like— naked with ludicrous black socks.

The devil spoke in a nasal voice: "Well, come on, get in the bed."

Physical revulsion turned to numbness. Something inside went dead. Cold. Like a robot, I undressed and walked to the bed. I lay back and closed my eyes, trying to think of beautiful music. *Scheherazade.* Putting my mind in another place, I transported myself away from this moment that I still couldn't believe was happening. Just get it over with. Put it inside and give me the money so I can leave. I opened my eyes to see him still standing. "Well, uh, go ahead," I stammered. He didn't budge. "Aren't you going to, uh, do, uh, it?"

"Oh, Jesus," he snickered as if to say even a ten-year-old could have known better, "you suck my dick."

And so I did it. As quickly as I could. I did not vomit or faint or die, though while it was happening, I was certain I would do all three of those things. Afterwards, this demon from hell transformed into a cheery, regular Joe, "Thanks, thanks a lot." I was dressed in seconds flat, taking the money from him, barely hearing him say, "You know, I really like you. When can I see you again?"

"Talk to Roberta," I said, already on my way out of the apartment, not stopping to breathe until I was in my own bathroom. I gargled and rinsed my mouth for thirty minutes. I counted what was my take for five minutes of torture—seventeen dollars.

When Berry came home and saw the cash in a pile on the dresser, his eyes burned bright, "Wow, great! We sure can use this." That was that. He hadn't asked where I'd gotten it, and nothing that I later did or said betrayed what I had just been through. We shared a wonderful dinner together, talking only of our great passion—music. That night, after we'd said our chummy goodnights and his snoring began, I noticed something funny about the moon that was glimmering through the bedroom window. It was shrouded in mist—compelling, mysterious, untouchable. Just like certain sides of Berry, I thought. Maybe I didn't need to know his secrets; maybe I should accept him from that day forward at face value, seeing only the sweetness and talent that he showed. But as I finally fell asleep, I also decided that there had to be other ways to survive besides those Berry, I hoped, would soon give up and those I'd experienced for five minutes of my life. And during the fitful sleep that followed I dreamt of faceless men in black socks, and from those dreams sprang the inspiration for Rayber. Survival—the mother of invention.

"You know, here we are just paying out and paying out, living from deal to deal. We have all this talent, Berry. Somebody should be paying us to do what we do. Why don't we start a music company?"

"Well, sure . . . ," he replied slowly. "But what exactly would the company do?"

I was thinking on my feet, improvising on a theme as I spoke, with Berry providing a backup vocal—like creating music. "I'll bet, with us struggling to find an outlet for our songs, that there are a lot of other folks out there who don't have half the resources we do," I speculated.

"Damn straight, that's what makes us unique," Berry uttered.

"Right. And there's really nowhere for them to go to get their song recorded. OK, there's Fortune, Sensation . . ."

"And J.V.B.," he added, and then, "So?"

"So . . . ," I took a breath, "say you're some kid with a song and you want to go to one of those companies and record your song. What do you need?"

"You've got to have a connection to those companies. A middleman. And then a tape." Berry nailed it.

"Bingo." I smiled. My idea was to start a service that would eliminate those immense obstacles. Anyone could bring us any song and pay us to record it. We'd go into a local studio and cut an actual record. With that, the client would have something to show, to take to the major New York labels and maybe—who knows?—get a deal for themselves.

"Our guys could do it. In the meantime, they'll be improving their skills. Helping with writing, singing, arranging. And," I emphasized, "it would give us a cash flow, which eventually could afford us a base to branch from and establish our own label."

Berry had gulped when I said the word *label*, whistled when I said the word *cash*. It was a damn good tune. Maybe overly ambitious, but it couldn't hurt to try. "Yeah," he crooned, "that's a great idea. You handle it."

"The Rayber Music Writing Company," I declared, christening the brainchild. From our two names, Ray-Ber. We shook hands on it. Now we were more than just roommates. We were business partners.

There are stretches in a person's life when time becomes a blur and memories of it fade, leaving only a vague feeling. Other times stand crystal clear in vivid detail, and you can return to those experiences and relive them as if they were happening now. Such was the day that Rayber ran its first radio spot. So come and get this memory:

It's 9:45 A.M. I'm sitting on the sofa in the living room. In front of me on the coffee table is a pad and pencil, the telephone, and the radio. I'm panic-stricken. What if nothing comes of it? No one responds? What if I was doomed forever to have unrealistic plans? What would Berry think? Meticulously, I go over every aspect of preparation.

The first step had been putting the word out. I'd contacted all the radio stations and rounded up their rates, finally settling on station WCHB. Good musical airplay and good listening demographics. Decent rates. I'd met with their ad rep, who'd helped me write the spot. We scheduled it to run twice a day, at ten A.M.—to nab the housewives at home—and then again at four P.M.—to hit the kids as they were getting out of school.

9:50 A.M. Berry comes to the door of the kitchen, where he'll be monitoring the phone and gives me a high sign. Well, at least he's optimistic.

9:55 A.M. I look at my watch. It's a surefire bet. We'll be a smash. I switch on the radio.

9:56 A.M. I look at my watch, again. What a jerk I am. We're just little peons thinking too big for our britches.

9:57 A.M. I take my watch off and set it on the coffee table. I'm not even going to look at it again.

9:58 A.M. Berry comes to the door once more looking nervous, his brow furrowed.

9:59 A.M. I'm staring at the minute hand on the watch, waiting for the precise moment that it crests at ten. I'm concentrating so hard that I get lost in the patterns on the face of the watch. It's just a jumble of numbers. The watch is ticking.

10:00 A.M. "Now," the voice on the radio says as I almost jump out of my seat, "an exciting new music company in Detroit! The Rayber Music Writing Company is here to service all your musical needs. If you have lyrics, we can take them and put a melody to them. If you have a melody, we can put words to it. Or if you have a singing talent and want to be a recording artist, we will personally write music for you."

My heart is pounding. I can't believe it's really happening. Now, I think, looking at the silent phone, ring, damn it, *ring*.

"Once again," the radio says, "that's the Rayber Music Writing Company, to service all your musical needs."

At the very second that the phone number is heard on the radio—not even a beat in between—our phone rings. I gasp. Berry comes running out of the kitchen, gaping over at me with his mouth wide open.

The ring has died out. Maybe it was a crank call, nothing having to do with the ad. There it goes again, a second ring. The room is swirling. I'm about to snatch the receiver off the hook. Calm down, give it a second, not too eager, I think. There's the third ring. I take a deep, deep breath, "Rayber Music, may I help you?" I can't believe how cool and collected I sound.

Berry rushes to my side.

"Hello," the voice of a young girl says awkwardly, "I've got this, uh, poem and I always thought, uh, it could be a good song."

I glance up at Berry with a grin, and a monster grin spreads across his face. Our eyes connect for a fraction of a second, mine telling his that it's for real. Our eyes are dancing a tango in that celebratory connection—victory. We did it.

"Well, maybe we can help you," I say, my tone professional and soothing. I ask her the appropriate questions, jotting down her particulars, and our first appointment is set for the next day. Berry's about to burst, his smile too grand for the size of his face. My heart wants to pump out of my chest. I want to jump up and swing around the house with Berry and shout and stomp for joy. But I'm restrained, giving our first customer our address, never betraying for one millisecond that she is our first. "Thank you, see you tomorrow. Good-bye."

I hang up the phone. "Berry, we . . . ," I start and before I can finish another word, the phone rings again. "Hello, Rayber Music. May I help you?"

"Yes, I'm a singer but I don't know where to begin."

At the end of this call, the same thing happens again. And then again after that. Berry gives me a kiss and leaves the room. We have to wait to hoot and holler, because it is well over an hour before the calls subside.

When the spot runs at four o'clock that afternoon, the same thing happens all over again. By five in the evening I have ten appointments set up for the next day.

And so it was that in less than eight hours, Berry and I had given birth to the Rayber Music Writing Company. We didn't know if this entity, this child born of a little idea I'd had, would grow up happy or sad, rich or poor. On that evening, that precipice of many more magical events to come, we didn't care what the child grew up to be. We were just proud to be parents.

Our child shot up like a weed. From our first appointment the following morning with a strong-voiced would-be songstress named Louvain Demps, there hadn't been a hitch. In Louvain's case, we'd rehearsed a few popular tunes with her. Then after hearing the versatility of her pretty, high soprano, we agreed to write her a song. Being our first client was an auspicious moment in her life—after paying us to get her career started, Louvain would later become one of the Andantes, the group that Motown employed as background singers on innumerable sessions.

The appointments took up the rest of the day, all of the next, and most of the remainder of the week. Some customers were like Louvain, singers wanting to get started or needing a demo to get recording deals. Others came wanting help with partial songs that they couldn't finish or arrange. A few arrived with completed tunes that were ready to be recorded. Some, like Eugene Remus and Wade Jones, two handsome male writers/vocalists, showed great potential. Most of our customers, however, came with poems that simply needed music.

It was astounding. Within one week we'd gone from nothing to more money than Daddy made at Cadillac in the same amount of time. And as it continued Berry and I easily assumed our roles as parents of the operation. We discovered we had authoritative yet nurturing traits, some of which came from our own parents and our experiences with our actual children, some of which lay intrinsically in our distinct personalities.

Berry was a born leader. His energy and charisma charged everyone who came to Rayber or was involved in our other projects. He knew exactly how to motivate people, how to detect and develop their strengths. He was a coach, inspiring and igniting enthusiasm. Along with his genius for timing—that instinct for spotting the right person at the right time—he had an unquenchable gift for infusing a group with such spirit that they'd all come out of a meeting fired up and raring to go. "Yeah, let's do it!" Like a ball game. And he was also a latter-day Socrates, an inveterate philosopher. He would spin beautiful, entrancing monologues about trust and sincerity and honor, all with a scholar's flair. Each would conclude with something relevant to the work at hand, and each embodied a theme of honesty. Liars were an abomination to Berry. He had his own father's wry sense of humor and almost every father's habit of avoiding sticky personal problems or complaints. "Go and talk to Ray," he would say.

That and just about every other order of business had been left to me. My primary concern was making sure that everyone in our talent base had an opportunity to share and benefit from the venture. Before we began, I sat down with each of the guys, explaining how it would work and how they could continue to develop artistically while earning a little money. Almost everyone was as excited as Berry and I were. I did the scheduling and assignments for sessions, which would last from thirty to sixty minutes: "OK, Smokey, this guy needs a ballad. You can handle that." Or "Brian, you and Robert arrange this song. If you need me for background let me know."

There were myriad technicalities to consider. For starters, there had never before been any legal documentation of any of Berry's deals. Obviously, if Rayber was to grow and mature into a real record company, it would have to be established legally. Having made several phone calls of inquiry, I headed down to the City-County Building and picked up a "Fictitious Name Certificate," which would enable us to register the Rayber Music Writing Company as a partnership between Berry and me.

Creating an efficient routine was necessary, not only because of our need for a profit but also to make the most of our somewhat limited resources. That became my undertaking also, scheduling what would happen when and where and with whom—there was, after all, only one piano and one tape recorder. Somehow I managed to set up the space to accommodate the ever-growing numbers coming in. We kept the tape recorder in the hallway. And when we were ready to do a demo, I gathered everyone around the piano.

Then when it was time to actually record the song, we rented time at Bristoe Bryant's house. A Detroit DJ, Bryant had a three-track tape machine and a small recording studio set up in his basement. We'd cut the song with a small combo—piano, bass, guitar, and drums. Any one of the guys might sing lead. I would arrange the background vocals, and we would perform them in a variety of combinations. A loosely structured group of us, usually including tall Robert Bateman and his inimitable bass voice; Brian Holland, whose musical versatility was growing by leaps and bounds; Sonny Sanders, with his clear, high tenor; and myself, began to call ourselves the Rayber Voices.

The total charge for the Rayber Music Writing Company's service: one hundred dollars. I knew that many people wouldn't have the whole hundred right away, so I allowed for installment payments. A deposit was required, but the installments could come in increments of twenty, ten, or however much the customer could afford.

Berry's mom, the lovable busybody and veteran business-woman, had been shocked. "Where's the guarantee that they'll maintain the payments, dear?" she had asked.

I showed her the records that were testimony of each customer's faithful installments. "See, Mother Gordy, if someone truly has music in their blood and a strong enough desire to commit to the whole hundred, I know they're going to want that record." Then I pointed to enough other instances in which people paid the full fee up front. So far, the ball kept rolling.

Money. That's what we set out to make, and we were doing it. Little by little. Compared to the mess that money would eventually create for us, the economics in the early Rayber days were amazingly simple. Bristoe charged us ten dollars an hour for studio time. At an hour or sometimes two hours a session, plus ten dollars weekly for radio advertising, we kept costs low. The musicians were given five dollars each, and our only other expenditure was for Rayber staff salaries. It was the first steady income that Smokey and Brian and the others had ever made working in the music industry—three dollars a week. We were grossing around fifty dollars a song.

I'd grown up watching Mama handle all of the family finances. As if having learned bookkeeping by osmosis, I started a ledger system for charting all income and expenses. I used a little five-cent notebook—one of those red spiral things that school kids use. The little red notebook became a mainstay of record keeping, and years later, when Motown was deluged by MBAs analyzing financial flow, all they had to go by was my notebook. But they were astounded by its accuracy.

The place was filled with shop talk, laughter, and camaraderie. Not to mention the good smells of whatever concoction I made for lunch. "Is that your special chili smellin' so good?" Smokey would ask. I had instituted a break around noon that we called "snacktime"; my cooking for the guys helped them make ends meet.

We were becoming the original Detroit commune. We ate together, rapped together, and sometimes a few stragglers would camp out in the living room together. But come early morning, we were up and cracking. Often I'd have Rayber customers scheduled for the entire business day, and our ongoing projects with the artists would have to be shifted to the night. Or Berry would have the Miracles in the bedroom and I'd have a Rayber customer rehearsing in the living room.

Regardless of who did what, whether you were a paying customer or an employee or employer, we were a family. From the beginning there was a feeling that the musical community of

Detroit was indeed a small world. And they were all in my living room.

That's exactly what one of our first Rayber customers said upon arriving; "Raynoma Liles, I can't believe it! Now, this is a small world."

"Mickey, Mickey Stevenson, well, what do you know?" I said to my old neighbor from Canfield who was looking as slick and hot-to-trot as ever, with those gorgeous silver threads running through his black hair. He'd brought some songs to play for us— the same enticing songs that I'd heard wafting through my window back in my newlywed days with Charles. We would go on to do some demos for him, including a lyrical number called "If Only the Sky Was a Mirror." Here was one talent that I made sure Berry met. They hit it off at once, and Mickey was eventually to emerge as a major player in the saga to come.

There were other visits from our past. Years before, I'd met Little Willie John—the super Detroit performer who'd scored with "Fever" and "Talk to Me." Also during that time, Mother Gordy had referred a coworker from the insurance company, a blues singer itching to get her career going, to Berry. It turned out the coworker was Mabel John, the female double and sister of Little Willie.

Cute as a button, redheaded and freckle-faced and without an ounce of ego, Mabel wanted so badly to be a part of the action that she was willing to do whatever she had to do. Since Berry didn't have a car, Mabel became his driver, chauffeuring him to radio stations, to record stores, to the barber shop. Whether he was heading off to a meeting with a distributor or paying a visit to his kids, she always made herself available. Little did we imagine at the time that Mabel was the first in a long line of personal assistants to Berry.

Blessed with an agile, articulate tongue, Mabel did the original on-air interviews with disc jockeys for our records. Berry was so impressed with her style that in return for the interviews he promised to help her with her career. Unfortunately, this was a long time in coming. In the meantime, she was content to attend to any of his needs. She brought him bag lunches, dug into her own pockets to pay for any extras he required. It was the kind of dedication Berry inspired.

Although the artists were a diverse group of personalities, they had a common denominator of youth, one more factor that made Berry and me feel parental. To have the futures of such young, unformed talent in our hands was a responsibility we didn't regard lightly. Little Freda Payne, for example, a musical child prodigy, started working with us when she was twelve. Berry had great hopes for her and had written her a song that, in retrospect, had a prophetic message. Called "Save Me a Star," its lyric said, "When you reach your goal of joys untold,/At least save me a star." These were words that Berry, then still struggling, had penned for Freda; yet I would later wonder to what extent he was speaking to the part of himself that would stop at nothing to reach those heights.

At any rate, there was little time then for such introspection. I was extremely fond of Freda, seeing something of myself in her, and the two of us bonded closely. Funnily enough, the guys used to call us lookalikes—petite, feisty, fair-skinned girls—just a generation apart. "Just be patient," I'd always say to her, and to her credit she hung in. It wasn't until 1970 that Freda had her big hit with the smash "Band of Gold."

Our artists weren't the only ones whose talents were being developed. Berry himself was honing and refining the skills that would one day earn him legendary status as a formidable song *meister*. From those first few weeks when I'd watched him work with the Five Stars, I was well aware that he had an instinct for knowing what made a hit song. He could listen to material, as he did initially to my fifty-some-odd songs, and detect where they worked and where they failed.

Generally, he thought my early songs were "garbage, Raymond, garbage." Unfortunately, I wasn't able to respond with my childhood quip of "you don't know what you're talking about," because his criticism was usually specific and valid.

As the Rayber Music Writing Company sprang to its feet, Berry began to solidify his attitudes about songwriting. At night when we could steal a few moments away from work, we'd sit down to a game of chess, which Berry was teaching me to play, and he'd hammer away at all his latest theories.

"You see, Ray," he'd start, moving the pawn harmlessly forward, "what nobody understands is format. Layout is crucial."

"Yeah, I agree." I'd seen an opening for my rook, moving it boldly out from the corner.

"Concentrate," he smiled and captured the rook with his

bishop. "Take every strong song and what you'll hear is basically a verse, another verse, a bridge, a chorus, back to the verse, one more chorus, and out. Damn, Ray, you don't want to move your queen there," he pouted as I took his knight.

"Now," he was wearing his poker face and setting me up to jump on his pawn, "what about the hook?"

I studied the board. "It's your move," he goaded.

I wasn't about to jeopardize my queen. "The hook is everything, I know that." Out comes one of my pawns.

"Sure," he said, his queen conquering the pawn, "but the key is in creating tension with the hook. You introduce it in the chorus, bring everything back to the verse, distract on the bridge—that's the tension—and then send the tune out with the hook."

"Oh, so what you're saying is that you can't overdo the hook?" I thought about it, moving my bishop. It was a brilliant formula, a commercial outline that even decades later many songwriters lacked.

"Good move, Ray, you little devil." I'd cornered his knight. Damn, he was letting me win. He launched into a dissertation on melody, pondering his next move at length. A beautiful melody that was simple and catchy would win him over every time. Berry thought the novel offbeat melodic ideas some of the guys were trying were wasted efforts. "You have to be able to retain the melody, keep on singing it afterwards." Now his queen leapt out aggressively.

"But, Berry, you're always going on about originality." I was no wimp. I faced his queen with mine.

"That's with the concept of the song. You can't just do the 'I love you—you love me' pattern anymore." Out came his second knight. Uniqueness of phrasing, rhythmic playfulness, Berry expounded, were marks of true artistry. Also, he continued as I worried about my next move, it was essential to tell a clear story without an excess of words.

Berry, I thought as my queen inched up, ready to pounce his king, had the lyrical notions of a real poet. "Check." I couldn't restrain my smile. Now it was his move.

Not one syllable would escape his scrutiny. Often he'd say to a writer, "You just used that word. Don't repeat it. Put it in a different way." Later, when the Motown aces—Holland-Dozier-Holland and Norman Whitfield and crew—were churning out songs, Berry would be frequently heard saying, "No, man, it's not saying any-thing." Or, "Continue the story. Don't say the same thing in the second verse that you said in the first."

Berry surveyed the chessboard, that old tongue of his wagging in his cheek. "So the student tops the teacher, huh? Damn, I taught you too well."

I felt a surge of glee. I loved winning and I was about to capture his king.

Smokey, who had been outside tinkering on his pride and joy, a beat-up Ford jalopy that sucked up his weekly paycheck for gas, stopped in to say good night. I gestured to him to come over and witness my triumph. "Surrender, Berry, she's got you right where she wants you," Smokey chuckled, knowing as well as I did how much Berry despised losing.

"Oh *yeah?*" Berry growled as Smokey and I dropped our jaws. In one fell swoop, Berry's bishop trampled my queen and my pitiful king was surrounded on all sides. "Checkmate." Berry rose from his chair, dusting off his trousers, and graced me with a nod telling me that at least I'd tried hard. "C'mon Smoke, I'll walk you out." Pointing back to me, he said to his young protégé, "Stay away from easy women."

From the door, I watched the two stroll arm in arm out into the muggy night. Under Berry's wing, Smokey's writing had ad-vanced tremendously. Young William "Smokey" Robinson had written prolifically before hooking up with Berry, but it was Berry who'd seen where the songs lacked focus. He'd take a tune of Smokey's and literally turn it around. "No, man, you should come from this point of view. Start here in the first person, get rid of that third-person voice." Then, when a strong theme was evident, Berry would guide Smokey further. "Yeah, that's good, very vi-sual," Berry would cheer the young poet on. "Now this line here, make it more of a picture. This is cliché. What about saying it this way?" And Smokey would incorporate the input and the line would be, "I'll build you a castle with a tower so high it reaches the moon. . . ." It was trademark Smokey—picturesque and unique. Or he learned to twist an old phrase into something completely new. "They say beggars can't be choosers . . . I'm a choosy beggar."

I smiled as the two made small talk down on the sidewalk. Smokey and I had also become fond friends. He was constantly pulling gags, keeping us all in stitches, or breezing through a room with a wonderfully warm green-eyed twinkle of a greeting.

I always knew I could toss him the ball and he'd run with it. He was as conscientious as I was about making a customer happy, making sure the product was the best that it could be.

Yes, I thought, as Berry waved good-bye to Smokey and turned to come back inside, we were quite a team. Now what had Berry meant about my being easy? Easy to beat in chess to be sure. But certainly not in giving my feelings away. About business or music or family I wouldn't hesitate to express myself to him; nor would he to me. And it was obvious that we held an overt admiration for one another. Sometimes, in fact, I'd been surprised to find him staring at me with a sort of reverence. It was conceivable that in his view I was some kind of magic. His lucky charm.

He was coming closer and the irrepressible pound in my heart began again. I loved his cocky walk, his happy whistle, his haphazard 'do, that turned-up little nose, those light-brown big round eyes, which now opened even wider at seeing me at the door. Go to him, Ray, one bold voice spoke in my ear.

I took a step forward, unsure, not knowing if I wanted him to see the wetness of my lips, the hardening of my nipples. Wait, another voice inside me warned, there is so much you don't know about him. Those secrets of his, his restless ways. He confides in you a lot, but what about that other private side of his? Are you ready to give yourself over to him, lock, stock, and barrel?

Berry was almost at the door. I was being drawn to him, the cooling night air blowing up my skirt, a sigh escaping my chest. Yes, I'm ready, I answered my own questions. I'm so in love with this man I can't eat or sleep.

Berry stopped short, inhaling deeply as we faced one another, the two of us squared off like two playing pieces on a chessboard, each of us allowing the other to speak first. "The stars are out," Berry finally said softly, eyeing me with a similar softness.

"Mmm," I looked up at the galaxy in the night sky, hearing one last internal voice, my proud and protective voice.

"It's getting late," I said out loud to him and walked back inside to check on Cliff, without so much as a hand to Berry's cheek.

I couldn't do it. I couldn't break through the wall that my own pride had erected. Besides, I had chosen to heed the message of that last voice of reason. Firmly, my instincts told me: Wait just a little longer, Ray. It's his move.

CHAPTER 3
BERRY
1958

"How do you feel about me?" Berry piped up out of nowhere one evening. Well, that was one hell of a loaded question. His eyes did have a certain shy, innocent cast to them, though. It was an expression that stoked all those maternal inclinations of mine. But his tone was flip. Considering the casual way he'd thrown the question out, I decided that if wits were being matched, I wasn't going to jump into his net. When it came to veiling emotions, I'd beat him to the punch any day.

"Oh," I sighed, drawing my hand absently up my leg, making sure he noticed how terrific those legs were, "I don't know." Then giving him a look of apology, I concluded, "You're too young for me." As it was, Berry was almost eight years older than me.

And he'd laughed outright. *Touché.*

I had it bad and that wasn't good. Rayber was on its feet, and laughter and music rang throughout the apartment. But couldn't Berry hear my heart pounding like a big bass drum? My emotions felt like a pendulum swinging back and forth. He loves me. He loves me not. Tell him how you feel. Don't tell him.

For weeks I hadn't had an appetite. At restaurants I'd order something light, and even then I'd barely manage to pick at it. My worst enemies had become that ever-narrowing double bed, that detestable light bulb cover hanging from the ceiling, and my own pride.

It was a Saturday in summer, nearly two months since Berry had first moved in. What a luxury not to have any work left over from the week. Damn, I thought, scrambling the eggs, now I don't have anything to distract me. Of course, lately even the demands of work could no longer calm the constant flutter in my stomach.

60

Yawning, Berry stumbled to the table, "What a beautiful morning." So it was. Sunny, a blue sky, a light breeze blowing the curtains. And his yawn was beautiful, revealing those beloved teeth.

"Don't forget you've got that appointment at the radio station." I joined him at the table.

"Oh, right, twelve o'clock," Berry said.

Then, suddenly seeing Cliff, the two of us broke out in peals of laughter. That impish child had slathered scrambled eggs all over his face and was looking back and forth at Berry and me. His eyes seemed to say, You two are acting like bigger fools than me. Mama, make a move.

All I could muster was a joke that Mabel John had told me earlier that week. It was hopeless. And all I got was Berry's approving laughter, instead of the touch of his hand, his kiss, or the embrace that I'd imagined a million times.

Maybe, though, today would be different, I thought as I walked him to the door. Oh, I was sick of maybes. Sick of examining his every movement for some hint. That was it. No more. I refused to notice how he paused with his hand on the doorknob. Or how he was turning back to me, or that strange way he was looking at me. Maybe something was wrong. I opened my mouth to ask and before I could, he stepped toward me. Took me in his arms and put his lips to mine. I pulled away in surprise. In disbelief. He brought my body close to his and we were kissing, slowly and lightly at first. What incredible heat. Then deeper and forever this kiss became. My pulse was his pulse, my mouth, lips, and tongue blending with his.

After an eternity, he simply broke from the embrace, smiled at me for a brief second, then he was gone. I collapsed against the door, shut my eyes, and tried to preserve for all time every iota of what had just happened. No dream I'd dreamt could have approximated the exquisite reality of that kiss. No *True Romance* story could have described the heights I was feeling. It was bigger and better than any romantic's view of a first kiss. A thousand violins, fireworks bursting all around, trumpets resounding. That prideful, polite wall that had kept us apart had come crashing down in a thousand pieces at my feet, and I was a lost cause.

I had no idea what he was thinking as he walked down the sidewalk away from the apartment or how he reflected on the encounter as he sat in his meeting. But it didn't matter, because when Berry returned that night it was my move, and I went to him with all that pent-up passion and ardor. Our lovemaking was like our music making. Respectful and admiring. Fun and clumsy and playful, too. Laughter and sighs.

The summer exploded into Technicolor. Each and every frame of our life together was happier than the next. In one scene the place was swarming with all the characters who were a part of our work. Berry would zoom through the living room calling out, "Ray, I need you and Brian in here." And I'd be running the other way saying, "OK, in a minute. Where the hell is Robert?"

"That damn Bateman," Smokey would groan. "He's using the bathroom for echo. And I have to pee."

Still watchful of every penny, Berry and I created free entertainment for ourselves. On treasured weekends we would just hole up, dreading the sound of the phone. "Don't pick it up," one of us would whisper naughtily. "Just let it ring." The chessboard was always set up, and I'd even started winning occasionally. There was also a deck of cards handy—sometimes in use for the entire weekend. Gin rummy, stud poker, once in a while a good game of go fish, it didn't matter; I never won.

Or the little family we'd become—Berry and Cliff and I— would meander down the street to spend a peaceful evening at Mama's. Dangling our legs off the porch, we'd shoot the breeze.

"What do you think, Lucille?" Berry might ask my mother, "Doesn't Cliff look exactly like me?"

"I think he needs to eat more," Mama would scold the two of us supposed adults, ignoring the fact that Cliff and Berry looked strikingly alike.

Then, of course, there were those languorous, relaxing scenes where the families would picnic together at Belle Isle Park. If there was any kind of competitive sport, no Gordy ever failed to show up. Our brothers and sisters were close in age, and the two clans meshed harmoniously. Birthdays, holidays, any excuse for a party, and all members of the two families would be crawling out of the woodwork. During these lazy, fun-filled outings I'd find myself looking over at Berry with tears of pure joy in my eyes, with a sense that our love itself was a matter of destiny, that our having come together was simply meant to be. The way his family took to me, mine to Berry, and to each other, was another sign that our love and all our endeavors together could only flourish.

In addition to Gwen and beau Billy, cousin Gwen, Anna, and Loucye, all of whom I'd gotten to know and love, these gatherings afforded me the time to get to know more Gordys. There was Esther, Berry's sister who would marry George Edwards, a Michigan state house representative. And then there were brothers Fuller, always wise and thoughtful, the energetic and proud George, and the somewhat straitlaced though ambitious Robert L. And two family members who would forever endear themselves to me with their loving, down-to-earth ways were George's beautiful wife, Rosemary, and Robert L.'s gorgeous wife, Theresa.

"What do you mean my mother's a busybody?" Berry wanted to know. There weren't enough hours in the day for us to talk. We talked about everything under the sun, and family was always a major topic of conversation.

"Your mother is the most tasteful, cute . . . the sweetest woman in the world. But, damn, she's always walking in here selling something. Kissing and hugging practical strangers." I'd perform a Mother Gordy imitation, " 'Yoo-hoo, I'm Berry's mother. I sell insurance.' "

Berry cracked up. She'd managed to sell several policies, even among our throngs of struggling musicians. "Talk about a busybody, your mother is audacious."

"What do you mean? My mother is a saint!" I exclaimed.

"She may be a saint but she's a cleanaholic saint." Now I had to laugh. Mama would sneak in the door while we were working and blaze a trail through the place, washing dishes and scrubbing floors. She was notorious for tiptoeing into the bedroom and organizing the closet and drawers. Berry was forever saying, "Your mother was here. We won't be able to find anything."

And Berry would one-up me again, "Now what about that father of yours? If I get one more lecture about how great his daughter is and how lucky I am to have you, I'm going to have to quit going over to the house."

"He's right. I am great and you are lucky to have me." I preened and turned the talk away from Daddy's impossible standards. "Look who's talking about fathers. What about Pops?"

"What about Pops? My father is a saint!"

"Your father may be a saint, but he's a flirtatious saint." Just the mention of Berry's tall, lanky, irascible father with his "hee-hee" laugh would send us both into guffaws. I'd stay on my roll by doing a Pops imitation: " 'Hello, Lucille,' " he'd telephone Mama's house, " 'how are you?' " How nice, Mama was thinking, he's calling to talk to me. Then Pops would ask casually, " 'Oh, say, is Alice home?' " Alice, who was oblivious to ulterior motives, never did get the gist of his interest.

"Now, listen to me, Ray. Seriously," Berry liked to change the direction of a conversation without warning, "about Cliff."

"What about Cliff?" My son was growing to be a very smart but mischievous three-year-old.

"He's always underfoot," Berry complained.

"Now, Berry, how can you say that? All you do is encourage him." Cliff was already famous for marching up to important visitors and saying, "Hi, I'm Cliff." Berry, his partner in crime, would pat Cliff's little head and explain to the startled newcomer, "Yes, this is my assistant." Then, lowering his voice, Berry might add, "Oh, and don't say anything about his height. He's very sensitive." The kid was becoming Berry's clone in the prank department, and within a few years he would earn a reputation at Motown as Berry's front-runner in practical joke terrorism.

So summer eased into autumn. That other child of ours—Rayber—would soon require a new change of clothes, a larger space. As business moved into full swing, we breathed a little easier about expenses and opened up the throttle on our own music.

CHAPTER 4
TAMLA
1958-1959

"This is pointless," I said. I was furious. Having just witnessed another of Nat Tarnopol's power plays, I'd had it. "These jerks act like you're a piece of dirt. You have to bow and scrape to get money that's yours. It's stupid. We're the ones with the talent. We've already proven ourselves, and now it's time to play ball with the big boys."

We *had* proved ourselves, damn it. Rightfully so, my confidence in our work and in my administrative skills was extremely high. I had become the harmonic expert in residence, in more ways than one. Smoothing tempers and soothing worries. Musically, I was frequently called upon to help with chord progression—which chord should follow which—and making the structure unique. Arrangement had always been my forte, and after so many hours hearing our different singers I instinctually knew whose harmony should go where. Like a symphony conductor I'd point my hand to Crathman Spencer to really wail, or to tall, dark Robert Bateman to slide under the lead with his pumping bass lines.

Sometimes we arrived at a discovery simultaneously, and we all felt the rush—the magic—of sharing in the creation. I'd look up from my piano to see the gleam in Satintone Freddie Gorman's big eyes. Or Brian Holland's ecstatic dimpled smile. Sonny Sanders's silken-voiced "yeah" or Smokey's expression of just having heard a musical miracle. And then, when the groove was really hot, Berry's approving nod. The collaborative spirit was astounding, the flow unstoppable.

Our product was getting out; we had quite a few licensing deals with different record companies. Thanks to Berry and his schmoozing with industry representatives, we weren't going unnoticed. Eddie Mesner of Aladdin Records and George Goldner of End were helpful. It was End, in fact, that released the Miracles' "Got a Job." Berry also had an amicable working relationship with Leonard and Phil Chess, who were based in Chicago and who also distributed End. Eddie Holland, still developing his career as a singer, recorded some songs he'd started when I first met him—"You," "Little Miss Ruby," and "Betrayed Heart." Even my group, the Teen Queens, qualified for a release with "From This Day Forward," the first legit recording of my written efforts.

The services that Rayber offered and the acumen of our talent stable were definitely now visible in Detroit. So, why, I reasoned, should we continue to give Nat Tarnopol and Jackie Wilson our best material, all for their benefit? We had other avenues. And Nat's attitude—that songwriters were at the bottom of the totem pole—was insulting. Anybody could write a song, Nat implied, and we should be happy having his star Jackie recording our stuff. Regardless of the pittance of a royalty he paid—when and if he paid.

I'd become well acquainted with both Jackie Wilson and Nat Tarnopol, who always cruised through our place in tandem. Nat was the silent controlling shadow to Jackie's flashy, overpowering "I'm here!" Jackie would call out "Come here baby!" to every woman in sight, grabbing and slobbering over his delighted prey. With me Jackie was somewhat subdued, as though our first encounter at Loucye's had signaled to him that I was unavailable. I couldn't deny my awe of his abilities, but I could absolutely turn down his efforts to get me in bed.

I reached my breaking point with Tarnopol the day he arrived at our place alone. "Hey," he nodded to me, with no acknowledgment that we'd ever met before.

"Oh, hi, Nat. Come on in." Under other circumstances, I would have said that Nat was good-looking. A tall, slender white man in his mid-twenties, he was young for the success he was attaining.

He stepped past me into the hallway, looking around, "Berry here?" How was it, I wondered, that Nat could spend so much money on his apparently costly suits and still look tacky?

"Sure, Nat, I think he's on the phone. I'll get him." Berry was actually still in bed reading the paper in his underwear and his 'do rag.

"Berry," I whispered, "Nat's here."

"Oh." He scrambled out of bed. "I'll be right out."

When the doorbell rang, I was at the piano with the Teen Queens and the Satintones flocked around me. We were in the middle of working on an arrangement. Robert Bateman, as usual, had just told a loudmouthed, raucous joke, and our laughter had been equally rowdy. But now, upon returning to the living room, I noticed an uncomfortable silence.

Hands in pockets, tapping his foot impatiently, Nat was surveying the crowd with an indifferent eye.

"Hey," I tried to be friendly, "let me introduce you to everyone. Folks, this is Nat Tarnopol, Jackie Wilson's manager. This is Brian Holland, Sonny Sanders, Marlene Nero. . . ."

To each Nat merely raised his chin, and before I was two-thirds of the way through the introductions we heard the bedroom door open and close. Nat turned immediately from the group, dismissing those who were still unnamed.

That was the extent of it. Berry and Nat conversed briefly and Nat left as abruptly as he'd come. Two hours later, still stewing, I stomped into the bedroom. Looking at Berry, who was seated at the side of the bed rubbing his temples, I let loose. Nat and Jackie were living the high life, and here was the man I loved all twisted up in knots.

Time to play ball with the big boys, I said, and I meant it. "You know, we aren't some mom-and-pop fly-by-night operation. What we have to do now is start our own label." It wasn't as if I was some Einstein; I was simply stating the obvious. And giving Berry a loving kick in the seat.

Berry was silent, staring down at his feet, still rubbing those temples. Not bothering to defend Nat or Jackie, he finally said, "I know."

Thus began a series of discussions in which Berry and I examined all that starting and maintaining a record label would entail. With the clarity of hindsight, I see that we didn't have a clue about the magnitude of our undertaking. We were, in essence, taking a wild stab in the dark. We understood that distribution, actually placing the records in the store, could make or break us. We were also aware of the importance of radio play. But we knew that owning the label would give us creative and financial control, and we were ready to win or lose to have that control.

That left the unpredictability of timing—finding that perfect moment to strike, and striking gold. It would take the right song, the right artist, the right audience, all at the right time. It was dumb luck that we really needed, something that could not be planned. We would make each move as intelligently as possible, but beyond that we could only hope that timing, fate, and sweet lady luck would be on our side. The stage was set. Berry and I were about to play the biggest chess game of our lives.

Enter Marv Johnson. We got lucky.

"Whatcha got there, man?" Berry asked the man sitting at the piano. It was a brisk, early winter evening, and Cliff, Berry, and I had walked into the back room of Prince Adams Records on Twelfth Street. Berry recognized Marv Johnson, who'd been kicking around Detroit for a while. A soulful, Clyde McPhatter–style singer, he had recorded a few songs on Kudo Records and also had collaborated with Billy Davis on some tunes. Berry first met him over at Specialty Studios, where Marv was rehearsing with a group called the Downbeats, who later became the Elgins.

As Marv, with a firm, confident air and smooth dark skin, plunked out the simple doo-wop chord progression, I noticed his strong presence, his proud posture. His song, though derivative of most fifties songs, had a distinctive melody and lyrics. Berry and I turned to each other with raised eyebrows, reading each other's minds. Even little Cliff looked back and forth at the two of us, as if he was thinking what we were thinking—Marv is great and this song could be a smash!

The following morning Marv came over, and we rehearsed his song, "Come to Me." Berry reviewed the lyrics and I arranged the backing vocals. Musically, it wasn't complicated. Fifties doo-wop songs usually fell into one of two categories that Berry and I referred to as either a two-beat rah-rah or a four-beat rah-rah. The difference was how many beats each chord had. "Heart and Soul" was the prototype two-beat, also known as a "round robin," or a cycle of repeated chords. "Come to Me" was a four-beat rah-rah in the mode of Sam Cooke's "Twistin' the Night Away."

A few days later, listening to the playback of the demo we cut at home, Berry said, "Yeah." Marv said, "Yeah." I said, "Yeah." Everybody else in the room said, "Yeah." A four-beat rah-rah of excitement.

For several late nights Berry and I toiled over a notepad itemizing the costs of launching "Come to Me" in a way that we had never attempted for any song before. Studio expenses, musicians' fees, trips to either Chicago or New York for that all-important distribution deal. No matter how we stacked the numbers, we couldn't get the bottom line under eight hundred dollars. No matter what regular expenses we didn't pay, we would never be able to amass that kind of cash from the Rayber income.

Besides, we had just upped our rent by moving to a bigger place around the block, at 1719 Gladstone, where we were busy setting up camp in the bottom half of a two-family dwelling. In a back bedroom we set up a small demo studio, thanks mainly to the electronic tinkerings of Brian Holland and Robert Bateman. Robert even saved us money by rigging up a microphone splitter from a cigar box. We established the closet as a sound booth and the bathroom as our echo chamber.

Through our improvisation we managed to keep setup costs down, but we still needed other things—like a car. A bank loan, unfortunately, was out of the question. Besides having no collateral, we had already run into trouble getting a checking account when we first established Rayber.

Having experienced very little racial prejudice before, I'd had no qualms about going to the Detroit Bank to open our account. To fill out the application, Berry and I sat down at a desk across from the large, imposing white bank manager.

"Well," he said after eyeing us critically and barely glancing at the paperwork, "I don't want you—uhm—folks to come in here and start bouncing checks, now. . . ."

"Fuck you," I said to the bank manager. Berry had never heard me use that expression before. *I'd* never heard me use that expression before. The Detroit Bank would never hear me use any expression again. "Come on, Berry, let's get out of here," I muttered, dragging him down the street to another bank. There at the Bank of the Commonwealth we were greeted most courteously, and we initiated a long-standing account, the one that one day would yield millions from Motown's success. As we filled out the paperwork, Berry was still getting over seeing my fighting pride in action.

We had to find capital for "Come to Me," so we weighed our options. There was an offer from George Kelly, a Detroit nightclub owner—ten thousand dollars in exchange for half-ownership of our organization. But no, as astronomical and tempting as that amount of money sounded in our hour of need, we had to reject it if we were ever to achieve autonomy.

"Wait," Berry suggested, "maybe we could borrow it from Ber-Berry." In the classic Gordy family entrepreneurial style, a savings club called Ber-Berry had been established for the purpose of purchasing real estate. Every week each family member deposited ten dollars into the fund; weekly business meetings were held with minutes, an agenda, and discussions of items that sometimes even went to a vote. Berry and I balked—borrowing money from family could be very touchy. Then again, we decided after a few more days of debate, "Come to Me" had enough potential that we were sure we could pay back the eight hundred dollars within a few months.

Once we made up our minds we met no resistance, and it was agreed at the next Ber-Berry meeting to give us the loan. Before I could stop to catch my breath, all the plans had been completed and I was standing in a sizable studio at United Sound. It was probably Detroit's best-equipped recording space, and as I inspected our personnel, I realized we were doing this shot with top-notch talent. Thomas "Beans" Bowles (he was tall and lanky like a stringbean) was set to go with his magic baritone sax and flute. Eddie Willis, with his kind smile and a noticeable limp, along with Joe Messina, a hip Italian kid, were ready to hit it on guitar. Benny Benjamin, high-strung and adorable despite a rugged pockmarked face, was about to blow us away with his drumming. And on bass we were graced with the genius of crazy-eyed James Jamerson. There was, of course, Marv Johnson himself on piano and lead vocal. And for backup there were none other than the fabulous Rayber Voices—Robert Bateman, who stood tall and sang low, Brian Holland, middle-sized and middle-ranged, and little ole me singing way up in a high soprano.

"Come to Me" and its flip side, "Whisper"—Marv's song as well—were recorded in one day of work that flew by without a hitch. Not one of us realized that we had just traced the outlines of what would later be identified as signature Motown. Using Beans Bowles's baritone sax, and putting persistent emphasis on the backbeat, which I played on the tambourine, had resulted in two elements that would be standard in all our future productions. Those, in essence, created the original Motown sound. History was now being written.

I was going to go out of my mind. It was Tuesday afternoon and Berry had been in New York since Monday for a meeting with the United Artists record label. Although I'd left repeated messages at his hotel, he hadn't called back with an update. Typical Berry, I thought, the deal probably went great and he's just torturing me by leaving me in suspense. Typical Berry, I worried, the deal probably went badly and he's avoiding calling me to report defeat.

'Round about midnight, I heard the front door open and close. Running into the hallway, I asked, "Well?"

Berry said nothing. But nothing could mean something. He marched me into the bedroom, our private sanctum for important discussions. Damn, I sensed bad news coming. "Well?"

His face was a blank.

"Didn't they like it?" I choked back my disappointment.

Suddenly, Berry grinned, and like a magician produced a bag, stuck his hand inside, pulled out a big handful of money, and threw it up in the air. Then he did it again. Soon we were laughing, hugging, dancing around the room with dollar bills fluttering down all around us. It was a dream come true—an old-fashioned cornball movie moment that was really happening.

Three thousand dollars, more money than we'd ever seen in our lives, had been the advance paid by United Artists for "Come to Me." Berry, God love him, had cashed the check into small bills to create this amazing shower of cash. Not only did United Artists love Marv Johnson's song, they loved Marv and wanted to sign him to their roster. In exchange, they would distribute the song nationally on their label. Berry had also obtained a 10 percent royalty for us. I was going to cry for joy, "That's incredible, Berry. Nobody in our league gets half that much."

And then there was the icing on the cake. "I retained local distribution rights," he announced. "We can put this song out on our own label in the Michigan area." I thought Berry was going to cry, "Our own label—d'ya hear that, Ray? Our own label!" This was the best of both worlds. All we had to finance were the copies for Michigan, and United Artists would handle all those thousands of others for the rest of the country.

Berry and I stood with our arms wrapped around each other, swaying to the music of our steady heartbeats. So proud of ourselves, we held each other like that for a good, long while. I committed these moments to memory—it was the sweetest song I'd ever known.

The label on which we released Marv Johnson's "Come to Me" in January 1959 was christened Tamla Records. *Tam* came from the song "Tammy" as Berry's tribute to the popular Debbie Reynolds movie, and the *la* was added to avoid copyright infringement. To some, it may have seemed inappropriate to name a sound that was rooted in black soul in honor of a pop song and a white teenage girl. To others, though, it made sense—we all really liked Debbie and that song. And to Berry, who had a knack for coming up with titles for everything, the name Tamla symbolized the crossover success—an appeal to both pop and R&B audiences—he hoped to achieve.

In January of 1959 I went to the City-County Building in downtown Detroit to pick up registration papers again. Berry and I were now establishing two more partnerships. While we filed legally for Tamla Records, we also registered our publishing company, Jobete Music, named with affection for Berry's three kids—Joy, Berry, and Terry. I was barely twenty-two years old when we signed the papers. I had known Berry less than a year, and I was three months pregnant with his child.

"Listen, I'm going to be at station WCHB with Larry Dixon. Turn on the radio at ten o'clock if you want to hear him play the song," Berry announced as he sped out of the house, running late as usual. I quickly switched our numerous radios to WCHB, looking forward to hearing "Come to Me" over the airwaves for the first time.

"OK," Larry Dixon announced on the radio, "we've got Berry Gordy at the station today with a fantastic record produced on his own Tamla label called "Come to Me" by Marv Johnson. Berry, tell us something about the song." I heard that familiar laugh of Berry's as he joked and talked about the song, and I smiled along with him.

"Thank you, Berry Gordy. And now for the new song. . . ." As the intro started up—"Yea yea, comma comma comma"—I began to chuckle. That was *my* voice on the radio. I got up from the spot where I'd been listening and walked into the hall where I could hear the song blasting from all the radios throughout the house. A delightful image of all the radios in the world playing the song at that instant flashed through my mind. The image itself made me laugh out loud. There was nothing dramatic or electrifying or momentous about it. It just felt right—and very real.

For anyone who has ever had a big dream, there are times when huge obstacles arise and it all seems impossible. During these bad times, gloom colors everything. Then suddenly the clouds pass, and the victories and jubilation and glamour and success explode across the screen of your life. Between those two extremes, though, is the very best vantage point, the place where the dream has become real. In the real world, good and bad things happen; you count your wins and try to cover your losses. Or, at least, such was my rationale for a few of those bad and sad things that had happened.

One of the sad times was back in the first days of our money struggles, in the early fall of 1958, when I had had a miscarriage. I had recuperated quickly in the hospital, with Berry sitting quietly and gently next to me the whole time. It had spurred me to write a song for him called "When I Really Need(ed) You." Later, still very touched, he had urged me to record and release it. It was a wonderful experience. The song and the love that prompted it remained in my memory and often served to strengthen me. And when, three months later, just after the initial success of "Come to Me," another bad thing happened, I found solace in the words of the song.

"Oh, say," Berry had begun, catching me casually in the hallway. Mama had been over on one of her cleaning binges and I was whisking about, making sure she hadn't filed away something important. I was in a heady mood, dizzily happy from the speedy series of events that had taken me from being Berry's protégée to his partner and lover. And I was carrying his child, no less. What was more, I was the co-architect of his dream. We had done it— Marv Johnson's "Come to Me" had been an instant smash.

I answered him with a smile, my eyes brightening, "Say what, Berry?" He'd just returned from spending several hours at his parents' house and seemed somewhat distracted.

"Uh, you know what I want you to do is, uh, change the paperwork on Tamla. Tomorrow morning you should go down to the City-County Building and change things from both our names to just mine."

I was stunned. A lump rose in my throat as I tried to respond, but no words came forth.

"I've been thinking about how it looks, and you said your-self—we're not some mom-and-pop operation." Talk about turn-ing a phrase of mine around. "Well, that's how it looks the way it is now. And it would be just simpler to have it in one name. For tax reasons and all that. You know."

Now I have very good hearing. I'm the lady with the perfect pitch, and for a second I heard something very off-key. My veins went icy and I felt as if the wind had been knocked out of me. Had someone told him to do this—someone in his family? Was Berry somehow threatened by me? To be sure, he knew that I was no weak-willed pussycat. But did that mean he had a shred of suspicion—that there was any possibility our relationship could fail? What kind of love did he have if he needed this protection, leaving me unprotected? What kind of a game was being played making it necessary for him to stack the odds in his favor?

And then I heard in my inner voice a stronger tune. We weren't opponents, we were passionate allies. I swore by a gospel of faith and loyalty and trust. We'd built everything we'd achieved so far on those premises. I had to trust Berry in this matter, or risk toppling the entire dream we shared together. "OK," I said in a small voice, the wind returning to my lungs.

The next day I went to the City-County Building and had new papers drawn up. As I gave away my legal entitlement to Tamla Records and Jobete Music, I'd ceased to question Berry's motives. Instead, I heard in my mind only what he had said after I'd agreed to do it, "It's just a formality. Nothing's going to change. You know that, whatever happens, I'm always going to take care of you." I looked up to see the face of the man who'd sat at my side in the hospital and who had been there when it really mattered. And heard the sincerity in that man's voice.

As I said, I have very good hearing, and for many weeks now I had been hearing the name Elsie Frazier. A girl who worked at WCHB, she'd been calling Berry often. Generally, I was never jealous about Berry's evening forays into the nightclub circuit. Socializing with industry reps, scouting out new talent, making contacts, it all came with the territory. Hanging with the top DJs—Larry Dixon, Larry Dean, Ernie Durham, Joltin' Joe Howard, Bill Williams—was one of the perks of having a hit song. Although this Elsie person worked in the business, my ears picked up an odd tone in Berry's voice every time she called.

One evening, as I was sitting in the bedroom watching television, Berry appeared at the door with the garbage: "I'll go stick this out in the alley." Well, that was a pleasant surprise—since when did Berry stoop to taking out the garbage? I guessed that because of my pregnancy he was being unusually considerate.

H'm, though, I wondered, what's the catch? On instinct I checked my watch. Garbage removal was about a one-minute job, tops. After two minutes, I allowed for extenuating circumstances—

Berry was always dawdling. He was probably chatting it up with a neighbor across the alley. I'd give him another three minutes for that. It was ten more minutes before he returned, and my gratitude for his kind gesture of removing the trash had long since vanished.

Coming in cheerfully with his little skip, he began to remove his coat, preparing to hop in bed to watch TV with me.

"Where'd you go?" I asked, my eyes fixed on the television screen.

"Where'd I go?"

"You took the garbage out?"

"I took the garbage out!"

"That's all you did?"

"That's all I did!"

There was a funky echo in the room. I turned calmly to him, a hint of steel in my tone, "I wish you'd answer straight. You did more than take the garbage out. You set it down by the garage, then you walked down the alley—in fact you ran down the alley to the drugstore on the corner. You went to the phone booth, the one on the right, and you made a phone call. Probably you called that girl Elsie who's been phoning you here." I hammered him, "I know because I followed you and watched your every move."

I waited for his response. He didn't speak. His expression went from surprise, to nonchalance, to shame, to out-and-out hurt.

The split second I saw that hurt I turned remorseful. How could I not trust him? Why was I so oversensitive? The mere thought that he could ever cheat on me was so devastating, I rejected it at once. What was I doing to myself and to us? I backed up, "I just made that story up. I didn't really follow you."

Berry's hurt now changed to anger, "I can't believe you did that."

"I'm sorry," I said to him as I saw him standing half-dressed, seething. "Berry, I'm really sorry, it's just that . . ."

He was walking out of the bedroom, shaking his head in disbelief, "We'll never be the same, I don't understand you, we'll never be the same."

"Come to Me" peaked at number six on the *Billboard* R&B chart. Marv Johnson became an overnight sensation in Detroit and was soon in demand by all the radio stations and local record hops. The Rayber Voices appeared along with him in shows that were precursors of the legendary Motown revues. A poster of one event at the Abington Theater, which featured Marv Johnson, the Satintones, the Miracles, Mabel John, Eddie Holland, and the Teen Queens, would one day be reproduced to illustrate a Motown songbook—even though the engagement predated the name Motown.

"Money," I'd whispered, holding our first royalty check in awe. It was almost obscene, more than ten times the advance we'd received from United Artists. It almost burned in my hands. "And there's more where that came from," Berry said. So right he was. The local distributors paid once a month and UA made quarterly payments from the national sales. It started pouring in, first slowly, then in a landslide.

The gold that we'd struck with "Come to Me" was making a difference. For starters, we were able to raise everybody to five dollars a week. Secondly, Berry and I had been out shopping for not just one but two brand-new cars. We weren't quite in the Cadillac bag yet, but we were mighty proud of the '59 white Pontiac convertible that we purchased for thirty-five hundred dollars. The other choice Berry couldn't believe. "Why a Volkswagen bus?"

"Look," I pointed to the ad in the newspaper, "they're giving away a free poodle with purchase!" Before he could argue, I dashed off and bought the 1959 VW nine-passenger van, one of the first of its kind, for nineteen hundred dollars. When I saw it, I just fell in love with it. And the poodle too.

It was a brilliant move to get the bus, I thought to myself, standing outside of the Apollo Theater one month later. The calls had been coming in from around the country, and Marv had even been booked on "American Bandstand." But when Berry, pulling strings through some booking contacts, had rustled up this latest event, I couldn't help feeling like a star-struck teenager. Even if I was six months pregnant with my second child.

We'd piled into the Volkswagen bus and headed off into the wee hours of the morning to New York City, home of the Apollo, where Marv Johnson and band were going to play. We were a motley crew. Jolly butterball Popcorn Wylie was at the wheel, driving as fast as his fingers tickled the ivories of his keyboard. Berry and Marv sat side by side trying unsuccessfully to keep a card game going. And the Rayber Voices in the back of the bus, warming up to sing at the Apollo, were newcomer and part-timer Gwen Murray, Robert Bateman, Brian Holland, and myself. "The

Apollo! We're playing the Apollo!" We chanted it the whole way there—everyone except for Marv Johnson who simply sat with his head held high, maintaining the pose of a star.

New York. The sights, the smells, the buildings, the crowds. We rolled right up to the Apollo, where Marv's name was splashed across the marquee. The Apollo was *the* place to see the greatest black entertainers. Ella Fitzgerald, Billy Eckstein, Sarah Vaughan. Billie Holiday and Charlie Parker. It was the black Carnegie Hall, the pinnacle of success. I was nervous, as there were still tons of preparations. We checked into the Theresa Hotel across the street from the theater, and I plunged into coordinating schedules, doling out expense money, and tearing through Harlem to find costumes for the Rayber Voices. Returning to the hotel with simple outfits of white shirts, purple vests, and purple pants for all of us, I gazed up again at the marquee. This event would be no easy gig. Apollo audiences were used to the best, and they were also New Yorkers: it all spelled out "tough." Horror stories abounded about decent artists who had been booed off the stage, and the Apollo even had a hook that forcibly pulled artists off the stage.

Berry, on the other hand, who'd been to New York as a small-time scrapper shopping deals, was full of confidence. Now he was a somebody—"Marv Johnson's manager, Berry Gordy, nice to meet you. No, I'm sorry, no interviews."

Unfortunately, the doorman at the back door of the Apollo the next morning didn't want an interview. He said, "I don't give a damn who you are and who you are managing. Marv Johnson, who the hell is that? Nope, can't let you in. Go buy a ticket and come in the front like everybody else."

We produced Marv Johnson and started yelling, "Look at the name on the marquee! He sings 'Come to Me'!" Nope, nope, couldn't let us in. By the time Berry finally found someone in the box office to vouch for us, our nerves were shot.

"Could you believe that guy?" Berry asked me on the way up the five flights of stairs to our dingy, dinky dressing rooms—one for Marv and one for all of the Rayber Voices.

"Lord!" I shook my head over that doorman. I guessed it meant we still had a long way to go with our careers. In the meantime, it was on with the show. Our debut was a noon matinee, one of four or five shows daily that the Apollo then offered. The audience would watch a cartoon and a movie before the live show began. Our bill included many performers, and because

Marv was doing so well, we weren't slotted until near the end.

Finally, with Marv in one wing and us in the other, we heard the announcer. "And now"—adrenaline was pumping, the band was playing, the crowd was cheering—"Marv Johnson!" Suddenly the nervousness disappeared as we glided out and met Marv in the middle of the stage and under the spotlight, exactly where we belonged.

It was sublime. "Come to Me" and "Whisper" were beautifully received. When we came offstage we couldn't get off our high. Hugs and laughter and shaking hands and slaps on butts—"Damn, we did it!" Cool hand Marv, of course, accepted congratulations with a "Well, it wasn't bad, not bad at all."

As our week-long stint sailed by, we were becoming favorites of the Apollo audience. Soon Marv was mobbed trying to get in the stage door, with that old doorman still standing by unimpressed. Just before one of the last shows, Berry raced backstage to tell us a new, unbelievable development. We were going to play Carnegie Hall.

A promoter who'd caught our Apollo act had selected Marv Johnson and the Rayber Voices to perform the fifties rock & roll music section for a concert featuring different musical genres. Berry agreed, and, still skeptical, we threw together a damn good arrangement of the Coasters' song "Charlie Brown," with Robert Bateman killing on the definitive line, "Why is everybody always picking on me?" It hit me the following night, as we occupied our pristine, spacious dressing rooms and as we walked out onto the grandest stage of the most opulent hall that I had ever seen: This was no joke, this was for real—we were performing at Carnegie Hall!

Back home, work took precedence as always. While the name Marv Johnson was spreading, Berry stepped up his push for Eddie Holland's campaign. With Eddie on a catchy ballad, "Merry Go Round," in the round-robin mode, the second Tamla record was born. Our next releases on Tamla were "Ich-I-Bon #1" by Nick and the Jaguars; "Snake Walk," which was an instrumental by the Swingin' Tigers, a.k.a. sax-playing Beans Bowles and band; and "Solid Sender" by Chico Leverett. To Chicago-based Chess Records we licensed a beautiful song that Smokey had penned and the Miracles sang, called "Bad Girl." On and on we worked, hoping with each effort to produce an heir to "Come to Me," that exact combination of ingredients that would move us up to the next rung of the ladder.

It was spring, ripe and fragrant—1959. A year had passed since Alice and I had traipsed timidly into Loucye's house to meet Berry and his little band of singers. Very soon, I hoped, looking down at my expanding stomach, I would give birth to a new family member. And every day our other family kept on growing. We'd gained one all-purpose member named Janie Bradford, a gal with a stupendous figure and a filthy mouth who doubled as a song writer/lyricist and a receptionist. Also, to my wholehearted pleasure, my brother Mike Ossman had climbed aboard and given us both his musical and his accounting expertise.

Time was an amazing kaleidoscope, I thought, sitting out on the front steps watching Cliff play. First we were hawking tunes from the trunks of borrowed cars. Next thing we knew we were performing at Carnegie Hall. Berry joined me on the porch, and I leaned against his shoulder as the two of us watched Cliff's antics. Not talking, we breathed in the aromas of the late spring afternoon, full of the rich possibilities about to bloom. I thought about Marv Johnson and saw his road to major stardom rolling toward the horizon. As fate would have it, Marv would fall from grace. So would others. But whatever events lay before us, the darkening day seemed to say only time could tell.

Berry, Cliff, and I went inside the house for dinner. I didn't look back to see the shadows on the lawn.

CHAPTER 5
MONEY
1959–1960

June 25, 1959. It was a boy; we had a boy! A beautiful bouncing baby boy, with blond hair and blue eyes. Now, wait a minute, roll that tape back for a second. I blinked, looking at the precious little thing. This child looks like a white baby. But there was no mistaking my small mouth and Berry's fine forehead on this handsome, tiny creature. It was a genetic wonder.

I'd been working nonstop until that moment, when in the middle of a Jobete policy discussion with Janie Bradford, Mike, and Berry, I stood up gasping, just as my water was about to break. False alarm, the doctors had told us at Detroit's Woman's Hospital, sending Berry home to wait for what they thought would be many hours. No sooner had he left than I'd gone into labor.

So when the nurse came to ask what we were naming our child, Berry hadn't yet returned to the hospital. We had been so sure it was going to be a girl that we'd only selected the name Tamla—the same name, in fact, that Claudette and Smokey Robinson would give later to their baby girl.

"What's your name, little boy?" I asked my newborn son. I already knew that he was a genius; perhaps he could give me some inspiration. Big blue eyes looked up at me. Let's see, I wanted to name him for Berry, but Berry, Jr., was already taken. So was Terry. I picked up a nearby newspaper. I'll name him for a statesman or an athlete. He should bear the name of a great individual, a man of letters, a hero whose contribution to mankind was substantial. At last, skimming all the way through to the comic strips, my eyes fell on the solution. Forever afterward Berry would swear he'd come up with the name, but the truth was that I named our son after a character who appeared in the funny papers, Kerry Drake.

I glanced up to see Berry racing into the nursery. I anticipated my bouquet of roses, boxes of candy, words of praise and congratulations. Instead he screeched to a halt, bedside, and looked down at Kerry, demanding, "Where'd he get the blue eyes? This baby can't be mine. Blue eyes?"

"Well then I guess you wouldn't want to hold this baby that isn't yours, would you?" As Berry took Kerry into his arms, the resemblance was immediately obvious, as was the joy that flowed between father and son.

"I think I'm in love," I said to the real-estate agent about a month later. Kerry was at home in the care of my good friend, Miss Lillie Hart, a motherly neighbor lady who'd promised, "Miss Ray, when you have that baby, I want to take care of it." Thank God for Miss Lillie, because two days after delivery it had been right back to work for me.

Since we'd long since outgrown Gladstone, I was scouting for a new headquarters for Tamla. On a sweltering July Saturday morning, I spied a gray house trimmed in green with a "For Sale" sign posted out front. Like so many others on the street, it was a fairly innocuous two-story family dwelling. But one structural distinction, a big showcase window gracing the front of the house, had caught my eye. I called the agent.

The house belonged to a photographer, the agent explained, as I saw that it was already set up for doing business: a reception area, just as you walked in the door; a medium-size office to the left of the reception area; and then, of course, the window the photographer had used to display his pictures. To the right of the reception area, the owner had knocked down some walls, leaving a space large enough for several desks. So far, so good. As the agent escorted me to the back of the house, however, I almost swooned. There was a huge cinder block room that had been added on as a darkroom. I couldn't have dreamed up a more perfect place for a recording studio.

After dragging my sister Kathy, who was now Kathy Bradfield, over to see the house, I got another vote of approval. The location, she said, was ideal. A socially acceptable neighborhood—one of Kathy's priorities, of course—that had commercial zoning so that we could now operate our business legally. Just across the wide, tree-lined street was a nursery school with a playground fully outfitted with swings, slides, and sandboxes.

"Yeah, now Cliff can leave his toys all over that playground," Berry pointed out the next day, giving me a quick hug of enthusiasm. And the upstairs second floor, with plenty of living space for the two of us and the boys, just cried out for a sign that read "Home Sweet Home." Pops gave the house a top-to-bottom structural check. "Hee-hee," his laugh rang out, "you found a keeper."

West Grand Boulevard—even the street name bespoke great things to come. Twenty-five thousand dollars was the purchase price. Three thousand down and payments of one hundred forty a month. Hopefully, I thought, standing out front on the walk not long after moving day, we'd pop another smash song out soon, and not have to worry about our burgeoning expenses.

"You guys ready to go to work?" I called over to my three recruits who were coming up the walk—soulful-eyed Ronnie White of the Miracles, hawk-faced country boy; Richard Morris who was a come-lately songwriter/producer; and Sammy Mack, a new Satintone. The four of us gathered up cans of paint and rollers and brushes.

Just then Berry scuttled out of the house, puffing, "Ray, they need you in the studio. O'Den wants to know where he's 'sposed to put the soundproofing." I'd found some old green velvet theater curtains to use for soundproofing, which another recent addition to the family, John O'Den, was going to help me hang. John, an ex-boxer and old pal of Berry's from Kronk Gym, was certainly fit for the job. At six-foot-two and 240 pounds and bearing a marked likeness to Joe Louis, John would wear many different hats in our enterprise. When he'd stopped by to see us on Blaine Street, he was so wowed by what was going on that he just stepped in as Berry's bodyguard. Later he would succeed Mabel John as Berry's driver, assist me in household and child-care tasks, and become everybody's beloved strong ox. John O'Den was heaven-sent.

"And another thing," Berry called, as the boys and I heaved the cans of paint from hand to hand up to the porch. "When is Bristoe bringing by the stuff?" We had already paid for Bristoe Bryant's recording equipment and baby grand piano to go in the studio. I reassured Berry that it was being handled.

"And another thing."

"Yes, Berry?"

"What color are you painting the place?"

We painted the building white with black borders. Perfect, if I didn't say so myself. Next I furnished the offices. In the larger space, I situated three desks—one for me, one for brother Mike, and a third to become the community property of the producers. Upstairs we dubbed one large room "the music room" and moved into it my dear little friend, the old mahogany spinet. Also on the upper floor were a kitchen, a master bedroom for the master and me, Cliff's bedroom, a third one that we converted into an office for Loucye, and a long narrow room that became a combination nursery/living room/auxiliary office.

The regular-size room to the left of the reception area was Berry's very first office of his own.

"And another thing," he said.

"Yes, Berry?"

"Where are my shades? If your mother lost my shades, so help me . . ."

"They're on your head, Berry."

"Oh, right. So what d'ya want?"

Now it was my turn. "And another thing," I said.

"Yes, Ray?"

"Do you know what today is?"

"It's Tuesday." I showed him the calendar. With Kerry and Cliff, projects and phone calls and meetings and errands and sessions and paperwork, and swarms of new people coming around, we were so busy we had to schedule a night for sex.

"Yea!" we both cheered. "Tuesday!"

I'd recently confided to a good friend that it wasn't just exhaustion that limited our sex life, but that Berry was hesitant about making love too often. "He says it depletes his business drive."

She just rolled her eyes and said, "Miss Ray, I beg your pardon, but, shit, if a man wasn't sticking it to me five times a day, I'd kick his black ass out."

I laughed high at that. No wonder she was single. What I couldn't explain to her was that Berry and I were making love every minute of the day—in making music and working together, in orchestrating the magic of everything that was happening. And with our new headquarters, we were both lustier than ever before, hungering for our next orgasmic hit.

"Miss Ray, the sign man is here," Janie hollered up the stairs to me. I jumped up from the desk to oversee the work. Berry had named our homestead, and it then occurred to me to order those big black letters to officially entitle the front of the house.

Up went the *H*. Next the *I*. It was funny, my life was rocking and rolling at such a feverish pitch, always leaping from one stepping stone to the next. The *T* and the *S* and the *V* were up. So many triumphs had been so welcomed, and yet before I'd had time to think about them it was on to the next goal to conquer. "Be careful with that *I*," I shouted. Sometimes, though, I could pause and feel the most amazing happiness and excitement from the smallest things. This sign was so beautiful and hopeful. Now hanging were the two *L*s and the *E*.

I was about to burst. "Berry, Berry, come and see the sign." He came out front with me, and as soon as he saw the partial banner there was that huge grin and those teeth of his. We stood on the sidewalk not saying a word and watched together as the last three letters were put in place. And then we read it in its unfolded glory: HITSVILLE, U.S.A.

Now began the legend of Hitsville. Motown legends, like any others, contain a lot of bent and distorted images, most of which get passed off as fact. But every once in a while you'll find one or two of these stories that just happen to be true. Such was the case with the first song we ever recorded at Hitsville.

Picture Janie Bradford, who had been writing songs with Berry since before Berry and I met. Janie was very tall, with medium-brown skin, short hair, a face that was passable but a body to kill. Her mouth was so murderous that it could have had her arrested, but it also poured out sensational lyrics. Now she and Barrett Strong went into the studio, about one week into our Hitsville residence. Barrett was actually one of Gwen's artists at Anna Records. He had a voice just like his last name, and he played a great, churchy piano. He was very fine-looking but ever so standoffish, maybe just to cover up shyness or some kind of cynicism. In the studio the two of them listened while Berry experimented with a riff inspired by the Ray Charles song "What'd I Say." Berry was in the mood to do something along those lines, something with the same funky feel.

Berry said, "Listen to this" and played the riff. It wasn't right. "No, wait," he said, "it's this." He tried it a few more times, unable to get the sound he wanted. Next thing Berry knew, Barrett had sat down and was jamming with him on that riff. He was doing so well, in fact, that Berry got up from the bench and let Barrett take over. It was hotter than July.

As soon as Barrett hit the groove, the sound vibrated up through the ceiling, right up into the room in which I was working and right into my bones. I bounded out of my seat to head downstairs.

"What should we call it, what should we call it?" Berry was asking them.

"Money!" Janie yelled out.

"Yeah, you would say something like that," Berry laughed.

"That's what I want," said caustic old Janie.

Soon they were improvising on a theme with Berry going, "Your love gives me such a thrill—"

And Janie answering, "But your love don't pay my bills." They kept bouncing these sassy phrases back and forth to each other.

I had now breezed into the studio, my heart doing pirouettes. Barrett had started singing too.

"Give me money," Berry blared. "That's what I want."

"That's . . . what I want," I echoed, carving out the soon-to-be immortal background vocal. Berry turned and smiled as he heard my voice. "That's the ticket."

It took us all of another hour to hammer out the second verse and refine the melody. That night I was up late doing the chord charts for everybody and sketching out the vocals for Robert Bateman, Brian Holland, Sonny Sanders, and myself. Midnight phone calls went out to line up the musicians.

Bright and early the next morning we were in the studio and I handed out charts to everybody. First to our two wild men, James Jamerson—the boss on bass—and drum maniac Benny Benjamin. Eddie Willis was back, still with a bad leg but a better than good guitar; and also on guitar was the proficient Robert White. Barrett, on piano, started the guys off. While they were shaping the band sound, I was over in the corner teaching the singers the song. Before long, we had it down all the way to the out-chorus.

We started to crank seriously, and we got set to record the basic track. Robert Bateman and Brian Holland doubled as engineers and hot-wired the equipment. "OK," I said, feeling like a traffic cop, knowing that when musicians are playing and can't hear the vocals they're apt to lose their place in the song. Following the chord charts, I signaled when to rest and when to come back in, using gestures and pointing and nods. "Second verse . . . solo . . . third verse . . . ," emphasizing rhythm, forming dynamics, and finally shaking my head and fist wildly at the break.

We were still working with Bristoe Bryant's three-track tape machine—instrumental overdubbing had not yet come into technological fashion—and the whole track had to be done live. Straight through without a mistake. "Take ten," Berry was saying. Then it was "Take twenty," and I counted it off again. Now it was "Take thirty-two."

Cleaning up the instrumental track, we moved on to the background vocals with Barrett playing a mean tambourine underneath. Sonny, Brian, Robert, and I had sung together so many times, our stuff was flowing like water. Now, with Brian and Robert back in the studio, Berry took over their spot running the sound board. "Take forty." Many takes later, we were moving into our third day, all of us disheveled, with Berry relentlessly keeping it going until he heard magic. Late that day we completed the last of Barrett's lead vocal. In the control room, Berry, Barrett, and I listened to the playback. "Money" was blasting on the studio monitors, piano pumping, drums pounding, Barrett screaming. The three of us exchanged cool nods. This baby is bad, and that is good.

But we were just over the first hurdle. Next came the stretch where if we didn't get the mix right the power of the recording would be lost. Berry decided he couldn't wait another day, so into the night he was at the mixing board with me at his side. Both of us entered that twilight zone of consciousness, spacy with exhaustion but more alive than ever before. Once or twice I tried to catnap on a desk just outside the studio. I heard the tape winding and rewinding, the click of the levers, Berry's measured breathing. It wasn't perfect until he could smell it. At last, the hiss of the machine dissolved and Berry stood, yawned, and padded off to bed. It was 7:00 A.M., time for me to get the place ready for the regular work day.

The marathon wasn't over, but surprisingly the toughest part—the deal—came together effortlessly. A few days later, Gwen listened to "Money" and said to Berry, "Let me have that record."

"What do you think of 'Money' going to Anna?" Berry asked me in a private moment.

"Great," I said. "Do it."

And so I sealed the fate of Barrett Strong's record. It was released nationally on Anna Records. In Detroit, of course, it was a Tamla record, the eighth release on our own label. Fueled by Berry's little riff, rich with Janie Bradford's cynicism, sugared and spiced by me, with help from the boys, and power-driven by the voice of Barrett Strong, it was an instant smash. "Money" peaked at number two on the *Billboard* R&B chart. Its immediate impact would be nothing, however, compared to what it would do over the course of the decades to come. And though we couldn't yet see into the future, what did it matter—we were really starting to be in the money!

"Miss Ray, the agenda please." With those words, Berry started our first Monday morning staff meeting. Later these meetings would gain an oracular reputation, a mystique for being a hotbed of creativity. The meetings began, however, as my attempt to handle the ever-multiplying problems of practical administration. As soon as we'd arrived at Hitsville, I instituted several new systems for operating Tamla. With brother Mike's assistance, I updated the payroll and accounting format. I designed schedules for studio use and building maintenance. Upon my suggestions, we lay down official work hours, job descriptions, and even a dress code. Berry and I took titles—president and executive vice president—first officers of Tamla Records.

Because all petty grievances and personal upsets were brought to me, I thought that the Monday morning meetings would be a nice way of resolving the beefs and still allowing the family feeling to thrive. John O'Den and I rearranged the studio into a meeting room, moving mike stands and the Ping-Pong table out of the way, replacing them with a long table and some folding chairs.

As Berry asked for the handwritten agenda I'd drawn up the day before, I could see John O'Den start to squirm. One of his many duties was helping me with snacktime, and it had been one of his complaints that instigated this first meeting.

Berry read out loud, "First item of business. John O'Den, general complaint. John?"

The muscle-bound he-man took a second to gain composure and then spoke with a frown: "Somebody's being a pig and leaving the kitchen in a mess." Though no one would admit to being the culprit in front of John, after a discussion we resolved the problem. John was more than glad to toss the baton of snacktime assistance to our old neighbor from Gladstone, Miss Lillie Hart, who was still keeping an eye on Kerry for us. In turn, John would have his hands full helping out with the care and guidance of Cliff.

Snacktime was probably the only predictable event at Hitsville. At twelve o'clock all work ground to a halt and every staffer would head to the kitchen to stand in line for Miss Lillie's lunch. Hank Cosby, who in the mid-sixties would become Stevie Wonder's chief producer and collaborator, started with us as a freelance musician. Often, down in the studio with an empty stomach, he'd hear the snacktime call and would jump in line with the other employees. "Sorry I cain't suv you Mista Cosby, you knows da rules," Miss Lillie would insist in her tipsy southern drawl. Free-lance musicians weren't considered staff.

"Oh come on, Lillie. Give me one of those hot dogs."

"No suh, no suh." She was a company woman.

Thus it was that one of the greatest triumphs in Hank's career came when he finally got a job as an arranger at a salary of sixty dollars a week—plus lunch. At last. "Lillie, *now* can I have a hot dog?"

We were a company and referred to ourselves as such. And, according to Berry, what was any company without a company song? So one Monday he asked Smokey to come up with a song for the meeting. A week later we all learned the first verse in one take. We'd belt it out like cheerleaders at the end of each meeting: "Nowhere will you find more unity than at Hitsville, U.S.A."

I'd look around the table, listening to everybody sing. And everybody *had* to sing. I'd ask myself how it was possible for my heart to just keep opening up and getting fuller and fuller, making room for the love I was feeling for everyone there. Every time I'd realize the same love was in other hearts for me, it would touch me all the more. I'd look at Janie Bradford, holding down the fort from that front reception desk; at Pops Gordy who held down the fort—literally—in building maintenance and repair. I'd think about how each person pitched in with whatever chores were necessary. And how welcome the schedule I'd made for those chores had been. Smokey, such a talented musician, still found time to sweep the floors on Wednesdays and cut the grass regularly. So grateful for Mike's smarts in money matters, I'd look down the meeting table and wink and kick him under the table, as we'd done as kids growing up. I'd find myself smiling over to the cute and skilled Loucye Gordy Wakefield, newly wed to sax player Ron Wakefield. Loucye had taken over responsibility for all manufacturing and dealings with distributors; I couldn't believe we'd ever managed without her.

Berry and I were running a well-oiled machine. When either of us saw a gap in personnel or expertise, one of us would find someone to fill it. Given our mutual respect and how alike we were, it was rare that we even had to discuss the hiring of new employees. When it became clear to me that he needed a personal secretary, I used my magic touch and caused the wondrous Rebecca Jiles to materialize. Extremely able and incredibly warm-hearted, Rebecca was one of the very few to become a permanent part of everything to come.

I stumbled on to a very young electronics whiz, a tall and curly blond-headed kid named Mike McLean. Upon becoming our chief engineer, Mike dramatically advanced our equipment and recording procedures. He was already hip to the importance of separating instruments in the studio. By barricading the drummer behind baffles—movable walls made of sound-absorbent material— and arranging the other instruments properly, leakage from one microphone to the next was drastically reduced. The result was a quantum leap in the quality of our recordings. Passionately in love with equipment of any kind, Mike kept the studio state-of-the-art and eventually built one of the first eight-track recorders ever used.

In time, the producers and writers would join the Monday morning meetings, making it an important creative forum for picking singles and assigning artists to producers. Another system of rating releases, however, had a different genesis. As the existence of Hitsville became more well-known, I noticed that quite a crowd of teenagers gathered regularly out on our front steps. Probably, I figured, they were hoping to catch some of the sounds they were hearing on the radio. So, why not? I invited them in to listen to the music. But here was the twist: after we played them our latest records, I asked them to select their favorites. Their opinions and tastes were such an accurate reflection of those of their peers that this event quickly became a regular Wednesday affair—our first quality-control entity. Soon I put together a tally sheet for scoring songs and writing comments. At times we'd ask the sharper kids to bring their friends around; other times we'd invite a whole class over.

Wednesday was also designated as the day for music class, which I offered upstairs in the music room to one and all. Smokey was my star pupil, Brian Holland a fairly faithful devotee. So many of the songwriters were self-taught and, though gifted, were limited to a hunt-and-peck knowledge of the keyboard. "Smokey," I'd ask while he played me one of his songs, "do you know what chord you're playing?"

"Not really."

"It's a G chord. This is G, the tonic, this is B, the third, and this is D, the fifth." I went on not only to teach them the keyboard but to lead them through key and time signatures, so that they could actually write down the music that they were creating.

I worried about Smokey. So cute, so charming, so talented. As he started to come into his own professionally, I was concerned that the attention he was getting would turn his head. So far, his absolute adoration of Claudette had been all we'd ever heard from him. In fact, after he courted her relentlessly, she'd finally accepted his marriage proposal just after the move to Hitsville.

Berry had first concentrated on making Eddie Holland a star. And then he'd taken up the crusade for Marv Johnson, whose early success had changed the course of destiny for everyone on board with us. After a few more releases from Marv, including the inimitable "You Got What It Takes," a controversial misunderstanding among Berry, Marv, and United Artists would contribute to the untimely deterioration of Marv's career. And so it would fall to Smokey to be the first to truly fulfill Berry's star-making dreams. A developing triple-threat artist, Smokey was a performer and a writer who would soon prove himself a worthy producer with the Miracles' "Way Over There." With this release he would emerge as a lasting, leading light in the company.

"Remember your wife," I would say if perchance those green eyes of his had been wandering. "Claudette is gorgeous and she loves you and she is worth more to you than any of these girls put together." Trust, I'd remind him, was the most valuable commodity in a relationship. "Look at me and Berry. We trust each other one hundred percent."

But trust or no trust, by the spring of 1960, with Kerry almost a year old, Berry and I were still unmarried. Mama and Daddy had long been up in arms about it, and now that I had Kerry's future to think about, I simply had to insist. Gun-shy after a failed first marriage, Berry really wasn't ready. But he also didn't want to lose me, and he accepted the edict without a fight.

Neither of our prior marriages had been legally ended, so I was briefly delayed by arranging both divorces—which Berry's ex, Thelma, didn't appreciate at all. Once I'd found a spot in Toledo,

Ohio, where you could get married in a day, I gave Berry the date.

Our wedding day was like none other. On a beautiful spring day we set out from Hitsville. In honor of my special day I wore a new dress and a little pillbox hat with a veil. Robert Bateman drove, and my mother, father, Mother Gordy, Berry, and I all crammed into the car. The drive was a rather scenic hour and a half, and when we finally got into town, about a block from City Hall, Berry suddenly spoke up out of nowhere: "Stop the car."

Robert looked to me to see if he'd heard what he thought he had. "Stop the car," Berry repeated, "I just want to get out for a minute. I have to go to the bathroom."

That seemed like a reasonable request to me, so I didn't pay much attention to where Berry went to find a bathroom. After a few minutes, we started giving each other wrinkled-forehead looks. Ten minutes later, it was getting really uncomfortable. Stuffed in the car, dressed up, we didn't say anything or know what was going on. Just as I started to have a panic attack, Berry returned to the car.

Robert turned on the engine, put the car in gear, and then Berry said, "I can't . . . I can't do this. I cannot go through with this."

Everyone was stunned. My father was particularly appalled. Mother Gordy was mortified, and Mama was in a state of shock. But me, I didn't miss a beat, "OK, Robert, turn this car around and let's go back." Not wanting to show how hurt I was, I played his rotten game. Robert hesitated and I repeated, "Take us back, Robert. I wouldn't marry this man if he was the last man on earth."

In another half-block, everyone suddenly got over their fits of frozen vocal cords, "No, Robert," Mother Gordy said, "turn this car back around the other way. They're getting married." Robert slowed down, not knowing what to do. My father, who had been shaking his head in utter disbelief, now said over and over, "Ridiculous, just ridiculous." Mama had not spoken, but if looks could kill Berry would have been very dead. Mother Gordy began screaming, "Robert, turn around, turn around." Daddy shouted, "Ridiculous, just ridiculous." Robert sped up and slowed down and pulled over and did U-turns. And I was yelling, "No, no, take us home. I wouldn't marry him." And soon nobody could hear anyone else in the confusion and din.

Berry sat through all this in a practically comatose state, no emotion apparent on his face. Robert at last figured that the verdict was back to Detroit, but no sooner did this sink in with the parents than the barrage began again. Mother Gordy tried reasoning with Berry. "Now come on, don't you love her? You know you do and this is a lovely girl." Daddy repeated a longer phrase at this stage: "I can't believe this, I can't believe this." A new round of instructions and shouting and yelling and screaming and nobody understanding anybody else began. After fifteen solid minutes of this, Berry exploded: "Stop! I can't stand this any longer. Stop the car and let me out. I'll walk back to Detroit. I can't stand this a minute more." We were now in the fast lane of the highway.

"Oh, no, motherfucker!" It was my turn to explode, "You're not getting out of here! This is your mess and you're riding all the way back with it. There's no way you're getting out now."

If silence was deadly, then nobody in that car would have survived. If it weren't for the presence of our families, maybe I could have handled the ordeal, but this embarrassment on top of Berry's ambiguity toward me was just too much. In the painful silence every breath and every flinch was magnified. Finally back in Detroit, we dropped off Mother Gordy first. As we let my parents out at their house, Mama turned back, leaned in the window to me and spoke, for the first time that day, in a whisper: "Don't you dare give that nigger his ring back." The fact that I myself purchased the ring is something Mama will never know.

Pulling up to Hitsville, we all stomped into the house. In the door, we saw the whole company standing by with a champagne celebration. "Congratulations!" they burst forth. One look at our faces and the glasses halted in midair. You could have heard a pin drop. Instead it was the sound of my high heels on the floor, marching past the party guests and up the steps to the second floor. Berry's feet took him down into the studio. I paused on the landing and said to Anna, "There's nothing to congratulate. We didn't get married."

The day continued in a cold war between Berry and me. Nobody else had the fortitude to speak to me either. That night, Berry came into the bedroom and finally spoke. "Do you want to get married?"

"No," I replied, thinking I'd never get over the morning's fiasco.

He sighed, "Look, let's get married. We'll do it tomorrow. Only please, do not bring any of our parents. And another thing—please do not wear that hat. I looked at that hat, and I just couldn't do it."

And so the following morning we returned to Toledo with Robert and without the hat. Berry grinned and kissed me. We walked out of the chapel, hand in hand, ran down the steps and into the car. The drive back was quiet and serene. In the backseat, Berry put his head in my lap and fell asleep. I placed my hand gently on his brow and studied his face. I thought about how far we had come together and how much further we would go. And for all the bounty of goodness and richness that God had given me, nothing could compare to this gift of love that I felt between us.

We returned from getting married and simply went back to work. At first, I resisted telling anyone, not wanting to spoil the tranquility. Then I called our mothers and told them to spread the word quietly. By the time everyone had heard the news, I estimated, Berry and I would be alone.

I prepared for our modest honeymoon at home by soaking in a luxurious long, hot bath, glancing at the clock every now and then to make sure I was ready and waiting by six, when he would be done with work. I adorned myself in lotions and perfume, thinking how sensuously we would make love. I perfected my hair and makeup, giggling already at how we would laugh and talk about our hilarious trip to Toledo. I arranged myself on the bed. In an exquisite two-piece white lace negligee, white satin slippers, and a pearl necklace, inhaling a contented breath, my lips already tasting his kisses, I waited for my man.

The door opened. My eyes followed him as he walked straight to the bathroom. After a few minutes, he was back in the bedroom and moving, not toward me, but to the closet. Of course, I thought, he'll put on those silk pajamas I'd given him. Instead he took out an expensive dark brown suit and began to change into it. I watched him. He ignored me. At the foot of the bed, he sat down to lean over and tie his shoes. I moved closer and touched his arm. "You're not going out, are you?"

"Yes, I am."

"Well . . . we just got married. This is our wedding night."

"So? What's the big deal?" Berry stood up and went back to the closet, refusing to make eye contact. Then he moved quickly, patting his wallet pocket, smoothing his jacket, fussing with his 'do. I was dizzy, nauseated, beyond conscious thought. Oh, of course, I calmed as I realized, this is a prank. He wasn't really leaving, I knew, even as his footsteps reverberated through the empty house and into the lobby. Each sound—the slam of the front door, his feet on the porch, the car door squeaking open—ripped at my heart. Only when I heard the engine start and continue down the street outside did it hit me with full force. He was gone.

Time and emotion and thought jumbled into a tornado of fury. Panic and paralysis set in. Hope suggested itself—he was off to get my wedding present. Someone probably told him that grooms give presents to their brides. Fifteen minutes. One hour. My stomach convulsing, my heart breaking, my lungs gasping. I paced, I threw the clock on the floor, I ran to the bathroom and saw myself in the mirror. The negligee mocked me, the makeup was insult upon injury. I tried to wash it off, and the tears came streaming out, mascara streaking and staining my face. Like a trapped animal, I stalked back and forth and around the bedroom. Two more hours. Another. And another. A desolate sadness, a loneliness, mingled with my rage. This man was a sadist. No man should be allowed to torture any woman this way. It was over.

It was eleven o'clock the next morning, when without sleep and back at work, I saw him from the window, pulling up in the car. In the bedroom, I headed him off at the pass. "Listen," I said, "I want a divorce. I'm going to have this thing annulled."

His stride to the bathroom was all business hustle, as if to imply my comment was too trivial to interrupt his busy schedule. I followed him to the bathroom door and watched him wash his face, my glare making it impossible for him not to say something. He grabbed a towel and then, "What's your problem? I married you, didn't I?"

"This is no kind of a marriage."

Berry dried his face, moved me aside, and went downstairs to work.

I spent the day, outwardly as efficient as always, inwardly devastated. "Where were you?" I confronted him coldly that night.

"What difference does it make where I was?" Now Berry paced. "I have things to do." He paced some more.

"Look," and he looked at last at me, "I married you. There are things I have to do in the evenings that don't concern you. They don't require an explanation and you have to trust me, or. . . . Regardless of where I am, I married you and I intend to keep it that way."

We talked for over an hour. He agreed to cut back on his evenings out. The socializing, he admitted, probably wasn't as necessary as it had been before. We stretched out on the bed, and he spoke close in my ear, the two of us like conspiratorial little kids.

I thought about leaving him, still, and then glanced down to see that he had on two different-colored socks. Without me to lay out his clothes, Berry couldn't even dress himself.

It was late when I went into the bathroom to get a drink of water and decide what I was going to do. I looked up at myself in the mirror; I was at my crossroads. On one hand, here was a man so starved for control that he could punish me shamelessly for having instigated our marriage. When I considered the alternative—life without Berry—I realized in a flash that my decision had been made long ago: I had decided to love him. Come hell or high water. Come fire and brimstone. And it was not only the man I loved, it was the music. And the dream. And I went back to bed.

CHAPTER 6
HITSVILLE
1960–1961

"Do you hear that?" Berry said, turning up the volume on the radio as he listened to one of our newest releases. It was late one winter evening and I let the sounds of the song sift through my senses. I wasn't sure I knew what Berry meant for me to hear. Yet my body warmed just thinking about how everything was happening for us; we were on a wild musical journey, not certain where we were headed but knowing that it was definitely onward and upward.

The period that followed the success of "Money" was one of experimentation for us. Though we may not have been aware of it, we were still searching for an identifiable sound, sorting out our roster, looking for a niche on the radio that no one else was filling. With the taste of victory on our lips from scoring regularly on the R&B charts, we were hungry for more—to perhaps even go beyond that market and have our records hit on the pop charts. Later it would be referred to as crossover success. All we knew was that there was a bigger market out there. Teenaged America, suburban and urban, white and black.

In August of 1960 we released Mabel John's "Who Wouldn't Love a Man Like That" on Tamla. Finally Berry's ex-chauffeur got her shot in the studio. While it didn't ring any big bells, on the basis of the song she was booked immediately for a week's engagement at the Flame Show Bar, which required that she have a whole show's worth of arrangements for Maurice King's sixteen-piece band. In preparation for her gig, I worked around the clock for two days, writing out the charts. Little redheaded Mabel bopped into the bedroom and saw the scatter of paperwork, "Why aren't you using the piano, Miss Ray?" I explained to her that Smokey needed it. Didn't I need a tuning fork or a pitch pipe? "Nope," I'd said slyly and had watched Mabel's jaw drop. It was still my best parlor trick.

And there had been some real magic in a song called "It," released in the same month as "Money." As "Ron and Bill" Ronnie White, who always struck me as imaginative, and Smokey Robinson had come up with the song. To live forever as one of the most charming yet obscure Tamla records, "It" told the tale of a young boy who befriends a homesick alien, an idea way ahead of its time as the success of *E.T.* would later prove.

These were all hot songs, but we hadn't found the big one yet. What we were seeing, however, with each Miracles release—"You Can Depend on Me" and "Way Over There"—was that Smokey Robinson was about to hit his stride. Or so we hoped with this new one that he'd written and produced for the Miracles.

To our good fortune, the music business in the early sixties was much simpler than it became in subsequent years. Postproduction work, as time went on, would become so bogged down with procedures that the time between cutting the song and getting it on the air could sometimes be up to a year or more. In our early days we could record a song and, if it was really great, have it out on the street the next day.

The Miracles' "Shop Around" had been in release for a week the night Berry asked me if I heard what he heard on the radio. But what *he* was hearing was "Shop Around" with an entirely different arrangement—nothing he could really explain, just an instinct.

Afterward Berry raced into the mixing room and started fiddling around, recutting the vocals with a faster rhythm track. Speeding up the tempo and deemphasizing the laid-back syncopation of Benny Benjamin's brush work brought out a straight-on backbeat, giving it a completely different feel. Looking like a mad scientist, Berry emerged in the wee hours of the morning with a new "Shop Around." He'd transformed it into a pop song. Eureka!

Berry had done well by trusting his instincts. Soon the new and improved "Shop Around" was in release.

To date, Tamla records had gone with B&H Distributors, run by a man named Bob West in Detroit. While B&H handled mainly R&B product, we'd known for a while that if Tamla was going to hit the big time we would need some heavy-duty distribution. I had a few ideas, and so did Berry: "Hey, there's this guy named Barney Ales who could help out with promotion on 'Shop Around.' I want you to meet him."

The next morning in Berry's office introductions were made. "Ray, this is the guy I was telling you about. Barney's interested in coming in to head up our promotion department."

As I shook the strong hand of this tall and boxy-built man, I saw in his attractive Italian features an expression of dark humor and shrewdness. "It's a pleasure to meet you." His voice was very smooth.

"Happy to meet you, Barney," I said. "Well, I won't keep you two." Closing the door behind me, I heard the murmur of their conversation break into loud laughter. Berry's phrase stuck oddly in my ear: "head up the promotion department." I had assumed that Barney would be coming in as an assistant to Al Abrams, who was in charge of that area. Al, who happened to be Jewish and, like Barney, was white, had been doing a bang-up job. Something felt amiss.

"Say, I like this guy Barney," Berry spoke out in bed that night, "but . . . he wants to start at one twenty-five a week."

"One twenty-five?" I sat up. "Loucye's only making thirty-five." And Loucye was our highest-paid employee. "For someone to just come in at that salary when others have been with us for a long time. . . . How are our people going to feel, Berry?"

"It's not their business and I don't care," he said, his eyes darting to and away from me. "That's what I'm paying him."

There was an unfamiliar rhythm here. I played my beat. "I don't think it's right."

"I don't care." Berry ended the discussion by turning over on his side with his back to me.

Somehow Berry had just changed the rules to how we arrived at all of our decisions. First he had asked my opinion; seconds later he had made up his own mind without me. But, I thought, if Berry was willing to pay the money, Barney Ales must be worth his salt. I'd have to trust Berry's instincts and overlook mine.

As Berry took Barney on the rounds of the company the following day, my extrasensory hearing was flashing warning signals. "This is Janie Bradford, our receptionist. She wrote 'Money'—well, she helped me write it," Berry began. Then, moving back toward my desk and Mike's, "This is Mike Ossman. He works with Jobete and accounting, and with Ray. Oh, you know Ray. You remember Barney, don't you?" Barney nodded. Without an invitation, I got up to join them as the tour continued into the control room. "Our engineers, Brian Holland and Robert Bateman, also members of the Satintones." As we moved outside to the building next door—which we had recently purchased—Berry and Barney's pace accelerated, and neither seemed to notice my effort to keep up. The two were gabbing away like long-lost friends. Berry was rarely this friendly toward practical strangers.

In the new building Barney met Loucye and Faye Hale, her assistant. I exchanged cheerful greetings with them as well; still neither man acknowledged my presence. Walking back to Berry's office, I held my own with their longer-legged strides, yet I was in their shadow. Finally, as the two entered the office ahead of me and as I prepared to follow, Berry spoke to me for the first time: "OK, thank you," and closed the door in my face.

Momentarily stunned, I felt confusion replaced by hurt and anger as again laughter swelled from behind the door. There was something about Barney that bothered me, and this new behavior of Berry's was making me very uneasy.

"Berry," I said later that night, "This guy Barney. He seems . . . it's not because he's white. I think the more integrated the staff the better. . . . Now, I know we need somebody strong like him. But he's . . . it's a lot of money, and . . ."

"Look, the guy is hired, and if you don't like it you can kiss my ass."

Before I could throw back the lowball, Berry had stormed off and out of the house. Since the blowup on our wedding night, he'd completely curtailed his all-nighters. I had an instinct that this was going to be one of those "I'll show her who's boss" nights. It was.

As it turned out, Barney Ales was phenomenal. Whenever anyone spoke of him it was with unflagging admiration. Within two weeks of his joining Hitsville, "Shop Around" started to move. Its success on the pop charts became a live-or-die crusade for Berry and Barney. Barney orchestrated the participation of all the major white distributors nationwide, and in so doing set up the machinery for us to repeat this success in the future. Besides being a landmark in the development of the hit Motown style, the Miracles' "Shop Around" blazed a path into that crossover frontier. It delivered us another influx of cash, it peaked at number two on the *Billboard* pop chart, and it won us our first gold record. We had crossed over, and Barney Ales had been our navigator.

I saluted him for his work, and he was equally admiring of

mine. Our professional relationship was respectful and friendly. Like Berry, he enjoyed telling a joke or two, and although his humor was a little coarse for my taste, Barney and I laughed together and appeared to be happy colleagues. Underneath that surface, though, was a silent, potent rivalry. I said nothing to anyone else. I sang his praises, giving credit where credit was due. But I knew that a knife in the hand of Barney Ales would find its mark. And I started to watch my back.

While Smokey had led the way, more and more of our artists were moving into the forefront with hits that took us to realms beyond "Shop Around." By mid-1961 we were waving our banners high.

Our next Tamla pop chart smash came from our first important production team, Brian Holland and Robert Bateman— known as "Brianbert"—who took a giant leap forward from being our house engineers. They would sometimes include another Satintone, Sonny Sanders, and be known as "Sonbrianbert," though not many of their songs together would stand the test of time.

Brianbert got their shot with a group called the Marvelettes. Originally know as the Marvels, they had auditioned for us as a group of five teenage girls from Inkster. Less one (Juanita Cowart), the Marvelettes were Gladys Horton, Wanda Young, Katherine Anderson, and Georgeanna Dobbins, who later dropped out. Their sound was sweet and young, their look cute and innocent. And their first song was our first number-one pop song, "Please Mr. Postman." Brian and Robert had been inspired by Freddie Gorman's job delivering mail. The Marvelettes, along with the Miracles, became consistent hitmakers. Their next several wins were produced by Brianbert. Then Holland-Dozier-Holland took over and later the producing wand was passed to Smokey.

Lamont Dozier was a cordial, broad-featured fellow with a country drawl who had come from Anna Records to sign with us on the short-lived Melody label. As a writer, he first worked with Brian Holland and Freddie Gorman, and it wasn't until later that, quite casually, he would collaborate with the Holland brothers on "Dearest One," a record released under Lamont's name in June 1962. The triple-threat threesome was born just as Eddie Holland's performing days were waning, and they settled in for an extraordinary series of hits. Holland-Dozier-Holland would become one of the most prolific hit-producing teams in history.

Mickey Stevenson, my wheeling and dealing old neighbor

from Canfield Avenue, had been movin' with the groovin' from the get-go. As a writer and producer, he would claim "Dancing in the Street," "Stubborn Kind of Fellow," and "Beechwood 45789," among many others. As an administrator, his tough and sharp tactics had proved him to be invaluable, especially with the row-dier of our musicians—the dice throwers, the booze guzzlers, the dope smokers, and the tail chasers. To keep them in line, get them to a session on time, and berate them when they didn't, he would haul them out of some of the darkest holes frequented by some of the stronger-stomached subhuman species of the world. For that, Mickey was given the affectionate name "Il Duce."

When Berry made him the first head of the artists & repertoire department, Mickey's influence was quickly obvious. The role of the A&R man is to oversee all projects—to coordinate recording and release schedules—and most of the producers tipped their hats to Mickey's high energy and frank communication.

That old music in my bones—I'd think about it often during the course of any Hitsville day. Not in my wildest dreams as a romantic little girl had I foreseen the caliber of musicians I would work with. Not to my surprise, the musicians who now formed such a vital core of the company were my favorites at Hitsville. My main men. Since I was a skilled musician, we spoke the same language, and because I never failed to recognize both talent and true grit, I became a favorite with them as well.

Many of the people at Hitsville then would become legends: on keyboards—Joe Hunter, Richard "Popcorn" Wylie, and Johnny Griffith; on baritone sax and flute—Thomas "Beans" Bowles; on guitars—Eddie Willis, Robert White, Don Davis, Dave Turner, Marv Tarplin, Dennis Coffey, Wah-Wah Watson, Dave Meyers, and Dave Hamilton on guitar and vibes. On bass guitar were Willie Green, Joe Williams, Bob Babbitt, and James Jamerson; on drums Benny Benjamin, Richard "Pistol" Allen, and Uriel Jones. Eddie "Bongo" Brown played bongos and percussion; also on percussion were Jack Ashford and Jack Brokensha. Bob Cousar, George Bohannon, and Patrick Lanier played trombone; Russell Conway, Floyd Jones, and Herbie Williams played trumpet. More saxophonists were Mike Terry, Hank Cosby, Norris Patterson, Teddy Bucker, and Loucye's husband Ron Wakefield, whose alto sax had soared on "Shop Around." Earl Van Dyke proved to be a monster talent on the keyboards when he came on board, through Mickey, to take charge of bandleading. Joe Messina, on guitar, already had a nice rep going from a regular TV studio gig he played. Joe, also a union musician, was an exception to the five-dollar rate; we paid him ten dollars a session—a whopping amount in those days. Occasionally we'd use my old alma mater harpists, Dorothy Ashby and Harvey Griffin. Most of the guys were seasoned jazz musicians, and worked with us on a freelance basis at first. After a few years, though, we realized that they were too valuable to lose and put them on salary.

Competition abounded among the musicians, and I often found myself protecting and helping a newcomer or substitute get acquainted with the others. I'd point out Joe Hunter, with his Cheshire cat grin and that everlasting cigarette dangling out of his mouth as he played. "They call him 'Fingers' because he can play anything and everything. Classical to jazz. Killer with the boogie-woogie piano too. Joe's played with all the heavy cats—Kenny Burrell and Paul Chambers. Berry met him ages ago and he played on all the first cuts of the Miracles' stuff."

Then Joe would look up from the piano and pass on his two cents. "Don't let Miss Ray fool you, she's the one that makes it happen around here. And she always knows what's happening. If somebody starts in a bar too soon or hits the wrong chord, they better hope she's not in the room. Nobody can get away with nothing around that pretty lady."

"And don't you forget it, Joe," I'd laugh. "You couldn't work with a nicer guy."

Unless, of course, you were working with Beans Bowles. "See that good-looking tall guy, the one who's about six-foot-four, 150 pounds? Beans is short for stringbean, and this man can blow. And he's an incredible bandleader. Berry found him at the Flame Show Bar—in Maurice King's Band. Found out he'd worked with Lloyd Price and Illinois Jacquet. But don't be intimidated, this dude is very laid-back. A real cutup. Until it's time to go to work. Watch him, he is a total professional."

Then I would warn the novice not to socialize with either Benny Benjamin or James Jamerson. "Those are the guys that Mickey is always rescuing from the fringes of hell. That Benny especially—the cute, hyper one with pockmarks—sometimes he's been dragged in here falling over drunk, hair a mess, clothes looking like he's slept in them. Mickey just props him up on the drum stool and puts the sticks in his hand. Once the music starts, though, he picks up the beat and comes alive."

Part of the magic of Benny's drumming, I'd explain, glancing over at the attractive, wild-eyed James Jamerson, was in how the two had developed an interplay between their instruments. Together, Benny and James established the blend of the bass drum and the bass guitar as the foundation of all great R&B-oriented dance music. Later, in the Supremes' "You Can't Hurry Love," which contained one of James's most-copied bass lines, the blend of the two would be perfected.

"James never ceases to amaze me," I'd go on. "Give him any key and he plays proficiently. Then he'll invent bass lines that turn out to be the crux of the song. Oh, and Beans tells a story that James used to hang with a dude named Washboard Willie 'cause he played washboard and harmonica. A lot of folks laughed at James for that—but he swears that's how he developed his sense of rhythm." From being the student of a washboard, James Jamerson· would go on to be perhaps the most influential bass guitarist of the sixties. Even in later decades, almost all the electric bass played on popular records would be rooted in James Jamerson artistry.

My conducting style had altered somewhat from my days at Cass, and as a rehearsal or session began I'd feel that funky rhythm and cut loose, my wild, excitable dancing driving the beat. James, I later found out from Beans, was particularly fond of his vantage point behind me. He would respond to my shimmy by shaking his thing, wagging his tongue, and mugging to the rest of the guys. The minute I'd turn around, he'd straighten up, and everybody would fight to maintain a straight face.

Usually, though, I didn't miss a beat, and my favorite expression was, "Next?" Early morning I'd zoom into the studio with the skeleton of a song—the writer's basic idea and my chord charts. The artist would sing it through, and the musicians would then run through the chords, suggesting patterns or shifts that worked. This was the family spirit at its best—when the concept came to life before our very ears. Sometimes one of the guys would produce a sound that changed the structure of the song: "OK, then, let's add eight bars here." Other times it wasn't that easy, and Berry became famous for his favorite line, "When I hear it I'll know it." Occasionally a mistake would be the honey of the song. The guitarist who was carried away in the heat of the musical moment would moan, "Oh, man, I busted a string."

Magically, on the playback, we'd find that the twang of the broken string actually enhanced the song. These mistakes became

integral to the distinctive Motown sound, and not many of our
early records were released without flaws. Another standard was
the use of two guitars—one on lead and one playing rhythm. And
because Berry was such a backbeat fanatic for the emphasized two
or four beat, we continually came up with new and outrageous
ways to hit it. Woodblocks, two-by-fours. Shortly down the road,
on "Dancing in the Street," bold producer Ivy Jo Hunter brought
in tire chains.

"Next?" I'd race to my desk to check scheduling of ongoing
and upcoming sessions. Before any producer could start work, he
had first to come to me to clear space and time. Then I would
require two more things: the song lyrics, so that I could write out
the all-important lead sheet for copyrighting, and a contract signed
by the songwriter. Nothing could be recorded at Hitsville unless it
had been copyrighted by Jobete. Later, when producers brought in
outside collaborators, I continued to insist that they publish with
Jobete. How fortunate for the heirs of Jobete that I was such a
stickler.

"Next?" I'd look up and see my husband. "Hey, Berry."

"Do you know what today is?" he'd ask, calendar in hand.

"Yea! Tuesday!" We'd both cheer.

And next on the checklist—another province that was largely
mine—was background vocals. The Rayber Voices had expanded,
to say the least. At one time or another almost every singer who
came to Hitsville had sung background. Members of the Tempts
and the Vandellas and the Miracles. For some of the young kids
who thronged out on that front porch, a chance to pitch in and
sing one of my oohs or uh-huhs or baby, babys was the chance of
a lifetime. A girl group called the Primettes got that chance on
many early sessions and continued to sing background on a few
more—even after their name was changed to the Supremes.

As the work for Jobete began to overwhelm me, our first
Rayber customer, Louvain Demps, got lucky when I asked her to
take over singing my parts. Her group, the Andantes—with Jackie
Hicks and Marlene Barrow—came into general use as house
backup vocalists. They cut one more definitive groove in our
sound: it would be their high, clear voices that backed most of the
Four Tops records—"Baby I Need Your Loving," "I Can't Help
Myself"—and the songs of many, many others. The other familiar
backing force, which developed when Smokey started producing
Mary Wells and wanted a masculine sound behind her, was a
group of three boys called the Love Tones.

"Next?" As the head of Jobete, I would forge through a mile-long checklist: listening to and filing the demos, determining and then verifying with producers which songs would be recorded. Furthermore: doing and correcting the lead sheets, procuring copyrights, obtaining and proofing and handling contracts, royalty statements, advances to writers, BMI contracts . . . it was endless. Since tracking every song copyrighted had necessitated a tape library, I got help from the very bright Billie Jean Brown to deal with the onslaught. Soon she became the first head of Quality Control, passing her tasks on to a sweet-natured girl from the neighborhood, Fran Heard, whom I'd hired when she came to me, without job skills, asking for work. I trained her to handle the tapes, and with time Fran found a niche with the company that lasted for twenty-five years.

By accident I discovered that Sonny Sanders knew how to do lead sheets and immediately offered him fifteen dollars a week to tackle a part of what I was doing. We were literally swamped. "Say, Sonny," I asked that handsome face later, "how would you like to do the chord charts too?" It wasn't long before Sonny inherited my responsibilities as our first house arranger. Later I recruited Dale Warren, my sister Ines's son, to work on arrangements. Dale was a terrific violin player, could write and arrange for strings, and was versed in the language of classical music. It was around then that Hank Cosby got his first hot dog from Miss Lillie when he joined the ranks as an arranger. Willie Shorter also arranged for a brief stint. And then, through the luck of the draw, Paul Riser, gifted beyond belief, emerged as the man most responsible for the gorgeous arrangements to be born in the classic Motown days.

"Next?" Toward the end of one day back before the arrangement staff had grown, I looked up and saw my husband. "Yes, Berry?"

Referring to a song of Barrett's that Berry had been developing for Eddie Holland, he said, "We're doing 'Jamie' next week. What do you hear arrangement-wise?"

I said, "I hear violins."

At this stage we hadn't used any strings yet. Berry thought about it, that old tongue in his cheek, and then said, "You got it. Whatever you want to do. Here's the demo."

That night I listened to the song over and over again as I created the string arrangement. I sketched out the figures that each string instrument would play, and in the morning I sat down with Sonny and showed him the figures as I hummed the different parts. What I wanted was a grand spiraling motion with the violins—to take the strings from a low tone and bring them up in a series of thirty-second notes to a climax and then, boom, Eddie Holland. It was certainly an ambitious undertaking, the most complicated score I'd attempted. The hardest challenge was probably the intricate syncopation I'd composed. It took me the rest of the day, with Sonny helping out, to refine and copy charts for the four violins, two violas, and two cellos.

The exciting day of recording the track for "Jamie" finally arrived. I had contacted the concertmaster of the Detroit Symphony, and he'd agreed to a booking of eight string players. Moreover, he'd stated that he was just delighted that they were going to work at Hitsville on "your rock & roll song."

It took every ounce of willpower not to laugh out loud when the concertmaster and his little bunch of sixty-five-year-old, bald-headed highbrows traipsed in with their instruments. Very polite and formal. Stifle yourself, Ray, I thought quickly, these are your heroes, pillars of the serious musical community. The visual contrast of these classicists sitting down with our wild, funky players, however, was priceless. I handed out the charts with a nervous glance at Sonny. Waiting to see how well we'd written the syncopated score for these musical dignitaries, I inhaled and counted the song off and . . . out came a nightmarish cacophony, like a violent cat fight. Everyone was playing something different, continuing through the score, exchanging looks at each other as if to say, What kind of music do they do down here?

Stopping the screeching at last, the concertmaster asked, "What is it that you want?" I sang it to him, and in two seconds he turned to the other gentlemen and said, "This is what they want" and gave them all their parts. We began again and it was a triumph, exactly as I had heard it. Eureka! That swirling, romantic, uplifting string sound in perfect syncopation with our regular band—the bald-headed symphony musicians and our motley crew playing as one. And the concertmaster proclaimed that he now loved "rock & roll."

"Next?" Oh, what a surprise, Saturday, my day off. That meant I had to get Cliff, now almost six years old, and Kerry, at a year and a half, ready for the company picnic in the afternoon. Also, Saturday was errand day, and it was time to stock up on supplies from the music store, Wurlitzer's, in downtown Detroit.

Just for fun, on the drive there I specifically did not turn on the radio, letting my ears breathe. The autumn colors were out and cool air rushed in the windows. Life was good. Berry and I were on a roll, in our work and in our relationship. The shadow cast by Barney Ales's presence had not gone away, but I kept it in perspective. It was not in my nature to stare long into shadows.

"Excuse me, Miss, do you know what that is?" The salesman asked me as I stood at Wurlitzer's transfixed by a strange contraption. It was a brown mahogany box about three feet tall with a keyboard on top. In the back of the keyboard was a ribbon extending from one side to the other.

"Oh, it's 'Mrs.,' " I said, now aged twenty-four, flashing that old wedding ring that I'd bought for Berry to put on my finger. "No, what is it?"

"It's an instrument simulator, called an Ondioline. You play this keyboard like an organ, and it actually sounds like violins." And the salesman demonstrated. Miraculously, it sounded like strings. I gave it a try. The keys were flexible, so you could shake them as you played and achieve a vibrato. With turns of a few more knobs and switches, out came the authentic sounds of French horns and trombones and more.

"What's this little ribbon thing in the back?" I asked.

He hit another switch, tapped the ribbon, and out came a percussive sound. A primitive drum machine. I was sold.

We used this amazing machine to simulate many different instruments. The sound was so true that, in his book *Temptations*, Otis Williams would mention that I had played a harpsichord on the Tempts' "Dream Come True." It was, of course, the Ondioline. The funniest thing about it was that amid all my comings and goings I would never see another one anywhere. Like other events in my life, I had just been in the right place at the right time.

In late 1961 Berry and I thanked every lucky star above for how far we had come in a little more than three years. And as a new and liberating decade came alive, we felt that our music was somehow a part of the progress that was afoot in the land. A great president, a member of a religious minority, was in the White House. To Berry and to me, President John Fitzgerald Kennedy symbolized the idealism we shared—the belief that doors would open for us, that anything was possible. We watched him and his beautiful wife on television and felt only more hope—for the country, for our little company, and for ourselves. Our black artists who'd been on the road, in the backwoods of the South and in tougher urban areas, had been disparaged because of their skin color, and we looked to this leader to end that discrimination. Already rumors of reform were in the air. It was an awe-inspiring time. JFK was new and fresh, young and exciting. So was his wife. And *we* were all those things. I'd look at their picture in the paper and think how romantic they were. Like us.

"And another thing."

Well, at least *I* was a romantic. "Yes, Berry?"

"C'mon, I want to show you something," Berry insisted with a very serious expression. What was it now?

I followed him upstairs to the music room, and together, unobserved, we watched an interesting scene unfold. By the time Kerry was a year old, he exhibited a love of music and we'd bought him a little record player, one of the old 45-rpm models with the big spindle in the middle. On it he would play DJ with his Tamla records for hours. On this particular day, the young DJ was crying mournfully as Cliff set up an imaginary bowling game using Kerry's 45s as bowling balls. I turned to Berry as he lost his poker face. I laughed, Berry laughed, Cliff saw the two of us and laughed, and finally even Kerry smiled as he toddled over to his father.

Berry adored his son. Of all the precious memories, the one that shines above the rest is the time I came into the control room one night and saw Kerry sitting on his father's lap as Berry was mixing. Kerry's small arms were reaching for the board, and then his little face lifted to gaze up at his daddy. It was such a peaceful scene, I hesitated to disturb them. After a while they sensed my presence and turned, both at the same time, father and son, to look at me.

Nothing has seemed as right with the world since that moment, nothing before or since.

CHAPTER 7
MOTOWN
1961–1962

There was nothing very dramatic or exciting or promising about it. To tell the story right, though, requires that I digress briefly for a little recording business background.

For several reasons record companies often establish more than one label on which to release various songs. One reason is to create a slightly different sound or identity from that of the mother label. Or a label might be started to feature the specific work of a certain producer or A&R man. In our day, an important reason was that radio stations were conscious of not playing favorites, in terms of the amount of airplay they would give to each label. So having more than one label would allow more of your product to get played on the air.

The Tamla label, of course, was our first baby. Then came Rayber, Melody, and Miracle, never to do that well, followed by the more successful ones—Soul and Gordy. There were later some attempts to start both country and rock labels, neither of which got off the ground. And in early 1961 Berry named a label for Detroit, the motor town. When we released "Bye Bye Baby" in February on Motown, we never intended it to be our dominant label.

The first Motown labels we stuck on the records were pink with stripes, and then in the summer we changed over to a blue map. As the calendar pages flipped by, we started referring to ourselves as Tamla-Motown. Even when the second half of the hyphenated name took over, none of our other labels fell from significant status. Nor were they characterized by any distinct sound, other than the uniqueness of the artists on those labels. Overall, there was, of course, the sound that we'd been developing, the music that had grown beyond doo-wop and R&B. "Shop

Around" and "Please Mr. Postman" were paradigms of that sound, which linked the inner cities and the suburbs, playing as brilliantly from a tenement window as from a brand-new car radio. We walked a fine line between an older-sounding soulful R&B and a teenage-oriented pop. We had struck oil with that precarious brew, and we began to look for artists and songs to keep the drill pumping.

Sometimes we erred; sometimes, because of timing and circumstance, great talents fell by the wayside. There were some early Tamla artists who, because they were too easily identified as blues singers, found themselves in an unhappy marriage with us, such as the fabulous Gino Parks and the sensational Singin' Sammy Ward. Mabel John, whose voice was rich with R&B feeling, would have done anything for a tiny foothold with us. Finally she became too frustrated. Stopping by my office one day, she shrugged, "Our directions are diverging. I'm R&B, Mr. Gordy's going pop."

"Mabel, go talk to him. He believes in you." Berry did try to record her doing pop songs, in some instances with the Temptations or the Supremes as background, but nothing clicked. When she decided to leave, she said a difficult good-bye to Berry, whose farewell was, "Don't worry. I'll always take care of you."

One female vocalist whose style did click with ours was Mary Wells—the first artist recorded on the Motown label. She had no intentions of being a vocalist, but rather had come to us with a song she'd written and wanted to sell to us for Jackie Wilson. We took her back to the studio and asked her to sing the song a cappella. Berry and I did our "by George, I think she's got it" glances at each other and decided to have her do the song. Called "Bye Bye Baby," it had a raunchy feel and only did so-so. It was Smokey who heard a softer voice in Mary and began to produce more sophisticated songs with her. With him in the production seat, Mary went on to string up the hits—"Two Lovers," "The One Who Really Loves You," "My Guy," and "You Beat Me to the Punch." With Smokey's help, Mary became a big star. In the midst of her career she married Herman Griffin, one of my dearest Rayberites and one of the first artists to record for Tamla in 1960.

Berry rushed in one day with the news that his ex-wife, Thelma, was going to start a record company. "We'd better start Gordy Records before she beats us to it." We did, leaving her to call her label—so imaginatively—Thelma Records. Born in March of 1962, the Gordy label ran close in breadth and success to Tamla and Motown. It was the home of the Tempts, Martha and the Vandellas, the Contours, and Edwin Starr; later, Undisputed Truth, Rick James, and Teena Marie were also on Gordy.

Martha Reeves, smart and sultry, was always hanging around, hoping for an opening. She got it when Mickey Stevenson, a.k.a. Il Duce, hired her as his secretary. She had already performed with a group called the Dell-Fi's which had put out a couple of singles on a Chess subsidiary. While at Motown, Martha watched and waited for a chance to reveal her true calling as a lead vocalist. Finally, the day arrived when Mickey was set to cut Mary Wells on a song of his called "I'll Have to Let Him Go" and Mary couldn't make the session. Martha proudly stepped forward. Soon she brought her girlfriends in, christened them the Vandellas, and, together with Holland-Dozier-Holland, scored the big time with "Come and Get These Memories," "Heat Wave," and "Nowhere to Run." Not a guy to miss out on a good deal, Mickey turned around and grabbed Martha back to produce her and the Vandellas on "Dancing in the Street."

The Contours, who would also record on the Gordy label, didn't come in with a bang at audition time. I was skeptical, as they looked like hoodlums, and Berry was about to borrow my phrase and say, "Next?" But after watching their very wild dance steps and listening to lead singer Billy Gordon's sock-it-to-you scratchy scream, I suggested we give them a shot as a novelty act. Berry nodded with his crooked half-smile and wrote them a song that spoofed the dance-hit style—and it was an instant smasheroo. It made the DJs crazy, though; they banded together and made sure it got an award as the worst garbage ever released. They would play the record and then break it on the air. But what did we care—the Contours' "Do You Love Me" was a charttopper.

Two groups who'd been knocking around, the Primes and the Distants, cross-pollinated and called themselves the Elgins. Their first lead singer was Paul Williams, who had that same kind of husky baritone as the awesomely talented David Ruffin. David brought his gifts—and his problems—to us from the Anna Records stable and formed a trio of lead singers with Paul and the high-voiced, handsome Eddie Kendricks. When joined by the deeper-voiced and delightful Melvin Franklin and the very polite gentle-man and fine singer Otis Williams, this group finally became the Temptations. They first recorded on the flash-in-the-pan label, Miracle. It took some time for the Tempts to cook up the right magic mix. Some things, though, as three decades of hit songs would prove, are worth waiting for.

Miracle was the same label on which I saw my last credited vocal recording. In early 1961, Berry, still enamored of the song I'd written for him while recovering from my miscarriage, decided to release it as "When I Need You," backed with "Continental Strut," by Little Iva and Her Band, with lead vocalist Raynoma Gordy. Later the record would become a collector's item, worth quite a pretty penny. But the monetary value would be naught compared to the emotional value the lyrics would always have for me.

Over on the Soul label, home to Junior Walker and the All-Stars, Gladys Knight and the Pips, and Edwin Starr, were my original accomplices in crime, the Originals—who later hit with "Baby I'm for Real." The group was composed of one ex-Satintone, Freddie Gorman; another guy from the early days, Henry Dixon; and two ex-Five Stars, Walter Gaines and Crathman Spencer. Damn, I'd think when I talked to Crathman, who was now going by C. P. Spencer, there's been a lot of water under the bridge since the fateful day that Alice and I peeked through the door at Loucye's and heard the Five Stars singing "Magic."

"Next?" Another audition was in progress, and my take was that these four girls were very cute and commercial. Their dance routine showed a lot of hard work, and their sound was pretty sophisticated, considering they were so young. That was the problem. Berry said, "I tell you what. I like you girls. Why don't you come back when you finish high school and maybe we can work something out?"

Well, they came back when they finished school—the very next day after classes let out. And every day after that. They got their first break on background vocals, and we eventually signed them and began the long process of finding the right material for them. One of their first recorded sides was a resurrected Teen Queens number, a song I'd had in my repertoire when I was a fledgling protégée of Berry's. It was called "He's Seventeen," a charming little two-beat rah-rah about teenage romance. "Seventeen, I've got a guy who is seventeen, I don't care because I'm just sixteen . . ." This would also wind up as a valuable collectible, but it didn't do much at the time for the four girls—Diane Ross, Florence Ballard, Mary Wilson, and Barbara Martin. They were known originally as the Primettes, a sister group to the Primes, but were renamed when we signed them. Even with a better name, it would be a long time before the Supremes had a hit.

"Say," Berry started, as we ran neck and neck in the ongoing chess championship.

"Say, what?" Half my pawns were gone and I was missing a bishop. Time to move one of the two remaining rooks and topple his knight.

"Ouch. OK, you know the blind kid? I'm going to sign him and get Clarence to see what he can do with him." A pawn of his took my rook. "Your move."

"Well, that's a fantastic idea. Clarence needs something right now anyway." My philosophy was it's always good to be sweet when you're about to win. Of course, Berry did have a fine plan. We'd just auditioned a little blind boy named Steveland Morris, who'd been brought in by Ronnie White of the Miracles. After we'd taken him into the studio, we watched as, one by one, this little prodigy played every instrument there. No wonder we decided to call him Little Stevie Wonder.

"Yeah, I think I'll do that. I'm not sure what direction to head him in yet, though." Berry moved his queen forward.

"Well, look, there's got to be something for a little kid with that potential," I smiled at Berry, capturing his queen. And using his favorite line, "You'll know it when you hear it." Then, feeling pretty cocky, I said, "I think we should hire that skinny kid with the freckles, about sixteen or seventeen, uh, Norman, Norman Whitfield." Well, so much for being cocky, there went my remaining bishop.

"That kid? I've caught him sneaking into the studio, just hanging around and listening." His pawns were chasing my queen.

I had to be a little cagey here. "He begs me every day to let him in. And, really, he doesn't bother anyone." I made a lame move.

"Persistence does pay off," Berry said happily. "I'll let Norman start in Quality Control helping the Kid out. That'll keep him busy." Norman Whitfield, who would become one of the most important producers at Motown, had just won a spot in the company. And I was about to lose. "Check," said Berry.

I was really stuck, looking at the board, laughing to myself over the "Kid," Berry's affectionate name for Billie Jean Brown, whose start with us had also been a fluke. She'd come over from the journalism department at Cass Technical High School, where she'd spotted an employment notice. The job listed was as an assistant to Loucye, helping to write press releases and liner notes for nine dollars a week. In June of '61, she'd written the liner notes for the very first Tamla album, *Hi! We're the Miracles*. In her spare time, she'd wander into other offices, idly playing various records here and there. One day a man she'd never seen before caught her engaging in this unauthorized activity. Pointing to the record, he asked, "Which side do you like the best?"

"You mean, which side do I hate the least." She punched her first words to Berry. He soon dubbed her the Kid, and had her work for him. He came to value her opinions about what songs should be released as singles. Eventually she became the first head of the Quality Control division, which made her a crucial figure in the Motown assembly line of decision makers. Every record that we cut went through Quality Control and was given a one to ten rating. Anything under a five was a no go.

"It's your move," Berry reminded me.

I was stuck, he had me in check. Suddenly, I saw the opening and rescued myself with a move of my knight. How sweet was the taste of victory. "Checkmate." H'm. . . .

"Hey," said Smokey, strolling up minutes later and placing his arm over my shoulder. "Aw, too bad, Ray, did Berry beat you again?"

Damn, I thought, even when I won I didn't get credit. Oh, well, a little walk and talk with Smokey always cheered me up.

Of all my long-running relationships at Hitsville, I probably felt closest to Smokey and Claudette Robinson. As Claudette had grown from a modest teenage girl into a young lady of strong character, so had grown my admiration of her. And I had strengthened my tone in those continuing lectures to Smokey on the virtues of marital fidelity. But sometimes those green eyes of his would only shine right back at me. Half-playful and half-lustful. Teasing.

"Listen to this, Ray," Smokey said on a hot, languid summer day in 1962 after luring me upstairs to the music room.

I sat next to him on the piano bench as he started the song, and his eyes were sly as he began, "I don't like you but I love you," going on to sing what eventually became "You Really Got a Hold on Me." When he finished he grinned. "What do you think of that one?"

"Oh, well," I said with extreme cool. "It's real nice." I couldn't even look at him as I said it, for fear that I would fall off the piano bench in a faint. Whether the sentiments expressed in Smokey's song had been inspired by me, I would never know. What I did know was that he was an irresistible charmer. And to protect both of us, I was out of that room faster than you could shake a stick.

"Ray, I need to borrow ten thousand dollars," Gwen stated on the telephone one day.

"Fine."

Gwen paused with a sigh of relief. "I asked Berry and he told me, 'Just call Ray, she handles all the money.' "

"It's OK," I said, not asking how long she'd need it or why she needed it. Gwen had always been there for us. For Berry, she'd gone beyond the call of duty as big sister when she'd provided him with shelter and a place to work, supporting him and paying the child support for his three kids. For Tamla, she'd helped by giving us Anna's list of distributors for our push on "Shop Around." Having been so busy at Hitsville, I hadn't really kept close tabs on Anna Records, though I'd assumed—what with Gwen and Billy's exper-tise—that they were faring well. Apparently I'd assumed wrong.

Part of the problem was our ground-breaking song "Money." This was ironic, because Barrett Strong was originally an Anna artist, and "Money" was released nationally on Anna. The song could have brought a sweep in for that company as well. But the distributors weren't paying on time, an old story for independent record companies. It often happened that a record would hit and there would be a huge demand for it. You then ran the risk of getting the big squeeze—on one hand the distributors wouldn't pay you the money they owed, and on the other hand the pressing plants wouldn't give you records without cash up front.

So Anna Records hit on hard times. The ten-thousand-dollar loan allowed Gwen, who had parted with Billy Davis, to join forces with her new beau, Harvey Fuqua, and briefly revive the ailing company.

Harvey Fuqua was downright sharp—tall, very dark-skinned, with a tasteful 'do, immaculate silver-hued silk suits, and snake-skin shoes. All the girls swooned when he was around. He'd sung with the Moonglows, who did one of my old favorites, "Sincerely." When the commercial appeal of that group started to fade, Harvey hired some guys called the Marquees, from Washington, D.C., to get some fresh blood going. One of these guys was a young singer named Marvin Gay (which he later changed to Gaye), whom Har-vey recognized at once as a fabulous talent. They had a hit with "Ten Commandments of Love," and when there were no subse-quent wins Harvey sent the rest of the group home to D.C. while holding on to Marvin for future plans.

Then the plot thickened. Gwen and Billy had been working with Leonard and Phil Chess on their Check-Mate subsidiary.

Through the Chess brothers, Billy Davis and Harvey Fuqua, who had once collaborated on some previous Moonglow songs, reconnected. In a quick succession of events, Harvey and Marvin moved to Detroit, Billy and Gwen broke up, Anna Records folded, and Harvey started his own labels—Harvey and Tri-Phi—mostly with Anna's artists and a few recruits of his own. Junior Walker, the Spinners, and David Ruffin were all part of this talent pool. Gwen and Harvey struggled through for a while, the ten thousand dollars having run out quickly, and then the old distributor nightmare began again. Soon Tamla inherited most of their artists and producers. By the time the smoke cleared, Harvey found himself married to Gwen and working at Hitsville. Just after that, Marvin started pursuing the heart of Anna Gordy.

"But that wasn't the original plan," Marvin confessed to me during one of our regular tête-à-têtes on the front porch. Our frequent conversations ranged in topics from family to religion to music and, of course, to love. Marvin Gaye was probably the most desired man at Hitsville. He was lovable, romantic, charismatic, sensuous, and brilliantly talented. Whereas the girls swooned over Harvey, they died over Marvin. What I loved about him were his many layers and his gentle sensitivity. He always spoke in a low, mellow tone, scarcely above a whisper.

"So what was the plan?" I found myself almost whispering too. I listened as Marvin told me of Harvey's plot: after moving to town, each would take one of the Gordy sisters. Harvey's original plan was that he would take Anna and Marvin would go with Gwen. There were to be differing stories about how the switch was made. The most popular theory was that Anna made the big push for Marvin, but I happen to know otherwise.

"Oh, God," Anna would stop by the office, "he's just a kid. He's much too young." Marvin would by chance walk by with an assortment of young girls dogging his heels, oblivious to them all. "Anna," he would say, practically speechless, a panting puppy himself.

"Well, hello, Marvin." Somehow Anna didn't appear so uninterested. But I happened to know that she had previously been married to a saxophone player much older than she was and that Marvin was seventeen years younger than she. So Anna continued to resist the charms of this irresistible man.

Marvin sought me out anywhere and everywhere. In the kitchen—"Anna is so beautiful." In the studio—"Anna is so intelligent." In the rehearsal room—"Anna, Anna, Anna." Finally back on the front porch, where we could talk—"She doesn't seem to understand how sincere I am. The age difference is meaningless to me. I don't want some little girl. Anna is everything I've ever wanted in a woman."

Thinking back to that excruciating time when Berry and I were falling in love, I beseeched Marvin, "Just don't give up. Keep on letting her know how much you really love her."

Marvin didn't give up, being the stubborn kind of fellow that he was.

"Ray, this man is chasing me down and chasing me down. Now he wants to get married. What should I do?" Anna's will-power was crumbling under the onslaught. And after pestering her relentlessly, showering her day in and day out with protestations of love, Marvin finally got her to succumb.

Marvin had arrived at Hitsville before Harvey. He began as a drummer, and a damned good drummer, doing such sessions as "Please Mr. Postman." But his real dream was to be a crooner, in the mold of Sinatra or Mel Torme. After proving himself to be vocally worthy, Marvin convinced Berry to let Harvey produce him on an album of standards called *The Soulful Moods of Marvin Gaye*, which offered such covers as "The Masquerade Is Over" and "Witchcraft." He also played piano on the album, and a damn good piano it was. But the album went nowhere.

"Look, if you're going to make any money, you've got to sing some of this funky stuff," Mickey Stevenson told Marvin, referring to a song that the two of them were writing together. Marvin wasn't convinced but agreed to cut the song.

It was the summer of '62 when I stopped by the studio to see how it was going. "I like it," I said, hearing the background vocals in my head immediately. "Now play that again." I began to sing, "Hold you tight, out of sight." I thought for a minute, "Wait, let's do, 'I wanna hold you tight . . . clean out of sight.' " Mickey did the opening bit, "Do do do bow," and I sang, "Yeah yeah yeah, yeah yeah yeah." How sweet it was—time always seemed suspended when the work was flowing like this. Marvin was banging out the chords and singing the lead, while Mickey and I ran down the harmonies. Ready to record some funky stuff.

For the session we got Martha Reeves, still pushing a pencil for Mickey, and a fellow Vandella, Rosalind Ashford, to do the backing vocals with me. Marvin used a husky voice almost as a joke; to him this wasn't the serious music that he truly yearned to do. But when the song "Stubborn Kind of Fellow" went nuts on the charts, Marvin stopped laughing at the funky stuff. Soon he had another hit, with background vocals by me and various Vandellas, called "Hitch Hike."

Marvin Gaye, a kindred spirit to me, didn't give up easily on his dreams. He still wanted to sing standards. Two years later, faithful to his own heart, he would record one album of show tunes and another of Nat King Cole songs. And he went down in early Motown infamy for a stunt he pulled at New York's Copacabana. The packed house waited excitedly to hear the live performance of all those wonderful Marvin Gaye hits—"Pride and Joy," "I'll Be Doggone," "How Sweet It Is to Be Loved by You"—and Marvin appeared in the spotlight decked out in white tux and tails and a top hat. And sang, "That old black magic's got me in its spell . . ." And then, "I've got you under my skin . . ." And Berry would be quoted in the annals of musical history: "What the fuck?"

Slowly I became aware of a new and volatile entity infiltrating the ranks of Hitsville. I didn't know what to do, because this emerging diabolical force was my darling son Cliff. The Motown Terror. Almost six-and-a-half years old going on twenty, he was growing up in the likeness of Berry to a frightening degree. I staged weekly interrogations of the little scamp on some of the reported atrocities. I wouldn't always get the full story from Cliff and would sometimes send him to Berry for what I thought would be a reprimand.

"You did what?"

"Aw, Mom, you know how everybody comes in trying to look good for you and Berry?" Cliff was still in his "Hi, welcome to Motown" stage.

"You know the guys, they look real sharp and sit down and hold their hats on their knees?"

"About the hat, Cliff? What did you do to that man's hat?"

"I said, 'Can I take your hat sir?' and then, 'Oh what a nice hat,' and I . . . pushed it inside out a little, punched the top open, and kind of mushed it in a ball . . . and I pulled the feather off and blew it. I said, 'Yeah, this is a swell hat,' and I gave it back to the man and said, 'See ya later.'" Cliff smiled proudly.

Of course, that poor man had wanted to thrash the boy, but, thinking he was Berry's son and waiting for the audition of his life, he was forced to paste a smile on his face and hold the pitiful remains of his hat on his knees.

Even I found myself a victim to the crafty devil's attacks. One time it was in the middle of a recording session, which, without multitracking and overdubbing yet available, had to happen in that one near-perfect take. The Temptations were singing and the Holland brothers with Lamont Dozier were producing and we'd been at it for hours. Finally we had our groove and thought that this umpteenth take would be our magic—and the power went off. "Ray, what's going on?" someone asked in the dark. And then in harmonic outraged unison, we all knew: "CLIFF!!!!"

The magical part of Cliff's mischief was that no matter how outrageous the pranks, he was so beloved by everyone that twenty-five years later they'd still be asking about "that Cliff." And no one more often than Stevie Wonder. The relationship between the two was marked from Stevie's first day with heartfelt displays of affection and plenty of shenanigans. It wouldn't be till Cliff was an adult that I would sit down and finally ask, "You did what?"

Cliff explained, "You see, when I first met Stevie, I thought he was faking it, being blind. We used to play hide-and-seek. I'd hide, and wherever I went he would come and find me. I thought, How in the world could somebody blind actually catch up to me all the time? Then I decided it was an act. So, I figured, he gets away with it and makes all that money, why couldn't I? I got me some shades—little kiddie shades—and since I didn't have enough money for a harmonica, I used a rubber band. I put that in between my teeth, stretched it, and played it that way with my shades on, moving like Stevie, with everybody looking at me. Then I went up to Stevie and asked him what he thought, thinking he'd laugh and give himself away. But he said, 'What are you talking about?' Oh, well, I guessed either this guy was really blind or he was just a damn good actor."

Then I would say to Cliff, "Stevie did what?"

"He never forgot anything I did. I'd pull some prank on him and then, two or three weeks later, I'd be sitting somewhere, listening to music and having a good time—and all of a sudden I would feel this slap upside my head. I wouldn't even see him coming. 'That's for a couple weeks ago,' he'd say."

Our financial situation was improving. We were far from tycoons, but life was much more comfortable than it had been in the early days. Although I handled finances with Mike and knew our net worth and potential, I didn't think of us as rich. It was just great to have the inflow so we could continue to create the out-flow—the music. But I was experiencing some sticky conflicts, within myself and with others, in regard to money.

Over at my parents' house, Daddy would ask, "How's Little Napoleon?" Daddy, of course, respected Berry immensely, but he'd always had reservations. "Are you protected legally?"

"Damn it, we've been through this a thousand times. Berry and I have a fifty-fifty split of the business. Twenty percent of my share I have elected to give to the original members. They've been at it as long as I have." My temper had a short fuse on these occasions.

Mama's tone would be just as testy. "You got all that in writing? And signed?"

"It's an oral agreement, but we'll get around to the paperwork. In case you've forgotten, I'm running a company and barely have enough time to go to the beauty shop, much less run around town to get documents signed."

"Raynoma," my Mama said, putting a slab of roast beef on my plate, "you are a damn fool."

"Oh, go to hell," I muttered inaudibly and went back home to Hitsville.

I knew on some level my parents were right. And I had been fairly persistent with Berry, bringing in proposals for stock issu-ances and profit sharing. His reply was usually that he wasn't ready to move on it yet. And as far as my protection, it was, "Don't worry, I'll always take care of you." So I didn't worry—there were too many other people's worries to mind.

"Miss Ray, I want to see my contract right now," Mary Wells had demanded one day. "It's my right, and besides I know how much the Miracles are making."

"Wait a minute. It's a standard contract, and it's just a formal-ity. What are you talking about, rights? We're not here to steal your money. You'll always be taken care of, don't even worry about it. This company is built on trust and, Mary," I looked at her ques-tioningly, "loyalty. We want you to have what you deserve, so please, trust me." I was quite firm. In later years, I would learn the importance of educating an artist in all the details of his or her contracts and career. But in these formative days, when the con-tracts were very straightforward, I took demands like Mary's to be

My father and mother, Ashby and
Lucille Mayberry, 1942. *(Lucille
Mayberry Collection)*

My brother Mike Ossman and I,
1937. *(Lucille Mayberry Collection)*

Me in 1947, age 10.
*Lucille Mayberry
Collection)*

Cass Technical
High School
graduation photo,
1954. *(Lucille
Mayberry
Collection)*

Demonstrating ballet prowess at
sixteen. *(Lucille Mayberry Collection)*

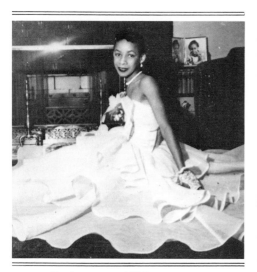

Senior prom, 1954.
(Lucille Mayberry Collection)

With my first husband, Charles
Liles, in 1955. I'm pregnant with
Cliff. (Lucille Mayberry Collection)

My son Cliff and I in 1960.
(Lucille Mayberry Collection)

Berry and I celebrate my twenty-
second birthday, 1961. (Lucille
Mayberry Collection)

Berry, his father, and I crowd into a
dime-store booth in 1960. *(Lucille
Mayberry Collection)*

Happy family: Berry, me, and our
son, Kerry, in Detroit in 1960.
(Lucille Mayberry Collection)

Berry's parents (Berry Gordy, Sr., and Bertha Gordy),
Mabel John, Berry, me, and Berry's sister Anna in
1961. *(Mabel John Collection)*

With my sisters and parents in 1961: Kathy Bradfield, me, Alice Wilson, Ashby and Lucille Mayberry, Juanita Dickerson, Roslyn Murray. *(Lucille Mayberry Collection)*

Stevie Wonder with Jackie Wilson in the early 1960s. *(Michael Ochs Archives)*

The Marvelettes in the early 1960s: Gladys Horton, Georgeanna Dobbins, Wanda Young, Katherine Anderson. *(James J. Kriegsmann/ Michael Ochs Archives)*

Mary Wells in the early 1960s. *(James J. Kriegsmann/Michael Ochs Archives)*

A Motortown Revue at the Apollo Theater in the early 1960s. *(Michael Ochs Archives)*

Smokey Robinson and the Miracles in the early 1960s: Smokey and Claudette Robinson (front), Pete Moore, Bobby Rogers, Ronnie White (back). *(Michael Ochs Archives)*

Smokey Robinson, me, and my brother Mike Ossman at the annual BMI Awards Dinner in 1962.

"your best bet is JOBETE!"

When Mike and I opened the New York office in 1963, the promotional pieces bore this logo *(Lucille Mayberry Collection)*

Berry and I doing "the Bird" in the early 1960s.

Holland-Dozier-Holland (Lamont Dozier, Brian Holland, Eddie Holland) in the mid-1960s. *(Michael Ochs Archives)*

Marvin Gaye in the mid-1960s. *(Michael Ochs Archives)*

The Temptations in the late 1960s: Otis Williams, Paul Williams, David Ruffin (front), Eddie Kendricks, Melvin Franklin (back). *(James J. Kriegsmann/Michael Ochs Archives)*

The Originals in the late 1960s: Freddie Gorman, Hank Dixon, Walter Gaines, Crathman Spencer. *(James J. Kriegsmann/Michael Ochs Archives)*

The Supremes in the late 1960s: Diana Ross, Mary Wilson, Florence Ballard. *(James J. Kriegsmann/Michael Ochs Archives)*

The Jackson 5 in the late 1960s: Marlon, Michael (front), Tito, Jermaine, Jackie (back). *(Michael Ochs Archives)*

affronts to our business ethics. I did understand, however, the disappointment many felt upon receiving their first royalties. "Wow, I've got a hit song and now I'm going to be rich" and then—after all the costs of recording the song, promotional monies, and advances are subtracted—they'd open the envelope, "Twenty-nine dollars and fifty cents?"

I was elated when an artist finally got his or her first car or put a down payment on a house. Especially the Brian and Eddie Hollands, the Robert Batemans, and my dear pal, Ronnie White, who through thick and thin had always been around to say, "Need anything?" Or "Can I walk you to the store?"

Berry had his own style of dealing with money questions. If he caught wind that, say, Gladys Horton of the Marvelettes had complained about her contract to Mary Wells, he'd call Mary into his office and say, "Gladys told me you said your contract with Motown was substandard."

Indignant, Mary would say, "That's ridiculous. Gladys was the one who said that."

It was a rather divisive form of getting the truth out, but it worked. For my part, I would caress the wounded egos: "Mr. Gordy only has your better interests in mind." It seemed I was often smoothing out the rough edges, stomping out potential fires.

The summer of '62 was a lot like heaven. Detroit was alive and green. We were a family, a very large one, and we were not inclined to miss out on any family tradition. The summer was studded with celebratory outings to Belle Isle and River Rouge parks, and I loved every bit of it—the food, the fun, the branches of our family tree.

The picnics rang out with the music of the children's laughter and the ruckus resulting from every competitive sport known to man. Cards, baseball, football—so that Marvin Gaye could show off his stuff. Sack races, volleyball, marbles, and then the serious event—the foot race—which invariably would be won by either Berry or his brother Bobby, whom we later called Robert L. At the height of the summer festivities, Bobby was the crowned champ. The prize? A fabulous cooking apron. "A cooking apron? Aw, shit." Then I sprang the gag. Reaching into the middle seam of the apron, I pulled out the tube of long, red cloth that made Robert L. burst out laughing, "An apron with a dick?" It then became a laughing contest between Gordy brother George, now producing and writing music with us, brother Fuller on board in administration, Bobby himself, and, as you'd expect, Berry, who was practically rolling on the ground with belly laughter.

For more dignified entertainment, we'd take the boys out to a show at the Fox Theater, usually to see one of our own Motown revues. Charming, soft-spoken Esther Edwards, Berry's older sister, had since joined the company to head our Artists Management division, International Talent Management, Inc., which was responsible for the artists' development and the nationally acclaimed Motortown Revue. Kerry would sit on my lap, Cliff between Berry and me. As an emcee would announce our presence and the spotlight swung down, I would duck, Kerry's bright blue eyes would sparkle, and both Berry and Cliff would crane their necks up to get as much acclaim as they could. Cliff honestly believed he was a company executive.

The glorious feeling of summer ended abruptly when bad news came in from the road that fall. We'd heard nothing but raves since our first Motortown Revue had set out to spread our sound to the far reaches of the United States. Berry had joined the tour on a few occasions and reported that the Revue was doing exactly what we hoped it would do, and more.

It was in the afterglow of this success that we received word of the tragedy. In South Carolina, late at night, with Beans asleep in the backseat, our driver, Eddie McFarland, had apparently fallen asleep at the wheel. He'd crashed into the back of a semi. Beans escaped serious injury but Eddie was killed instantly. Esther quietly relayed the news to us and swiftly made arrangements to have his body shipped back to Detroit.

Eddie was a distant relative of Berry's—a most pleasant, happy-go-lucky guy. And young. It seemed impossible that he was gone. The night before the funeral we held a wake in the studio. His parents were there and were inconsolable. The rest of us were in a state of shock, still unable to come to grips with the loss. Suddenly the door was opened by someone laughing loudly. I looked up to see Barney Ales entering the room, still laughing.

He was always a put-down kind of guy, with a relish for insult jokes. Polish and Jewish and black jokes. Now he had some dead jokes to tell. In a stage whisper, he stood by Berry, leaning down, loading the jokes into his ear. And Berry was laughing. Everyone else was appalled, and it wasn't long before I could take no more.

I strode over to the two of them and said through gritted teeth, "Will you please shut up? You have no respect. This boy's mother and father are here." I was enraged.

They were momentarily subdued, only to begin again, whispering and shaking their heads like two naughty boys after being scolded by an old schoolmarm.

The kinship between Berry and Barney had deepened, and I felt distrustful. "Just watch him, that's all," I told Berry. Barney, in turn, was watching me.

Life in general, with its many ups and only a few downs, was indescribably good. I loved Berry with a love that was endless, a love that encompassed our work, our family, our music. I loved him unconditionally, completely—for his humor, his vision, his drive. I even loved the fight in him. Lord knows I had it too. The music of Motown was our love song to each other every minute of the day. Our love was Motown. I remember thinking that it couldn't get much better. What I had no possible way of knowing was that my life was about to become a living nightmare.

CHAPTER 8
MARGARET
1962–1963

The first phone call came on a night when Berry wasn't home. But that wasn't anything out of the ordinary.

I'd made a lot of concessions about Berry's all-nighters, understanding how important they were to his style of doing business— being on the prowl, looking for action. When his nights away began to outnumber those at home, I asked only that he not stay out all night: "Just come home, because I worry about you and I want to know that you're OK."

He'd tensed at this tiny attempt at control, "Fine. What time do you want me home?"

To ease his defensiveness, I said, "Well, just be in before six in the morning."

After that, it never failed. Like clockwork, he would arrive at one minute to six. There had been many dark nights alone in the house with the boys asleep and odd creaks on floorboards and a rough wind blowing the branches of the trees against the windows. After too many sleepless nights, I admitted my fearfulness to Berry. His response was, "That's crazy."

"I don't care if it's crazy. I don't want to stay alone in the house." I threw it right back at him.

"All right, I'll take care of it," Berry said, somewhat reluctantly.

"Really? You won't go out?"

"I didn't say that," Berry explained. "I'll get someone to stay at the house."

Robert Bateman was one of the only Motown guys that Berry felt he could trust in such a personal matter. Berry decided that since Robert and I were wonderfully dear friends, Robert's large size, deep voice and warm company were sure to make me feel safe. And on the first night of the job, Robert demonstrated to the boss's satisfaction that the kids and I were in good hands. While Berry prepared to depart, Robert systematically checked all the windows, locked all the doors, inspected the household, and switched on the floodlights. He escorted Berry to his car—a sleek turquoise '62 Cadillac convertible—and I went up to my bedroom to watch TV.

"Oh, hi, Robert," I said, when I saw him in the doorway.

"Hi," he said very casually, stretching out beside me on the bed. We watched some TV and then talked for what turned into hours. I found myself confiding in Robert about my recent loneliness, something I'd done with no one. And suddenly a question arose in my mind, one that had never been allowed to form. "Robert, where is Berry? Who's he with? He must be with somebody, he can't just be at some club. Not three, four, five nights a week."

He looked away, and back. "Miss Ray, I know where he is. And I know who's there with him."

"Oh, my God, Robert. Who? Who is it?" I was on my knees on the bed.

Robert was lying on his side with his head propped on his arm. "I'll give you that information," and his eyes went from sympathetic to calculating. "But not for free."

"What do you want?" I sighed. I knew damn well.

He just grinned.

Well, pretending he wasn't serious, I laughed and sent him downstairs. But my lingering question was whether Robert really knew something about Berry or was just baiting me for his hook. The following night, it appeared that the latter was the case. No sooner had the drone of Berry's engine faded down the street than Robert flew up the stairs.

"Hi," he said, and I turned to see Robert standing in the doorway with a ridiculous lewd grin on his face.

"Now stop—this is silly." I couldn't help but giggle a little.

"Come on," he teased in his deep voice, "I have information you want, and you have something I want."

"Why don't you tell me what you know, and then we'll discuss the price?" I thought I'd try outsmarting him. Nothing doing. Next thing I knew, this strapping funny guy was bouncing on the bed crooning, "Ah, come on, I want you so bad. Just let me slip it in."

"Robert!" It took me an hour and a half to get him to go downstairs. Every time I mustered a serious, insulted frown, Robert would tickle me. By the third night, he'd developed a routine. From the second Berry was gone, Robert was up in my room, moaning and groaning. The more put off I tried to act, the more outrageous he became. "You think this is hard for you, Miss Ray, well what about me?" And then he'd point. "You want to talk about hard?"

To a certain extent, these fights were welcome. I was so lacking in male attention, and Robert was one of my all-time favorites. Sometimes his compliments felt like music in my ears: "Miss Ray, I've always wished I could have a lady like you." But then he'd get out of hand: "Here let me take it out and just show it to you."

"Robert!"

At the end of the week—and at the end of my wits—I surprised Berry one morning by saying I'd gotten over my nighttime fears. That day the disappointed Robert was told his security services were no longer needed.

I never found out what Robert knew about Berry. I also never told Berry about Robert's outlandish advances. That was a mistake I'd made long before—"Berry, Sonny is really a flirt," or "Obie Benson hit on me at the picnic."

Berry always blamed me, of course: "It's your fault," or "You must have been leading him on." Only later did I learn from James Jamerson that anytime I reported such misconduct, Berry would fine, ridicule, suspend, or threaten the guilty party; James himself had been on the receiving end of Berry's punishment many a time.

So I opted not to tell Berry about Robert's advances. And I settled in for some more long nights by myself.

That was when the phone calls started.

"Hello?" I answered, just on the brink of sleep. There was silence. "Hello," I repeated and yawned. "Who is this?" A longer silence. I looked at the clock. It was three-thirty. A prank, I thought, and hung up the phone and soon drifted back to sleep.

"Hello?" The second call came twenty minutes later. As before, there was only silence on the other end.

The third, fourth, and fifth calls came in shorter intervals. They continued until morning, and the next day I was slightly uneasy—and exhausted. When I retired for bed, alone as usual, I was sleepy enough to forget my plan to take the phone off the hook.

"What do you want?" This time when it rang, I was up like a shot. Again there was an interminable silence, and this time the caller hung up. I almost left the receiver off the hook, but my curiosity got the better of me. When the next call came, there was again silence, despite my repeated demands to know who was calling. The calls continued all night. The following workday was difficult, the next night even more so. For four nights the calls came. With each menacing ring I would become increasingly angry and frightened and even more unable to simply disconnect the phone.

I hadn't yet told Berry about the calls, as I didn't want to be accused of being crazy again. But I did tell him about the next development. On the fifth day the calls came with a voice.

"Hi." The woman's voice was soft and friendly. "I'm calling to let you know that your husband just left me and will be home in about twenty minutes. Listen for the key in the lock in twenty minutes and see if I'm not right." And then she hung up.

There was the key in the lock. It was exactly twenty minutes later.

As he walked into the bedroom, I swung out of bed. "Some woman just called here and said you were with her!"

"That's ridiculous," Berry said. "Don't start this crazy shit again."

I shook with anger and desperation as I ran down the particulars of the conversation and the calls. But Berry, acting as if I was unstable, blew the whole thing off and dressed for bed. I went to the window and stared into the darkness outside, gripping the windowsill, trying to get a grip on myself and what was happening.

And that was only the tip of the iceberg.

"Well, did he get there in twenty minutes like I told you he would?" That was the opener of the next call.

"Who is this?"

"Your husband and I had a great time again tonight." Her soft singsong was thunder in my ears.

I thundered back, "How dare you . . . how dare you call in the middle of the night like this?" I slammed down the phone, but a second later it rang again.

"Why are you getting mad? I thought you would want to know."

"Who is this? Why are you doing this? Stop calling, leave me alone," I screamed. And the line went dead.

It went on for a week. "Berry and I went to the Twenty Grand to see the Impressions. What did you do?" I tried everything. I didn't answer some calls. Or I picked up the phone and put it down again. Or I refused to speak. It was torture. During the day, when I saw my own reflection in a mirror, I didn't even recognize myself—I looked haunted.

"Miss Ray." Janie Bradford handed me the phone as I passed her desk. It was Barrett Strong's sister.

"I hate to be the one to tell you this," she started, "but Berry is fooling around with this girl Margaret. You know, when you're upstairs working, or downstairs, they're in the back, all over each other."

It took a second to sink in. "Margaret Norton? That girl who comes down here with Barrett?" Margaret had been here nearly every day since we'd recorded "Money." She was one of the prettiest girls ever to set foot in Hitsville. About seventeen, with flawless features, always dressed very well, and very polite. "I thought she was Barrett's girlfriend."

"No, she comes around with Barrett, but she's there to see your husband."

Suddenly it all made perfect sense. That sweet little voice, all those nights out. Reality hit, then shock followed with a violent downpour of humiliation. I had built my role as the mother figure, always advising the young men how to treat their women. Waxing on about faith and love and trust and saying, "Look at me and Berry." Oh, my God, everybody knew. Everybody had watched Berry and Margaret together. They saw me every day and never said a word even though they knew.

Janie's eyes were lowered. She knew.

"Where is he?" I growled.

Janie muttered her reply.

"What did you say?" I steadied my voice, taking in deep breaths.

"At the barber shop."

"Is it true?" I stormed into the barber shop. There were a lot of people in the shop, but I immediately spotted Berry in the back. When I spoke, the whole place stopped dead, "What's this I hear about you and Margaret? Is it true? Is it true, goddamnit?"

The barber stood next to Berry with a hand towel and looked at me uneasily. Berry said nothing out of the ordinary: "I don't want to talk about it."

"C'mon," I said. "Let's go—right now!"

"Well, let me finish getting my hair done," he said with irritation.

I saw that irritation and quadrupled it. *"No!"* I snatched the bib from around his neck and dragged him bodily out the door.

I drove like a maniac with Berry sitting silently as I told him what I knew. Crying, screaming, banging my hands on the steering wheel, I begged him to tell me the truth. "Let me drive," was all he said, as I sped the wrong way down a one-way street. I saw an oncoming pickup heading for my windshield and threw the wheel to the left, careening into an alley, the screeching brakes of the truck drowning out my sobs. Berry said nothing, neither denying nor confirming.

The next thing I knew, we just walked into Hitsville and went back to work. Everything slowed down; time did not seem to pass. I looked at score paper, copyright applications, contract copies, and they dissolved like mist in front of my eyes. But I wasn't crying. Before I knew it, day had turned to night and Berry was up in the bedroom getting ready to leave. Though my heart felt too heavy to even walk up the stairs, I somehow entered the room and closed the door behind me. I looked at Berry. Our history together burned between us. "Are we going to talk about this?" I asked. But no, there was nothing to talk about, he said. I was the one with the problem. "Don't wait up," he said and left.

That night Margaret called and I told her I knew. "I'm hurt and shocked," I said. I reminded her that I had welcomed her into my place of business, was always kind to her. I told her I had nothing more to say to her. And still she asked in that sweet, soft tone, "How does it make you feel, me and your husband?"

The nightmare refused to end. Margaret stopped coming around to the studio. Maybe she sneaked in with Berry, but I never saw her. But now she called the office on my private line. Two, three times a day. "Hi, how are you?" she said. "How may I help you?" I bit back. This was psychological terrorism at its worst. Images passed of Berry's profile; he was unwilling to look me in the eye. The weapon of silence was lethal. And there were more phone calls at night from Margaret. I began to anticipate them, getting into bed and waiting for the phone to ring.

Then came a call from Margaret that stood apart from the rest. It began no differently from the others. "How are you?" asked the usual cheery voice, as if we were friends.

"I'm fine. How are you?" I said, numbed by the routine.

She hesitated and then said, "Everything you've heard is true. He loves me." More silence. I said nothing. She started again and told me it had been going on a long time. That Berry married me, but "the only reason was that he needs you to work in the business. As far as love, he loves me."

Past caring whether it was all true, my heart having heard enough, I only wanted this woman gone from the earth.

"We have great sex together, too," she added. "In fact, that night you got married . . . was he home?" My stomach clenched, a sick taste entered my mouth as she asked, "What does that mean to you that your husband slept with me on your wedding night?"

My marriage was over after this conversation. It could never be the same. I could never be the same. I confronted Berry as soon as I saw him, and he called me a liar, said I was crazy. But it no longer mattered. I knew the truth.

One day blended into the next. I had never worked so hard in my life, doubling up on all my usual responsibilities. A part of me had died inside, but another part was still hopeful. I wore that hope like a life jacket. I didn't know what I was going to do; I only knew that I couldn't make decisions in a state of despair. I had to wait and mend. I was still the strongest person I knew.

But then the phone calls escalated. At the office, at night. I changed the phone number and still she called. There was now a disturbed edge to her voice. "Let him go," Margaret would say and hang up. Soon she began detailing their sex life.

One afternoon I stopped by a shop called the House of Nine. Trying to go on with the business of life, I decided to go shopping. I must look especially decked out today, I thought, since the saleslady was staring at me. "Are you a singer?" she asked.

"No," I smiled. "I'm with Motown. I'm Mrs. Gordy."

"Oh, Mrs. Gordy. That's funny. Which Mrs. Gordy are you? Because Mrs. Berry Gordy was here just ten minutes ago."

"Mrs. Berry Gordy? That's impossible, I'm . . ."

"Yes," the saleslady insisted. "Margaret. Margaret Gordy . . ." She stopped talking when she saw me breathing fire, then watched as I bolted out the door.

Now everywhere I went in Detroit it was the same—Margaret had been there just before me. At Kauffman's Furniture—"Oh, you must know Margaret Gordy, she just bought the most beautiful French Provincial dining room set." At Saks—"Mrs. Berry Gordy?

Margaret Gordy, you mean." I started seeing Margaret on the street ahead of me. At the hairdresser, the dance studio, my dressmaker's shop, the Twenty Grand—she left her trail everywhere.

As the phone calls increased, they became more and more bizarre. I almost wanted them to come, as though, by talking to her, I might understand what had poisoned Berry. I saw him very rarely, and there was death in his eyes. How could he justify not talking to me? What demon had possessed his soul? I avoided my friends and family and coworkers. I felt I had been betrayed. And I was ashamed.

Somewhere around this time, Smokey started following me and talking in my ear, touching me lightly and playfully. At first I thought he was making fun of me; only later could I see his concern. I brushed him off, but the gestures continued. One night as I walked through the dark passageway from the studio to the house, he suddenly grabbed me from behind. With his arms around my waist, he pulled me to him. "I really love you," he said with a half-serious grin. I looked at Smokey, I wanted to cry so bad, I wanted to cry and grab him and have him hold me to his chest. But I couldn't. If I did that, I thought, I would lose the last shred of control I had left. So I pulled away and walked into the house without him.

I had been swallowing the rage, holding it back, and now it was time to let it out. Berry was upstairs getting ready to leave, and I decided not to let him. I knew it would mean a fight, but I had to take a stand.

He came down the stairs.

"Berry, where . . . where are you going?" My anger sounded like hurt. He pushed past me into the lobby without a response. I fought back my tears, saying, "Why, Berry? I don't want you to go, please don't." I felt as if water was filling my lungs.

"That's your problem." He turned back to me, with a face that dared me to go on. As we stood face to face in the lobby, I became aware of a third presence in the room and turned to the desk to see Smokey sitting there. He looked back and forth between us.

"Fine, then. Get out!" At last my anger found its voice. As Berry stomped to the door and jerked it open, a rage as big as Detroit seized me. I rushed forward and pushed him with every ounce of my strength, "Get out!" Completely surprised, he fell down the step onto the porch. I retreated, slamming the door shut. When I turned around, I saw Smokey with the most sorrowful look on his face. In a flash keys rattled in the lock and Berry burst in with his own fury, pushing me down on the floor. He swung around, and as he left with a reverberating slam of the door, I sat on the floor, stunned. Finally I looked up at Smokey, still at the desk in the half-darkness. His face said everything. We sat there for a long while in silence.

My sense of self-preservation finally demanded that I retaliate. I decided to be productive at work, laugh, pretend I was back to my old self—and have an affectionate man all to myself. I initiated an affair with Sonny Sanders—so sweet, very handsome, and obliging. We met in motels, then I would rush home at five-thirty in the morning, just before Berry walked in. My coldness matched his. I enumerated all his shortcomings. How he had never said "I love you." Never bought me so much as a flower or told me I was pretty. How he just took, took, took my very best.

Many more weeks slipped by. And then I woke up one morning and thought, damn, Ray, this isn't you. This isn't fair to Sonny. Revenge wasn't a solution, and I told Sonny I couldn't continue. I decided to try to save my marriage.

That morning Berry came home at fifty seconds before six. Seeing me awake, he made an acknowledging sound, a sort of grunt. I told him we had to talk, that I couldn't go on. He grunted again and said he was tired. I insisted, and he committed to talking after a few hours of sleep.

He undressed quickly and crawled into bed, face down in the pillow. When I looked over, I couldn't believe what I saw—his entire back was covered with lip prints. The hard-core evidence of his cheating was staring me right between the eyes.

"Berry," I said, "your back. You've got lipstick on it."

He mumbled into the pillow, "That's crazy, what are you talking about?"

"No," I said, "I'm serious. You have red lip prints all over your back."

"Shit," he replied and just to shut me up, got out of bed and walked to the mirror, not expecting to see what he saw. He was appalled. I could tell his mental wheels were turning, and then, wearily, he said to me, "OK, I'm going to tell you the truth. I have been seeing Margaret."

I could only pause and ask, "Do you love this person?"

Berry exhaled with difficulty, "I don't know. I think so." He was quiet again. And then, "I always dreamed of a Cinderella.

When I saw this girl, I knew she was my Cinderella. She was beautiful. All the things I ever dreamed of having." He went on to tell me that it didn't mean he didn't want to be with me. He was in a dilemma, he said. A good wife on one hand, a fantasy woman on the other.

"Well, don't feel so upset about it," I started in. "Because you know all those nights you've been getting in at six? Well, I had just gotten in myself. Some nights I hadn't even taken my clothes off. I went to bed in my slacks, 'cause you got here too quick." Berry was dumbstruck. "You've been doing that?" he said.

"Oh, yeah," I said. "I've been laying out every night. I've been with one of your best friends." He was in shock, and I lit into him. All the despair and hurt and outrage exploded in a stream of abuse. As I spoke, my anger compounded itself. My words developed a rhythm, a pulse, a groove, that expanded and climaxed as I pounded away. I was delivering an amazing musical solo of fury, propelling my words into him. I wanted him wounded.

At last I struck a nerve. Berry's face suddenly distorted, and, breathing fire, he charged at me. Dragging me out of bed, he hoisted me up high over his head and threw me on top of the dresser. Perfume bottles and glass jars and metal hairbrushes and mirrors fell to the floor in a single enormous crash. A dead and sickening silence filled the room. He stood in the middle of it, breathing heavily. In seconds, he was dressed and gone for good.

Within days, I moved out of Hitsville.

We agreed to get a divorce. I wanted it over and done with as fast as possible. In the middle of the arrangements, Berry said, "Listen, regardless of what Margaret is doing or what her involvement is in my life, I'll always take care of you. No matter what I do, when we get to be ninety years old we're going to be together." In the meantime, Sue Weisenfeld, an attorney at Motown, arranged a Mexican divorce. It happened very quickly.

Another nightmare began—a new barrage of phone calls from Margaret to my apartment. Numbers were changed, and still she called. "Why are you calling me now? We're divorced. The man is free." She didn't believe me—Berry hadn't told her.

And that singsong voice was polluting every good memory I had. "You know, Berry and I have great sex, but there's one thing missing. I want you to teach me how to suck a dick, because I know you're good at that and I don't know how." Then she asked if we could get together so I could show her how to do it.

It was a true-to-life possession, a contagion of my whole being by this seventeen-year-old disturbed girl. To cope, I started taking tranquilizers. After several bouts of painful hemorrhaging, I was in the hospital three times and had a cyst the size of a grapefruit removed from one of my ovaries. I saw every recognizable part of myself slip away, and I entered a twilight zone of unnatural, unrestful sleep and depression. Still the calls came, and still I answered them. I was late to work, then I'd miss a day, then a week. When I returned everything would feel foreign. Many of my responsibilities were being taken over by others, the system that I had set up no longer had room for me. I became expendable at Motown.

Friends and family were distraught. But I trusted no one. Sick and paranoid, I imagined they were in collusion with Margaret. When I became fearful at night, I took out the two guns—a .25 and a .38—I'd bought long ago to protect Berry. Some crazed artist that he'd rejected might try to attack him, I'd once thought. That was the old me, always obsessed with his needs. Now I would have to learn to defend myself. I cut off all my ties of support and wouldn't talk to anyone, except the one person who had been my nemesis. I became obsessed with her, and obviously she was with me. She told me everything and asked me questions about everything. I took her calls, caught in a web of her insanity. It was as though a part of me wanted to be her, to be the Cinderella of Berry's dreams. And she couldn't stop making her calls to me, as though she had to learn what it was that I, an intelligent businesswoman, musician, and mother of Berry's child, had offered to him.

I was sinking fast. Coming up for air, I started dating again. Berry had a Cinderella; I would find my Prince Charming. And I would make sure that Berry saw me with him.

"Who's there?" Someone was trying to come in my bedroom window. My apartment faced an alley and a parking lot. In order to make his dramatic entrance—and there was only one person I knew who insisted on those—he would have to take a running start and jump up high enough to get his fingers on the ledge. Then he would have to pull himself up by his fingers and raise the window with his forearms perched on the sill. Berry was strong enough to do it and, of course, it was Berry. Now I was the forbidden lover. And he was keeping other men from being with me. There was a bad sickness spreading in Detroit.

One of the first Prince Charming candidates was a great-looking, intelligent, sophisticated fellow named Tony Brown. A psychologist who would later become a New York City–based television talk-show host, Tony had many of the trappings of the kind of man who could win my heart. Unfortunately, Tony didn't have the stamina to withstand the barrage of phone calls sprung on him by Berry. These calls, which came to Tony's home two or three times a night, sometimes at three and four in the morning, were Berry's ostensible attempts to be pals with Tony, to discuss various psychological and philosophical ideas. Tony's reaction to them, however, was to put an abrupt end to our short-lived romance, saying apologetically, "Ray, that man is never going to let you go."

Not long after Tony there was another beau, the very debonair and gorgeous Ron Vance, who was in bed with me the night of Berry's impromptu visit. As it happened, Ron was wearing Berry's beautiful black silk pajamas.

"Oh, no. Get up! Get up!" I urged Ron, managing to hustle him into the living room when I realized who was outside the window.

"Hi. What's happening?" Berry said, dusting himself off.

"Nothing," I said coolly.

With his very good instincts, Berry smelled a rat, "Who's here?"

"Nobody . . . ," but Berry was already out of the bedroom.

I followed him into the adjoining room, where Ron—a tall, handsome guy—sat dressed in Berry's pajamas, trying to look casual as hell.

"Who's this?" Berry asked, and when I told him, he bellowed at Ron, "Listen, you get the fuck out of my pajamas and get the fuck out of this apartment."

"Be cool man, be cool." Ron was out of the pajamas and out the door before I could even get a sentence out to Berry.

"You and I are not married anymore. I like Ron. You put him out like you own me, but Ron and I are going to be married." I had no intention of marrying Ron, but this was the punch I had to throw. It's your move now, Berry, I thought.

His move, it was later rumored, was to threaten Ron Vance and then offer to pay him five thousand dollars to stay away from me.

A few weeks later, Berry made an unexpected play. "Just give me some time. This relationship is not going to last. I need six months to phase it out." Berry was discovering how disturbed

Margaret really was. Once when he was at my apartment she called and I had him listen in on the extension. And she had started pulling stunts with him to get his undivided attention. She would slash her thighs and call him; when he came running over she would be lying with blood all over. He felt responsible though. She was so young, he said. As if my being twenty-five made me over the hill.

"When we get to be ninety, we'll be together." He really believed it.

Who gives a damn about being ninety? I thought. To hell with that. While I'm young he's spending his thousands on furs and jewels and cars and furnishings for another woman. What's he going to give me when I'm old—a set of false teeth?

With every ounce of my pride and strength, and the tiny vestige of sanity that was left, I reignited my love affair with Motown, with my own creation. I started taking back the jobs I'd delegated to others, and I started to heal.

But with one blow the effort was squelched. Margaret called to say she was pregnant with Berry's child.

I'd been in a frenzy all night. I was in the car, outside her house. I tried to quiet my feverish brain and think back over the past six hours.

On a Friday night, at eight o'clock, Claudette and I set off for the Westside Bowling Alley. She had begged me to go out, and I'd finally given in. Unlike all the Berry Gordy devotees who had carried on as if Margaret had always been Berry's woman, Claudette had stuck up her nose at the politics and stood by me. She couldn't stand Margaret and had never made any pretense about it.

Walking into the bowling alley, we saw Smokey and Berry standing at their lanes, absorbed in the game. And there was Margaret just behind them. Claudette's face practically turned blue as she grabbed my arm to lead me out again. Shrugging her off, I walked directly over to Margaret and sat down next to her. She was caught off guard, stiffened slightly, and then regained composure. Claudette veered over toward the guys. "Hi," Margaret said with a thin nonchalance.

From this point on, all I could think about was her last call: "I'm pregnant with Berry's child." I was thinking about it when I felt my pocket to see if the gun was there, the .25. I was thinking about it when I felt the bulge of the .38 in my purse. These were the instruments of protection I'd bought because I wanted to defend the man I loved. The man whose soul Margaret had robbed from me. I leaned to whisper in her ear, "Listen, bitch. What are you doing here with my husband?" There was a smile on my face for everyone to see.

She was nervous,"But I'm not here with your . . ."

Only Margaret saw the gleam of the pearl-handled .25. I jammed it in her side. "OK," I continued to smile, "I want you to get up slowly and walk outside with me. I'm sick of you. I'm sick of your phone calls. So get up now, bitch, and walk out. Make one whimper and I'm going to blow you away."

As we walked slowly to the door, every word of every phone call pounded in my head. Cinderella, huh? Once we were outside, I would bash the handle of the gun into the Cinderella face, until all the Cinderella qualities that Berry so adored were pulverized into one hideous, gory mass. We were nearing the exit, and I was planning how I would make her the ugliest hag in the world, with the face of the despicable person that she was.

We were outside. My adrenaline pumped. Her expression was fearful. Her eyes darted around and then were glued back on mine, transfixed, as the tiniest hint of a satisfied smile crossed her lips. I raised my hand to strike that smile and—a pair of strong arms locked around me. A voice was shouting, "Run! I've got her. Run!"

It was Smokey. I couldn't even see his face, but I knew that voice and I recognized the arms that held me as Margaret ran down the street for dear life.

"Let me go, damnit, let me go," I screamed with frustration. I cursed, and kicked, as Margaret disappeared from sight. I slumped in resignation and Smokey let me go.

A small crowd gathered, their faces aghast. My humiliation was total. For an eternity, no one said anything. And then Berry pushed through the crowd, still at a distance from me, with the light from the doorway angled over him. His face searched mine, and he saw in it everything that had happened between us, the victory and the devastation. Then I turned and left.

I sat in the car in front of Margaret's house with a plan to kill us both. For hours and hours. She never came out. By mid-morning, I decided to leave Detroit.

It was a Monday staff meeting. At its beginning, Berry made a brief announcement. "Miss Ray will no longer be with us at the Detroit office. She's leaving to open our office in New York, and this will be her last meeting with us here."

At the end of the meeting, they sang the song, "At Hitsville, U.S.A. . . ." I went around the room and hugged everyone. No one said very much. It had happened so quickly, maybe the realization that I wouldn't be there hadn't yet set in. There wasn't much to say.

I had already said good-bye to Cliff and Kerry. My older son was with Mama, and Kerry was in the good care of Miss Lillie. Until I got myself together, I wasn't going to be much of a mother to anyone.

As I was going outside through the front of the house, an entrance I had passed through a thousand times, I thought about the first time I'd walked in. A million memories threatened to slow me down. Finding the house, painting it, sitting on that front porch with Marvin or Janie . . . I stopped the memories; I let them go. I rushed out of Hitsville and didn't look back.

CHAPTER 9
NEW YORK
1963

As swiftly as my life had been plunged into hell, it rebounded, all in the span of a plane ride.

I hadn't wanted to leave Detroit. When I went to Berry to propose that I go to New York to launch a Motown office there, I was scared to death. I wanted him to beg me to stay, to tell me that he needed me. Instead he chuckled. Relieved, he said, "That's a terrific idea. That's the old Ray I know."

And I guess the old Ray was still with me, because although I hauled my bags wearily onto a plane in a gloomy, overcast Detroit, leaving behind the wreckage of a heart, I did a quick-change operation in the sky and came out on the other end as . . . Miss Motown! I had made it to the Big Apple, and I was going to make some music.

Feeling about as big as my pinky finger, I gazed at the Manhattan skyline from the cab. We drove over the Fifty-Ninth Street Bridge and plunged into the hustle of the city, weaving our way to the Americana Hotel on Seventh Avenue. By the time I was up in the hotel room looking down at the swarms on the streets below, I had been transformed into a New Yorker. Detroit was a damn cow pasture in comparison.

One phone call to George Schiffer, a Motown attorney in New York who had secured the office for me, and I was standing in the lobby of the Brill Building on Broadway and Forty-Ninth—in the hub of what was being called the new Tin Pan Alley. Reading the names of all the successful songwriters and publishers on the directory, I had an urge to caress its bronze finish. Leiber and Stoller, Phil Spector, Gerry Goffin and Carole King, Burt Bacharach and Hal David. Songwriting home base for groups like the Drifters, the Coasters, and the Shirelles.

139

"George, it's perfect!" I sang out. I'd told him I wanted Jobete-New York to be an exciting office, and he had gone to town. Modern, high-tech, chrome and glass, bright colors. I skipped through a tour of it—two big offices, a reception area, and a small demo studio. Glass desks, big round-cushioned chairs in fuchsia velvet. Vases and bouquets of flowers surrounded the entryway. Telegrams were piling up, and the phone wouldn't stop ringing. "Congratulations." "Good Luck." "Welcome to New York."

A rock & roll kind of guy stuck his head in the door saying, "Welcome to New York." I blinked. It was Bobby Darin, whose office was across the hall. To the left of us was Elvis Presley Music. It was as if all of New York's music industry had come to meet and greet me. I felt the pulse of life in me, the fearless Ray returning. And now, I thought—let the show begin.

"Next?" Another gentleman who came to see me was Lloyd Price, the R&B great from New Orleans, of "Lawdy Miss Clawdy," "Personality," and "Stagger Lee" fame. Lloyd strolled up to my desk, his arms laden with candy and ice cream. After batting around some musical ideas, he said, "It would be an honor to escort a lady such as yourself to dinner."

Sounded like a date to me. "Well, sure . . . ," I began.

"Fine," he interrupted. "My chauffeur will pick you up at nine o'clock this evening."

The driver arrived in a red suit, with gold tassels and buttons, and escorted me to a bright red limousine with lush red velvet upholstery and a glittering fully stocked bar. This boat of an automobile floated us to the Upper West Side to Lloyd's penthouse suite, where we sat down to enjoy a catered feast and a spectacular view of the city.

Life certainly was getting better.

"Ray," my indispensable receptionist, Joan Miller, buzzed me in my office, "your brother's here." Her whisper came through the intercom: "I think I'm in love."

I raced out to the reception area. "Mike!" That brother of mine was always a welcome sight. He picked me up and twirled me around, "How's my baby sister? You OK?"

"I'm better than OK. C'mon, let's get to work." I pulled him into the office. "Now, you're going to take care of my appointments, set up auditions, listen to demos and bring me the good stuff, do the payroll, help with the books . . ."

"Whoa," Mike laughed. "Slow down, how long you been in this city anyway?" And then he took my hands and said, "Did I ever tell you how proud I am of you?"

I beamed at him as he rubbed his hands together, "OK, let's make some music."

Together we soon assembled a writing staff chock-full of promise. George Kerr, an aggressive, fast-talking guy, had a strong portfolio of songs. And Sidney Barnes was a real find. Handsome, refined, and shrewd, he was also one of the most versatile singers I'd ever encountered. His voice ranged from the lowest bass to the highest tenor, and he could imitate just about anyone's style. On demos he could sound exactly like Smokey or Marvin Gaye or any one of the Temptations. Berry was impressed when he met George and Sidney, and he would eventually steal them back to Detroit, where they would stay with Motown for many successful years.

The purpose of Jobete–New York was to find new material for the established Motown artists. To that end, I cultivated a nurturing and stimulating environment in which the writers could take all their New York creativity and let it blossom in a down-home Detroit style. I seldom sat behind my desk during a meeting; rather, I'd pull up a chair alongside the artist and the collaboration could begin.

As I signed up writers, cowrote, and arranged, I also produced their demos. In the process, I wound up hiring many musicians, some of whom would later acquire stellar reputations. Some familiar faces in the studio were pianist Richard Tenryck and arranger Bert DeCoteaux. Then there were Eric Gale, a guitarist, and Bernard Purdie, a drummer, two New York scene knockabouts who would grow to be key figures in the late-sixties soul era.

"Ray," Joan buzzed, "Mr. Gordy's on the phone."

It was our weekly conference, strictly business. During each rather formal oral report, I recapped new talent found, projects on the boards, song titles. The slightest innuendo, even a hint of intimacy in his voice, would force a tightening in my chest. And his business updates weren't any easier to hear. The old family didn't seem to be hurting without me.

By summertime, though, I was building a new family in the big city. These artists had become my people, New York Motowners. Each artist brought his or her own individual sensibilities, and the sound had a whole different feeling. The songs were unique, yet the spirit that had cooked in Hitsville was here as well. Plus, another old family member had come to New York to stay for a bit—my sister Alice. "Wow!" She said at the office. Quite a little lady these days, Alice was full of enthusiasm and pitched in to help on the phones.

"Now when George Clinton comes in, let me know." I told her. "That guy has great commercial potential. He's also clean-cut, soft-spoken, with a beautiful smile. Tailored pin-striped suits and a briefcase. Just buzz me when he shows up." I was betting that George was going to be our star writer, for he kept churning out smooth, mainstream love songs. He was also producing and putting groups together, as Berry once had done. And I was right that a great career lay in store for him—but dead wrong about how he would ultimately hit. Years later, I went to see him in one of his Parliament/Funkadelic groups, and he walked on stage attired in only a diaper with the back cut out of it. "Ray, I've changed," he said after an all-in-your-face funk spectacle. "Yeah, I guess *so*," said I.

In addition to gathering up the songwriters and producers, I also stumbled over some smashing performers in New York, and I assisted them in getting deals. I warned Alice when I introduced her to Tim Wilson, lead singer of the Serenaders, "Watch out, he's a charmer. I mean very slick. Oh, man, though, do I love his voice." Tim, who looked like Nat King Cole and sounded like Anthony Gourdine of Little Anthony and the Imperials, shook Alice's hand and checked her out. As Tim was very dark-complected, he definitely didn't meet her requirements—which included the yellowest, the fairest skin, and the lightest, greenest eyes—and she just rolled her eyes at his attentions. No sooner did she hear that wondrous voice of Tim's, though, than she fell in love and started going out with him on the sly. All of a sudden, she was in my office telling me they were going to get married. Which in two years was exactly what they did. I just shook my head. Next?

Life was a never-ending series of twists and turns, I thought, as I sat quietly with Smokey in a darkening hotel room.

I had been in New York less than a month when he called me. He was in town and wanted to get together at his hotel. Even as I rode up in the elevator, I felt a clamp on my emotions. How could I divorce Smokey from the trouble between Berry and me? He and Berry were more of a team than Berry and Margaret were. I almost turned away at his hotel room door.

But the door had opened, and the clamp inside me released.

"Smoke. . . ." He embraced me with love. At every crossing of the road, almost, Smokey had been a witness. So there was no need to ask questions or pass judgments. We were just quiet with each other for a good stretch, and then began to talk. The afternoon wore into evening, the room darkening, and neither of us made any effort to turn on the light. It was late when Smokey took my hand and broached the subject that we'd been avoiding, "You know, Ray, that day you left . . . Berry cried. He couldn't stand to see you go, but he didn't know how to get you back. He didn't know what to say."

I didn't know what to say.

"Berry loves you," Smokey said. "Honest. You're the only woman he's ever really loved."

That was news to me. Berry sure had a funny way of showing love. I squeezed Smokey's hand, a gesture that made up for my loss of words. In my eyes I thanked him for being a friend.

There were more visits and more conversations, and Smokey campaigned for me to come back to Detroit. Motown was incredibly hot. "Don't be a fool," he said. "I'm loyal and faithful to Berry, but I'm not a fool. There's money in Detroit, and this money is yours. Come and get it."

"Smokey, I haven't left Motown. This is Motown too. Nothing has changed between me and the company. There's money here too. Maybe more than there. With me and Berry, too much has changed." Thoughts surfaced of Berry and Margaret, now living in some luxurious home in Detroit. "I'm starting over, Smoke, and I'm happy to have gotten out of Detroit alive."

I was definitely starting over in the boyfriend department. I was dating Lloyd Price and various other fellows in his circle and was having a fine old time. As far as any serious entanglements, however, I was a no-go. This old heart of mine had been through enough for a while, and all those old defenses had been revived to protect it.

"Listen, I came here to protect you," a guy named Ed Singleton said to me. Oh, please, I thought.

He was a songwriter and manager who had heard tell of the Motown lady and had decided to stop in and pay his respects. He was very attractive, approximately five-foot-ten with a medium build, a tan complexion, and neatly styled dark hair. His light-gray gabardine suit was tastefully coordinated with a black silk shirt and a matching handkerchief placed carefully in his jacket's upper pocket. He smelled of French cologne and carried himself like an Arabian prince. We chatted, and I was secretly impressed by his articulation. I enthused over the music community of New York and the warm welcome I was being given. That's when he dropped the line about his real motive for coming to see me.

This interesting-looking, compassionate fellow had decided I needed someone to be my knight in shining armor. What a line. As it turned out, this baby was for real. Though the men I'd been dating were good buddies and associates of Ed Singleton, he described them as "a bunch of hard-core shysters disguised as fairy godfathers."

As he explained to me, his concern wasn't only for my virtue; the bottom line for these cats was to get next to Berry Gordy's money. Part of what he was saying made sense. The New York music industry was much more cut-throat than what I'd known in Detroit. It would be wise for me to beware of suitors bearing gifts. I appreciated the advice but still was skeptical about Mr. Singleton's intent to protect me. Sounded more like he wanted to get me into bed himself.

A few months later I was pestering this man to death to get *him* into the sack. That was certainly a turn of events that I hadn't seen coming, but he had a lot of appeal. From the offset, in addition to his overall appearance I liked his shoes. I happen to have a weakness for men's shoes. Call me crazy, but when I looked down and saw his tasseled loafers, I figured he couldn't be all bad.

It was an uncommonly cool summer night in 1963 when Ed came up to visit me at the apartment I shared with Mike in the Presidential Towers on Eighty-Sixth Street and Riverside Drive— any New Yorker's dream address. Lo and behold, he had on Italian gray suede Antonio Brotini wingtips. He was racking up points right and left and didn't even know it. We talked, and without effort, I started to pour out everything to him. This man was a great listener, emotional, sympathetic, a strong shoulder to cry on. I gave him high marks for that. It got so late that he slept over on the couch, without even making a pass at me, earning himself several points for respect. The next night he came back after work, and the same thing happened. And then the next, and the next after that. For a couple of months, he spent the nights on the couch as I slept in my bedroom, and by day we were the dearest of companions and confidants. He got a very high score on the friendship charts.

Then there was his business acumen. From his office on Broadway he managed the careers of various artists, including Tony Orlando and Flip Wilson. His managing style was compassionate, personal, and patient.

When Ed turned to me one day early in our friendship and said, "You should really have your boys here," he won a place in my heart. He was right. I was starting to get on my feet, and as much as making music was important to my being, so was being a mother.

I was shortly thereafter introducing Cliff, now eight, and four-year-old Kerry to Ed.

"Hello, young man," said Ed.

"Where's Lillie?" Kerry asked, noticing for the first time since we had flown in from Detroit that day, that his lifelong caretaker was absent. I explained to Kerry that Lillie was at Hitsville taking care of other little boys and girls (later she would actually raise Smokey and Claudette's three kids), but Kerry wouldn't have a word of comfort. "I want Lillie!"

Cliff, at this first meeting, strode right up to Ed, "Say, Ed, where's all the action?" Soon he was up to his old tricks again: impersonating the elevator operator, turning off the power in the building, dangling Kerry out of our fourteenth-floor window. The usual—"You did what?"

Ed's manner with the boys reminded me of my father's with those six kids of Mama's: he treated Cliff and Kerry as his own. I threw away the score sheets and decided I really liked Ed Singleton. And that's when I started making discreet suggestions that he really didn't have to sleep on the couch every night. When those didn't work, I made less discreet suggestions. Finally I started nagging him to have sex with me.

Ed surprised me. "If I have sex with you, I want you to understand that you have to marry me."

"What?" I said. He repeated himself. "Wait a minute," I exclaimed, "just because I have sex with you, I don't have to get married." I had never heard such logic coming from a man. Come to think of it, I'd rarely heard that logic coming from a woman.

"I'm telling you," Ed laid down the law, "you can leave me alone or not. But if you insist on having sex, we're going to have to get married."

That night we went to the Lincoln Plaza Hotel in Manhattan and booked a room with stars on the ceiling and rhinestones and glitter everywhere. There were mirrors over the bed and a heart-

shaped tub. I finally had my way, and in the dawn hours that
followed, after we had fully exhausted ourselves, I realized that I
was going to end up married.

At the office one morning, I turned around and saw Berry
gliding through the entrance doors. "How's my New York office?"

It was his third or fourth visit. He loved popping in unannounced. The first sight of him was always the hardest—like a
rush of wind suddenly transporting me to so very long ago. But
then, after his breezy hellos to Mike and Joan and whatever artists
were on hand, we'd settle down to work.

"No, man," Berry would say to the writer, "put this line here."

"Right," I'd add. "How 'bout sticking the hook here at the
end?"

We had learned well from one another. From time to time I
would find myself glancing over at him. In the context of music, it
was painfully obvious to me how well matched we were, like right
and left shoes. I knew he was still the man I loved. But he represented Margaret and the pain of the previous year, so I clung to the
warmth of Ed Singleton, to the autumn cityscape outside the office
window, and to the sense that this was my town and my operation
was a good one.

My visits to Detroit were tough. There was more and more red
tape coming between the employees and Berry. Barney Ales
seemed to gloat as I passed his office. I shivered, feeling odd ghosts
around the house.

"Heat Wave" was all over the streets of New York. Hearing the
familiar beat made me intensely homesick and I'd dream of being
back in the studio with the guys. When I saw them in Detroit, they
all did their best to make me feel at home. The musicians were still
my main men, very generous with their time and talents on the
demos I'd brought. Eddie Kendricks sang on them for the same ten
dollars a session I was paying the guys in New York. Everyone
seemed genuinely happy to see me, but there was so much left
unsaid. As if the history that had caused me to run had been
erased. And so I ran back to New York determined to write a new
and better history.

Summer had turned into autumn, and during the first months
the trees in Riverside Park were a glorious sight to behold. You

could look toward the George Washington Bridge and see a thin strip of burnt orange and rusty reds leading north toward the upper Hudson Valley. Good things lay in store, I hoped.

By mid-October the rain had come, and everyone was on edge. But still I trudged along with hope. Moving into November there was still more of the same. It was cold and wet and windy. A harsh winter was coming, and yet I knew by spring all would be well.

November 1963. For those of us who lived through it, there will always be that memory of where we were when it happened. I was on my way up to the office in the Brill Building, which stood at the edge of Times Square. And it was as though the shot in Dallas rang out through the city streets of New York. The news was blasting everywhere, from stores and car radios and offices. People were pushing and shoving to get to the newsstands. Faces were wet with tears. The city was shrouded in despair. And collective shock. President Kennedy had been assassinated.

My first reaction was disbelief. He had represented the idealism of the country. He was our hope and our spirit and now he was gone. I thought at once of Berry, and at that moment the phone rang in the office.

"I guess you heard about Kennedy." His voice was strained.

"Yes." There was a long silence.

"I thought about who I could call to talk to about this," he said slowly, "and the only person I really wanted to share my feelings with was you."

"I understand." There were tears streaming down my face. Neither one of us could form words. And then it sounded as if someone had come into his office. "I'll call you back later, if that's OK," he ventured. "Of course," I said softly, just before we hung up.

I spent the rest of the day listening to the radio or talking with Mike and Joan. I was unable to come to grips with the fact that Kennedy was dead.

Berry called that night when I was home, shortly before Ed was due back.

"You won't believe it," Berry said. "Marvin Gaye and I had a fistfight today." Berry had been sitting in his office, alone with his grief, when Marvin had suddenly burst in.

"Hey, man, give me my money." Marvin apparently felt there was a discrepancy in his royalty statement.

Berry took a second to find his voice, "Come on, what are you talking about? President Kennedy has just been killed, and here you are talking about your money?"

"Give me my money, motherfucker."

They argued back and forth, Berry aghast at Marvin and Marvin spitting anger at Berry. On the umpteenth go-around, Berry jumped over his desk, and they had a knock-down-drag-out fight, rolling on the floor of Berry's office.

"Can you imagine?" Berry asked me. "People are crying in the streets, and the only thing he can say is 'Give me my money.'"

He and I talked about our huge sense of loss, and Berry was sentimental with me in a way he hadn't been in a very long time. And when the topic of Kerry came up, as it often did, Berry spoke hopefully of getting to spend time with our son, whom he missed dearly. Only toward the end of the conversation did I hear the deep weariness in his voice.

It was quite late when I put down the phone. Ed hadn't come home yet, and I wandered around the kitchen listening to the noises from the street. It had been almost two years since Berry and I had talked like that. Never before had I wanted so badly to turn back the clock. I filled up the bathtub and soaked in it for a long time, feeling nothing but a profound emptiness.

CHAPTER 10
BUSTED
1963–1967

The president's death continued to affect us. That day in November cast a darkness over the nation for months to follow. The future seemed more uncertain to me than it ever had before, as though the world needed to start all over again.

The year-end review for the New York office loomed several months down the road, and I felt my survival was at stake. This was my proving ground. I'd come here to get myself together, and, by God, I had to make it happen. Even more, I felt the *company* needed me to succeed. Motown had to take hold in New York, the pulse point of the music industry, if we were to keep pace with the rapidly changing industry. I put the pedal to the floor in every aspect of my work. And with fuel from the more amicable contact I was having with Berry, I began to feel encouraged. I knew that we had two potential gold mines in Tim Wilson's group, the Serenaders, and George Clinton's Parliament gang. Determined to ignore my few gnawing anxieties, I scheduled a trip to Hitsville to stoke the enthusiasm there.

There had been a couple of strange omens from Detroit. One night, several months before, I had picked up the phone to hear a familiar voice. The hairs on the back of my neck stood on end.

"Hello," she said. "How are you?"

"I'm very well, Margaret." She was calling to tell me that she and Berry were going to have a baby. I'd heard it from her before, but this time it was true. After that, she'd started making periodic phone calls to the office again. I was, fortunately, hardened to her pattern and managed to keep the demons at bay.

But then Ed began to get a series of unusual calls. Not from Margaret but from Berry. "Ray's not going to stay with you. All she cares about is money, and you don't have any." He was full of divisive tactics. On one call Berry even offered Ed fifty thousand dollars to leave me. It seemed that, although Berry didn't want me for keeps, he'd be damned if anyone else was going to have me. Ed and I tried to laugh about it, but as the calls continued we started to feel the strain.

My zest for the New York scene gave me a thrill, but my hopes weren't paying the bills. It had been a problem before, but now it was becoming particularly acute. Berry had no concept of the cost-of-living differences between Detroit and New York. The contrast in rent alone was astounding. When I'd left Hitsville my Motown salary was twenty thousand dollars—pretty nice for Detroit, but in New York, less taxes, it was nothing, especially with raising two boys. Rent on my Detroit apartment had been ninety-five bucks a month; in New York rent was four hundred. Plus rent for the absolutely necessary space in the parking garage. In Detroit I parked my car in the driveway for free.

Then there were my struggling writers, most of whom were totally broke. At first I had budgeted fifty-dollar advances for them here and there. Soon that money stopped coming, and I fronted them the money out of my own pocket. But before long my pockets were empty and funds for the demo sessions were dwindling daily. There was simply no getting around it—the budget had to be updated. Yet Detroit continued to turn a deaf ear to my repeated requests for money.

I was optimistic, though, as I led my New York crew onto the airplane. Their performance at Hitsville would be sure to wake everyone up to what I was trying to do.

I was there for a day when I placed a call to Mike. "It's going great. Guess what? The minute we got in, Berry took us straight back to the studio. Both of the groups did some numbers, and Berry flipped."

Mike chuckled, "That's great. What did he say?"

I was charged up. "He said he was definitely interested. We're going to record a couple of the songs and, as Berry put it, 'We'll see where we go from there.' And, Mike, everybody went nuts for the Serenaders. We're going to cut that song I love, 'If Your Heart Says Yes.' Berry said Tim Wilson's voice is as strong as Martha Reeves's. The guys are psyched, sitting out on the front porch, hanging with the natives." Mike was rooting for me all the way.

On the flight home, I was still positive but not as high as the first day. For one thing, I had to deal with Berry's capricious tactics in the personal arena. There was one night in particular when, hearing a commotion out on the railing of the hotel window, I went to investigate. Who did I discover but Berry, in a three-piece suit, climbing hand over hand like a monkey—trying to relive his amorous days of yesteryear.

On board the plane, Tim noticed my preoccupation. "Well, did they mention any deals?"

"No, but I wasn't expecting any. And everyone is impressed—you guys were fantastic. The song is really strong. They should probably move on it in a couple weeks." I wasn't sure about the record, as I felt we hadn't really captured the essence of the song. But I had fulfilled the goal of the trip—I was being taken seriously. So on with the show, and probably by review time we'd have enough under our belt so that that green light would shine.

"Hey, Berry," I began casually. This wasn't an easy phone call. But the money situation was very tense. Our review was now only three months away, and Detroit was dragging its heels on picking up our projects. "Listen, we need a budget update and fast. We're on the verge of some great things here, but we're being squeezed tight."

"That's out of the question," he said. I started to laugh, almost nervously. "Let's be serious," I told him. "I've been trying to tell you what it costs to do this anywhere near right in New York. We've got something going that could be huge. You've been here. You've heard the material. We just need more money to get it off the ground."

"That's your problem," he said harshly. "You either come up with a way to do it or close the office."

Stunned, I dropped the phone. Never in my wildest fears had I anticipated this. Standing in my office, time stood still as a fleeting and awful premonition washed over me. I had witnessed this emotional unpredictability before in our marriage and personal communications, but when it came to money and business decisions, Berry had always respected my judgment and given me full backing. When and why and how had this sudden change occurred? Close the office? Like hell. I resolved to make it fly, no matter what.

Mike and I trimmed the operation down to the bones. There

wasn't enough pocket change to take an artist downstairs for a corned beef sandwich. We couldn't afford to hunt down new talent, and still there was no word from Detroit on our existing projects. I wavered between trying to hold my breath until review time and flying to Detroit to throw an official temper tantrum. I decided to try Berry again, on the chance that our last exchange had just caught him in one of his bad moods.

"I can't do it," he said.

"I'm not asking for that much. And I know that the money is there."

"It's out of my hands," Berry stated in a flat voice. "I don't have anything else to say. Good-bye."

I threw the phone across the office, shouting to myself, "God-damnit, that's my money too!" Pounding my fists on the desk in complete and utter frustration, I couldn't believe that I'd been maneuvered into such a ridiculous position. What was I doing begging this man for money? If it hadn't been for me, he wouldn't have a dime. And then it dawned on me—this was just another game to him. Now, for the first time in our history together, it was a money control game, with his tight fist on the purse. Out of his hands? What did he think I was, stupid? I knew this game of domination, this irrational contest of wills. Berry knew me to be one of the very few who had always refused to kowtow to him. And he was daring me to defy him now, saying to me, "I've got all your major playing pieces. I took your love, I broke your heart. Now I've got your money locked up where you can't touch it. It's your move."

While I contemplated that next move, overcome by physical and emotional horror at what was becoming a brutal, devastating game, I didn't realize it would take me decades to fully understand the cause and the extent of Berry's monstrous transformation. What I wouldn't be able to conceive until some twenty-odd years had passed was that somehow Berry had twisted the story of what had happened to our marriage and our perfect partnership. Some-how, Berry had convinced himself, or others had helped convince him, that *I* had abandoned *him*. For this imagined abandonment, I would be punished in ways that were beyond the comprehension of even the most insightful individuals. Only in retrospect would I be able to pinpoint this moment as the one where I caught the first glimpses of this frightening side of him.

Meanwhile, however, I didn't have the luxury of even trying to fathom Berry's motivation, caught up as I was in trying to keep the

New York office afloat. So the move that I finally decided to make in response was many more weeks in coming. In the meantime I called Berry with one more plea for a two-thousand-dollar-a-month increase. I detailed the survival struggles of my writers and told him how physically distressed I was becoming—unable to eat, unable to sleep. It was all to no avail. I had the harsh realization that Berry wanted me to fail, that he was looking forward to relishing the moment when I admitted defeat. But Motown was my child, and what I was doing with my writers in New York was part of that. To let Berry deprive these young talents of their oxygen supply was to me like killing my children. No mother would let that happen without a fight. It was unthinkable. I came up with a last-resort plan.

When I arrived at this solution, a part of me was adamantly opposed. It was unethical. And yet, I asked myself, how many times had additional records been pressed to sell directly to record stores to make some extra cash? Bootlegging came with the territory in the music business. By-passing distributors and artists' and writers' royalties for direct payment to one individual was as routine as the sun coming up in the morning.

I took my last stand with Berry. I called to ask for five thousand records a month. If he couldn't give me the two thousand dollars and wouldn't give me a budget update, he could give me that. I needed that for six months. In six months I could show what New York could do. Berry was impenetrable. He said, "You figure out how to keep things running without bothering me for money."

With his crisp hang-up of the phone, all my ethical reservations dissolved.

It's your move, Ray.

Ed argued with me; I argued with myself; Mike had no knowledge of it. In the end, I chose my favorite because it was the hottest-selling record in the stores: "My Guy" by Mary Wells, written by William "Smokey" Robinson. And because I didn't have a master, I took a copy of the record from a Times Square record shop, made my own master, and planned to have the records pressed from that.

"Are you sure you want to do this?" Ed asked one last time.

"Yes," I said. "As executive vice-president and co-owner of Motown records, I'm going to have some records pressed up. I have the authority to do it, and I'm going to do it."

When I called the owner of the pressing plant, whom Ed had

contacted earlier in the day to let him know I would be in touch, his receptionist asked, "Who is calling?"

"This is Mrs. Berry Gordy, executive vice-president with Motown.'

"I'll put him right on, Mrs. Gordy."

I was to the point. "I want five thousand records pressed. I need them within the week, delivered to my office." That was that.

I found an assistant who knew the record stores and some distributors and sent him off to sell the copies of "My Guy" for fifty cents apiece. As I handed him the keys to my car—a beautiful silver Lincoln Continental that I was still paying for—now laden with five thousand records, I gave him a thumbs up. This was the hardest two thousand dollars I'd ever make.

I was in my office when Mike came back to tell me that two men in the reception area were insisting on speaking to me. I went out to find two sober-looking types. Must not be record people, I thought.

"Mrs. Gordy?" one of the men asked.

"That's me," I said.

"We're from the FBI. You are under arrest," he said as he flashed his badge. I felt cut adrift. This isn't real, this isn't really happening. Mike, who knew nothing, was having a similar reaction. Five minutes earlier it had been just a normal day. All of a sudden, the sister he admired so much was being handcuffed by the FBI. Within a few minutes, Ed was called in his office across the street to come over for questioning. When he arrived, he too was placed under arrest, and the two of us were taken away in their car.

We rode through midtown in silence. This is stupid, I thought. Something Berry, or that scumbag Barney Ales, is pulling to scare us. Nothing is going to happen. They'll slap my hands and make me turn over the money.

It would be a while before I would know what really happened that fateful day. Apparently someone at a record store had spotted a very beautiful silver Lincoln Continental and thought Barney Ales would be interested to know just exactly what had been unloaded from its trunk. The car hadn't been hard to trace.

"Stop pacing," Ed was saying, after we were booked and put together in a holding tank in a lower Manhattan jail. The numbness had passed, and I was now livid at this game of Berry's. I stalked the perimeter of the tank, with Ed's eyes following me.

"This is my company too!" I shouted, passing him. "I started this fucking company." Ed had never heard me use this language before, and he was about to hear me use it a lot more. "They have no right to do this to us. I'm the fucking mother of this whole fucking thing. Without me, Berry would still be licking Nat Tarnopol's fucking shoes."

Ed was gritting his teeth, his face somber.

"Oh, come on, Ed. This is just his game. As soon as we make our calls we'll be done with the punishment."

"Yeah? I don't know about that."

I paced some more, "When can we make our fucking calls?"

"Listen, Berry, I'm in jail." We'd been in the tank an hour before they came to put us in the cells and let me make my one call.

"I know," Berry said.

"So get me out of here," I said. "This is ridiculous."

"No, it's not ridiculous," Berry stated. "You bootlegged my records, and that's where you belong."

All around me were cell doors banging, guards' footsteps tromping, keys rattling, walkie-talkies and loudspeakers sputtering. My life was a bad cops-and-robbers movie. I yelled all the way to Detroit, "Come on, you know that's a bunch of crap. You've got people stealing money right and left and you're treating me like some felon. Why are you doing this to me?"

"Because you're stupid," he seethed. "Stupid and careless. I'm not going to help you. My hands are tied. You're just going to have to stay in jail, or get out the best way you can. And if you don't ever get out you can kiss my ass."

"Are you finished?" the jailer asked me. My one phone call had just told me to kiss his ass. Ed stood there shaking his head back and forth. I started to think that the matter might be serious after all. The realization walloped me in the gut: They had me right where they wanted me. Right where they had wanted me all along. I had played right into their hands, and I was done for. Everything that I'd tried to hold on to was gone, and now I was going to go to prison for twenty years for selling a Mary Wells record.

Luckily Ed had his own realization, which was to call an attorney friend of his who had us released in the morning. That night in jail felt like twenty years.

"Hello, Barney," I said, not surprised to see Barney Ales standing in front of the office door the next morning. The door to the office was padlocked. Barney's face was a mix of impatience and disdain, as if I had disappointed him by being such an unworthy opponent. "It was far too easy beating you," his eyes said.

"What the hell is this?" I said.

"We're closing the New York office. I'll wait while you remove your personal belongings."

The piano was a personal belonging, having been purchased with my own money, but there wasn't enough time to remove it— or several stacks of valuable creative work. These were items that I would never retrieve.

Next?

The cold war had begun. I was summoned to Detroit. Two days later, Ed and I and our attorney, Halsey Cowan, sat down in a meeting room from which Berry was notably absent. In his stead were Barney Ales, George Schiffer, and the Noveck brothers.

"Do you understand your options?" One of the Novecks asked.

"Yes, I think so," I answered.

"Fine," said the other Noveck. "You have forty-eight hours."

In forty-eight hours I was to make one of two choices: either to be prosecuted and face a jail sentence of a probably lengthy duration or to sign a general release from Motown and all its entities. Upon signing I would be given a settlement, which was fully dictated to me: a flat sum of ten thousand dollars, thirteen hundred eighty-two dollars a month for ten years, and child support for Kerry of one hundred fifty dollars a month until he was eighteen years of age.

I went first to my family, to Mama and Daddy and my sister Kathy. It had been a long time since I had been able to allow others to be there for me—to share anything painful. I had been too proud. As they gathered around me, I saw my mother cry. I couldn't remember having seen that before. They were devastated. They had always been wary on my behalf, distrustful of Berry. If only they had pressed it a little further, Mama and Daddy now said. They blamed and berated themselves. And though Kathy, especially, could see how outrageously small the settlement was, they saw that the matter was way out of their control.

Halsey Cowan, a prominent attorney who at one time had been Frank Sinatra's lawyer, advised me to take the settlement. Later I would wonder if he had been in collusion with Schiffer and the Novecks. The hotshot legal guns and dumb old me. That wouldn't have taken any stretch of the imagination. Motown was big business now. The amount of money behind it was enough to grease anyone's palms.

I had been defeated. The proud little soldier I was—having marched and fought and led one and all to victory, having survived the terrorist tactics of Margaret Norton, and having picked herself up and relocated to New York to try to make music—had been shot down. Finally, Ed, who had been with me during every step of the turmoil, said, "Let's just take the settlement and go. We can start our own label. Washington, D.C., has a big market, a lot of music, and nobody is down there recording." I looked at Ed, a man of remarkable goodness, my jaw dropped, and I thought, "Hope." That was all I ever needed.

In my mind, I equated Motown with the love I'd had for Berry, and the music our love had made. For me it wasn't about the money. Even with men like Barney Ales circling Berry's door, I could not hurt Motown; it was still my child. I blessed it and hoped that it would prosper and be well. And I decided to take the settlement.

Back in New York, we were waiting for the lawyers to draw up papers, and Halsey called with a new twist. "Ray, I've been checking into the divorce you received from Berry. It was done in Mexico; it's not legal. You're still married to him."

Berry was on that phone, too, faster than you could shake a stick. Fit to be tied. This was all my doing. I was out to destroy his reputation and drag Motown through the mud. Money was all I wanted, he accused me.

He had dealt me the final blow. His love was all I ever wanted, along with a chance to make my young dreams come true. To make music. We were standing on opposite shores. In between us now was an ocean of hurt. My war was over. "Oh, Berry." I tried to stop my tears, but it was useless. "I hate this so bad. I hate what's happened to us." I told him that I would sign anything they wanted me to sign. He calmed down and sang me his old standard: "Don't worry about the future. I'll always take care of you."

I went by myself to an office in New York and sat down at a conference table amid a battery of lawyers and accountants. Papers and documents were shoved at me. "Sign here" and "Sign there" and "Thank you." I took my copies of the paperwork and left. I wandered through the milling crowds on the street, not knowing my name or the day or the time or the year. I had just signed away my whole identity. I looked up at the towering buildings. "Who am I?" I asked the sky.

"Oh, Miss, you dropped something," a man's voice said. A kindly little black man handed me back the papers. I clutched onto the fragmented remains of who I had been and resolved to hold on even tighter to the one thing left to me that could tell me who I was—a tiny shred of hope.

Well, I also had Ed, my two beautiful sons, a little bit of money, and I soon would have a lovely new address in Washington, D.C. We first occupied a townhouse on G Street, and it wasn't long before we lucked onto an old six-bedroom mansion on Argyle Terrace that was a bit less expensive than the townhouse. It was on the northwest side of town just across from Rock Creek Park. Talk about making childhood dreams come true—the house looked exactly like a castle.

"Mike," I said to my brother in the spring of 1965 as we readied to go down to D.C., "go to Detroit, get your wife and child, and come on down." Let's make some music.

Shrine Records. I loved the sound of our new label's name, and I loved the sounds off those records that we were starting to make. But about seven months into our sojourn, before we really got those discs spinning, there was still a big bill left to pay: the debt that I'd incurred making wild whoopee in a hotel room in New York.

"It's time to get married," Ed had stated in no uncertain terms. I wasn't so certain. I'd flunked out of marriage twice; maybe it was a school that wasn't meant for me. But this was Ed, a man of no modest determination, very masculine, and very persuasive. Tender, and an ardent lover. A man who had always been there for me, with whom I could talk to about anything. I let go of my doubts, said yes to this fairy-tale Prince Charming, and had myself a sweet old-fashioned *True Romance* story. So we traipsed off to tie the knot in Arlington, Virginia—another place where you could do it in a day.

We accomplished something else that night, and soon I saw one more side of Ed Singleton. The moment that I confirmed the news, he ran out to buy cigars. He walked around our castle with his chest puffed out, painted the nursery blue, and raced around town to buy a crib and teddy bears and little toys for the baby. On October 23, 1966—almost nine months to the day after our trip to Arlington—our son, William Edward, Jr., was born. His daddy was more than just proud; he was a total participation man—"I'll mix the formula" or "Hand me that diaper, Ray. This baby needs a change" and "Don't worry, I already washed the dishes" and "Here's your dress, dear. I went ahead and ironed it for you. Come on, get out of bed, it's time to go to work."

With my ten thousand dollars, we'd set up Shrine and immediately had begun to draw in acts. There was an interesting hub in Washington, a pool of young, fresh talent with no outlet for their potential. No one was offering a label anywhere close to the level of Shrine, and our roster was full within the first few months of the operation. In total, we would have somewhere between fifteen and twenty quality releases, songs penned primarily by Ed and Mike or Harry Bass, one of Ed's New York artists who had migrated to Washington with us. And, of course, several of the arrangements were knocked off by none other than Ray Singleton. Just like in the old days, my creative and business juices were flowing. "I have a great idea," I piped up one afternoon and picked up the phone. I placed a call to my nephew, Dale Warren, the violin genius, also of Motown arrangement fame.

Three weeks later he was in the office, all set to wow us with his fantastic arranging abilities. Dale had come a long way since I'd given him the job at Hitsville. He did wonderfully by us, and would go a long way further still. In time he would move on to Stax Records with Al Bell, and ultimately be the visionary arranger on Isaac Hayes's "Shaft." From there he would arrange for Holland-Dozier-Holland and Fantasy Records. By 1989 Dale Warren would become conductor and musical director of the Southeast Symphony Orchestra, in Los Angeles.

Though I lived it like a fairy tale, it wasn't all violins and roses. The music business was changing rapidly, a far cry from the days when Berry and I had taken a loan of eight hundred dollars from his family to produce Marv Johnson's "Come to Me."

It was a whole different ball of wax in the mid-sixties. The stakes were higher and the risks were bigger. On the plus side of the ledger, Shrine had a sharp, sexy product, and Ed had been able to attract some enthusiastic investors. On the minus side, many were business folk new to the music biz. They wanted their hits, and they wanted a say in every cent that was being spent trying to crank out those hits. Yet they didn't know two cents about the process—"How come the demo cost so much?" "You told me this singer was great; why did he hold up the session for two hours?" Unable to convey to these conservative fellows that making music wasn't much different from gambling, we soon found out that they were often the ones slowing down and blocking the wins—and losing the money they had invested with us.

Though our Shrine geese weren't laying any golden eggs and we were basically surviving on a week-to-week basis, the cocks were crowing and the chicks were clucking on my old ranch in Detroit. All the ranch hands with whom I'd worked were breeding hits like rabbits. In 1965 the Supremes were living high on the hog, having strung up a series of five successive number-one hits. Each act was hotter than the next—Marvin Gaye, Martha and the Vandellas, Junior Walker, the Marvelettes. The Tempts recorded "My Girl," the Miracles did "The Tracks of My Tears" and "Ooo Baby Baby," the Four Tops had "I Can't Help Myself" and "It's the Same Old Song." Smokey and the Hollands were writing hit tunes in their sleep. In 1966 the promise of Stevie Wonder sprang to life with "Uptight (Everything's Alright)" and the Tempts entered into a dazzlingly fortuitous relationship with producer Norman Whitfield. The Isley Brothers recorded "This Old Heart of Mine," and Jimmy Ruffin floored me with "What Becomes of the Brokenhearted." These were the glory days. My perspective on all of Motown's triumphs was a powerful mix of feelings. While I certainly wished our labors with Shrine were yielding similar fruit, I couldn't begrudge the success of what I still saw as my family. It was with enormous maternal, professional pride that I watched hits top the charts and that I saw the careers of artists—all with whom I'd worked—come to life. Whether or not I was being acknowledged, I couldn't help but cheer Motown on.

This strange array of emotions was difficult to contain when, a couple of months after the move to D.C., I'd flown to Detroit alone to handle some loose ends and pay a visit to Mama and Daddy. Being in such close proximity to Motown, I was forced to confront again the history that had sent me into exile as well as the resulting hurt and anger.

One night while in Detroit, I got together with one of my old girlfriends at a local club. Never having been much of a drinker, I needed only a couple of drinks to get tipsy. My defenses were wearing thin as she goaded me on, provoking the flow of the memories of relentless torturous phone calls from Margaret, the demise of my marriage to Berry, my abrupt departure to New York, and the circumstances surrounding the exile from Motown. She kept talking and the drinks kept coming. We became more and more inebriated and decided to go file a formal protest.

"We're here to see Margaret," I said as the two of us exhaled flammable fumes on the Spanish maid at the entrance to Berry's townhouse.

"Meester Gordy, no in the casa."

We pushed right by the maid into the casa, as I shouted out, "OK, bitch, I know you're here, come on down."

"Shit, there's nobody home," my girlfriend announced after a full inspection of the premises.

"Well, hell," I slurred, stumbling over to a table. On it, I spotted a scrapbook just begging to be pillaged. With amazing manual dexterity, considering that I'd never been so drunk in my life, I managed to extract several pictures of Margaret—photos of the Cinderella with the flawless features—and to rip them into a ticker tape parade's worth of trash. With each rip and tear of the pictures, I was conscious of tearing out the memories of the person who'd caused so much damage in my life.

Having thus left my mark of Zorro, I grabbed my friend and, with menacing expressions, we exited past the maid. "Oh," I said, turning back to her, "you can tell Meester Gordy that Mees Ray was here."

The next morning, feeling like some beast was upstairs playing timpani in my head, I awoke to the phone ringing.

"I heard you came by to see me last night," Berry said.

"Oh, yeah," I said, remembering. "So where were you?"

"I was at the hospital."

Oh, God, I didn't want to hear about another Margaret drama. What I wanted was someone to deliver me an ice pack. "So, Berry, what were you doing at the hospital?" Lay it on me.

"Loucye was sick," Berry said in a low tone, and I remembered that I'd heard she'd gone in for tests or something. I was surprised that Berry had taken time out of his busy schedule to accompany her. I asked him how she was doing.

"Well, uh . . . Loucye died."

A wave of remorse and grief swept over me, a horrible lump caught in my throat. Loucye had it all together. She was smart and pretty and ambitious. If not for her house and her help. . . I shut out those images. Berry explained that she had been suffering from headaches and had passed out at her desk at work. At the hospital she hadn't made it through the week. In the final medical analysis the doctors called it a cerebral hemorrhage.

There was a long silence. It wasn't necessary to say anything. Berry knew how devastated I was by the loss of his sister. She had been family to me too. "I'd like to see you," he said, his cadence soft and slow. "Why don't we meet at the Travel Lodge and we can talk?"

Though he didn't explain it, I assumed Berry had checked into the motel to avoid dealing with Margaret during this sad business. He and I talked at length about Loucye, whose passing was the link that made it possible for me to put our pained history aside and end up staying with him at the motel. I remained there until just after the funeral. There were many familiar faces at the funeral—saying good-bye to a friend.

The engine of the limo was already running when Berry paused and said to me, "Thank you." He looked tired. "Thanks for staying with me. I always feel better when you're with me."

The wind was blowing as he and I faced one another.

"Well . . . ," he said and sighed. He gave me a kiss and turned to walk toward the long black limousine. I almost called his name. But I stopped myself. There was nothing to say, nothing to do but watch him go.

The next day, I returned to D.C. and to Ed and the boys.

"Look," Ed was saying somewhere past the middle of 1966, "I have an idea."

We definitely needed one. Our last Shrine investor had just bailed out. What was more, we were hearing reports from various DJs that Berry had been campaigning against us. Apparently he had put the word out that his troublemaking ex-wife—the "My Guy" bootlegger—was trying to run him out of business. Whatever Berry was or wasn't saying, all we knew was that the best distributors, who didn't want to lose Motown affiliations, wouldn't help Shrine.

No one of sound mind would think that Ed and I had the will or the clout to bury Motown—it was preposterous. We wanted to make music and make a little money. Maybe we were idealistic, but it was our belief that there was room for everyone in the business. But our investors were causing us grief, the many moods of Berry Gordy were wreaking havoc with our promotional network, and the one thing that Motown had in spades we couldn't seem to get an ounce of—luck.

"So what's the idea?" I asked Ed, hoping he was carrying some loaded dice.

"You know, I could probably get us jobs in New York. Florence Greenberg has been trying to get me to come and work for her, and

I'll just bet I could swing something for you too." I seconded his emotion, and soon we'd hopped on a commuter flight to New York, anticipating fair weather ahead. As I watched the passing clouds from my seat next to Ed's, I thought about his latest frustrations and felt a special warmth for him and for how he was attempting to improve our straits.

I was especially touched because I knew that Ed had been feeling insecure about being supported by my monthly settlement check. Not that it bothered me in the least, but Ed and I did share that sinful trait of pride. Compounding the fact that his wife was footing the bills were those unpredictable phone calls from Berry. Strange as it was, the same man who was rumored to be doing his best to keep us off the radio was also still calling up Ed, wanting to hash over life with Ray. The many faces of Berry Gordy.

There was little I could do to explain Berry's behavior to Ed; my own understanding of the causes behind Berry's swift changes of mood—from bully to pal to private confidant to foe again—would continue to evade me for years. Maybe, I sometimes thought, Berry was simply bored and unhappy, and by poking at the embers of our feelings he gained a sense of excitement. He was probably already exhausted and even remorseful of having Margaret in his life. As I was to eventually realize, Berry's cruel manipulations were actually the controlling games of an abandoned, angry little boy. Having told himself enough times that I was the one who'd left, he could justify to himself such hot-and-cold behavior.

For Ed to have withstood the pressure from Berry's constant interference should have earned him a medal of honor. To reassure Ed and to affirm my commitment to him, I tried to minimize my own phone contact with Berry, restricting conversation to the topic of now-seven-year-old Kerry. Father and son hadn't seen one another for three years, nor would they come into contact for another three years, and then only in the coincidental and dramatic circumstances that always seemed to surround my life.

Flying to New York, Ed and I met with Florence Greenberg, and a happy threesome was formed. Her company was Scepter Records, which she had started in 1959 specifically for the Shirelles, whom she managed as well. The Shirelles' fabulous hits on Scepter had been "Will You Love Me Tomorrow," "Dedicated to the One I Love," and "Baby It's You." Florence also had, on her Wand label, Chuck Jackson, the Isley Brothers, and the Kingsmen (of "Louie Louie" notoriety). But Florence's biggest success was

with Dionne Warwick, who had marked the sixties with a snow-
ball of hits by Scepter's A&R men, Burt Bacharach and Hal David.
Wow, I thought, I get to work in this environment and get paid for
it too. What a deal!

Three days a week, Monday to Wednesday, we'd leave the kids
with a nanny and fly off to work for Scepter. In fair Manhattan we
resided in a gorgeous midtown fourteenth-floor penthouse apartment. From its balcony I could admire the expanse of the entire
New York skyline. Then, late Wednesday night, we'd go back to
D.C., where Shrine was still hanging on.

Florence kept us busy. We worked with the Shirelles on several
projects, including a pretty tune of Ed's that I arranged, a song in
the groove of "Will You Love Me Tomorrow."

Ed, as it turned out, knew Nat Tarnopol. There was that
twisted hand of fate, all of a sudden pushing me in the direction of
a familiar voice—"Come here, baby!" Jackie Wilson, who else?

Soon Ed and I found ourselves working with Jackie and
knocking off some fairly successful projects with him at Bruns-
wick, a division of Decca. We produced two of Ed's songs, "She's
Alright" and "Watch Out Baby," for Jackie—with my string arrangements and recorded with the New York Philharmonic. The
songs scored well by us, and the work was a real shot in the arm. I
was in my element. But all things being relative, it was hard not to
compare a moderate hit of a star in decline with that ever-spread-
ing comet trail of superhits coming out of Motown.

After six months of commuting between New York and D.C.,
and with all the difficult and variable odds going against Shrine,
I took full stock of the situation and knew what I had to do. I'd
been a gypsy for almost four years. The nightmare and the heartbreak and the war and the bust were behind me now. It was time to
have some peace, to live with my husband and three children on
solid ground.

Regardless of my lack of legal entitlement, in my heart Motown had never stopped being mine. I made the necessary phone
calls, alerted Ed and Mike and the kids, and started packing.

I was going home. Home to Detroit and home to Motown. I
had a feeling that it needed me.

CHAPTER 11
WAR
1967–1969

Where were you in 1967? Think about it. If you can remember hearing any one of the following songs, you might remember something of the world around you. The Supremes were cresting with "The Happening," "Love Is Here and Now You're Gone," "Reflections," and "In and Out of Love." Nineteen sixty-seven was the year for "Jimmy Mack" by Martha Reeves and the Vandellas; the Marvelettes' "The Hunter Gets Captured by the Game"; "You're My Everything" and "All I Need" by the Temptations; Stevie Wonder's "I Was Made to Love Her"; Gladys Knight and the Pips' "I Heard It Through the Grapevine"; and "Bernadette" by the Four Tops. In that same year Smokey and the Miracles recorded "I Second That Emotion," "The Love I Saw in You Was Just a Mirage," and "More Love." Wherever you were, it would have been hard not to catch the name Marvin Gaye, whose "Your Unchanging Love" and whose duet with Kim Weston called "It Takes Two" led him right into the smashing Tammi Terrell duets: "Ain't No Mountain High Enough," "Your Precious Love," "If I Could Build My Whole World Around You," and—my absolute favorite—"Ain't Nothing Like the Real Thing."

Hair was starting to get longer and skirts were definitely getting shorter. I know mine began to border on illegal. Black men's 'dos were history and Afros were becoming the rage. There were peace symbols, love beads, bell bottoms, and headbands.

But that was only one side of the coin. In another part of the world, a war was being fought that nobody understood. Our young men, black and white, were marching proudly off to Vietnam and being sent home in body bags. We were spraying napalm and Agent Orange on innocent civilians; we would also be poisoning ourselves.

On our own soil another battle was being waged, fueled by the spirit of anger that had been growing for years in black men and women all across the country. Martin Luther King, Jr.'s, dream of equality through nonviolent resistance had given way to an unquenchable rage. Blacks were tired of waiting, tired of being spat on while walking down their own streets, tired of having a brother or sister shot down for little more than a white man's sport. The courts of law and ministers of justice tossed out crumbs they called civil rights that were unenforceable. For blacks, the sentiment was, What good was the right to sit at a lunch counter if you couldn't afford to eat there?

For three summers in a row, the nation's cities had been seized by rioting in the black ghettos—outbursts of the welling rage that resulted in massive burning, looting, and tragic loss of life. In '64 disturbances flared in seven major cities; in '65 the Watts riots in Los Angeles became a show of unprecedented violence that, in one week, claimed thirty-four lives, triggered at least four thousand arrests, destroyed more than six hundred buildings, and caused an estimated thirty-five to forty million dollars' damage. It was Watts, burning down in front of our eyes on the television screen, that made it clear to me and to everyone watching how serious the racial unrest had become. In 1966 the number of incidents accelerated and spread to the smaller cities and towns around the country. As the summer of '67 approached, there was an undercurrent of energy much like a time bomb waiting to explode.

Motown reflected this state of the nation. For all its outward appearance of having a groovy happening, inside it was seething. Berry had isolated himself from the people who had helped him build the company, creating a houseful of discontent. He had appointed people who had no history with the company, people with little or no experience making music and with little or no respect for those who knew how, to prominent positions in the company. They were businesspeople, pure and simple. That they were given power in creative decisions was insulting to the Motown veterans. The fact that they were white only aggravated the situation, and the whole thing resonated deeply among the black ranks who were being pushed back to the rear guard.

One might wonder how it was, after being on the outs for a few years at this point, that I knew so much about the state of the company. Well, let's just say that I heard it through the grapevine—vague rustlings in the brush telling me that all was not happy in paradise. I didn't know the specifics, but old mother wit was whispering in my ear again, telling me I could be of help, saying "Get your butt to Detroit. There's trouble in the wind."

My only hesitation was because of Margaret, whose phone calls had continued through the Shrine years. I knew that she was now the mother of Berry's child, a little boy, Kennedy, named for Berry's hero. I'd heard that, though Berry still supported her in grand style, their involvement was lessening.

After making the decision to go, it hadn't been hard to come up with a strategy for dealing with Berry. I didn't ask him; I told him, "Listen, we're not cutting it in Washington. We're coming back to Detroit, and we both need jobs. We also need a two thousand-dollar advance to move."

And, by George, it worked. Of course, the grapevine would pass the buzz back later that Berry was taking it as a personal win, joking to everyone that he'd hired "her and her husband." It was as if he'd finally bought us out. But making him feel like he had won was all part of the game. And it was becoming more and more important, as I was soon to discover back at Motown, to know how to play ball with the big boys.

"Juanita," I said at the airport, after embracing my sister, "I hate you."

"What?!" Ed, Cliff, now twelve, and Kerry, almost eight, were aghast at my statement. Even baby Eddie, who wasn't even a year old, looked shocked.

Juanita burst out laughing, "I know what she means. It's because of my hair." Nita had the most beautiful head of long hair, and I had coveted it since I was a child. She was also one of the warmest and most generous women on the planet. With my hordes moving into her house in Detroit, there was simply no question about whether or not we were welcome; Juanita's arms were open, food was on the table, and the beds were made.

"Thank you, Nita," I said, packing the troops into the car. I held Ed's hand as we drove through Detroit with the rush of memories flying by the window. My hometown, I thought, I love it. I had looked forward to sharing it with Ed and having him get to know my folks—and here we were.

Monday morning had been D day. On the way in to work with Ed and Mike—who was being hired as well—I explained the status of Hitsville. "It was bound to happen—the people just outgrew the space. But it's still being used for recording, and there are rehearsal rooms and a tape library." I sighed. The move from Hitsville marked the end of an era. That family front-porch feeling had been magical.

Now on to the next era. We stood in the lobby of the Donovan Building, Motown's new headquarters, a cavernous, ten-story gray brick structure at 2457 Woodward Avenue. The worn marble floor hinted at the glamour this building must have once had. The dingy halls were painted an institutional olive green and lit by dim round bulbs hanging on long poles from the high ceiling. It looked like a psycho ward, and I immediately had all sorts of redecorating ideas. Leave it to me. Still, I had no idea what to do with the creaking antique cage elevator that had a wrought-iron gate and, apparently, a wrought-iron will. At an arthritic pace it lifted us to our fifth-floor destination.

We were met by our immediate boss, Motown's current A&R director, who introduced himself as Ralph Seltzer. Berry was out of town. Since he was spending more and more time at his new office on Sunset Boulevard in Los Angeles, and out touring with the Supremes, Berry had delegated many of his duties to Ralph. And greeting us was one of them.

Ralph sure didn't look like the man most responsible for the creative output of the world's most successful black record company. A white man in black-rimmed thick glasses who seemed to be examining us closely, Ralph had a vague expression on his face that I assumed was a smile. I'd heard that Ralph, a lawyer, had been hired first for administrative purposes, and even on that level was thought to have a difficult temperament. How he had made the move to A&R was beyond me. In any case, he seemed fairly benign as he escorted us to our suite of offices, which had been recently vacated by Suzanne DePasse—who had gone off to California with Berry as his creative assistant.

"Hi." We looked up and saw a cute, big-eyed, brown-skinned girl sitting at a desk in the middle of our main office area. She was very perky, and appeared to be in her early twenties. "I'm Venida Adams," she said. "I was Suzanne DePasse's secretary, but she's gone, so I guess I belong to you." I had just met a key player in my future. Spunky, fun-loving, Venida and I would be inseparable friends for many a year to come.

"All right, Mike, you take that office." I immediately started choreographing. "Ed and I will take this one. But first let's sit down and figure out a job description." Clarifying that matter would have to wait, though, for I spotted a familiar face popping through the double wooden doors.

"Hey, baby, I sure am glad to see you." It was Norman Whitfield, freckles and all and a few extra pounds. "We sure missed you. Don't go nowhere no more, stay right here." I introduced Ed and Norman, and talk and laughter about the good old days chimed up at once. Norman was the creative king at Motown now, having just begun a batch of hits for the Temptations. He would eventually become one of the most successful producers in history.

"And Ed," I giggled, "this boy started out begging to be let in the front door."

Next?

Johnny Bristol swung through the double doors, looking as sleek and handsome as ever. Originally coming from the Anna Records stable as an artist, Johnny was now a house producer working primarily with Junior Walker. He had also since married Berry's niece, Iris Gordy, the daughter of Fuller. Upon leaving our office, he said "Ray, when you get a chance, I want to talk to you."

As Johnny left, he was almost knocked over by Ivy Hunter, my wild and talented old pal, who rushed in, picked me up, and twirled me around. He was still wearing his hair in dreadlocks, and this was long before they were fashionable. Ivy had taken a vow years before that he wouldn't get a haircut until he had a hit. I wondered what he considered "Dancing in the Street," which he'd cowritten with Mickey Stevenson and Marvin Gaye. Maybe he decided to keep his hair for luck.

"Ray, we sure are glad to see you back," Ivy smiled in his rugged way. Then he added, "Things are a drag around here."

Ed was surprised to hear this sentiment. Somehow I wasn't, but I asked, "What do you mean, Ivy?"

"Later," he promised, ducking out.

Our next visitor was Robert Bullock, the attractive, tall son of Berry's sister Esther Edwards. I couldn't stop hugging him—he was truly a long-lost relative and was overjoyed to see me. He also alluded to the status quo being off kilter at the Donovan Building.

"Wow," Venida chimed, "you know everybody here."

Ed said, "I'm having the tour without leaving the office."

One by one, all the producers trooped in to say hello. The very sharp Harvey Fuqua. Hank Cosby, who used to beg Miss Lillie for a hot dog, now a respected producer/arranger. Clarence Paul, who'd helped Stevie Wonder make it to the top. Richard Morris, producer of Martha Reeves's "Honey Child," who had won a place in my heart long ago when he and Ronnie White helped me paint Hitsville. When he asked to take me to lunch so we could talk, I didn't have to ask what about.

I took a spin around the halls, knocking on those double doors, not knowing who was going to be inside. It was better than opening presents on Christmas morning—each one more delightful than the next. "Janie!" "Ray!" Behind another door was Billie Jean. One door opened to a group of faces who just stared, until a voice cried, "Ray!" and I saw who it was—"Tommy Gordy!" George Gordy's freckle-faced son, the love of my life.

It was old home week, all in a day—a ten-hour-long reunion that put me on such a high, it wasn't until we got back to Juanita's that I realized who was missing. There had been absolutely no artists there, not even Smokey, who was part of the administration. Mickey Stevenson and Beans Bowles, I knew, had already left after misunderstandings with Berry. The absences of Brian and Eddie Holland were particularly glaring. These names were synonymous with Motown. Well, I would soon find out where they all were.

Over the next few days I pieced together, by talking to various people, the circumstances afflicting Motown. With the phenomenal growth of the company, the sophistication of certain "tests" Berry administered had increased. Mickey Stevenson, the wheeler-dealer of the decade, should have been able to combat the pressure. But he got angry when Berry didn't develop the career of his wife, Kim Weston. Furthermore, Mickey was tired of Berry's refusal to share the spoils of victory. "I left because I wanted a piece of the company," Mickey would explain later on. "Berry wanted me to stay because I was a powerful force, and he offered me a big raise, but I wanted the power to go with the force."

I could see that the gaming had become mean-spirited. Berry always had consciously fostered competition between our creative people. And Motown had first thrived on those healthy, friendly challenges because it was understood that we were all winners. There was no longer a strong family atmosphere. The competition had turned into fighting, and the playful aggression was now actually overt hostility.

All those I talked to told me they missed the intimacy of Hitsville. From a sunny, tree-lined neighborhood street to the impersonal, gray building downtown. Gone were long talks on the porch as summer days came to an end; instead, the moment you stepped outside the new address you found yourself in the company of skid row bums.

Gone also were the days of picking up the phone and talking to the boss. The more insulated Berry became and the less available he was for day-to-day creative decisions, the greater the void in which no one knew what to do. It left producers bickering among themselves with nowhere to go for valued direction.

The story was that when Mickey left, Eddie Holland was made the next A&R director. Eddie's ascent led to dissent. Holland-Dozier-Holland were in an incredible hitmaking groove and were benefiting from one of Berry's game rules: if a producer had a hit with an artist, he automatically produced the next release on that artist. This meant that H-D-H maintained a stranglehold on the Supremes and the Four Tops, even before Eddie was given the job of handing out production assignments. Week after week, the other producers found themselves without access to the artists, unable to get their material heard. To add to the situation, Brian Holland now worked in Quality Control, exercising even more power over what records were released. I could easily see why the other producers felt they were being locked out of the system.

But even with circumstances so favorable for them, the Holland brothers and Lamont Dozier, shortly after my return, came to the same decision that Mickey had made. Berry wasn't going to share Motown's profits with anyone, no matter how instrumental they were in the company's success. So H-D-H began a work slowdown program in protest, which landed them nothing more than a rupture in communication with Berry. Lawsuits soon would be initiated by the company and countersuits would be filed. As usual, the only winners in this ongoing battle would be the lawyers.

Eddie's exit had signaled Ralph Seltzer's entrance into the power vacuum at the top. "And guess who brought Ralph into the company?" someone, probably Ivy, had asked.

"Why, it wasn't my dear friend Barney Ales, was it?" I guessed that right.

Ralph's first position was as special assistant to the president, with power to revamp systems throughout the company. In the process he made many foes with his aggressive, abrasive style. He was a lot like Barney, who, in reaching for power, had impressed Berry with his administrative smarts. Berry considered good articulation, organizational skills, and a large vocabulary signs of intelligence. His opinion, one that would later run rampant in the entertainment industry, was that a good administrator could administrate anything—a plastic-bottle factory or a record label. With this reasoning, without a shred of creative experience, Seltzer had been appointed head of the Creative Division.

The fact that he was white added to the resentment, but that wouldn't have mattered if his personality and policies had been different. Everyone described him as abusive and foul-mouthed, a man who had no rapport with his people and no respect for their work, treating them like bums or babies. One of his first policies was to charge producers twenty-five percent of the cost of the recording sessions they supervised. Normally the artist is charged for the session against his or her royalties, but in Seltzer's accounting, the producers were to be docked their percentage in addition to what the artist was paying. The upshot was that the company made back one hundred twenty-five percent of its recording costs.

With Ralph, it was a closed-door policy; rarely did he promote a collaborative climate. At Hitsville, of course, where most of the Motown producers had come of age, the atmosphere had been one of openness. The oppressive, hostile environment of the new regime, where producers were treated like second-class citizens by a superior who didn't give a damn about their problems, was fertile soil for revolt.

A decade later, Ivy Hunter would put it succinctly: "Once Berry brought in Ralph Seltzer, the family atmosphere was finally destroyed." In the long run, Ralph was held in contempt by almost everyone at Motown except for a couple of people. Sylvia Moy, one of the best Motown staff writers, remained with him for years. Explaining it to me much later, Sylvia said, "Ralph was a brilliant company man, a Motown man, a Berry man. Everything he did was for Motown and for Berry." So the big bully could exploit the producers because he was making money for his boss, alienating most everyone in the process. "I could understand both sides of the quarrel. I loved the guys," Sylvia would say, "but Seltzer appeared to me just to be doing his job."

No one knew how Berry felt about the situation or if he even realized a mutiny was brewing. Very few came forward for fear of losing their tenuously held jobs. There had even been whisperings of surveillance tactics organized by Ralph against those who complained. Producers were not the only people with complaints.

On the road, Motown artists compared notes with singers signed to other labels. Finding their royalty rates substandard, and being treated like children when they questioned those in charge, the artists too were feeling subversive. Times had changed, yet provisions for the artists had not. In the old days, we all thought we had a stake in the company, that everyone would receive his due down the road. With the new ruling junta, that had become a big joke.

On the artists' behalf, Clarence Paul attempted to address these problems through company channels, and when that failed set up meetings, first with Ralph, then Berry. Ralph was out-and-out rude; Berry cut short Clarence's two-minute prologue to take a phone call. The president, after all, was a very busy man.

Sylvia tried to help by calling a meeting at Clarence's house to soothe the artists' unhappiness and discuss the producers' beefs. That meeting ended prematurely when it was reported that there were two men in a car out front writing down the names of those in the house.

Berry wasn't ignorant of the general malaise in Detroit even though he was often absent. The company was riding high, yet production was way down and the Hollands weren't at the office. After much deliberation he apparently decided that the situation was out of control and flew from California to Detroit, where he called a surprise meeting.

"OK, I understand you have some complaints, that there are some problems." Berry opened the floor to the assembled, then sat down with his hands folded and waited. A chorus line of shrugs danced before him. "Oh, there aren't any problems," said most of the previously outspoken critics. Glancing to one another, they asked "Did you have some kind of problem?" Ivy became incensed; fear had rendered his fellow workers mute.

"Yeah," Ivy stood up, "I'll tell you what the problem is." With no mincing of words, Ivy described the current state of affairs in the Creative Division, emphasizing the problems with Ralph Seltzer. Berry, it seemed, took Ivy's presentation with a grain of salt, since the others didn't seem so troubled. He thanked him for his candor but did nothing to address his grievances, much less protect him from Seltzer's retaliation.

Reprisal then came to Ivy, not in the form of firing, but in a Seltzer-orchestrated limbo for Ivy's projects. Despite his talents and his contributions to Motown, he became a marked man, and no one wanted to risk his own neck by collaborating with him. Two others who did back him at the meeting, Morris Broadnax and Shorty Long, found their next checks withheld.

Within our first two weeks in Detroit, our office had become a complaint department. The producers were instantly comfortable with Ed, seeing that he was trustworthy, sympathetic, and wise. And an ally. Impromptu bull sessions became standard fare during the course of a day, as we offered support to those venting their anger.

"Ray, you came just in time to help us get some of this shit straightened out," Ivy said after a long recap of the civil war that was brewing.

"Yeah," Ed said, "We better start calling you Joan of Arc."

I had no intention of becoming a martyr, yet I knew something had to be done. This was no mere chess game. But I knew that to succeed I'd have to beat Berry at his own game, using the same tactics he'd used on me. In the meantime, Ed and I looked for projects. We now faced a challenge shared by the other producers— finding a place for ourselves in the system. And coming in as we had, without appointments to specific artists, we certainly had our work cut out for us.

My heart was pounding as Ed and I walked into the London Chop House for dinner with Berry. Berry had initiated the meeting, and it would be the first time Ed and Berry would actually meet in person, as well as the first time Berry and I had seen one another since I had become his employee. I couldn't help but feel overwhelmed, thinking back over what had happened. Damn, I thought, as Berry approached, there's a civil war going on in me. But the moment Berry and I caught sight of one another, wide, affectionate grins spread across our faces. We embraced, and then the two men shook hands. "Hey, man, it's great to meet you after talking on the phone all these years," Berry began. Ed echoed the sentiment.

The evening came off without a hitch. There was much laughter and talk and real warmth. "I'll tell you what," Berry said, "when you first called me about jobs, I thought it was, well, funny. Then, I started to feel excited about it. In exchange for helping you out of a jam, you guys are going to add a lot to the company." He then said what a terrific couple Ed and I made. No details were discussed, but Berry implied he was aware of the storm clouds gathering in Detroit.

Driving home from dinner Ed remarked, "I'll bet our hiring has a lot to do with Berry's desire to deal with all this trouble." Two decades later Ed would recall: "In his heart, Berry was hoping for the best from our being there. He was aware of the turmoil in the company, and he needed someone to come in and still the waters, someone who could give him a link to his people. And who was better than Ray, the cofounder of the company?" Even so, stilling the waters would be a delicate undertaking.

Berry's return to Detroit signaled the advent of a producer's meeting. The troops assembled in a pseudo-conference room that was actually more of a classroom. The pupils sat in their little chairs facing teacher's desk. Behind the desk was Headmaster Gordy. Everyone involved in the creative side of the company was present. The assistant to Ralph Seltzer, a well-liked man named Harry Balk, was close to the front. All the familiar faces were there: Smokey Robinson, Harvey Fuqua, Johnny Bristol, Iris Gordy, Norman Whitfield, Barrett Strong, Clarence Paul, Ivy Hunter, Richard Morris, Sylvia Moy, and Billie Jean Brown. New-comers Nick Ashford and Valerie Simpson, producers and writers with loads of promise, engineer Cal Harris, and several secretaries, including Rebecca Jiles, were all present.

Berry, always a casual chairman, announced, "I guess you guys have noticed that lady over there, who you probably all know is back with us. Miss Ray. Stand up." I stood to hearty applause. "And also Ray's husband, Ed Singleton." More applause for Ed and a certain amount of fond amusement at the phrase "Ray's hus-band." Venida had told me we were the hot subject on the office gossip wire.

Creative processes had changed since I left town. I noted that the original three-meeting system—producers, Quality Control, and Sales—had been modified to accommodate Berry's absences. The producer's meeting now combined some of the Quality Control functions. Once a week, the producers met to listen to all current material, critiquing songs in the works, demos meant for specific artists, and records vying for release as singles. With a chronic backlog of items to discuss, the meetings, I was told, could last as long as five hours.

Rebecca Jiles assembled the agenda, as I had originally done. Before the meeting, the producers let her know what songs they were planning to submit and she listed exactly what was to be played at the meeting, something that had not been done before. I discovered that this had come about because the previous method of having the producers introduce their own songs had deteriorated into a Keystone Cops folly. All the guys would rush in with records under their arms—"Hey, man, I've got the next single." "No, man, I've got the bomb." So a decision was made to omit all identifications and play the records without the others knowing who produced what. Discussions were led by Berry after each song, "OK, uh . . . Norman. What did you think?" Norman stood to say, "Man, that was a bunch of garbage." Berry then asked, "What did you think, Johnny?" "The track was loose, no one will dance to that shit." There was little charity to spare among these guys.

The anonymity didn't really help reduce the rivalry, though, as they could always tell each other's work. Raised voices came close to thrown punches. "That's junk." "What are you talking about, asshole, this is a smash. What the fuck do you know?" "OK, what hits have you had lately? You don't know a goddamn thing, and you're telling me this is a hit?" With all these creative personalities contending for such high stakes, the meetings were volatile and sometimes chaotic.

Politics were always an issue too. Over the years Billie Jean Brown, the head of Quality Control, had assumed more and more responsibility in the company. Taking a leave to get married in '64, she was temporarily replaced by Brian Holland. When she returned in '66, it was with more authority than ever. As Berry's absences increased, so did her freedom in selecting what singles were released. It was not surprising the producers were extremely friendly to Billie Jean.

Another rule of thumb was: when you're hot you're hot, and when you're not you're not. Norman Whitfield was on a winning streak as very few producers ever had been. Like a batter who connected with pitch after pitch almost as if bat and ball were mystically attuned, Norman had been hitting on every record brought into the meetings. Ballads or funky numbers, it didn't matter. He had found that his particular home-run-hit swing was in how he set up the songs. You knew when you heard those tracks, "This could only be a Whitfield production."

He had virtually been handed the golden bat from H-D-H, who were now gone, and Norman was one of the main reasons that Motown was still on top. Like H-D-H before him, Norman had become the chief beneficiary of the follow-up rule, monopolizing and hitting with the Tempts, Gladys Knight, and Edwin Starr: "I Heard It Through the Grapevine," "Ain't Too Proud to

Beg," "War," and "Papa Was a Rollin' Stone," and on and on. My instincts told me Norman was going to be the man at Motown for many years.

I attended another producers' meeting, during which Johnny Bristol sprang to his feet with an accusation that the company was playing outright favorites with Norman by giving him sole access to artists and overlooking a lot of other talented guys. Then Norman leapt up into the fray: "Hey, man, the company ain't giving me shit. I just happen to be the best. So sit down and shut the fuck up." Johnny erupted, and if he hadn't been escorted out he would have gladly beaten Norman's "just-happen-to-be-the-best" ass. Berry shook his head in disgust, then just looked out the window, as if wishing he was anywhere else but there. California dreaming, I'd say.

The general discord, in fact, seemed to have spread to every aspect of business at the Donovan building, and the company had been transformed into something I could barely recognize. Motown was now an organization rife with back-stabbing. Nervous to protect his or her own job, each person was fearful of who might run into Berry or Ralph and repeat a comment that may have been made, even in jest. Anger and paranoia permeated the atmosphere like a virus lingering in the carpet, incubating in the heating ducts. No wonder production was down.

There were a few gems, however. Harry Balk, Seltzer's assistant, was a hip, down-to-earth white man, a record pro who had been in the business forever. I had known him originally as Little Willie John's manager. For years Harry and a guy named Irving Michnik, as the Talent Artists agency, had represented Little Willie, Del Shannon of "Runaway" fame, Johnny and the Hurricanes, and the Royaltones. Harry, who knew good music, was liked across the board.

The money men were a different story. Ed Pollack, the head of finance, was an uncooperative, uptight conservative. The thought of Gwen going to Pollack for a loan, as she once had to me, was totally absurd.

Then there were the Noveck brothers, Harold and Sidney, the Motown accountants. Bald-headed and pudgy, the Novecks were very serious about money—the definitive "no" men. Any proposals for company improvements received an automatic "negatory." Of course, Berry thought they walked on water, and anybody looking at Berry's bank accounts would think so too. However, in the long run, the Noveck brothers would show some short-sightedness in important areas. When I later tried to convince them, around the time cassette tapes hit the market, that Motown should manufacture cassettes, I was turned down by a pair of pudgy frowning faces shaking their heads in tandem like Tweedledum and Tweedledee.

The Novecks were as much a symbol of the new Motown as Ralph Seltzer was. The administration of company finance seemed to result in only Berry's accumulation of wealth and no one else's. As the tension mounted between the inflamed rank and file and the entrenched white executives, the Seltzer contingency was circling the wagons. Instead of breaking down the barriers, Seltzer concentrated on reinforcing his authority in abusive ways. Those of us who had known the freedom of the old Motown realized that that freedom had been traded out from under us. The old feeling was of having our own piece of ground and working it with known pride; now it was turning into a plantation.

What I spent many months trying to understand and address at the company was similar to the sense of frustration that was prevalent in black America. It was the same helplessness turned to rage that was coming to a head on the streets of Detroit.

Ed, the boys, and I were living in a new development called Regency Square in what used to be the East Side ghetto but had benefited from urban renewal and had become a relatively elite section of Detroit. To the west of us, in the area around Blaine Street, where I grew up, and in the other less fortunate areas of the city, incidents of crime-related violence were on the upswing. Any hope that the summer of '67 might be free of the awful inner-city clashes that had plagued the previous summers was dashed as soon as the weather turned hot. By June the season's rioting had begun, and it was immediately clear that it was going to be even worse than expected. Tampa, Boston, Chicago, Cincinnati, Atlanta, and Dayton had been hit first. Buffalo, Milwaukee, Minneapolis, and Plainfield, New Jersey, had followed with major disturbances, lasting for days and requiring the intervention of National Guardsmen and federal troops. The government later estimated a total of one hundred sixty-four separate riots over the summer. In mid-July Newark was devastated by an outbreak even worse than Watt's: twenty-six people were killed and three hundred fires caused nearly fifteen million dollars in damages.

I walked the halls of the Donovan Building during the first weeks of July, waiting for air-raid sirens. They were coming, I knew it. Just as I knew that race relations were heating to an all-time high within our walls. Somewhere a gauge on the pressure cooker was about to blow; there was no mistaking it. It was only a matter of when and how.

On Sunday morning, July 23, at 4:00 A.M., police raided an after-hours bar on the West Side and arrested seventy-three people. A crowd gathered at the scene as rumors began to circulate that a woman had been kicked and a man beaten by cops. Voices shouted out questions, confusion grew, questions turned to curses. One person picked up a rock and threw it at a cop; soon a storm of rocks rained down on the policemen. When one rock went through the window of a clothing store nearby, part of the crowd began looting the store. Within an hour, dozens of stores in the area had been looted and torched.

All day the looting continued. By nightfall it had spread to the East Side. Snipers began shooting at police and firemen. With the firemen unable to stop the bullets and the Molotov cocktails, fires burned from block to block. Detroit was engulfed in a cloud of smoke. In the middle of it all, Daddy, with the invincibility of a man morally outraged, was on top of the house with a garden hose, determined to keep it from going down in flames.

By Tuesday morning, Governor George Romney had mobilized the National Guard and President Johnson had sent in army paratroopers. At first these forces simply took positions while the rioting continued. Mama and Daddy were in the center of the worst of it. The streets were absolute chaos: rocks and bottle-bombs and burning cars and neighbors running down the street with televisions and sofas. The soldiers sat in their tanks and watched.

I have never seen anything as terrifying as when they finally did move in, with bayoneted guns drawn. Countless tanks rumbled down Twelfth Street, and people scattered out from in front of them. Helicopters buzzed the roofs of buildings, trying to flush out the snipers. Guardsmen sprayed barrages of machine-gun fire at the rooftops. Many innocent people who were trying to sit out the action in their apartments were hit. It was a war zone.

Seven days after it had begun, the last of the soldiers left. Forty-three people were dead, thirty-three of them black. Thirty-eight hundred people had been arrested; five thousand people were homeless. There were fifty million dollars in estimated damages. It had cost more in damages than any other race riot in U.S. history and was the bloodiest in a half a century. In the aftermath there was only more resentment. And the smell of smoke was in the air.

In the middle of all this, like a lit fuse near a keg of gunpowder, was a Motown staff writer named Abdullah. He had been a street performer in Brooklyn and as a troubled youth had been in and out of jail. Along the way he had turned to the Black Muslim faith and transformed himself into Abdullah. He strode the halls of the Donovan building outfitted in a head rag, bedouin clothing, and a scimitar in his waistband. Chief among the beliefs of his faith was the notion of black supremacy, to which Abdullah adhered militantly. Newly signed to Motown, a black company, he had proudly planned to be the biggest thing we ever had, the greatest performer in the history of the world, and march his people on to glory. "Columbia Records wanted me, man. I could have went anywhere, but I came to the brother so I could help him build his thing." Imagine his militant surprise when he found that Berry Gordy was nowhere to be seen and he was pointed instead to Ralph Seltzer's office.

Their tug-of-war was known to all factions at Motown. To some it was a running joke; to the more sensitive it was a potentially lethal combination. When the surveillance rumors had begun to fly, Abdullah started filing oral reports that he was being followed: "My civil rights are being violated. If Seltzer don't do what I want him to do, I'm going to kill the blue-eyed devil." Abdullah used the phrase of Malcolm X and Elijah Muhammad for the white man rather loosely.

At 6:30 in the morning, soon after the riots, Ed and I were awakened by the phone. Ed picked up the phone.

"Hi. Mist' Singleton?" It was Abdullah.

"Yeah."

"Hey, brother. Listen, the shit gonna hit the fan. I've had it. I ain't going another day."

Ed asked what was the problem, to which Abdullah related that he had been in the studio with the Four Tops and had come outside, and there *they* were.

"Who is *they*?" Ed wanted to know.

"There's a car sitting there, man. There's some guys sitting in there. They followed us, and I did a couple things just to be sure. I tried to duck them and I led them on a path, you know, I wanted to be certain. I wanted to have all my facts."

I heard Ed tell him to cool down. And I watched him listen as Abdullah went on for several minutes about wanting to get his money and leave, then about killing the blue-eyed devil. Ed sensed real trouble and made Abdullah promise to stay put until we came to pick him up.

Once we had him in the car, Ed tried to calm him down while I tried to think of something. This guy was a walking, talking burning riot. Half a block from the office we stopped at a red light, and Abdullah saw one of the producers heading into the building. "Hey, hold there Mist' Singleton. I'm going to talk with my man a minute. I'll meet you upstairs." And he hopped out of the car with his guitar case.

"There's something wrong here," Ed said. "You park the car. I don't trust that son of a bitch."

While Ed ran in after Abdullah, I parked the car. In the meantime, this was going down: Ed asked the secretary if Abdullah had gone into our office. No, she said, he went straight to Mr. Seltzer's. Oh shit, said Ed, running down the hall. When he got into the office, Abdullah was seated in front of the desk, screaming at the top of his lungs. Seltzer, behind his desk and as red as a beet, was scared out of his mind.

"Abdullah . . . ," Ed started.

"Brother, stay out of it. I told you, man, this blue-eyed devil . . ."

Ralph started screaming, "I don't have to take this shit." Ed knew the crash had come, and as he lunged forward Abdullah jumped on top of Ralph's desk. In a single motion, Abdullah snatched a letter opener from the desk and grabbed Ralph by his collar, pulling him out of his seat. The blade was inches from Ralph's face when Ed jumped in between them. The three fell to the floor wrestling. Ed heaved Abdullah away from Ralph and saw that Ralph's shirt was ripped off, his glasses were askew, and he was convulsing in fear. Ralph shouted, "The last man who slapped me was my father, and I just buried him." Ed looked down at his ruined suit. He had cuts and bruises all over, and his hands were bleeding. Then suddenly Abdullah jumped up, grabbed his guitar case, and stalked Ralph again. Ed tackled Abdullah, the guitar case opened—and a machete fell out. As a security guard walked in the office, Ed looked over at Ralph and saw that at least there was a recognition in the other man's eyes that Ed had just saved his life.

Ed shoved Abdullah into our office and closed the door, making the guard stay by the door, then raced back to Ralph's office. "Look, draw up a release for this kid. Get me a ticket, some money, let me take him to the airport and away from here." For once, Ralph obliged and Ed scooted back to our office, calling for flight info with Abdullah ranting and raving, "My man, I just couldn't take it no more. Best thing is to give me my shit and let me go before I burn this place to the ground." Meanwhile the guard was nudging his gun at Abdullah as if to taunt him. Ed was on the phone, trying to get it all together before another eruption. He heard "I'm gonna blow this place" and spotted Abdullah about to grab the guard's gun. Over the top of the desk Ed flew, and another skirmish ensued, with the letter opener having been replaced by a loaded gun.

At last, security reinforcements arrived, and Abdullah was somewhat pacified. He was given a temporary release, a little money, and his things. After we had packed him and his guitar case—less the machete—on a plane to New York, we returned home ready to collapse. Before we could get our shoes off, the phone rang.

Berry, calling from L.A., said to Ed, "Well, I heard about all your dramatics today." He was using his testy voice.

"What are you talking about?"

"I heard how Abdullah put you up to that."

Ed pulled the phone away from his ear, and then back, "You've got to be kidding."

"No, you're clever, man. You're a clever dude. That was great. You're fantastic." Berry laughed without humor.

"Let me tell you something," Ed said. "It's a good thing you're in California, 'cause if you were anywhere close, we'd have a dance today." Ed was starting to boil. "My nerves are fucked up enough as it is. Got my suit fucked up, my hand is bandaged . . ."

"No, but that's the way you set it up. You're clever."

Ed was in no shape to match Berry's cool cockiness, and a conversation followed wherein a few unpleasant phrases were uttered. Berry maintained that certain insiders had told him what had gone down. I knew better. It was the game, the perfect way to cast off his own responsibility in the events he had set in motion at Motown. It served him even better because it was Ed, my husband. From then on, their relationship, which had never been solid, would slowly deteriorate.

It had been a lousy summer. Motown played the sounds of young America—pissed off. Bedlam. At one point Bobby Taylor of the Vancouvers started coming through with his pet lion. Talk about the natives getting restless. In another time and space, it would have been hilarious. In our current state of anxiety, it only fed the fevers.

By 1968, as far as my work as a "martyr" went, I had more or less come up with a plan for reconstruction. But before I made that move, I needed to get caught up on some creative work with the artists.

"Ray, if I don't get five thousand dollars right away, the mob is going to break my legs." Ron Miller burst into my office as white as a ghost. Ron was a gambler always about to get his legs broken. Gambling almost came with the Motown badge. And poor Ron had downright horrible luck. Yet he couldn't stop himself. The same old song. On this occasion, however, I was able to get him the advance.

Besides being a gambler, Ron was a frustrated writer who specialized in pre-rock hit-parade pop songs, pretty melodies without much emphasis on the beat. He probably would have been more suited for someone like Dionne Warwick than the funkier Motown artists. Most of the producers thought his material was too square, and, as a square white guy with corny songs, Ron had trouble getting their respect. But Berry liked him and believed he could get his ideas across. And his funny temperament completely endeared him to me. The songs he had written for Stevie Wonder, "A Place in the Sun" and "Travelin' Man," were early examples of what Ron could do. And, just around the time I got him his advance, he wrote a tune that was about to change his fortunes.

"I can't do this song," Stevie Wonder said when they went to record it. It sounded too much like Andy Williams, especially with Ron singing it in Stevie's face in the style of a Vegas lounge lizard. Hank Cosby, who was producing, finally convinced Stevie, saying "Look, do it, and do your own arrangement." Which is what they did, sticking a big beat behind it and making it funky. When Ron walked in and heard how they were changing his song, he almost died: "That's not how it goes!" After many such upsets, Hank had to kick him out of the studio.

Finally, they finished it only to discover that Berry didn't like it. It sat in the can for a year, until Billie Jean, who knew it was a hit, insisted it be released. "For Once in My Life" was a smash, a number-one pop hit. It would become overwhelmingly popular—the most recorded Motown song ever. Because it sounded like a standard, Berry published it under a newly invented company, Stein and Van Stock, which he named to sound like an old Tin Pan Alley publisher. For Ron it was a godsend, the lucky strike that would keep him rolling in clover for decades. He would strike again with "Heaven Help Us All," "Yester-Me, Yester-You, Yesterday," and in a big way with Diana Ross's "Touch Me in the Morning," which would be cowritten with Michael Masser.

Sylvia Moy had brought me up-to-date on Stevie Wonder's career. His had probably been the longest gestation period, with only one hit, "Fingertips (Part II)," happening as a kind of fluke. Sylvia told me, "When Stevie's name came up at the producers' meeting in '65, nobody wanted to work with him. That's when I spoke up and said, 'I'll take him.'"

Sylvia, a singer and songwriter since she was very young, had a friend, Barbara Wilson, who had a friend, Gwen Gordy Fuqua, and Barbara made the suggestion that Sylvia try out for Gwen's brother's record label. Before she'd done anything, Mickey Stevenson and Marvin Gaye heard her singing at the Caucus Club and talked her into auditioning. She was then signed as an artist and a writer. But once the producers saw what a good writer she was, they lost interest in her as a singer. She wasn't just good; she was a terrific writer and would have many Motown hits over the years. Collaborations with Hank and Stevie would include "My Cherie Amour" and "Never Had a Dream Come True"; Sylvia also had cocredits on "It Takes Two" and "This Old Heart of Mine." What she really wanted to do, though, was to produce, an ambition that was constantly frustrated in a typically male chauvinistic way by Mickey and the other producers. Told she could coproduce with one of the guys and receive royalties, she still couldn't get label credit. So the shot to take Stevie when no one else would was her big opportunity, and she had stipulated that she'd do it if she could produce and get the credit. Finally, Mickey gave her the green light.

She had immediately gone through every song Stevie had ever written, asking him to play every riff, every single verse, every line. Nothing impressed her. "Stevie, don't you have anything else?" Stevie had one last line, and then it was—eureka! "Play that again!" "Baby, everything is alright, uptight, out of sight." They played the line over and over and together fashioned a song. Sylvia cut a demo and proudly presented it to Mickey, who took one listen and said, "That's great. I love it. Sylvia, thanks a lot but . . . it's going to take a real pro to produce this record the way it should be done." Mickey Stevenson and Hank Cosby produced "Uptight (Everything's Alright)," and Sylvia was devastated. And she would never break that circle.

In the spring of '67, Hank Cosby had been directed by Berry, who was dissatisfied with Stevie's progress since "Uptight," to get to work with Stevie. So Hank sat down with Stevie to hear what he had to play, exactly as Sylvia had done before. All he had to play was a four-bar musical phrase. "That's it?" "Yeah," said Stevie, "I was born in Little Rock, had a childhood sweetheart." That was the genesis of "I Was Made to Love Her." Together, Hank, Sylvia, and Stevie developed more lyrics, but the heart of the song, musically, was only those four bars. The record hit number-two pop, number-one R&B that summer. And those three would continue their collaborative hit-writing spree for the next few years, while Stevie learned, under their tutelage, to become a phenomenal writer by himself.

It became apparent to me that even though the artists weren't directly involved in the turmoil at the Donovan Building during that previous summer, they hadn't escaped the fallout. For those on lengthy tours and returning to Detroit, there was less and less of the Motown they knew. Part of the problem was that there was nowhere at the Donovan Building, as vast as it was, for the artists to hang out. I'd lobbied extensively for an artists' hospitality suite, a place where they could drop by, which would benefit both the artists and the producers. Of course, these proposals were met with uncomprehending stares by the Noveck brothers: how on earth could a capital layout of x amount of dollars be justified except when it leads to y increases in productivity? "No."

Meanwhile the artists were harboring their own license to riot as they experienced certain separate-but-equal issues during that summer. On a marquee in Las Vegas, the same week as the Newark riots, the billing "Diana Ross and the Supremes" had appeared for the first time. Everyone knew that Diana was being groomed by Berry for a solo career, but the amount he would invest to make her a star would result in highly divisive problems. A couple of weeks later, while tanks rumbled through Detroit's West Side, Florence Ballard was dismissed from the Supremes. We'd all seen it coming.

When Diana was given the Supremes as a star vehicle it caused Flo great difficulties. Her reaction was to rebel, and she'd rebelled so self-destructively that Berry could justify ousting her from the group that she'd helped to create.

Berry had a dream. If Motown's success stemmed from its crossover appeal, what he saw in Diana Ross was the biggest crossover potential of all: star quality. A hungering, driving ambition to be famous. Diana was talented enough, though others were much more talented. What she did have was an aura that projected on a mass level. As Berry's vision became fixed on the West Coast and the movie industry, he saw Diana as the leading lady in the films he wanted to make. He would put everything into his dream of taking her all the way from the ghetto to the heights of sophisticated society and of making her the biggest star in the world. As Berry would do so, many talented people would be discarded. And his obsession would cause irreparable damage to Motown.

Flo was only the most visible one cast aside. All of the female stars felt abandoned—Gladys Knight, Kim Weston, the Marvelettes. Valerie Simpson, who could never make the company take her seriously as an artist, would also face Berry's indifference. All of Motown's performers, male and female, with the exception of Smokey Robinson, would bridle under the relentless Diana Ross elevation and their increasing inability to reach Berry. Martha Reeves was more of a fighter than the rest, but her status would soon plummet. The Vandellas' last hit was in 1967 with "Jimmy Mack"—and it had been recorded a few years before. With H-D-H in defection, Martha had to struggle to get good material.

The Holland brothers and Lamont Dozier, in self-exile for a year, made it clear they were not returning in mid-1968. This time Berry was spooked. His main concern was for Diana Ross and the Supremes, who'd been practically married to H-D-H's hit songs for years. Reaching the end of the line with "Forever Came Today," a song recorded the year before, the Supremes didn't have any more material from their most successful writers to draw upon.

From L.A., Berry called Hank Cosby to say, "We've got problems. But we can't let them get us down. We've got to kick ass anyway."

Hank called an emergency songwriting session. For three days he holed up in the Pontchartrain Hotel with Deke Richards, Paul Riser, Frank Wilson, Pam Sawyer, R. Dean Taylor, and Dennis

Lussier. When they emerged seventy-two hours later, they handed over a song as tough as any Norman Whitfield/Barrett Strong Tempts tune, a song about determination and pride called "Love Child." That song was Berry's baby. Just as he'd done with "Money," Berry personally supervised everything about the recording, including the mix. He mixed the hell out of that song—more than anything I'd ever seen—keeping Cal Harris down in the studio for days on end. And it paid off. In the fall of '68, "Love Child" put Diana back on top. And the orchestration of this regained stature would forever stand as one of Berry's great and shining moments.

During the turbulent times of my first year back at Motown, I'd been blessed with two shining stars of my own. One was Ed, who became a compatriot in the ongoing struggle. And Ed was responsible for the other star, on one of the happiest days of my life—"It's a girl!" Seven months after my thirtieth birthday, on October 4, 1967, I gave birth to our beautiful baby daughter, Rya, in the Detroit Woman's Hospital. I hadn't thought anyone could be more thrilled—I'd been dreaming of this moment forever, my own little girl! Of course, a few hours after they brought her to me, Ed was grabbing her out of my hands, "My own little girl!" Next comes Mama, taking the baby away from Ed, "My own little girl!" Ed's mother, who was staying with us at the time and watching over little Eddie, started to take Rya from Mama. "Hold it right there. I'm going to help take care of this child," my mother warned my mother-in-law. Oh, the beautiful harmony of family. But I knew from the moment I saw this perfect little creature, that she was going to be pure music.

For Motown, we were making music too. Ed had written a song called "Don't Bring Back the Memories," inspired by our relationship. "Don't bring back the memories of a love that couldn't last." I'd helped somewhat with the lyrics and the structure, but it was mainly Ed's creation. A song from the heart and soul, we envisioned it for the Four Tops, hearing it as one of those flag-waving, four-beats-to-the-bar tunes à la "I Can't Help Myself." Harvey, who was about to go into the studio with the Tops, heard it and went nuts. So when the cut was done, Harvey brought it up and played the track. "Well," I said.

"Well," said Ed. Instead of that straight four sound, Harvey had syncopated the song in the old doo-wop fashion—with a

Moonglows feel that was Harvey's style. Gulp. When it was released, Ed insisted it be credited to my name; his feeling was that if Berry heard it as his, the song would be sabotaged. What, Berry sabotage the efforts of those trying to help the company? Need I comment?

Ed and I put together proposal upon proposal to combat the growing provincialism of Motown's output; the proposals only occasionally were acknowledged by Berry. There were, however, a few ideas that got a nod. With the more advanced technology he'd learned in New York, Ed was able to make helpful suggestions that improved the engineer's handling of stereo mixes. He also made it his special task to do something about Motown's album jackets. In the late-sixties era, when brilliantly colored pop-art album covers lined the record stores, we were still turning out the cheapest, most outdated covers imaginable. Another accomplishment of Ed's, an accomplishment that few others could ever claim, was to have somewhat befriended Ralph Seltzer. Ralph was always grateful to Ed for saving his neck.

I had built my part of the old Motown on a dream, on an idealism that ignored heavy odds of opposition. In attempting to reshape the new Motown, Ed and I may have been overly naive. I was shocked to discover that there were certain individuals at different levels who were engaged in their own illicit form of profit sharing. I stumbled over people making those little under-the-table deals—tidy sums arranged with various suppliers, record pressers, radio stations, label printers, all the way down to pen-and-pencil vendors.

One plant operator whose company pressed both records and labels paid a visit to my office trying to offer Motown his services. A big fat guy with a huge cigar, the perfect Hollywood cliché of a sleazy businessman, he ran down his rates, and I told him I would consider them.

"I can tell you are very particular about your product, and I respect that," he said, with a puff-puff of his cigar. "I can guarantee you superior workmanship for Motown. And," he played his other card, "I'll guarantee you, personally, for Motown's contract, two cents per record."

I knew a bribe when I heard it. It brought to light the scope of what was going on in our hallowed halls. Even after I told him, casually, that I'd get back to him, he started to estimate: "Let's see, with ten thousand units a week, for four months alone, that would be for you alone—"

"Thank you, I'll be in touch."

The second the operator left the room, I looked up to see a very breathless Barney Ales running in. "Who was that guy?" I just waved him off casually. Many times I'd been given an opportunity to let Barney know what I thought of him or to confront him about the part he'd played in my being cast out of the Motown inner circle. But I'd passed on those impulses. The games were going strong, and part of playing the game was doing it without emotion.

For all the feelings of resentment and betrayal that Barney conjured in me, I also felt a kind of pity for his particular brand of power lust. He typified those who'd stop at nothing to receive their thrones, and now he sat high atop his in the kingdom of sales, stroking his now silvery beard. I could have almost felt sorry for him, if it hadn't been that it was his kind of mentality that was ripping Motown apart.

There was another kind of stress that, by 1968, even as Ed and I worked intensively on my latest plan to stabilize the company, began to bear down badly on our marriage. It was a Berry Gordy kind of stress. Statements he'd broadcast such as, "Yeah, Ray went out and got this really handsome guy," may have sounded generous to some, but with my extrasensory hearing I could detect a trace of jealousy.

It was well known that any man connected to a woman in Berry's life—whether she be wife, sister, mother, artist, or girlfriend—was in for more than his share of trouble. Ed was forewarned by many who said, "Once a woman is Berry Gordy's, she's always his." Both Harvey Fuqua and Marvin Gaye knew that rocky road well. Stories abounded of the terrible fights between both men and Berry; Anna and Gwen were terminally in the middle, wanting to alienate neither brother nor husband. Harvey and Gwen would finally split. As a result of this, and the general turmoil of the day, Harvey would make his exodus from Motown. The breakup of Marvin and Anna wouldn't come for a few more years—which meant there was that much more time for hostility and bitterness to mount.

Berry's attitude about the Abdullah incident had opened a fresh wound for Ed, a wound that was available for salt sprinklings from Berry's innuendos. And Ed wasn't a grin-and-bear-it kind of guy, either. Nor was I a sit-down-and-take-it kind of gal.

I jumped up when I heard the screaming. It was coming out of Seltzer's office. Ralph was blaring like a siren, "Get the hell out of here! Take your shit and get the hell out of here!"

Running toward his office, I saw the door open and saw George Gordy, Berry's brother—now writing and producing— emerging. George's face was dark with anger and humiliation. I realized that Ralph was asking for it, that he was living danger- ously by deflating the spirit of everyone who worked for him and cutting off all possible allies. To emasculate George this way was cutting close to the bone. Ralph's was powerlust gone sick—if something wasn't done soon, his days would be numbered, as would Motown's.

I finalized my strategy for unity. It was time for me to take my stand. All systems were on red alert—your move, Ray.

"What do you guys think?" Ed, Mike, and I reviewed the epic report and proposal, a blueprint for restoration. It was a bitterly cold day in the winter of '68. Bad warning winds were blowing outside. I knew that presenting this to Berry needed to be handled with the utmost care. Berry's whole attention now seemed to be on implanting Motown in L.A. and on launching Diana to the skies. Convincing him that the preservation of the crumbling Detroit battleship was worthwhile required perfect timing. Succeeding at this was everything to me—the crumbling battleship was still my creation, my child. And now, with this report, we stood a chance. There was hope.

"I don't know," Ed said skeptically. Ed was becoming suffo- cated by the war within the Donovan building, by the push and pull of the past. He too was already looking to the West—longing for sunny skies with room to breathe. One of the issues in the report, however, was his idea of improving the record jackets. "You know, before we go and present this, I'd like to go in and talk to Berry about it," Ed decided.

"Ed, you don't know Berry. He won't listen," I told him.

But Ed was at that moment on the phone making an appoint- ment with Berry. "Hey, look, everything has gotten way out of proportion here, and I've got to talk to you."

I also understood Ed's logic, but we weren't dealing in a game of rational logic. I also knew the meeting would have added friction because of me, and I planned not to attend. I didn't want to jeopardize the success of the report.

"OK, it's time," he said, as he readied to march down the hall. "Aren't you coming?"

"No," I answered. "This is your meeting."

Ed was adamant that he needed me to come with him. I gave in, feeling I couldn't let him walk into the lion's den alone. I followed him reluctantly into Berry's office, past the bodyguards, up to Berry's imposing, regal desk in the middle of the well-appointed room. As soon as we were seated, Ed immediately went into his monologue, describing the problems and how they could be resolved. After the first syllable left Ed's mouth, I saw Berry's face harden and I knew what was coming.

"Who the fuck are you to tell me anything?" I could lip-sync along with the entire album of this meeting. "Well, look, mother-fucker, kiss my ass." And then, "Oh yeah, fuck you."

The two of them were now performing in loud vibratos, and the guard stuck his head in the door to ask if there was a problem. "Oh, no," I told him. Just my husband and my ex-husband spoiling for a fight they'd both wanted for a long time. And I knew who was going to win.

The lyrical content was predictable as the volume increased, "Kiss my ass!"—"You kiss *my* ass!"

Finally Ed turned to me with, "Let's get the fuck out of here."

"Yeah," Berry echoed, "get the fuck out."

By the time we arrived at home, Ed and I were still playing it out. "I'm not working for this motherfucker, the ignorant fool, here they are ready to burn his building down and I can't even tell the motherfucker what I did, so fuck him. . . ." Ed walked from room to room, slamming doors, throwing everything that wasn't nailed down, kicking everything that was. My heart was heavy. Our relationship was being caught in everyone else's crossfire. His anger was legitimate. And yet I couldn't say anything. My silence fed his fury. "You got me here. I came here because of you. This was your move. Here I gave up everything I had, then I find myself blackballed for something I didn't do. I almost get killed trying to protect some other motherfucker." And then Ed stopped. "I'm leaving. I'm going to L.A."

What happened next I would not remember or understand for many years. I only knew that I ran. I was out of the house some-how, without a coat or socks or shoes, running through the night on the ice and the snow of the ground. I was running to Mama and Daddy's, where the kids were being watched. And I was running to my parents, to be taken in their arms, like a little girl who had been away from home for a long, long time. I was running away from the war. From Ed's disappointment and his anger. From Berry's power over me and over my life, and from my disappointment and anger at him. I remember that the cold and snow bit through my bare feet until my bones were frozen. And that I didn't make it to my parents' house. I remember that I knocked on a door of a cousin of my mother's, an eighty-year-old man. And shivering and gasping, I was let in and given a couch on which to sleep. I blacked out and slept the sleep of death. I vaguely remember being awakened by the old man's hands on my waist as his voice asked me to come and get into his bed. I forced him off me and tried again to sleep, now in fits of anguish, waking from my dreams to find myself in tears.

In the morning I called Mama from her cousin's house and asked her to watch over the kids for a few days. I also called Ed many times. Every time he answered I hung up. Finally, after two days, I borrowed a coat and some shoes from the old man, and I went home. On our bed I found a note from Ed. "I've gone to Los Angeles" was all it said. I felt a dull ache in my bones and a sensation as if I was still running. Running from everything, fleeing over the ice and snow to nowhere. Nowhere to run, I thought, it was a song, a Motown song. I could never run away; it would follow me everywhere. In a world falling down around all of us, in a time of war, there was nowhere to run.

And, so for a while longer, I would stay. And face the music.

CHAPTER 12
HOLLYWOOD
1969–1970

"Miss Ray, the agenda please." Berry opened the meeting. After all my work and planning, I was being given my day in court. And my court turned out to be a conference room at the Sands Hotel in Las Vegas. Having survived a feverish, and self-inflicted, cold and still being extremely confused about how to respond to Ed's hope that I would join him in L.A., I'd opted to put everything into my save-Motown mission.

Feeling that my report was finally ready to present, it dawned on me what an empty gesture it would be to simply hand Berry a document. I took a wild shot. I called him and told him we needed to have an overall company meeting. There was one second of deadly silence and then, "Yeah, let's do it. But let's go somewhere, let's make it a big company gathering."

Masking my great surprise I asked, "Well, where? You mean, like Hawaii? Bermuda?"

"No, no," he said. "Let's go to Vegas. That's it. You and Suzanne and Ralph organize it. Let's do it." I'd been delighted, to say the least, to feel the old highs of working side by side with Berry on a venture. And on top of his enthusiasm about the company event, he knew he could also get some gambling done in Vegas. What a deal.

As the meeting began, all our months of preparation became immediately evident. One by one each department representative stood to present his department's problems, goals for the future, and suggested improvements. Having worked with everyone beforehand to help organize their presentations, I'd made sure emphasis was placed on practical solutions, as opposed to futile complaints. At the end of the first day the general mood was quite buoyant. And besides, we were in Vegas—most Motowners' hog heaven.

At the end of the second day, it was my turn. Glancing at Mike, who'd just finished distributing copies of the eight-page report, I took a deep breath. In bold print, the name Ralph Seltzer appeared on the printed report as a number-one problem. "I'm here to represent the artists, writers, and producers of the Creative Division, regarding the protest over our inability to communicate with Ralph Seltzer and the problems it has caused."

I hadn't looked forward to being up at the podium by my little old lonesome, yet as I got into the report, momentum gathered, my words increased in heat, and my eloquence soared with the intensity of my beliefs. "While Ralph Seltzer may have a legitimate place in this company, it is not as head of the Creative Division. He cannot handle creative personalities, he knows nothing about the process of making music, and he gets no respect from his employees. Ralph is a catastrophe. He is the wrong man for that job." As I spoke, Ralph's face turned twenty shades of purple and his glasses steamed over. For the first time, he was forced to endure criticism without cursing out the critic. I had never questioned how my presentation would affect my relations with him back in Detroit. All I'd cared about was letting Berry know how serious the situation was. If it meant out-and-out war with Ralph, it would be worth it.

I looked at Berry, who was expressionless but listening carefully. No one had ever presented such a well-organized, detailed report. At my closing, he nodded and then asked, "Ralph, do you have something to say in defense?"

"Yes, I've got a lot to say." Ralph stood, addressing the room as if staving off an angry mob. "I'd like to say, in the first place, Ray doesn't know what the hell she's talking about. I'm dealing with these people the best way that I can. I think my record shows I've done a great job for the company, and I don't think anyone else could do better. Mr. Gordy placed me in this position because he knew that I'm the best."

As Ralph spoke, Berry's face registered neither sympathy nor anger. Several times he looked over at me and our eyes met. I'd made the big play. Now it was his move.

This meeting was a catharsis for me, a culmination of almost two years of being back at Motown. Also, the general spirit throughout the company was being uplifted by this meeting, and the Creative Division was relieved to have had its voice heard. I guessed that Ralph's days were numbered. Little did I know that mine were numbered too.

Arriving home from work not many weeks after the meeting, I found a package from Ed. Inside was a record called "Can I Change My Mind" by Tyrone Davis. "Baby, won't you change your mind, so we can start all over again." I played it a couple times and then I changed my mind about sticking it out in Detroit. "Can I Change My Mind" became our theme song; with it Ed seduced me out to California.

My parting with Berry was short and sweet. He thanked me for what I'd accomplished, particularly in Las Vegas, and his tone seemed to say that, no matter what games were being played, he knew I was in his corner. "It's great whenever you're here. Your spirit is part of Motown. No matter what happens, I'll always be here for you." The only love song Berry knew how to sing to me.

I gazed at Ed at the Los Angeles airport. California was making a new man out of him, and he was ecstatic to see me and the kids. We embraced and he said, "C'mon everybody. Let's go home."

We all piled into the car. Cliff, now almost fourteen, was as charming and devilish as ever. At nine and a half, Kerry was an amazingly perceptive, shrewd, and ambitious kid. Considering there hadn't been any contact whatsoever between him and his father in many years, it was startling how much he was like Berry. And Eddie, two and a half, was a total love. I couldn't tell yet about Rya, just past her first birthday, but something told me this little girl was going to grow up strong-willed.

Our first glimpses of Los Angeles were disappointing. Freeways, cars and more cars, suburbs, tract houses. A couple of palm trees. Our hopes picked up as we hit Sunset Boulevard, with its seedy kind of glamour. Then we turned north, traveling up from Sunset into the hills, through narrow, winding streets, past grand Spanish-style houses with perfectly manicured lawns. Bougainvillea, cacti, palm trees. I was getting enthusiastic—this was really Hollywood. Every dream house we passed increased the suspense a little more.

"Here it is," Ed said, as the car slowed, and into my vision rose one of the most dazzling homes I'd ever seen—a huge, contemporary, gray-brick structure set majestically atop a climb with the other houses like peons beneath it. It promised an interior of splendor and luxury. "Wow," I said. "Yeehaw," yelled the boys.

"Ed, I can't believe . . ." Just as I was ready to burst into song, the car stopped short of the palace's driveway and I looked to see a tiny white bungalow with tiny windows, like a gingerbread house.

The house was so small that the moment I stepped into the living room, I nearly stumbled over a pile of bedclothes, which in fact turned out to be a person sleeping. The rattle of the keys, the kids, and the lugging of the suitcases roused the pile of bedding, and a yawning head rose from its nest.

"Good morning," said Ed cheerfully. "Ray, this is Rick Matthews, one of my artists. We're going to do some great things together. This guy's going to be a big star. Rick, this is my wife, Ray."

The head bobbed with mild comprehension. While Ed banged on into the bedroom with the suitcases, Rick pulled himself up to his feet and tripped forward to shake my hand. As it turned out, Rick (who was originally from Buffalo, New York, and was born James Johnson) was connected to Motown from some experiences a few years before. Calling himself Rickie James, he had sung at the time with a Canadian rock & roll band called the Mynah Birds, which also included Neil Young, later of Buffalo Springfield and Crosby, Stills, Nash and Young. They cut some sides at Hitsville that never got released. What a small world, I thought, as the new California smells wafted through the window. Motown was everywhere. It wouldn't be until almost a decade later that Rick James would finally break through at Motown and have huge success.

The kids and I immediately dug Rick. He was funny and warm, with tons of talent pouring out of him. At this juncture, he was a very nice, clean-cut, ordinary-looking guy with short hair. He didn't think of himself as an R&B or soul singer at all. He was a black kid who loved rock, probably idolized Jimi Hendrix, and hung out with all the rowdy white boys. Ed, who knew a potential star when he heard one, would work very diligently to develop and sustain Rick's career. In the process, he would cut about eight masters with Rick—and would be sorry to see them collecting dust in his garage forevermore.

After my initial reaction, I became enchanted with the little house on Miller Drive. It was a cheerful, sunny house with a patio. In the cozy living room was a beautifully polished wood floor, a big white bear rug, and a fireplace. Coming from the war zone at the Donovan building, life seemed exquisitely quaint and comfy.

This was the first stint, since my nightmarish phase with Margaret and Berry in Detroit, that I wasn't working. I felt just fine being an at-home mother and wife for a change. After giving birth to four children, without one real vacation from employment, I thought I deserved it. And I knew that Ed deserved it. Maybe this time we could shake loose the shackles of the past and do it right.

As I began to explore this new land of opportunity, I wasn't quite sure what to make of it. On one hand, there was a lovely serenity—that laid-back California cool. On the other hand, the seasons never changed, and there was a flow about the days that became surreal, as though something darker and more ominous lurked below the surface. Being in the heart of the movie world—with its ostentation, glamour, and power, there was also a wild, anything-goes kind of drama in the air. Soon I would see how this unpredictable, complex environment would affect every aspect of my family's life.

Within a few months Ed hooked up with an investor to put together a record label. So, with a little money to spare, we decided to house-hunt for a larger place. We went to see a house closer to Beverly Hills on St. Ives Drive. Like many Hollywood homes, it was all but hidden from the street. As we approached with the agent, through a gate and down a walkway, it looked small and hemmed in by its neighbors. But once inside, the place opened up like magic around us, with a huge expanse of space spreading out in front of our eyes—a beautiful, sunken modern living room and beyond it a big picture window with a breathtaking view of the city below. The house was a tri-level, which enabled construction of one of its most unique features, a pool with one glass wall. The agent explained that it was originally built to film scenes of people swimming underwater. Now *this* was Hollywood.

"Oh, this house has a history," said the agent. "We only rent it to entertainers." Pointing to a desk, she whispered to us, "Elvis Presley stayed here; this desk belonged to him." And then she name-dropped some more. "The Rolling Stones and, oh, one of the last occupants was a record producer named Terry Melcher, the son of Doris Day. He would have stayed but he found a bigger place in Laurel Canyon." What a deal. We took a lease for two years, only too proud to reside with Elvis's old desk, and it would become one of our favorite homesteads in California. Soon after moving in, Ed was able to realize a lifelong dream of having his family nearby. Leaving Ed's brothers Ronnie and Jesse at home in Ashbury Park, the rest of the Singleton clan, including Ed's mother, Mary, and siblings—Richard, Jimmy, Pierre, and Ida—all joined to live with us in the illustrious home on St. Ives.

After the riots of Detroit, our new home in the hills seemed unbelievably safe—until one morning in August when we awoke to the media buzzing about a gruesome collection of bodies in Laurel Canyon. The news reported that a gang of people had entered a house on Cielo Drive, and five people, including actress Sharon Tate, were slain in a brutal, ritualistic massacre. It was frightening enough to know that these killers were roaming the hills. But when we read the following day of police speculation that the murderers may have actually been looking for the previous tenant of the house—Terry Melcher—we were terrified. Later we learned that Charles Manson may have indeed wanted to take action against Melcher for rejecting some of his songs. Not only that, but Manson knew Melcher wasn't living in the Cielo house—he just wanted to send a message to the producer. It didn't matter who was there, they were going to die. It would be many, many months before we slept soundly in bed at night.

It was ironic, of course, that although we didn't have much—if any—contact for some time, Berry was living not very far away on Curson Drive. He had purchased a sprawling, two-story contemporary house from one of the Smothers Brothers. It was quite a spread. Completely invisible from the street, it was approached by going up a long driveway and finally coming to a huge iron gate, which opened up onto a paradise—palm trees, ferns, flowers, and a little arched bridge over a lily pond. The house itself was a miracle of modern architecture, a gorgeous, harmonious blend of glass and wood. It was a long way from Loucye's house.

Because of all the ghosts that Motown represented to Ed, and because I wanted so badly to give him the support he deserved, I attempted to minimize my past ties. While it gnawed at me constantly that Berry hadn't seen Kerry in six years, for Ed's sake I chose not to do anything about changing that unhealthy situation. Simply pretending the past didn't exist, however, became increasingly more difficult to do. You didn't have to look any further than Cliff's school bus to see signs of the ever-present connections. In the fall of '69, Cliff and Jermaine Jackson were in the ninth grade together. Jermaine's brother, Jackie, who rode the same bus, was in high school. Little Michael Jackson stayed for months at a time at Berry's house. The kids were all friends.

It was in Hollywood where Berry again worked his magic. The Las Vegas meeting had been instrumental, I hoped, in alerting him to the crises embroiling the company. Whether or not that was the case, he recognized, just at the last minute, that there was no one to catch the ball except himself. Even given the trauma of Motown's departure from Detroit, the company rode into Los Angeles on a high. The last few years of Whitfield-produced hits for the Tempts and Marvin Gaye, Ashford and Simpson's beautiful work with Marvin and Tammi Terrell, and Stevie Wonder's string of smashes all provided great momentum. And Berry, from his new command post, was about to spring on the world a whole new surprise that would send the company into major overdrive again.

The five brothers from Gary, Indiana, the Jackson boys, were already veterans of the road—pros—by the time they came to Motown. Papa Joe made sure of that. Apparently Gladys Knight had spotted the boys and recommended them a couple of times to the company, but there had been no follow-up. It was Bobby Taylor of the Vancouvers who got them their first audition. Of course, they knocked everybody out. Berry signed them up, moved them to L.A., and made them Suzanne DePasse's special project. But it was Berry, rolling up his sleeves again as he'd done with "Love Child," who really put the company fire behind the new act—contributing to the songwriting and producing and pushing as hard as he had in our early days. Bringing in the exceptional talents of the Corporation, a writing/arranging/producing team composed of Freddie Perren, Fonzie Mizell, and Deke Richards, Berry's old instincts for selecting the perfect supporting players were right on target. And so, the first Jackson 5 single, "I Want You Back," came out in October and went straight to number one. So did the next one, "ABC," and the one after that, "The Love You Save." The Jackson 5 was Berry's triumphant coup.

My boys often walked down to a West Hollywood park to play with the Jacksons and their other school friends. One day Kerry went down to the park, saw all his pals on the field, and started trucking toward the game. A man stopped him saying, "I'm sorry, you can't play." Kerry did not introduce himself even though he knew who the man was. Instead he dashed into the game. The man ambled after Kerry, and pulled him back, "Now, go on home, kid. This is a closed game." Kerry, like Cliff, loves any potentially dramatic situation, the more angles the better, and there was no stopping him. He hightailed back into the game, and the man—

who was close to the boiling point—gave chase, picked him up, and started to remove him from the park. All of a sudden, Kerry asked the man, "Do you know my mother?"

"Who's your mother?"

"Ray Singleton is my mother," Kerry said.

"Ray Singleton?" It took the man a beat longer to make the connection. "Oh, my God! You're my son!"

"Yeah, Dad," Kerry said to Berry.

Berry was stunned. I received a call from him that night. "Guess what, guess what?" he tripped over his words. "I saw Kerry. Kerry. And I didn't even know the kid." He was beside himself with the emotion of it.

Both Kerry and I were given more pause for reflection when one day, as I was dropping him off at school, I saw another ghost from the past. From the car I saw a beautiful young black woman with a flawless face, walking with a little boy around five or six years old. My stomach tightened and my breathing grew short. I knew that Margaret and Berry no longer lived together, that she and Kennedy were living in lavish style in a beautiful home in the hills, provided and maintained by Berry. But seeing her was an unpleasant surprise. "Kerry, do you see that little boy? That's your brother Kennedy." Kerry said nothing, though I could see his wheels turning. I didn't tell Kerry that this was the same woman who'd driven a stake between me and Berry, who'd been partly responsible for the earthquake that jostled my share of Motown out of my grasp. These were the shadows I refused to look into and from which all children should be protected. So all I said to Kerry was, "That's your brother."

Years later Kennedy would describe to me his first year in school. Shy and insecure, he'd received abusive treatment from the school bullies, who pestered him wherever he went. He would have felt completely terrorized except that sometimes, on the playground or in the hall, when the bullies were taunting him and roughing him up, an older boy, a sixth-grader, would suddenly appear and rescue him, sending the tormenting crew into flight. And then, without a word, the older boy would turn and walk away. This happened over and over again, and Kennedy was mystified. When he got to second grade, the older boy was no longer around, and so his identity remained unknown until a few years later when Kennedy was staying at his father's house and Berry introduced him to his brother: "Kennedy, this is Kerry." Kennedy's jaw dropped open. "You're that guy."

The constant tide of the past continued to wash destructively against the shore of my marriage with Ed Singleton. We seemed to be sinking into an inevitable abyss. I lived in a state of guilt. Ed had given up a promising business in 1963 to, as he'd put it then, "come to protect" me. It was just after that that Flip Wilson and Tony Orlando made killings in the entertainment market, and so Ed missed the very boat that he'd set sail. I felt it was my fault. There were also the lingering suspicions of Berry's interference in our Shrine venture. And then I'd sent him into battle at the Donovan Building, fighting for a cause that wasn't his to fight for. But as my guilt increased, so did Ed's exaggeration of my culpability. He became suspicious of my every motive, my every word.

Money problems were a big burden too. Ed was so eager to prove himself with investors that he pushed too impatiently, and when things floundered he was furious at himself and would send the investor packing. Soon we were living only on my alimony money—thirteen hundred eighty-two dollars a month. Ed endured the whispers of his peers, real and imagined, that he was being supported by Berry Gordy's money. His self-esteem hit the bottom, and I felt only helplessness. My guilt, his frustration, and the towering yet unseen presence of Berry meant that our civil war raged, with fights that seemed out of our own control and friendly fire turning into full-scale attacks.

"That's it! Don't you ever call me a 'motherfucker' again, Ed. Whatever I've done, I've tried to do right by you." That was my first departure, as I scooped up the kids and headed to Detroit. Two weeks later: "Ray, I'm a lost man without you and the kids. It's because I love you so much that I go crazy. Please come home." We were on the next plane to L.A.

A couple of months later: "Goddamn it, Ray, don't fucking tell me how to run my . . ." And it was back to Detroit. This time I enrolled the kids in school, thinking we were back to stay. This time lasted a month: "Ed, you are one of the finest men in the world. I know we can get through. The kids and I are coming home."

In L.A. the warring resumed and the periods of reconciliation grew shorter and shorter until soon I was on the road once more. Sometimes I left the kids with Ed and his mother, who was living in. Most of the time I took them with me. Other times I got in the car and drove with the same feeling that I'd experienced running in the snow that night in Detroit.

I took long walks on the beach in Santa Monica, wondering

where my home was. My home with Ed was loaded with land mines—a man struggling to hold his head above water and a woman who knew she couldn't quell the undertow. My home with my parents in Detroit was only a temporary stopover. And my home I'd built with Motown, well, I no longer owned the keys. Sometimes, lulled by the smell of sea air and the sound of rhythmic tides, I slept in the backseat of the car with the windows open. Then in the morning I would walk some more.

I'd sit on the beach and stare at the ocean, thinking of dramatic movies in which the heroine can fight no more. And step by step, inch by inch, she would walk to the water's edge, the tide washing over her feet, her ankles, up to her waist. As she walked further out, her eyes still on the horizon, slowly, very slowly, the waves crept over her until finally she was seen no more. And in the last frame there would be that vast endless sea and a setting sun. Then the credits would roll. Nope, I thought, with the water only up to my calves and a refreshing ocean spray on my face, that's not the movie of my life. Coming out of the water, I decided to make my movie a high-adventure intrigue. What the hell, this *was* Hollywood, right?

In the first scene of my movie, I go to a telephone booth with just enough change for one phone call. I place it to the Beverly Comstock Hotel.

"This is Mr. Gordy's secretary, Rebecca Jiles, at Motown. Mrs. Gordy is coming into town and she'll be staying with you for a few nights. And we want her to have everything, whatever she wants— just charge it to Motown Record Corporation. Now she doesn't have any luggage and she has been through quite an ordeal, but don't pay any attention. Just give her the best." It was uncanny how much I sounded like Rebecca Jiles.

As the scene continues, I walk in barefoot, without a purse and only the clothes I am wearing. Visualize the glamorous, fabulous Beverly Hills hotel. Rooms for two hundred dollars a night. Swimming pools, movie stars, all the high-muckety-mucks. Picture me, a little waif with sand in her hair strolling in and being shown to a suite with the greatest of deference. There I station myself for days, taking bubble baths, ordering from room service, watching television, and waiting for my alimony check to arrive at the Motown office so I can grab it, round up the kids, and fly out of town.

Well, the first scene is such a smash success, and goes completely unnoticed by the authorities, that a couple of months later it's repeated, with even more style. "Miss Jiles at Motown again. In addition to the room, could we get Mrs. Gordy a rental car, please? Say, a Cadillac convertible? What color? Well, she does have a weakness for powder blue." In this scene I also make trips to the dress shop and pick myself up a lovely new outfit. Powder blue, naturally. These two visits to the Beverly Comstock are so revitalizing that I decide to return again, and then again. It is so easy, simple as one-two-three and do-re-me. What wows the audience is that, while I'm taking bubble baths, I don't even have bus fare to get to the office to pick up my check when it does come in. What a wacky show business life.

To interrupt this madcap movie, I should explain that I was, quite simply, emotionally exhausted. Those hotel stints, about six of them all told, were my only way to get the kind of rest that I hadn't experienced since I was a teenager living at home with Mama and Daddy. Ringing up a tab at Motown's expense seemed completely justified in light of everything that had been denied me. At first, in fact, Berry unofficially indulged me in these delightful episodes. Once the company was formally wise to the number of dollars I was wracking up, however, I became persona non grata at the Beverly Comstock, and Motown put its foot down to similar VIP privileges for others. I felt badly for having caused the crackdown, but later Berry would make a humorous quip about me: "This is the only woman in the world," he joked, "that can travel all over the country without a dime, using my name." In the meantime, and until he confronted me, it was on with the show.

Everything about my life then was cinematic. Each time Ed and I reunited, it was tender and romantic, with tears of hope streaming down my face. Each time I walked out the door, our shouting matches had raised the roof. And usually those scenes of flight were wild escapades with my happy throng of kids, jumping on and off airplanes, trains, and automobiles. Later Cliff and Kerry would sit down and count a total of nineteen different schools they attended during this period.

What was so surreal about this stretch of time was that my children were not aware of the turmoil. On the outside I was their buoyant and fun mom, offering them one adventure after the next. But, of course, on the inside my desire to have some stability somewhere was clamoring to be fulfilled.

Using Cliff's and Kerry's tally, I must have left nineteen times. The nineteenth time, Ed was sitting in the bathtub. After having his usual blowout and kickout to an investor, he was in a mood— frustrated, trapped, exhausted. He called me into the bathroom and started in on me. "Listen, I don't like the way you are handling things and you've got to straighten up and fly right and change your ways," and on and on.

I stood in the bathroom while he raved, and then I broke in, "Excuse me. Could you hold that thought right there. I see you're without a towel, so let me go get you one. I agree that I'm inadequate, that I haven't been doing the right things to support you, but . . . let's continue our discussion when I get back with the towel."

Ed waited and waited for that towel—because I never came back. Ed's mom was watching the kids, and I hopped in my car, barreling down the street for my last stay at the Beverly Comstock, where I booked myself in for an indefinite run. In the past when I had left, I usually called Ed back to get in my side of the argument. But this time I didn't call Ed. I took a couple of bubble baths and called instead another important male character in my saga.

"Berry, this is it for Ed and me. I've left him for good. Now, I got you your divorce from Thelma, so I want you to help me get my divorce. I want to give Ed five thousand dollars, because he's over there in that house and he doesn't have any money. Send me that five thousand and I'll get divorced."

The money arrived the next day. I'd never received money that quickly in my life. Having so kindly obliged my request, Berry also let me know, in no uncertain terms, that the gig was up and that this was my final stay at the Beverly Comstock. I didn't call Ed for a couple of weeks, and when I finally did it was to tell him I was leaving once and for all. In a small but firm voice I said, "Bring the kids to the airport. We're going back to Detroit. I want a divorce."

There was a dramatic exchange when Ed objected. We both delivered high and low blows over the phone. At first he refused to bring the kids; then he wanted to keep Eddie. In the end he said that he'd bring them all. As I waited at the airport on the appointed day, I paced back and forth, thinking that he had backed down. There was no sign of the kids, and our plane was due to depart. Then, finally, at the last minute, Ed's right-hand man dropped off my children, and we raced to catch our flight to Detroit.

Once back, I anticipated that the divorce proceedings would be long and drawn out. When I returned for the divorce a couple of months later, I walked up to the judge alone and waited for the hours of hell to begin. The judge asked me if I wanted the divorce. "Yes," I said. It seemed only seconds later when he said, "Divorce granted." It happened so fast, and that was that. Well, it was Hollywood, after all.

After it was over, as crazy as it sounds, I felt great. I still loved Ed Singleton very much and sorely regretted all the circumstances that led to the breakup. But I was inexplicably happy. I felt young and free, as if I could hear and smell and see again. I felt as if my life was truly starting over again. To celebrate, I did something completely out of character. Although alcohol usually makes me sick, I drove from the courthouse to a liquor store for a bottle of vodka. Jumping back in my car, I flew down the freeway with the window open and my left foot propped against the open window. The radio was blaring, and I was singing at the top of my lungs and waving the bottle of vodka in the air while the wind of possibilities rushed in my ears. And for the first time in a while, I started to hear the music again.

CHAPTER 13
DIANA
1970–1971

"You did what?" I shouted at Berry a few weeks later.

"I already set it up. You're hired," he said. Well, if that didn't beat all.

The kids and I were staying, once again, at the home of my sister Juanita and her husband, Dobbs, in northwest Detroit, just down the street from my parents' new house. Dobbs, in fact, was the handsome real estate agent who'd sold them their house—only to make the next sale to Nita, and marry her. He and Nita would forever open their arms and home to us, and whatever else we brought along—German shepherds, sheep, goats, chickens, and even sometimes Venida, my secretary turned-best-friend from the Donovan Building, and *her* animals.

Knowing that, above all, I needed to be doing music and earning a living again, I'd just sat down to scope out possibilities when the phone rang.

"I can't handle being on the road with Diana Ross," Berry began. "I want you to go in and work with her. She opens tomorrow night at the Cocoanut Grove, and she's expecting you."

"Wait a doggone minute, what about the kids, the . . . I've got things to do . . . I . . . Diana Ross? I need twenty-five thousand a year on this and two hundred fifty dollars a week expenses."

"Just be at the Grove tomorrow night. The show starts at eight o'clock. Good-bye." Berry's hang-up sounded like a ball thudding in my court. In our last exchange, I'd called him asking for help with my divorce. Now it was his turn to ask for a favor. Well, I thought, I guess it's time to play ball.

"Come on, kids! We're going back to California!" To their general cheers of enthusiasm, and Nita and Dobbs's mutual rolling of eyes, I worked like a team coach, blowing that whistle and directing the mayhem of traffic. And at once a flurry of activity snowballed us through packing, reservations, two international airports, and to a hotel room in Hollywood—with a baby-sitter. Some thirty hours after Berry's call, I was walking into the Ambassador Hotel looking every bit the part of an artist's stylish manager. And yet I didn't have a clue as to what Berry expected of me.

Amazing, I thought, what a lot of water had passed under the bridge since those days in 1960 when skinny little Diane and her group, the Primettes, came forward hoping to be part of my company. Sweet, polite, and respectful, Diane then knew me only as Miss Ray, her employer and her other employer's wife. Now a decade of smash hits and international fame later, she was quite another person. She was no longer a Supreme, and her solo career was soaring on the wings of two recent phenomenal Ashford and Simpson hits—"Reach Out and Touch (Somebody's Hand)" and "Ain't No Mountain High Enough." Now she was Diana Ross. She was not only Berry's greatest female star sensation; she was also his lover. That powerful pride of mine suddenly stopped me at the door of her dressing room. This is insane, I thought. I'm walking into a hornet's nest. And then, from the stage of the Cocoanut Grove, I heard the strains of the band warming up, soothing all my hesitations and rousing my desire to again be a part of the only world I really knew.

"Hello, Diana," I chimed and received an extremely warm greeting in response. There was no acknowledgment of our history or the dramatic reversal of our roles. And as I immediately attempted to help out in the dressing room, it struck me that, above and beyond these new circumstances, we were family. All the hubbub now surrounding Diana had grown from the tiny seed that Berry and I had planted almost twelve years before. In the eighteen months to come, I would need to hold tenaciously to the knowledge of those roots.

"Oh, Ray, may I speak with you?" Diana called to me after the show. I was just saying good night to Roger Campbell, road manager and technical director, and his assistant, Les Peterson— both old friends. In addition to helping them with their various duties, I had volunteered to take over sound coordination, something I'd already handled that night. I'd also spent some time conferring with Liz Moran, Diana's capable administrative assistant, with whom I'd grow to be good friends during the next few months. While pitching in on everyone's behalf and assuring that everything ran smoothly, I was also conscious of the necessity of creating a supportive atmosphere for Diana. I knew all too well that Berry habitually criticized her mercilessly after a show. So I trotted backstage to congratulate her on a beautiful performance.

Before I got a word out, Diana said, "Look," and lifted her eyes away from her own reflection in the makeup mirror, "I know that tonight was your first. But I do expect that from here on in you will perform to the best of your ability. Also, from now on, I would prefer that you refer to me as 'Miss Ross.' I know that you have known me for some time, but in my position I need to be treated with more respect."

My reaction was a strong mix of nausea and pity for her. In molding Diana into a superstar, Berry was shaping a monster. Now I knew I'd have a calling—to remind her of her humanity. Instead of reminding her that she wouldn't have been in her "position" if not partly for me, I replied, "Berry has asked me to do a job here, and you can be sure I'll do an excellent one. However, in my position," and I echoed her haughty articulation of the word, "I too require being treated with some respect." Taming wild horses would have been a far easier task than the one I was about to begin.

When I returned that night to the hotel, my jaw clamped tight, Cliff, now all of fifteen, sensed my mood and reminded me of an episode from the past. "It was just before we went to New York. I must have been about seven, and Diane was no big deal, skinny legs and pigtails. Then all of a sudden she was Diana, and she had these beautiful bouffant wigs and gowns, and everyone thought she was the most unbelievable thing ever walking. Remember?"

"Yes, I remember," I said, also remembering my horror at the time.

Cliff went on reminiscing. "It was that time that the Supremes were performing at some really great hotel, and a few hours before the show, when I was scoping out the hotel, I happened to get on the elevator with Diana. She had on a gorgeous gown with all these little sequins—I remember I could see myself a thousand times on her dress—and a big, elaborate wig. There were about six or seven people in the elevator too, and they were going on, 'Oh, Diana Ross, oh we love you, you're beautiful, oh we're on an elevator with Diana Ross.' She was eating it up. Meanwhile I was thinking, what's the big deal about her anyway?

"That's when I got the inspiration. Let's make these people really get excited. So, just as the elevator was coming to a stop, I maneuvered my way up to the front and waited. When the door opened there were more people there—'Oh, Diana Ross, oh!' I hopped out, checked my escape route, and then as soon as she stepped off I jumped up—remember, I was really short then—and grabbed the top of her wig and snatched it away. Well, I turned to run, but before I got too far, I looked back to see her reaction. Under the wig was a stocking cap on the crown of her head, holding some hair down; the rest of the hair was in these little pigtails, which were going 'boing, boing' all over the back and the side of her head. Standing in her gown, half in shock, her mouth opened and she said something like 'Aaagghhhh,' and the people watching either had their mouths open in shock or they were laughing up a storm."

In hearing the story retold, I too laughed uncontrollably, especially when I recalled Berry's reaction. Cornering Cliff a few hours later, he'd said sternly to the little boy, "Diana came and told me you pulled her wig off." For one frightening beat, Cliff believed he was finally going to get it, but then Berry began to stagger, hold his chest, and laugh uproariously.

Cliff's recollection would serve me well in the weeks to come, but soon I was surprised to see a nice relationship developing between Diana and me. Aside from having the overall responsibility for her and her sixteen-member entourage—dancers, backup vocalists, musicians, wardrobe mistress, cook, technical and security people—I became her traveling companion and, as it turned out, her confidante. There was also a longer list of duties that included troubleshooting, sound checks and coordination, and organizing transportation and accommodations. She now performed in the larger venues—the Cocoanut Grove, New York's Waldorf-Astoria, Chicago's Theater in the Round. Noticing there were usually many celebrities in the audiences who wanted to meet Diana, I created a system allowing for such introductions. John Wayne, Jimmy Stewart, Ella Fitzgerald, Barbra Streisand, Ed Sullivan, Liza Minnelli—when I'd bring them backstage, one by one, each star, no matter how successful, seemed to be in awe of Diana. She relished all this attention, even when we had to sneak her out of theaters or travel with fans plastering their bodies over the limousines.

I admired the hell out of Diana's drive; her ambition reminded me of my own when we were building Motown. During the course of my twenty-four-hour-a-day job, I would accompany her to TV tapings and recording sessions, where she was always impeccably professional. Backstage, with the help of her wardrobe mistress, Pat, and myself, Diana would sometimes have as many as eleven costume changes a show. And, onstage, it was clear that she'd learned her lessons well. Her performances were executed to perfection, with unparalleled timing, gestures, and expressions. During "Reach Out and Touch (Somebody's Hand)," with the audience holding hands, swaying, and singing along, Diana floated among them with a follow spot behind. The light was like a halo behind her as she spread stardust kisses on the audience and blessed them with her smiles. No one could pull it off like she could.

Unfortunately, there were other sides to her that made my role as her personal assistant hard to take. One was her selfishness. Though she made a hundred thousand dollars a week in some venues, she thought my two-hundred-fifty-dollar-a-week road salary was excessive. And praise or popularity to anyone other than herself amounted to treachery as far as Diana was concerned. I tried to keep in mind, however, who'd groomed her for this success. Therein lay another problem—Berry.

I'd played some rough chess games with him in the past, but this one took the cake. There was Diana, queen of Motown yet still playing to be Berry's queen—to be his wife and have his child. There was me, the ex-queen, the previous wife and already a mother of one of his children. The only thing I was playing for was to be heard and not forgotten. It was an absurd game, brilliantly devised by Berry. And the moves were not friendly ones.

One night Berry showed up without notice right before a show, taking everyone by surprise. As he sauntered in, the whole entourage, Diana included, scattered. What did I care? Holding a role of tape and with a nail in my mouth, I fiddled with some wires. Wearing old work jeans, a sweatshirt, and sneakers, I concentrated on my project. I was interrupted by Berry, who in all our years together had never once told me I looked anything but unsatisfactory. Now he gazed at me with an expression of worship and said, "Ray, you look fabulous!" Yeah, right. As Berry spoke those loving words of praise, I turned to see Diana, a woman who spent hours on makeup alone, standing in the wings with a look of horrified resentment. With this good play, Berry won—getting me to work for her, yet making her detest me.

Another way he played it was when, again showing up unannounced, he walked in just before Diana's opening at the Waldorf. She had on her latest four-thousand-dollar Bob Mackie gown, one of those feathered, sequin-studded, plastered-on dresses that practically required a team of workmen to get on properly. Preparing to make her stage entrance, she turned to Berry and gave him her "Yes, I'm a star" smile. He did his little tongue-in-cheek, cocked-head look and said, "You know, you look just like a chicken in that thing." Again, Berry won—Diana ran into her dressing room in tears, and I felt sorry for her. Great.

As the game went on, Diana's plays included having Berry on the telephone at the drop of a pin. Then, instead of confronting anyone on the crew, she would play tattletale. "Do you know what she did?" And, "There's a light bulb out in my dressing room, you'd think that someone could . . ." Anything to have his attention.

Berry reacted by phoning me in two seconds flat, "What the fuck are you doing out there? I send you out because you're the only one I can trust, and you know she's a big star, and if you can't give her the respect she deserves, then I'll just have to get someone else."

Diana's strongest move for control was always to ignore the fact that I had a personal life. And it was with the utmost relief that I made it into L.A. as often as I could to spend time with the kids—away from the mind games and back to the family I loved so well. Cliff was now almost fifteen, Kerry was eleven, Eddie was soon to be four, and Rya around two and a half. By now, even the babies knew how to order from room service. "Rya, you ordered what?"

At first, since there hadn't been a spare second to go apartment hunting, we based ourselves at the Continental Hyatt House, and, man, was there a pancake bill. When I finally found the time, I moved us over to an apartment at the Fountainview West, with a terrific housekeeper and guardian for the kids—my dearest friend, Venida, who had her baby girl, Shirene, with her. Each time I came home, I'd then find myself out on the road longing for them even more. I also missed my own parents something awful. Here I'd been a gypsy, traveling around to all these exotic places, and not once had Mama and Daddy visited me. "We'll come when you get settled," they'd always say.

When I found out we were going to be at the Frontier in Vegas for a week, I called Mama a month prior to the engagement and invited her and Daddy to come. I thought it would be perfect. She gave me her pat answer about only coming when I was stable, which in my mind was an insinuation of disapproval. All my other brothers and sisters were married and settled down with families. I was the wild one, the damn fool. Married three times, divorced three times. Thirty-four years old and still doing that crazy music stuff. Dragging her kids around the country and back a zillion times. Underneath her tone was also her unspoken sadness for the losses I'd suffered in my greatest venture.

I was practically in tears. "Mama, please. I want you to come. I'm sending you the plane tickets and making the hotel reservations. I've listened to your excuses all these years, but now that's it. You have to see Las Vegas—you'll love it."

"No, no, we can't come right now. Ash and I are getting old. We're comfortable here."

"Fine, I tell you what. I'm going to send you the tickets and I'm not going to call you anymore. I'll be at the airport to pick you up. If you're not on that plane, you'll never see me again." If there was one person in the world more stubborn than my mother, it was me.

I'd been pacing at the airport for an hour. Over the past month my parents had left messages everywhere for me, but I'd refused to return calls or to contact them. Now, as the plane touched down my heart was sinking. I should have known better than to throw an ultimatum at my own parents. I watched through the windows as the passengers filed down the steps from the plane onto the tarmac. No sight of them. Tears were welling in my eyes. And I'd planned such a wonderful week. Wait, now, wasn't that Mama in . . . why, she was all in her finery. Her prized little mink stole, a powder-blue pillbox hat, and a pretty silk dress. "Mama!" I began shouting through the windows. And there was Daddy in his Easter Sunday navy blue suit, still one of the most handsome men on earth. And then—wait just one minute—it was Nita and Dobbs!

In the terminal I bounced up and down, squeezing and hugging each and every one of them. "Well, Daddy," I asked, knowing that this was the first airplane ride either of my parents had ever taken, "how was it?"

"I'd have to say that it was up-to-date, Raynoma, up-to-date." My father beamed at me.

Everything to Daddy was up-to-date—the blue Cadillac convertible, the Las Vegas strip, the marquees and flashing neon signs and billboards. When my parents stepped into their hotel suite, they were speechless. The best surprise was, however, when I took them to my room and there were all the kids. Then that afternoon I took everybody backstage to get a chance to see what I did, all the intricacies of lighting, sound, and stage production.

I put them at a front table for the show, and Miss Diana Ross came over to welcome them, telling them how thrilled she was that they were in town. They could hardly take it all in, it was so much.

It was a week of heaven. Then our whole gang flew to Los Angeles for another week. Deplaning, we were met by a chauffeur and valet. "Welcome to Los Angeles, Mr. and Mrs. Mayberry," said the chauffeur and whisked everybody out into the limo while the valet collected the luggage. "How did he know we were coming in, Ashby?" Mama whispered.

"It's very up-to-date, very." Daddy shook his head. So off in the limo we rode, with buckets of champagne and ice-cold sodas for the kids, all the way to the Century Plaza hotel. Their week in Los Angeles flew by all too quickly. In the years to come, especially after my father passed away, I would remember those bright and glorious two weeks. I would have given them the world if I could have, and their appreciation of that trip was the jewel of jewels to me.

"No, I said 'no' and I mean 'no.' " Oh, the many moods of Diana Ross. The same woman who'd graciously acknowledged my parents in the presence of an audience was now undergoing a personality costume change. There were twenty-five blind children in the audience, whose chaperon had just approached me, "Please, could you try to arrange for the children to meet Diana? Just for five minutes. For them to be able to say they'd met her or touched her or even been in her presence would change their lives. Can we arrange this, please?"

Diana cringed. "I don't want to meet them."

"Why not?

"I don't want to, that's all," she replied.

"Oh, Diana, come on. Just two minutes or whatever for these blind kids. These kids worship you—you're their queen. Just say hello, that's all you have to do. No one's going to make you build them a hospital or anything."

She was in a fury. "I'm not going to do it. I refuse to subject myself to being depressed by seeing a bunch of blind kids, OK? I'm tired and don't want to be bothered with it. So I don't give a damn what you tell the lady. The answer is 'no.' "

I was heartsick when I returned to the children's chaperon and too disgusted to even make up an excuse for Diana. All I could do was fabricate excuses to myself for why I didn't climb on the next vehicle home.

The sole reason I didn't was Berry. I was being tested, I kept telling myself. If I quit the job, I would lose. If I get through, I will earn the right to go on to the next test. Well, score me an A-plus for tenacity, because I did carry on a little longer. And, to her credit, Diana showed softer sides. There were times when, after spending many hours together, our relationship was like that of conspiring teenage girlfriends, and she and I had some good old-fashioned fun.

Being her confidante, though, certainly had its drawbacks. She sometimes confided things I didn't want to hear. Her affairs with Smokey and Brian Holland were discussed occasionally, but most of the time, she talked about her main obsession—Berry. Theirs was a love-hate affair. They needed one another and recognized the other as the fulfillment of their ambitions. She worshiped and reviled him. He'd molded her and her success. For that she loved him, resented him, and was dependent on him.

Then there was a series of detailed descriptions of how great she and Berry were in bed. I heard the one about the first time they made it together several times. When the Supremes started to really hit, Diana at one point was sick in the hospital and Berry, a.k.a. Dr. Feelgood, paid her a visit. After a careful examination of the patient, he made his diagnosis, adeptly filled her prescription, and soothed away the pain.

I learned to laugh, to put aside the hurt from my own saga with Berry, and, yes, to feel sorry for her. I came to realize that, for everything that belonged to Diana, she was envious of me—for my intelligence, for my business skills, for my being a mother, especially of one of Berry's children. To assuage her own insecurity about their relationship, she needed to constantly reaffirm the affair by talking about it. She also worried incessantly that she was too old—twenty-eight to her was shameful. And yet the man whom she wanted to sire her babies was beyond her grasp.

Unbeknownst to Diana, Berry was sleeping with Chris Clark, a Motown artist—one of the first white singer/songwriters to be signed by the company—whom Berry was trying to fashion as the white Diana Ross. A tall platinum blonde, Chris was soft-spoken and charming. She was also an avid photographer and would contribute greatly to Berry's portfolio of pictures taken during the years that they would be together. And it would be years. Even as the affair with Diana continued at length, Berry was able to juggle the two women.

When the rumors made their way to Diana and she immediately confronted Berry, his response was eerily familiar: "That's crazy." Her decision, as mine had been in the Margaret era, was to believe Berry. History, they say, has a way of repeating itself. Then, one night when Berry was entertaining Chris in his bed, Diana showed up unannounced, hot for her man. In a bind, Berry made a real original move—he shoved Chris into the closet. And there was no claiming a headache or an early morning at the office to Diana. She spent the night in Berry's bed, and Chris stayed in that closet. But after too many close calls, and too many unexplainable coincidences, the truth about Chris was finally pried from Berry. He also confessed about the closet episode.

"See that tree that's leaning over," Diana said to me the next time we were both at Berry's. "Yeah," I said and turned to look at it out the window. The tree's bent-over condition was a result of the terrible love triangle, said Diana. "I kicked that tree so hard when I found out."

I'd hardened myself to such a degree that I almost laughed one day when I heard Diana pick up the phone and demand, "Berry, are we getting married or not? I have to know right now. Yes or no?"

Of course, as our history together proved, Berry was not the man to be on the receiving end of an ultimatum. Only he could write the tests. Part of the rules were that no one could give him an ultimatum. Even if it killed him, he'd answer no. So to Diana it was, "No, absolutely not."

Two days later Diana announced that she was marrying a man she'd been dating off and on: Bob Silberstein, an incredibly attractive white guy also in the music business. She asked me to please call Berry with the news.

"Congratulations, Berry," I said.

"What are you talking about?" he asked, completely in the dark.

"Diana and Bob just got married in Las Vegas."

Berry took the blow like a real soldier. "Great, that's absolutely great!" He sounded as if he was throwing streamers around his office.

For a long while, the public sentiment was "poor Berry Gordy—getting the shaft by the hard-hearted Diana." Berry told me later that Diana's wedding day was the happiest day of his life. He said that at an earlier point she'd almost forced his hand, until at the last moment he'd realized, "I can't marry this woman. This woman is as selfish as I am. I'm going to have to be kissing her ass all the time. I need somebody to kiss my ass." Berry revered the star but basically didn't like the woman.

In the meantime, Bob Silberstein, the Prince Charming that Diana hoped would rescue her from the Berry Gordy no-win games, was getting his dose of tests. A perfect Hollywood mismatch, their marriage was all to accommodate Diana's needs. Bob, who at the time they met was managing Chaka Kahn and Rufus, wound up on Diana's payroll, a fact that became unbearable to her. I found Bob to be a warm, soft-spoken guy, and it was sad later on to hear Diana say that the only way she could tolerate him was as an escort. To complicate an already loaded situation, Berry became a sort of third party to the marriage, accompanying the two of them everywhere. Another weird triangle, like the one of Berry, me, and Margaret, followed by that of Berry, me, and Ed.

Soon after Diana married Bob, a new light was shed on the ultimatum she'd given Berry—she was pregnant. When Rhonda was born, she looked enough like Berry for those of us who knew the situation to figure it out, but whether or not Diana told Berry at that time is unknown. An extremely devoted mother, Diana shielded Rhonda from the knowledge until she was seventeen years old. In the meantime, Rhonda had grown up the daughter of a white man—and had to rethink her identity upon finding out her father was a black man, and one with whom she'd casually shaken hands over a hundred times.

But there were moments when these soap operas were so outrageous that I could only laugh. As if power and money and fame were all license to play out fantasies, no matter who got hurt. Just a bunch of ego-hungry adults acting like hormonal teenagers. I'd think back to all that counseling I did at Hitsville, preaching loyalty, honesty, and fidelity. I must have been a hopeless romantic, thinking those virtues could be upheld in a world that never really wanted them. But when it came to hurting innocent children, even unintentionally, it cut sharply against my grain.

Later in 1973, two years after Rhonda was born, Berry held a wedding reception at the Beverly Hills Hotel for his daughter Hazel and Jermaine Jackson. In the entertainment industry, and particularly in black high-society circles, it would be the event of the decade. Hazel Joy was the ultimate belle of the ball, an extraordinary vision in white—a white mink train and white mink cuffs, the entire dress adorned in pearls and costing somewhere in the vicinity of twenty-five thousand dollars. Toward the end of this beautiful affair, Berry stood to say a few words. Telling some humorous and poignant stories about Hazel, his eyes fell at last on Diana, Bob, and their baby girl. "And thank God I only had one daughter," Berry finished. Diana immediately drew herself up, signaled to her husband they were getting the hell out, and made a hasty, conspicuous departure.

As my patience for working as Diana's assistant began to wear thin, I became aware that her relationships with other Motown artists were awkward as well. She did become very close to Suzanne DePasse, who had a similar temperament and priorities. They would work closely together on *Lady Sings the Blues*, and Suzanne would become Diana's project manager at the company. And Diana would have that undefined close relationship with Michael Jackson. But very few Motown artists came to her shows, and I never witnessed her asking any of her peers to come onstage and sing with her.

So it came as no surprise to me when, a few years later, Diana and Marvin Gaye locked horns. Marvin was just as temperamental as Diana, probably more so. They were alike in their ardent competition for the company's attention and the public's love, but in all other ways they were extreme opposites. Diana was thoroughly professional; Marvin was chronically undependable. She didn't touch drugs; Marvin was in his early bouts with cocaine. She kept her personal turmoils far away from work; Marvin's ran wildly out of control. Diana, the teacher's pet, deferred always to Berry Gordy; Marvin had an attitude problem with authority in general and with Berry in particular.

And yet, at the time, the two were the reigning romantic prince and princess of Motown. So, someone suggested, why not have these two superstars do an album of duets together? The timing couldn't have been worse. Berry and Diana were having strained relations, and she was pregnant with her second child. Berry and Marvin were always testy with one another. But Marvin was still the wild card, and it all depended on whether he wanted to make things rough for Diana and Berry.

As they arrived at the studio, Marvin, fortunately, was there on time. However, he was sitting on his stool surrounded by a cloud of pot smoke. Diana stormed out of there and into the control room to find Berry. "Listen," she said, "I cannot sing with this man smoking weed. I'm pregnant. I do not want to be around any drugs. I won't go on until you make him stop."

Berry chose to act with diplomacy. "Man, don't smoke no weed. Diana's pregnant. She's going to have a baby, and you don't want the drugs around the baby." Berry continued with gentle persuasion as the smile on Marvin's face just kept getting bigger.

"Fuck Diana Ross," Marvin said. "I'm going to smoke this weed or I don't sing."

Neither would back down, so all the duet vocals—those tender words of love—were recorded separately. For the entire *Diana and Marvin* session, Diana refused to be in the room with Marvin.

Berry figured he'd lost his investment on this deal and threw the album in the can. But Russ Terrana, an engineer who would spend twenty-two years at Motown, and Hal Davis, the album's producer, kept listening to the tracks. Finally, after tinkering with them, line for line, verse for verse, mixing and matching—one verse of Diana, one of Marvin, their voices together on the chorus—they got it down and convinced Berry to release it. And, the album, thanks to the splendid mix by Russ and Hal, was a big hit.

While the fact that they'd clashed so strongly came as no surprise, I was given pause, later in 1984, when after Marvin's death, Diana recorded a song called "Missing You" written by Lionel Richie about Marvin. In the song she would sing about the road to heaven and how much she loved him. Maybe she regretted the hard things that had happened between them, but, as far as most people remembered, they couldn't stand each other.

"Diana," I said to her one afternoon, "you're really doing great." Whenever we were in L.A. with extra time on our hands, I'd teach her some things on the piano. Not musically trained, but with lots of energy and enthusiasm, Diana enjoyed it tremendously. Soon we found ourselves with a regular lesson going. This was what I had so sorely missed on the road, actually doing something creative.

"You know, you keep going like this and you could eventually write songs of your own. Or we could collaborate and book some studio time and record them," I suggested. She was more than capable of turning out some good work.

"Really, you really think so?" She seemed so flattered.

Behind his desk, Berry was glowering at me as I walked through the door. Diana was seated facing him, legs crossed, staring straight ahead at the wall. I sat down next to her, though she would not so much as look at me.

Berry stated, "Diana tells me you're trying to steal her away from the company."

I almost laughed. "What?"

"She has told me that you want to record her yourself, avoiding the company's producers and furthering your own career at the expense of Motown."

I was about to spit. "What? That's ridiculous. All I did was talk to her about learning to play the piano and suggest that we work on some songs and maybe go in and produce a couple of things together. I didn't say anything about leaving the company. Or," I spoke directly to Diana, "furthering my career. You know that's a lie."

Diana stared blankly ahead.

Berry responded for her. "Nevertheless, Diana Ross and I have decided that you're fired."

I again turned to Diana. "Is that what you want?"

Diana stared blankly ahead.

Berry again responded for her. "Yes."

"Fine then." Standing, I spoke with careful articulation, "Fired's fine, as long as this doesn't affect my overall position in the company and you continue to pay me my salary of twenty-five thousand a year." For one second my eyes locked with Berry's. Unspoken was his awareness of how bogus my being fired really was. And for that he couldn't contest continuing my salary. Holding my tongue in those silent moments wasn't easy, as I looked a last time at the two of them sitting there gloating. As Berry himself had said, they were very much alike. Two children, really, into their capricious power trips, lording over my life and booting me callously from my own house. What was even more infuriating was that they were doing it to spite themselves. I'd finally proved myself as one of the very few who could actually work productively with Diana. Now all the effort was down the tubes, and Berry would again be stuck for finding someone competent enough for the job. A no-win situation for both sides.

Obviously, three couldn't play at chess. Berry, as always, came in with a setup in which I was doomed to lose—at his own expense. Diana played exactly how he knew she would. The funny thing was that, as hurt and disgusted as I felt, I still felt sorry for her.

A few years later, I ran into Diana and asked her what the hell happened in the end. "Oh," she grinned sheepishly, "you were great." Not a profoundly enlightening statement. About ten years after that, I saw Diana standing with Michael Jackson and Suzanne DePasse at the party for Michael's *Thriller* premiere at the Los Angeles Forum. She broke into a big smile, as though we were the oldest of friends. Pointing me out to the other two she said, "That's the lady that started Motown, right there. She is a great lady."

She and I were never actually on opposite sides, and so I would retain an affection for her. And even as I walked out of the office the day I was fired, I made a choice to forgive and forget as far as Diana was concerned. Berry, on the other hand, had just knocked me down for easy slaughter. That man better be on his guard, I thought, because guess what—the next move would be mine.

CHAPTER 14
JOBETE
1971–1977

The next decade was to contain some of my highest highs and some of my lowest lows. The war in southeast Asia was over, only to be followed by the scourge of Watergate. Black America was a house divided. There were those with new freedoms who believed that strides had been made, and there were the disenfranchised, with knives in their hearts and in their belt loops, who believed the heroes had died in vain. The sixties slogan "make love not war" gave way to that of the seventies—"make money not babies." This would be the decade that spawned some of the most far-reaching musical innovations, as well as some of the most ridiculous commercial trash.

There were now two Detroits. The old Detroit lay almost in rubble—with only dying embers left of the family town whose industries had once given birth to two American dreams, the automobile industry and Motown—motion and music. That was the Detroit whose heart and soul had raised me, and that fed into the music I'd made with Berry. The new Detroit that was being built on fear was a vision of contrasts. I saw the residential pockets of luxury, where doors opened only to a privileged few, against a darkened skyline of new ghettos and tenement housing, hotbeds of crime and violence. Blurring into the distance were the suburbs of the middle class, whose doors and windows were locked and barred at night. The automobile industry was fading fast. Plants were closing and many jobs were being lost. Motown's departure, which by 1972 was all but final, twisted the knife into the city, which grew to blame the company for deception, for only pretending it would stay.

Upon my return to Detroit, once again descending with my

family on Juanita and Dobbs, I labeled myself a "consultant" to what was left of Motown locally. It was also a time for me to regroup and rethink, to take a little shelter with family from the storms that I'd fled. As the months went on I would be reading these tales of the two Detroits and, as always, the tales of the two-sided Berry Gordy.

One tale told of the feeling of betrayal in Detroit after Motown, one of its major arteries, was gone. There was an alleged comment of Berry's circulating among the local black radio stations: "If a black disc jockey never played another one of my records, I wouldn't give a damn." Whether this was in fact a direct quote, a fabrication, or some quip that was misconstrued, it didn't matter. The black DJs retaliated by boycotting all Motown songs, with the exception of Stevie Wonder's, for many months.

In Detroit's new historical district, Indian Village, once an illustrious haven for the Dodge family and their strata, I stumbled over a piece of fool's gold in the form of a red-brick nine-bedroom mansion, which I rented for four hundred fifty dollars a month.

"Alice, how'd you like to come live at the Waldorf-Astoria?" I called my sister, who was newly separated from Tim Wilson and who had returned to Detroit with their little Tim André Wilson. I was thrilled at this opportunity for us to reunite. Of course I invited Venida to move in too, along with her young daughter, Shirene, warning her, "Better come fast—knowing Alice she'll take dibs on the biggest room first." Not that it mattered, for all the bedrooms were huge. The layout was incredible—white columns outside, butler's and maid's quarters, and a chauffeur's room in the carriage house out back. The dining room was so big that we didn't bother trying to furnish it; we just let the kids ride their bikes and trikes through it.

In the same new Detroit, our next-door neighbor received a knock at his door one night and, with the chain latch still secured, was stabbed to death through the opening of the door. His door was then knocked down and the home robbed. The following day we bid a hasty farewell to Indian Village.

"Kids, you're not going to believe this," I said, standing in the center of our new four-bedroom apartment in a high-security building with eighteen stories, a swimming pool, and tennis courts. The renovated area in downtown Detroit was probably the finest address available. "Look out there, over a couple blocks by Mullett and Russell. That's where I lived when I was a little girl. It was a ghetto then." The kids couldn't believe it.

"What exactly is a ghetto?" asked six-year-old Rya. I prayed that she would never know.

Having settled in, I set to work on a couple of projects I was doing to help out my sister Roslyn, a Lena Horne look-alike. Now Roslyn Murray, she'd started a nursery school with five students in a rented room over a store—the Michigan Institute for Child Development. Eddie and Rya were receiving free tuition in exchange for my assuming some of the business responsibilities—applying for licensing, making sure it met legal nursery-school requirements, recruiting clients, and organizing a transportation system for the children. Roslyn's vision of having one of the most educational and creative preschools in the nation would eventually materialize. With a curriculum that included the three Rs, a foreign language, music and ballet training, and martial arts, the Michigan Institute for Child Development's enrollment would reach fifteen hundred students, from preschool to junior high school, with six locations in the Detroit metropolitan area.

Sometime later, Berry's accountant notified me that they were cutting my salary to fifteen thousand a year. As if it wasn't hard enough raising four kids. I remembered one of my old riffs— "Next?" What humiliation did he have up his sleeve next? At another time I would have been completely incapacitated by this action. But, probably as a result of all the game playing that had gone down over the years, especially the last assault when he and Diana had fired me, I knew better than to react as if this move by Berry and his lackey accountants was the result of sheer cruelty. Something was up. Maybe it was Berry's perverse way of expressing that he missed me, a way to get my attention and of drawing me back into his clutches. Maybe not. All I knew for sure was to be on guard, that I'd be hearing from him again soon.

"You did *what*?" This call of Berry's was the last straw. Nothing could have prepared me for this. I was no longer amused.

"Listen," he said. "I'm setting up trust funds for all the kids to have when they reach twenty-one. I'm giving the three older kids,"—meaning Hazel Joy, Berry, and Terry, his and Thelma's kids—"a million dollars apiece. And I'm giving Kerry a hundred thousand."

That was it. I didn't say anything to Berry, but when I hung up I knew that it was time to do what I'd been avoiding. Berry could come at me all he wanted, but when it threatened to damage the children, I would come right back at him in a way that he could never anticipate.

I talked it over with Kerry. I held my fourteen-year-old son's hands and peered into those hazel-green eyes and gazed at the kid who looked more and more like Berry every day. His father's renewed interest in him, begun at the baseball diamond, hadn't endured longer than a season. Yet, despite the lack of contact, Kerry was his father's son. Terribly sharp, very witty, he was a natural-born salesman—in grade school he'd been the local bubblegum dealer. And, filling me with pride, Kerry was already starting to write songs.

Kerry protested, naturally. The two of us had never gone long without being together.

"C'mon," I said at the airport in the summer of 1973. "It's just a few months. And besides, I'm not sending you off to Siberia. You're spending the summer in Bel Air. If you're really unhappy at the end of August, you can come back. But your father has got to spend some time with you to get to know you." I watched as Kerry walked up to the gate with his head bent low, an experience that would wrench any mother's heart. My prayer was that he could melt his father's. As he disappeared from view, I continued to wave, wishing the best for the Motown son—the heir apparent.

The transition between the two Motowns, the one in Detroit to the one in California, left some tragic casualties. The company's biggest stars took the ride to L.A., sooner or later, but for those who were more expendable the relocation became a convenient way of booting them from the train. Case in point: Ivy Jo Hunter. Having never recovered from being pegged a troublemaker in the last of the Seltzer days, Ivy was cut off from projects as punishment. He asked to be released from his contract, but the company refused— giving him nothing to do but walk the halls of the Donovan Building. Double indemnity. When the release was finally issued, Ivy left in bitterness.

Another case was a real puzzler: Hank Cosby. In '72, as shop was being shut down altogether, Hank was dragged into Ewart Abner's office. Abner was the black man who Berry appointed as president of Motown to deflect critics of his white executive policy. Without warning or reasons, Hank was fired. For the rest of his life, Hank Cosby would have no idea why.

And a little closer to home was the case of my brother, Mike Ossman, who'd begun making music with me and Alice on our old Webcore wire recorder in the basement. Mike was a leading player in Tamla's ascent, and an even more critical player to Hitsville and to Jobete in New York. Yet after the war at the Donovan Building he was cut adrift. With a family to support, he took a job with the Water Board in Detroit. From a young man of enormous creative promise who'd been my rock through thick and thin, to a man who by 1973 was discouraged and let down. Oh, God, I thought, everytime I saw him—the Water Board?

The contrasting images of what was then and what was now continued to haunt me. Martha Reeves was once sultry and sexy, a tough fighter who'd gone to work for Mickey Stevenson, found her chance, and proved herself. That fantastic voice. Outstanding performing abilities and—as all the producers could tell you— inventive and unique in her interpretations. A workhorse in the studio, Martha had had more spunk than a lot of the others who weren't let go. I kept comparing this image to that of the woman I went to visit in the hospital, where Martha had returned to several times after suffering nervous breakdowns.

I was led into a chamber with thick iron bars on the door. An attendant opened the door as I followed along down the hall to a room where, strung up in a straitjacket, Martha Reeves waited. Oh, no, dear God, I thought, as a wave of shock rippled through me, don't let this be true.

"Ray, don't let these doctors come back in," Martha whispered. "They're trying to kill me."

"It's OK, it's OK." I tried to comfort her, repeating my words. "Martha, it's OK. We all love you, you have all your friends." For a long time she rocked back and forth. And I could only say, "It's OK, nobody's going to hurt you."

It wasn't OK. And for others it would be worse than for Martha. Case in point: Paul Williams of the Temptations. Paul and his buddy Eddie Kendricks had come up from Alabama with great dreams. Paul began as the lead singer of the Primes, his husky baritone mixing perfectly with Eddie's high falsetto. Paul was handsome, funny, a driving force with the Primes, and the innovator of the Tempts' marvelous stage moves that were later polished by choreographer Cholly Atkins. Contrast that with the tragic news we got in August of 1973, not long after I visited Martha, that Paul had killed himself. Over the years he'd battled drugs and alcohol, but Paul's problems involved more than substance abuse. When David Ruffin left his group in '68, followed by his best friend, Eddie Kendricks, in '71, Paul went into a downward spiral.

Drugs made him too sick to perform. Richard Street was brought in to sing Paul's parts, at first from offstage, then in Paul's place. For awhile the Tempts watched out for him, then Berry tried to help by putting him on a consultant's salary. Nothing helped. An attempt to run a boutique failed, and he wound up owing some $80,000 in taxes. One day he sat in his car a few blocks from Hitsville and shot himself.

The new Detroit was a fortress of hell. Crime was so prevalent that the kids weren't allowed to go out and play anymore. If we could only hold out until Cliff graduated at the end of spring, I was working on a plan that would have us back to L.A. by summer and that would get me back to Motown. Not to mention reuniting with Kerry, who, as I'd foreseen, had become a full-fledged son to Berry and, by '74, was entering his second semester of school there.

"You did what?" I received another call from Berry's accountant suggesting that another salary cut was in the wind. This was an outrage. It wasn't part of my plan to call Berry this soon, but I refused to have the company that I had helped build cut off my already thin air supply.

"Berry, I'd like to come back and work with Jobete. You know that I belong with the company. The whole Diana Ross fiasco was completely absurd. I was unjustly fired and you know it. I'm ready to go to work and show you what I can do." I was a little too needy, and this wasn't the swift move I'd wanted to make.

"You can't come back," he said. "You stay in Detroit. Whatever you're doing, just stay there."

"Fine," I said. There were more ways than one to skin this rabbit. In four months, I pledged, I would be back at Motown. I was overestimating—it would actually be more like a month.

"Mommy, Mommy!" My children were banging on the apartment door. Every day I watched from our fifteenth-floor window as Rya and Eddie went to and from school, which was just across the street. Today was no different, and I had just observed the two entering our building. But as they ran in the door, they were screaming, "Mommy, it's a bad man in the elevator. It's a man laying there and he's got a knife stuck in his throat."

I went down to the elevator, and, sure enough, lying there was a man with a knife thrust into one side of his neck and protruding about six inches out the other.

"OK," I said a short time later. "We're getting out of here.

Venida, you and I are going to work for Motown in L.A."

"Really?" Venida asked me, "Did you call Berry?"

"No," I explained, patting my friend on the back. "You're going to call Berry when we get to town. You're going to call him and call him and call him. I'm not going to talk to that man. At all. You're going to be my mouthpiece and you're going to get us jobs at Jobete."

In less than a month, after finding a safe place for Cliff to stay until he graduated, we'd escaped the towering inferno of Detroit and were in L.A. with new digs in Northridge, almost an hour from the Motown office. And we were working for Jobete. Venida had completed her first mission. Shaking that girl's hand, I thought to myself that in a game of chess two knights were better than one.

Here's how the moves had been played: After arriving in L.A. and shelling out for our living setup, I was virtually penniless. So we honed a fabulous technique that eventually landed us our jobs. Whatever Venida's mission, whether it was keeping the electricity on, paying emergency medical bills for the kids, or covering any one of the endless stream of expenses known all too well to single mothers, Venida would pick up the phone and call Mr. Gordy's office. Standing over her, I'd feed her the lines, never allowing her to accept no for an answer. Berry would put her through every test in the book, dragging her through a roller coaster of resistance. On that ride she'd hold the phone to her ear, perspiring from concentration, trying to juggle the information coming at her from both directions. Her approaches ran the gauntlet, from perky and polite—"Hello, Mr. Gordy, how are you? Yes, it's Venida again," with a whisper to me, "He's in a bad mood"—to a more testy approach—"No, I can't call you back. Just put me on hold," her eyes imploring me to tell her what to ask.

Berry would inevitably pull out the expected, "This isn't my problem; you tell Ray to find a way to handle it."

Upon my urging, Venida would roar back, "Oh, yes, this is your problem. That bill has to get paid." Or, in the winning play, "Oh, yes, this is your problem. We need those jobs." And so on, until through sheer staying power we'd have Berry relenting. He was partly amused at her audacity, and also impressed. Well, hell, I was impressed—Berry never accepted calls from any other than the top VIPs of the business. However, he knew that Venida was with me, and he also knew that it was me talking through her, which brought him to his regular question, "Where is Ray? How come she can't come to the phone?"

"Oh," Venida would say woefully, "she would love to talk to you, Mr. Gordy, but she's just not feeling well. Maybe it's the flu." Berry, being fully hip to the trick, could only chuckle in response. For the first months of my return to Motown, I protected myself from the hurts of the past through this unusual means. But there was a method to the madness, and my main need was fulfilled—we were going to make some music.

On our first day of work, Venida and I stood in the middle of the Jobete offices, now under the direction of Robert L., Berry's younger brother. It was like a morgue, and ticking away was the time clock—Robert L.'s obsession. I looked at Venida with raised eyebrows. It appeared we had our work cut out for us.

Jobete was my original baby. I had pioneered it and run it all the way up through my days in New York. And how this baby had grown. By now, after almost fifteen years in existence and multi-tudinous copyrights and top-ten hits, it had given birth to off-shoots such as Stone Agate, Stone Diamond, and Stein and Van-stock. Jobete was by far the most profitable arm of the company; publishing is, in fact, where the money is made in the music business. An artist stops making money from a song when the record stops selling, but the publisher makes it every time the song is played on the radio, television, or in a movie; every time it is performed or covered by another artist; every time that particular record is played; and every time its sheet music is sold. Because Jobete controlled the rights to almost all of the Motown catalog, it was astronomically prosperous. On more than one occasion, Jo-bete would actually keep Motown afloat.

After I had left Detroit in '63, Jobete was handled by Berry's sister Loucye Wakefield. When Loucye died in '65, Berry's brother Bobby, who became Robert L. on the job, took over Jobete. Robert L. had entered the company earlier, during the heyday of Marv Johnson's success, with a cute song he'd written called "Everyone Was There." The record, licensed to Carlton, was a big hit, and Robert L., under the name Bob Kayli, became a main attraction for us. But, when his follow-up records bombed, Bob Kayli went back to being Bobby Gordy, waiting for his future administrative job to open up.

After Motown picked up momentum, Jobete—in addition to administering a catalog of songs—assembled a staff of writers whose job it was to generate new material for the company's artists. That was something I'd initiated in the New York office, by organizing a separate Jobete staff. In recent years, though, with the growth of corporate Motown, there had developed an ever-widening division between Jobete and Motown. The Motown producers, more and more, weren't relying on Jobete writers and were either writing their own songs or getting them outside the company. It had reached the point where, though both entities were in the same building, there was no communication between them. I discussed the problem with Venida: "Say you're a writer who has struggled to get your material heard, to earn a living from your craft, and you're out there competing with a million other songwriters. Finally you end up as a staff writer with Jobete and you still can't get anything to a Motown artist, even though you're right there. As far as I can tell, Robert L. hasn't developed any relationships with the creative people at Motown, people like Suzanne DePasse. These writers at Jobete are losing their drive. OK, how do you solve the morale problem?"

"You get rid of the clock," answered Venida. "The place looks like a damn insurance company. The way it's run with all that whispering—I could have heard a pin drop. And that Robert L., with his hair all in place and the pin-striped suit and the tie and the way he stands by that clock and locks the door if someone is one minute late."

"I have an idea," I said.

"You do?" said my sergeant at arms. "Well, so do I."

The next morning Venida walked into the office with a bunch of balloons tied around her waist, and I followed with a big bag of refreshments. Singing "Hitsville U.S.A.," the two of us marched past the clock, proceeded to our office in the back, and turned on some loud music. Pulling off my shoes, and plopping on the floor, I waited to greet the staff. The message was clear—"Here's for creativity! This is not a bank. Let's make some music and have some fun." Bit by bit, all the writers were down in our office and there was a party going on. Even Robert L. came back to welcome us.

My first goal was to address the communication problem between the writers and the producers. The way things were going, nobody told Jobete who was working on what projects. In the old days, everybody knew that, say, Mickey was going to cut a song on Marvin, and all the writers would compete to come up with the best one. I remembered one such contest between Smokey and Berry, to see who could write a hit for the Temptations, who hadn't scored yet. Berry cut his song, while Smokey and Bobby Rogers cut another one that they'd cowritten. Presenting both songs for a producers' vote, the winners were . . . Smokey and Bobby for "The Way You Do the Things You Do," which then became the very first of numerous Tempts hits.

So my first move was to get the head of the Creative Division, Suzanne DePasse, on the phone, "Hey, listen, I'm here at Jobete now. What I want to do is bridge the gap between us and Motown. I need to know on a weekly basis who's going in and out of the studio. I just want the writers to know what's happening."

"Great," she responded. "Just check with my assistants every week and we'll give you an update." It was so easy, I wondered why it hadn't been done before. I looked over my list of the next steps— meeting with all the producers in their offices to reestablish that contact, then bringing the writers in to connect with them. Also, I needed to educate the writers about how to deal with the company. Soon that list was completed, and I was pulling writers into my office. "OK, Frank Wilson is going into the studio in four weeks to work with Eddie Kendricks. Get your material ready and we'll present it to Frank, and Gwen Gordy needs a follow-up song for High Energy, something similar to their last hit, "You Can't Turn Me Off."

Next? I beheld the end result of my latest project in all its glory—a mini-demo studio, with a piano, tape recorder, and microphone system. A demo room was an extremely valuable resource, and before long the writers were using it to its full potential.

It wasn't long before a mysterious catastrophe occurred. Robert L. was beside himself, a nervous wreck. Someone had stolen the clock. How could he maintain law and order without his precious clock? Days went by and the poor guy was almost reduced to tears. In addition to being comically stodgy, Robert L. was at times a little paranoid. What if the thief was an angry songwriter whom he'd rejected or whom he'd denied an advance? When a package was delivered by messenger and Robert L. was called to the front to sign for it, he refused to open it—the package was ticking! Robert L. immediately called security and everyone flocked to the scene. Andrew Davis, the head of security, arrived telling the crowd to "Stand back, please," and tried to gingerly open the ticking package while Robert L. held his breath. Finally they opened the box, with people in the room closing their eyes and plugging their ears. Andrew reached in and pulled out the missing clock, and then a note. It read, "The clock is back and the bitch is black." Venida was probably the only person in that room laughing harder than I was.

There were distinctly two Motowns. The Hitsville spirit of the first Motown was long gone, along with most of its original producers and many of the artists who'd scattered after the fire in Detroit. The new Motown, though, was not without verve. Much of that was due to the Jackson 5 and, through them, Berry's renewed involvement in the company; Berry's coming down from the hills tended to wake everybody else up, too. With a new staff of writers and producers in California, he brought Motown into a new phase based on the awesome coming-of-age of its favorite son, Stevie Wonder, together with its two most durable veterans, Marvin Gaye and Diana Ross, and its hope for the future, the Jackson 5.

Marvin Gaye altered the face of the new Motown forever, when in 1971 he recorded the masterpiece of his career. *What's Going On* was totally unlike any Motown music before. An ambitious suite of thematically linked, jazz-influenced songs, profound and prophetic lyrics, the album was produced by the artist, which was unprecedented at Motown. *What's Going On* was the real Marvin Gaye. It reflected his personality, his vision, his inner soul, his total being. And his great sadness. It was the best work of his life, and Marvin knew it. When Marvin died thirteen years later, I could barely stand to hear it.

Berry thought that it was the worst garbage he'd ever heard, and he refused to release it. Well, Marvin was a stubborn man. He then made an amazing move—he took a stand not to record another note for Motown until *What's Going On* was released. After much combative deliberation, the album came out, and of course in every way—artistically, critically, and financially—it was a phenomenal success, probably the best album Motown ever recorded. Marvin had paved the way for artists' control, so much so that Stevie Wonder, who turned twenty-one shortly thereafter, won a contract giving him an unprecedented amount of money and autonomy. Before Marvin stood up to Berry, it would have been impossible for artists to gain such control. These artists were the ones whose music would carry Motown into the future.

With his house in order, Berry was ready to make the move of his dreams—Motown Pictures. This was his bid to be a true Hollywood mogul and to make Diana Ross the biggest star in the world. His first movie, *Lady Sings the Blues*, was a great success, a good start to the land of his fantasies. After that, things went steadily downhill. In 1974, some months after I returned to Jobete, he started filming in Rome the next Diana Ross vehicle, *Mahogany*. From the get-go, there were problems on the set—Diana's hysteria and Berry's backseat driving to director Tony Richardson. When Richardson left, Berry took over directing, something he'd never done before. Months and months went by, stretching into the next year, and millions of dollars were spent. Box office was great on its first week of release but died soon after that, and ultimately *Mahogany* was a flop. As Berry would later tell me, it almost broke the company.

And, as they say, when it rains it pours. While Berry was away in Rome, the Jackson 5's contract came up for renewal and Papa Joe Jackson went to Motown president Ewart Abner for a substantial amount of money to re-sign the boys. Abner apparently didn't communicate the immediacy of the problem to Berry, who didn't intercede. Using bad judgment, Abner offered Papa Joe an insultingly low counteroffer. Berry came home to find that Joe Jackson had signed his boys to Epic, where they'd been given a contract for more than three times the amount Papa Joe had originally asked from Motown. Ewart Abner, of course, was history after that. And for Berry, who had invested so much energy into the Jackson 5, only to have them disappear when his back was turned, it was a nightmare that would haunt him for a long time.

The company sued the Jacksons for jumping the gun on their contract. After five years in court, six hundred thousand dollars would be awarded to Motown, which was possibly equivalent to its legal fees. Motown also won the right to the name "Jackson 5," which was like owning the rights to the name "Frank Sinatra," and then tried to promote an imitation. Jermaine Jackson, married to Berry's daughter Hazel, loyally stayed behind at Motown when his brothers left. Unfortunately, his career with Motown would never quite take off.

In the tale of the new Motown, Suzanne DePasse emerged as a pivotal figure. In time, the province of Motown Pictures would fall to her. Starting out as Berry's creative assistant, she was a young woman of fierce ambition who'd step on whatever toes or incur whatever resentful feelings necessary to climb the next rungs.

What was more, she tolerated Berry with twenty-four-hour-a-day dedication. She knew that if she could put up with him, she would make it to the top. And she did.

"Suzanne," Berry called to her. It was during a meeting at his home in Bel Air one day in the summer of '75. Suzanne, though pretty and attractive, battled a bit of a weight problem. Berry often teased her about it, always waiting for a crowd to be around for the occasion. At this particular meeting there were about twenty of us on hand when Berry said, "Suzanne, get up and show 'em how fat you are. Get up and pretend you're an ape—be a gorilla for everybody."

These were the tests of our lives. Berry pushing people beyond the limits of abuse. I knew these tests well, and back during our years together I'd frequently tell him these were unacceptable— kicking him under the table, pulling him into bathrooms and saying, "Hey, look, don't be talking about Lamont's nose in front of everybody." The victims' reaction to these so-called tests ran the gamut—some shrugged them off, others would be horribly humiliated, and a few became explosively irate.

But Suzanne didn't hesitate; nor did she look around. She stood up and began to do this gorilla routine, "whoo, whoo," scratching her armpits and everything. The room roared with laughter, but Suzanne passed the test. I was mortified and embarrassed for her. But it was highly revealing. She didn't give a damn what she had to do; she'd do whatever it would take to make it. And she would later attain the presidency of Motown, having certainly earned it the hard way. Watching her go through with that gorilla act, I was also aware of the complexities of my relationship with her. Personally and professionally, we got on fine. She commanded my respect as a hardworking, proficient individual. But there was a vague rivalry that would surface from time to time. I saw that, with Suzanne, Berry was reshaping a less threatening version of me. Less threatening because their relationship didn't have such a complicated past and less threatening because she never questioned him. And I did.

A few years earlier, when I was still with Diana Ross, Berry had invited a group of people to his house for dinner. Joy, Berry, and Terry, his three oldest kids were there. So were Suzanne De-Passe and Chris Clark, who, in between trips to the closet, was still Berry's girlfriend. A choice setup for Berry: three women with overlapping functions in his life, all vying for his attention. Put them together, start a little fire, and see what happens. We were sitting around the table during dinner when Berry thought of his next game. Explaining to us how he was trying to write lyrics for a song, he passed around a piece of paper for each of us to write down our conception of his lyrics. The paper made the rounds, each of us participated, and it returned to Berry. He studied it in silence while we waited to have our visions reviewed. I watched as his face wrinkled in a combination of disgust and disbelief, and I wondered who was going to get the sting.

"Oh, this is so ridiculous. This is the stupidest, dumbest . . . Listen to this, everybody, listen to what Ray wrote."

Hairs on the back of my neck bristled, a clammy flush burned my face. But I tried to smile as he ridiculed my entry. The smile dropped as his barrage continued. He read through my comment and picked it apart mercilessly. My eyes lowered, I tried to hide my anger and hurt. Why must he punish me in front of these people— Suzanne, the woman who had replaced me as his closest business associate, and Chris, one of the women who had replaced me in his bed? Clinging to the hope that one of them, as I would have done, would stand up to him for me, I heard them begin to laugh. I looked up at them and saw them for who they were: Berry's women, with clownlike faces and puppet gestures.

A tightly coiled spring that had been locked inside me for ages unleashed as I bounded out of my seat. I grabbed the beautiful white linen tablecloth that graced the dining table and pulled with all my might. Crystal glasses of wine, china plates laden with food, silverware, and large serving trays, everything shot up like fireworks and fell to the floor in an unholy splatter and crash. Food and drink on laps and faces. Eyes wide and mouths gaping—first at the mess and then at me. I interrupted the lethal silence to address the host.

"Motherfucker, I told you, don't ever do that shit to me!"

For my grand finale I overturned my chair, pivoted on my heels, and raged up to the room where I was scheduled to spend the night. Five or ten minutes later, I wasn't surprised to hear a knock at the door. As Berry entered, a million messages were exchanged in the connection between our eyes. "See," Berry said, "that's the reason you don't have anything. Suzanne would have never done that." Truer words were never spoken.

Like some kind of artillery training, these were the episodes that helped me to develop a whole new system of defense. When I returned to work at Jobete, I enlisted allies, refusing to leave myself in open fire. Although Berry had punished me for loving him, our son, Kerry, could carry on my message of love without fear of reprisal. And because Berry had punished me for being unwilling to slither on the ground, for rising up and facing off to him, the audacious and irresistible Venida would be our intermediary. So far, with these two buffers, Berry and I were having an all-time truce, and I was free to put 100 percent of my being into work.

There were many issues at Jobete that Robert L. and I differed on. As a musical strategist, I liked to take calculated risks while Robert was conservative and afraid to try anything that was the least bit innovative.

I'd signed up a very talented writer, Miles Gregory, who had been recommended by Robert L.'s administrative assistant, Carol Ware. After a few months working in the demo studio, Miles, at a whopping fifty-dollar-a-week salary, composed a musical track for a song and came to me for some help. The two of us went over to Janie Bradford's house and tried to knock off some lyrics. After five hours nothing much was on the table, except a title, coined by Janie, "Love Don't Live Here Anymore."

Two weeks later I'd written a melody and lyrics on top of Miles's chords, and he and I were putting together our demo in the studio. When Robert L. happened by, he expressed great enthusiasm and then returned two or three times daily to check on the progress. It was exhilarating to see him standing there nodding his head in approval. We all knew this song was a hit. But I was in for a surprise.

"You did what?" I asked Robert L. The renewal for Miles's contract had come up as we were working on the song, and I was astonished to hear that Jobete was dropping Miles.

"Robert, what are you thinking about? What about this song?" I continued to protest, but nothing would budge Robert L. to renew the contract—for fifty bucks a week. So Robert dropped Miles, and the writer took his song over to Norman Whitfield, who now had his own label and publishing company. Norman knew a hit when he heard one, published it, and recorded it with Rose Royce, and as we all had foreseen, "Love Don't Live Here Anymore" was a smash success. I soon heard from Robert L.

"That's the song you were working on," he said. "This song belongs to us because you were working on this song when he was under contract."

"Robert," I reminded him, "I told you this song was a smash. I begged you to keep Miles because of his potential. We hadn't even finished the song when you dropped him. For you to drop a writer who costs you fifty bucks a week and then claim his song is outrageous." Robert tried to contest me, but he was at a loss, not wanting to openly admit that he'd dropped a good writer.

I was at my own loss. Even though I was cowriter of "Love Don't Live Here Anymore," I couldn't claim it because I was tied to Jobete. Later I sorely regretted my lack of interest in the money, but at the time I was more upset about Robert L. losing such a promising writer. So I told Miles, "Take this, this is your song. Jobete is going to fight you if I say I'm involved in it." The first royalty check Miles received from that song was for an astronomical amount of money for a fledgling writer. Years later Madonna would cover it, bringing to Miles an amount of money that made the first amount look like peanuts.

In some respects Robert L. did have a kind of begrudging admiration for my efforts and abilities. In his eyes my real coup was the demo studio. The writing staff had also shaped up beautifully—Don Fletcher, who would cowrite "Dancing Machine," my old pal Ron Miller of "For Once in My Life" fame, Pam Sawyer, Marilyn McLeod, Kenny Hirsch, Kay Lewis and her sister Helen, Terry McFadden, Larry Brown, Elliot Willensky, Brenda and Mike Sutton, Harold Johnson, Elgee and Kenny Stover, Angelo Bond, and, last but certainly not least, Janie Bradford.

With the constant support of Venida, my work at Jobete rolled merrily along, as did my homelife, especially when Cliff returned from Detroit. And out on the wide ocean of the past that lay between Berry and me, the waters were still.

While on the set of *Mahogany* in Rome, already millions of dollars over budget, Berry received a call from Pops. "Your mother's had a stroke at home. She's in the hospital now, but we don't expect her to live."

It was a terrible dilemma for Berry, for each single day away from the set would cost a hundred thousand dollars. The family understood, though. "Really, there's nothing you can do. Mother might not make it through the night. If she does, she won't know you. We're sure she wouldn't want you abandoning your work needlessly. Stay in Rome and take care of your responsibilities there."

Even with the distance between us, geographic and emotional, I could almost sense Berry's anguish in this decision. He loved his mother so. He simply couldn't bear the thought of not being in Los Angeles with her when she died. But by the time he arrived at the hospital and went in to see her, she was already hooked up to life-support systems and the doctors had declared her brain-dead. Berry stood by the side of her bed, looking at her. Such a proud, intelligent, graceful woman. Then he took her hand and kissed her cheek. On leaving the room, Berry was informed he was the one who had to decide whether or not to stop the machines and let her die.

The thought of Mother Gordy not surviving anything seemed impossible to me, and the news filled me with immense sorrow. She'd been such an important part of my life. Even after Berry and I divorced, I'd always kept up with her and all the family, never breaking the bonds between us. Knowing Berry was probably at the house, I left the office early to go by and pay my respects.

As I stepped into the elevator at the seventeenth floor, I found Berry there with Roger Campbell and Les Peterson. I looked at Berry and he looked at me. I hugged him, his head leaning on my shoulder. We held tight to one another while the elevator descended to the first floor.

Outside the building I kissed him good-bye, saying what needed to be said. I pulled away to go to my car and felt him reach for me. He held me close. We stood for some minutes, not saying anything, and then I heard him sigh.

"Today," he said softly, "my mother will die." My face was quite near to his as he added, "I have to make the decision to cut off the machines." He fell silent once more, then asked me if I could stay with him for a few days. I agreed and helped out while the arrangements for the funeral were made. It was almost exactly ten years since Loucye died. Again a tragedy had produced a haven in which no weapons were allowed—and all that existed there for the two of us was love.

After our closeness during Mother Gordy's funeral, however, Berry and I fell quickly back into a respectful, professional relationship. He'd begun working at home, so it was only now and then that he'd come by to survey the scene at my spot in the building. Even so, Berry's approving nods and thumbs-up to the music we were creating reinforced my belief that he was glad to have me back and churning out the tracks.

"Next?" I asked Venida to read me the list of my ongoing projects, while I replaced some of the cork on the wall in the demo studio.

"You have a note here—Stephanie Mills?" Venida asked. Berry liked to brag that I was the only one in the company who could get anyone, no matter how unapproachable, to come in and work with us. Now he'd given me a dare to find someone for Stephanie. I had an inspiration. "Venida, I'm going to get Burt Bacharach and Hal David in here!" Within a couple weeks, the name of that prolific songwriting duo had indeed been attached to a Stephanie Mills project, giving me another notch on my belt.

Another undertaking, which would later become a regular practice, was reviewing unreleased masters from the company's vault. It was thousands of hours of work. I'd hatched this notion after many writers complained that they'd composed terrific material that was just sitting down there gathering cobwebs. Among the many pearls I found were some gorgeous, lush instrumentals written by Paul Riser, Motown's greatest arranger. I cataloged them and made a note to myself to look for something to do with them. Wasting music like that was a crying shame.

"Ray." Venida was holding up the phone. "It's a man named Emmett Cash. Says he's working with Fred Williamson and wants to talk to you about working as musical director for a movie!"

Visions of Hollywood sugarplums danced in my head as I tried to prod my memory, whispering to Venida, "Isn't Fred Williamson that actor who used to be a football star?"

Turned out Fred was more than that. He'd just received a contract from Brut/Fabergé to write, produce, direct, and star in six films. Emmett invited me to a screening of the rough cut of the first film, *The Hero*. Well, I thought, while viewing it from between my fingers, at least it has a basic message—how to sleep with as many women and kill as many bad guys as was cinematically possible in ninety violent minutes. How was I going to put music to this? Then, remembering the Paul Riser instrumentals from down in the vault, I hired arranger Coleridge Taylor Perkinson to adapt them for *The Hero*. If Fred was going to knock off scores of bad guys, he might as well do it to beautiful music, I figured.

Then came a dream-come-true tale in which I found myself rubbing shoulders with one of my real-life heroes, Bill Cosby. His secretary, Marlene, a friend of Venida's, was living with us briefly, and I told her I'd do anything to meet Bill.

Well, he and I were soon buddy-buddy, and he'd taken to calling me "boss." "Hey, boss," he'd greet me. "Sure, whatever you want to do, boss." Now, one of Bill's great unfulfilled dreams was to be a Motown producer. Perfect, I thought, he could produce something, and maybe later I could talk him into doing some albums himself on Motown. Stu Gardner, Cosby's talented music man, had already produced a couple of singles for Chisa, a Motown-distributed label in 1969, and Stu was raring to work with the artists. Plus, Bill told me that he would take any act that I wanted and feature them anywhere in the world where he was performing. I rubbed my hands together, knowing that the company could strike gold having Bill involved.

I arranged a dinner at Berry's and invited Bill, with his wife, Camille, to discuss some ideas. I also did some heavy prepping with Berry, always prone to waxing poetic for hours about his own greatness. "Berry, if you start talking about how great you are, I'm going to kick you under the table." Berry promised me he'd be a charming host.

Instead of using my Pinto station wagon—indicative of my current financial straits—to pick up Bill and his wife at the Beverly Hills Hotel, I collected them in a limousine—courtesy of Motown. The three of us sat down with Berry to a pleasing meal, compliments of Berry's French chef.

Berry forgot his promises immediately. "So, I went to this guy and I told him, 'Look friend . . .' " My high heel poked Berry's shin. "Oh, oh yeah, Bill . . .you're great" and "your scholastic achievements, wow," and "finishing school like you did." I'd smile for a while and then Berry would stumble, "Yeah, well, me and Diana Ross . . ." I kicked him again. "So, uh, and, Camille, Ray tells me you're quite the businesswoman." My under-the-table action worked like a charm and the night was a success.

As it turned out, the thick skulls at the company nixed our project. And the many talents of Bill Cosby would not be tapped until a few years later, when he would be brought in by Steve Barri, then head of the Creative Division, to do some comedy albums.

By 1977 Berry and I had established a pleasant business relationship and had even begun more casual contact, usually involving the kids, especially Kerry. Our son, still residing with his father—though spending stretches with me as well—had played an important role in our improved communications. That summer was Kerry's graduation from Beverly Hills High School. The commencement ceremonies were held on the long, sweeping lawn of the school. The sun was bright and the sky was blue. As I looked for a seat, I spotted Berry down front. He was standing, shielding his eyes from the sun, and looking about, probably for me. I didn't really want to sit with him. Call it a protective device, but I'd healed so much I figured the less proximity at a time like this the better. So when he turned in my direction, I ducked to the side, hiding in back of someone's hat. Then I noticed Berry speaking to Les and Roger, who were now taking off down the aisle, scouting for traces of me. Damn. Well, I'll be a sport. I stood and waved, removing my sunglasses. Berry came to take my arm and led me back to the seat he had saved for me.

Looking up ahead at the many chairs set up for the graduating class, I sat down. Berry nudged my elbow. "You know this guy next to you?" I turned to see if I recognized someone and indeed I did. It was my father, and next to him, my mother. Berry had flown them in from Detroit. I was so moved, I didn't know what to say. I looked over at Berry and then back at my parents. As the band struck up a rousing graduation march, so did my heart.

It got better. Berry took all of us out to Chasen's, one of Beverly Hills' finest establishments, in honor of Kerry's graduation. And as the week continued, my parents and I stayed at Berry's house as his guests. There we got the royal treatment—the housekeepers and the cars and the French chef's gourmet specialties. Nothing was too good for my parents as far as Berry was concerned. They were delighted, except I could tell that Mama was dying to get in that kitchen and teach the cook some of her own specialties. And, while they didn't say anything directly, I knew what they were hoping. Through the years they had believed that Berry would one day see the light, and at some point he and I would be together. Although I knew better, it did seem as though our deep ocean of trouble had all but gone away in that one week, and I too began to hope.

"Ray, listen," Berry started, just before I left to drop the folks at the airport. I forgot about hope, thinking he was going to say "see ya at the office." But what I heard was, "When you're done saying good-bye at the airport, why don't you come back? I'm enjoying our being together." He smiled his enigmatic Berry smile. "Like old times."

Later that night I was back at his house and, just like old

times, we were talking and laughing, and it was truly amazing. After all the games, the tests, the nightmare, the war—here we were, just us. That guy with the raggedy clothes and the bad 'do and those unbelievably sexy teeth. And me, the little girl who came from out of nowhere to change his life forever. Because we both loved music.

Berry yawned, "Well, I'm going to go to bed now." For a moment I forgot my place in time, thinking just like the old days that we'd both turn in together. And then he said, "Come on, you can sleep in my room." A voice that I hadn't heard in a long, long time, the one that used to caution me in the early days, whispered inside, "It's OK."

His bedroom was pretty sharp for a man who used to walk around in raggedy clothes. It was a king's chamber in colors of a deep, majestic forest: greens and dark polished woods. A fire crackling in the fireplace. Freshly cut flowers in vases. Exquisite antiques. Louis XIV chairs and tables. An easy touch of a remote-control button revealed a hidden closet with a customized built-in stereo and big-screen television. His bed was four times as wide as the double bed we once shared in our first apartment. This boat-sized creation for sleep—and other pursuits—had a mahogany headboard with a family crest carved into it. I was about to pinch myself, for this must be a dream.

"Take off your clothes, get ready for bed," Berry said, seeing me standing like a lightning-struck statue.

"Well," I said shyly, "I don't have anything to wear."

The next thing I knew, we were wandering through a closet twice the size of my bedroom. There were actually two closets, one for the casual man, the other for the perfectly tailored executive. Hanging neatly were suits already coordinated for business meetings—coats and pants, shirt and tie and hanky in pocket, all on one hanger—while directly underneath were matching shoes with socks tucked into them. Exactly as I used to lay out his clothes for him, this presentation was the work of Billy Davis (no relation to the songwriting partner and beau of Gwen's), one of Berry's old-time buddies turned valet.

Berry saw me staring like Alice in Wonderland at his shoes. "Yeah, Billy keeps me absolutely sharp. He keeps himself sharp too. I give him a budget and every time he buys me something he gets one for himself, too."

Changing into the splendid burgundy-striped silk pajamas

that Berry found for me, I looked at myself in the bathroom mirror. Me and me had a talk. One me said, "Run," and the other me said, "Now, how in the hell are you going to go anywhere in clothes that are hanging off you like that?" One me said, "Ya look pretty damn sexy for a forty-year-old broad." The other me agreed, "With your heart pumping like that you're nothing but a damn teenager." The cool voice of reason still sang to me that it was OK.

And so began a tale I never would have written in my wildest fantasies. Each morsel of the experience was more surprising and luxurious than the next. When I went with all my courage to his bed, his laughter at me in those big pajamas rang out, as did mine at his regal attire—and those same old skinny legs. We lay in bed together while he played music, which we discussed with more laughter and more rhapsody. "We still have the same opinions about music," he said. The music and our harmonious laughter drowned out the noise of the past. And when he shut off the tape player, turning the lights down low, a boyish look of innocence came over him as he asked, "Would you mind reading to me for a while?"

He handed me the book. I opened it and began to read with the soft, sensual voice of one reading from *The Arabian Nights*, even though this book was on building stereo components. "Berry, this is what you want me to read?"

"If you wouldn't mind."

It was the most boring material I'd ever read, and Berry was snoring in minutes. Those snores were the most beautiful things I'd ever heard.

When I opened my eyes in the morning, I was alone in bed. The dream was over, I supposed. And then I saw Berry out on the sunny deck, sitting at a table on which breakfast was spread out royally. "Morning," he called and walked to the foot of the bed, studying me. "Do you know that's the first time in eighteen years that I've ever seen you with your eyes closed? When I woke up this morning, I saw you and all of a sudden it made me upset." I smiled at him, with tears in my eyes. Berry took my hand saying, "I thought to myself, damn this woman went to sleep. She really doesn't give a damn about me anymore."

The nights and days turned to weeks and months. There I was in Bel Air, one of the most exclusive residential areas in the world, sleeping chastely with Berry Gordy in the same bed. During this time we never became lovers. There were, in fact, other women—

possibly two others—staying in the house. Berry would visit them early in the evening and then come up to bed with me. They were his concubines and I was his queen.

Once again I was Miss Ray, and I accompanied Berry through his full days of meetings and was a part of every decision and event in the company, from the creative to the financial. I took notes as in the old days, and later he and I bounced around ideas, evaluating everything that was happening. Our rapport was as natural and flowing as a steady stream.

In the evenings there was a never-ending string of galas, parties, shows, and political events. Late at night we would sit by the fire with tea or wine and talk about our day. He shared the intimate details of his life apart from me, his love life and his restlessness. We stopped short of discussing the painful past. Our dark history was hid far away behind closed curtains, where also lurked my fear that this would soon come to an end.

It was beyond amazing; it was stupefying. "Where are you going?" he'd ask.

"Just to get a glass of water."

"Oh, no. Let me." He'd pick up the phone, "Will you please bring Miss Ray up a glass of water?" Soon the butler, wearing a white jacket and black bow tie, would enter carrying a silver tray with a goblet of ice water and a vase with one red rose. Damn, I'd think—next?

I kept trying to leave, to get some perspective. But Berry would frown. "Where are you going? Don't leave unless Les and Roger know where you are." It was a form of romantic house arrest, to which I succumbed happily. The best part to me was the return of my lost child—the music and the company. We treated it again as ours, instead of his alone. I'd been in touch with Robert L., making sure all was in order at Jobete and he'd affirmed that it was. Venida would come each evening with a daily report, and I would give her instructions for what I knew she could handle in my absence at work and at home with the kids. On weekends she would bring Eddie and Rya to stay with me at Berry's. As with everything else, my two youngest accepted this latest turn of events as an exciting new adventure.

The fact that Berry and I were not sexually intimate felt natural to me. Physical lovemaking was never the height of our passion; rather what connected our souls was our love of family and of music, and our dream of etching out a great volume of history. There was a certain reverence gained by not pressing into the sexual, as if by remaining platonic, nothing could taint our relationship. Maybe I kept myself untouchable, but if I did, it was with the hope that we would reunite again as Kerry's mother and father, as man and wife.

One night we were returning from the home of Lew Wasserman, the chairman of MCA, where we'd attended a political fund raiser—five thousand dollars a plate—for presidential candidate Jimmy Carter. In the car Berry and I were silent as we drove by the multimillion-dollar estates of some of the most famous people in the world. Berry was now a part of this world. Contrasting images came to mind of what was then—the guy who'd counted quarters for the bus—and what was now.

He broke the silence. "You know, I never told you this . . . but," his eyes were on the road, "I loved you."

To have these words withheld from me for eighteen years and to have them suddenly blurted out like this was staggering.

Berry talked slowly at first and then his words began to pour out. "Do you remember that night when you were pregnant with Kerry? I'd taken out the garbage, or so I'd said? And you pretended to have followed me to the phone booth and made up that story. Well, you were almost on the nose. But not quite. First of all I was calling that girl Elsie. But I was calling her to tell her I couldn't see her anymore. That I loved my wife. Oh, and you were wrong about something else. You guessed I'd gone into the phone booth on the left. I'd gone over to the one on the right. That's how I knew you were testing me." Berry shook his head with a sad sigh, as if to say what a shame we'd played all those games. Seventeen years later, the mystery was being solved.

I held my hands in my lap, trying to still my longing to touch his cheek.

"And when we broke up, at first I was relieved. I thought I wanted Margaret. But then . . . remember the day you came into my office and said you wanted to go to New York? I wanted to stop you but I didn't know how. And when you left I . . ." Berry paused. "I cried."

I swallowed, not wanting to cry myself. "I never wanted to go. You knew that." We both were silent again, sitting in the idling car in front of the house, the electric gate closed protectively behind us.

Again Berry spoke. "I was angry for a long time that you

could leave me. I depended on you, and all of a sudden I found myself dealing with all these people I wasn't used to. I really was mad at you."

It wasn't necessary for me to say that I'd been a little mad myself.

He went on, "Another thing. Your leaving me made it impossible for me to ever really be happy. I mean, I've gained all these riches, but I will never have another woman who will love me for just me and not because I'm Berry Gordy."

"Berry," I turned to him, almost gasping for air to speak words that were so long in coming, "I came to your office, praying that you would stop me. I didn't want to leave you, but I had to save my own life. It would have been so easy, all you could have said were two words—'don't go.' There never would have been all this heartache."

Behind us now, the past ebbed and faded. This precious peace in the car was our present. And his house stood in front of me as a future, a home again for the two of us. We left the car together in silence and walked into that house. We climbed the staircase slowly and went into the bedroom, not needing to turn on the lights. So familiar and so meant to be, I thought, we could always find our way around, even in the dark.

Under the covers, I opened my mouth to ask what hadn't been asked, and yet the words wouldn't come. And then I heard the voice of my instincts, singing sweet and soft, "It's OK." And so I said to him in the dark. "I love being here with you, Berry. Maybe . . . I need to make a decision about the future, and I can't pretend I don't have kids . . . Maybe we could . . . I mean if you want . . ."

It was the greatest risk I'd ever taken—my tiny voice, my broken sentences, those words now dangling in midair, up in the uncertain darkness of the room. My heart was pounding, what had I done, what had I asked?

And then I heard the glorious sound of his soft voice—as if in the middle of a fall I'd been caught by his strength and his certainty. "Yes," he began, "why don't you go back to your house for the time being? I understand that you need to be with the kids. I'll think about what you said and I'll get back to you and we'll work something out." Berry's honest and gentle words lulled me into sleep, a sleep wherein I lost the instincts that once protected me. The last pieces of my defenses dissolved in that sleep, like a crumbling house. I burned those sticks of resistance in a pyre of hope as I slept that night with Berry at my side. And also on that night, way out over the ocean a bad storm was on the rise. The tide, as it had been known to do before, had shifted, and was about to take its most drastic change for the worse.

CHAPTER 15
APOLLO
1977–1980

Of all the ups and downs I'd encountered in my life, I was about to plummet to deeper depths than I'd ever thought possible. But no dark vacuum was too awesome for Miss Ray. I'd find a way to build a ladder and slowly climb out.

There had been a warning sign, something that had happened not long before I heard that jubilant orchestral promise of Berry's that "we'll work something out." But I'd chosen to overlook this warning sign even though it was witnessed, to my complete embarassment, by Hugh Hefner, whose Playboy empire included his own palace of Versailles—to which Berry was regularly invited for evenings of very serious backgammon games.

"Listen, I want you to go with me to Hef's," Berry said, not wanting me to be out of his sight for a moment. I protested, insisting that I didn't play that game, nor did I think I would be comfortable mingling with all the bunnies.

"Don't worry," Berry cooed, "you're with me." So I got decked out in anticipation of some stiff competition and waited for Berry while he plucked a cool ten thousand in cash out of his safe. Pocket change for the gambling table at Hef's. Enough money to put Cliff through college.

At the opulent, sprawling estate, we wandered through the game room, which conjured up images of ancient Greco-Roman days. Waiters roamed with trays of orgiastic food and drink. Most of the men sat absorbed in their games, and a sprinkling of scantily clad women whose breasts were like sculpted marble melons wandered about. Finally we caught sight of Zeus.

"Hey, Berry," Hefner called over to us, "how are you?" Berry began shaking hands with a small group of men surrounding Hef as I saw our host giving me an approving eye.

"Oh, Hef, this is Ray, my ex-wife," Berry said as Hefner and I both extended our hands. Just as our handshake began, Berry added, "She may be ugly but she's smart." The host's hand was withdrawn, and the circle of onlookers fell silent. But I, after an embarrassed smile, let it pass. A bad move.

But it was on the following day that Berry, in an act of generosity and concern, had plunked down twelve thousand dollars for me to undergo dental treatment that I'd sorely neglected for lack of funds. One night I was getting slapped upside the head, the next day I was being caressed with support. Not that the dental work was any romp in the woods.

The morning following the amazing serenade of "we'll work something out," I went home to spend some time with the kids and to await Berry's game plan. I also went in for the last of the dental surgery, which proved to be a trauma to my entire system. My body was wracked with extreme pain and constant nausea. Only able to consume liquids I saw my weight plunge to a frightening seventy-eight pounds, and I landed in the hospital for two weeks. There it was determined that I was suffering from malnutrition.

Released from the hospital with a prescription for very addictive painkillers, my physical condition only spiraled downward as the vomiting and nausea increased. My emotions were so out of whack that I found myself, over a small misunderstanding, having a parting of the ways with Venida.

"Do me a favor," my doctor warned at last. "Stop the medication and just deal with the pain." So I did, although my condition would last six months, and all the while I clutched to the life raft of hope that Berry had inflated for me. We were going to be together again, and soon I would return to work as co-skipper at the helm of the good ship Motown.

"You did what?" I asked Robert L., who telephoned me a few weeks after my hospitalization.

"You're fired."

"What are you talking about?" I asked.

"You haven't been here in five months. I can't have people popping in and out when they want to."

"Wait a minute." I reminded him, "You know that I was with Berry that whole time. Venida was taking care of the office and I was with Berry. You can call the man and ask him yourself."

"I don't give a damn where you were," Robert concluded. "You work for me and you should have been here. You're fired."

My son Kerry playing ball with a young Michael Jackson in Hollywood in 1969. *(Juanita Dickerson Collection)*

Smokey Robinson with my sons Cliff Liles and Kerry Gordy at a 1983 recording session. *(Cliff Liles Collection)*

Berry and I with Jimmy Carter at a fund-raising dinner in 1976. *(Ray Singleton Collection)*

My daughter, Rya Singleton, in Hollywood in 1978. *(Ray Singleton Collection)*

Ed Singleton with our son, Eddie, Jr., and Daren Singleton at Eddie's high school graduation in 1984. *(Ray Singleton Collection)*

Apollo in the late 1970s: Benny Medina, Lenny Green, Cliff Liles, Larry Robinson, Kerry Gordy. *(Cliff Liles Collection)*

Stevie Wonder in the late 1970s. *(Michael Ochs Archives)*

A Jobete office party in the early 1980s: Kenny Hirsch, Ron Anton, Berry, Ron Miller and friends, Robert Gordy, me, and (front) Tommy Gordy. *(Ray Singleton Collection)*

A 1983 reunion party. Above: Eddie Holland, me, Lamont Dozier, Berry, and Brian Holland. Below: Holland-Dozier-Holland, the Four Tops, the Temptations, and Norman Whitfield surround Berry. *(Ray Singleton Collection)*

Diana Ross and Berry in 1985. *(Ray Singleton Collection)*

Berry and Suzanne DePasse in
1985. *(Ray Singleton Collection)*

Guy Costa and I in 1985.
(Ray Singleton Collection)

Desiree Gordy, Jermaine Jackson,
Marchella Liles (peeking through),
Cliff Liles, and Michael Jackson at
"Motown 25," 1983. *(Cliff Liles
Collection)*

Sherrick and I in London, l
(Ray Singleton Collection)

Berry, Kerry, and I at Kerry's Wedding, 1987. *(Ray Singleton Collection)*

Crathman Spencer and I at the
1989 Motown Family Reunion.
(Ray Singleton Collection)

Marv Johnson and I at the
1989 Motown Family Reunion.
(Ray Singleton Collection)

With Martha Reeves at Hitsville,
U.S.A., in 1989. *(Ray Singleton
Collection)*

With Wanda Rogers of the
Marvelettes in 1989. *(Ray
Singleton Collection)*

Back to where it all began: Hitsville, U.S.A.
(Ray Singleton Collection)

Knowing that Berry was in my corner, I called him up. "Listen, your brother just called and fired me because I wasn't in the office. As I tried to explain to him, I was working as your executive assistant all this time."

"I know," said Berry. "Were you at Jobete?"

"How could I be at Jobete when I was with you?"

"Robert fired you?"

"Yes," I answered, waiting for Berry's master strategy on how to right the wrong.

"Well," he decided, "there's nothing I can do about it. You should have been at work."

From out of a lofty dream, living in Bel Air with a man whom I loved and no longer feared, I fell. Like being shoved out of an airliner speeding through the clouds, I tumbled down without a parachute. From the vantage point of my spiritual and financial crash landing, I looked back up at Berry. He, that demigod, who with one hand giveth, hath now with the other hand taken away. I should have known better—what idiot would place her trust in a man with a track record like Berry's? My belief in an impossible love was my only excuse.

Why and when and how Berry could have again undergone such a Jekyll/Hyde transformation were questions that had no rational answers. Like the weather, Berry's mood had simply shifted. Maybe in those months, as he contemplated having me back in his life, he foresaw having to make undesirable adjustments from bachelor life. Or, maybe, on a deeper level where he was that insecure small man who'd somewhere along the way convinced himself that I'd abandoned him, Berry questioned my motives for wanting our reunion. Or, maybe, as his tone had suggested, backing Robert L.'s decision to fire me was just a business decision.

Whatever the case was, I had to drag myself out of my sickbed to stand in line at the unemployment office. I had no money to support my family and no job. And that old pride of mine prevented me from turning to anyone for a loan. On the way home from the humiliating experience of signing up for a weekly pittance—one hundred twenty-two dollars—something quite mystical occurred.

Stopped at a traffic light, feeling sorry for myself, I saw in my rearview mirror a chauffeur-driven automobile approaching on my left. It was a white Mercedes limousine with tinted windows and

golden hubcaps, driven by an attractive older woman with mirrored sunglasses and a pert black chauffeur's hat. As it pulled up
next to me, I cursed it and all that it represented. I cursed the
demon Berry, whose refrain, "I'll always take care of you," had
become nothing more than a lure that had propelled me over the
edge of a precipice. I snarled at that female limo driver. But then,
through a slightly opened rear window, I heard the limo's stereo
cranking out a very familiar song, one on which my own voice was
singing, "That's what I want!" Berry's little riff, Janie Bradford's
words, Barrett Strong's churchy organ and vocals, and my own
background arrangement and chorus sung with the Rayber Voices.
Like a sickness passing out of the body during sleep, my bitterness
evaporated in seconds, as my entire being was cleansed with a
rainshower of new hope and glory. I had done it before, I could do
it again.

"Money . . . that's what I want," I sang out, rushing into the
house, startling Cliff and Kerry and his friend Benny Medina, all
of whom were in the middle of band practice. Even Eddie and Rya
got worried looks on their faces—has Mommy really gone over the
edge?

"Hey, Benny, c'mere. I want to talk to you," I called, as all the
kids gathered around, wondering what the hell had come over me
and why I was singling out Benny. Of course, as I soon explained,
I had just had a brainstorm. Benny, who was already registered
with the Toni Kelman Commercial Talent Agency and had nailed
several commercials himself, was always suggesting that I take in
Eddie, now eleven, and Rya, ten for a shot at representation. My
two younger ones—adorable and bright kids—were enthusiastic
about the idea.

After registering them with the agency, the phone began to
ring immediately. Audition after audition, call-back after call-
back, from once to twice to every evening of the week. Soon they
were sick of seeing me outside of school when they walked out.
"Oh, no, we're going to an audition."

That year the two did twenty-four commercials, and it soon
spilled over into actual acting jobs. "Little Lulu," an ABC After-
School Special, and "Cindy," another special with Nell Carter, as
well as "Happy Days" and "Diff'rent Strokes" and a Richard Pryor
special and his movie *Blue Collar*. My two little champions were
unstoppable as each tried to outdo the other.

One day, though, Eddie really scored. "Guess what, Ray?" The agent called to tell me, "Eddie's got a series."

"Great," I said, not exactly sure which one of the auditions had yielded this job. "How much does it pay?"

"Seventeen-fifty to start."

What did that mean? Seventeen dollars and fifty cents? "Oh," I said, very disappointed.

"Don't worry. If the series stays on a year, it'll go up to five thousand dollars a week."

"Well," I said, incredibly relieved and thrilled at the same time. "I guess we can accept the terms of seventeen hundred and fifty dollars a week to start."

So, after thousands had competed for the role, Eddie had been selected. I stood at the sidelines, shaking my pom-poms and cheering, while the little guy went running into this television series called "Harris and Company." Starring Bernie Casey, it was an optimistic show about a black man raising five kids on his own. What a miraculous turnaround in our lives, I thought. And what an amazing trouper Eddie was, basically supporting the household, hopping in the car with me to get to Universal Studios at six A.M. and skipping out in the evening at seven P.M. when I came to pick him up. Although it was a terrific experience, I was actually relieved when the series was canceled and he could return to his normal life of school and play. I decided to end their acting careers for the time being, and Rya and Eddie agreed. "Yea! No more auditions!"

I'd been avoiding Berry like the plague for well over a year. And, suddenly, in one of those crazy show biz turnarounds, I was being beckoned back to work at Motown. Well, this was Hollywood, after all.

As Cliff would remember and relate to some of the Motown staff, "Well, it all started in '71, when Mom was on the road with Diana Ross. At one point, when she was in town she went to some pawnshop in L.A. and bought me a bass and Kerry a guitar. I started playing along to records, just sort of picking out things. One day I was trying to figure out this bass line on a song called 'Want Ads' by Honey Cone, and Mom comes into the bedroom and says, 'Give me that bass. Let me show you how to do this.' The next thing I know my mother is all over the place, jamming on this great bass line, the first time through. 'That's all you have to do,' she says while I sit there in total shock. 'If Ma can do this, I can too,' I thought."

Well, happy as I would be to take credit as Cliff's musical inspiration, there were other influences as well. As he continued to practice daily, he soon emerged with a hero—the inimitable James Brown. Those funky yet simple bass lines rang through our place—wherever we were living—night and day. Finally I got another bass hero, James Jamerson, to come over and give Cliff some lessons, which, although it was a major ego boost to the kid, wasn't always the easiest of experiences. "You did what?" Between James's impatience and Cliff's mischief making, I was never sure there would be a house left standing by the lesson's end.

By the time Cliff finished high school and returned to L.A., there were more developments. Cliff would later explain, "Kerry at this point had switched from guitar to keyboards and he was pretty good, too. One day I went up to visit him at his father's house and saw that he had a little setup that also included some drums and a tape recorder. Pretty soon we were making up songs and recording them. Kerry was finishing up at Beverly Hills High and knew Diana Ross's brother, Chico, who was playing drums. So he started in with us, too. Next thing we know, we've got two more guys from Beverly—Benny Medina, this high-energy singer and bongo player we call Mr. Personality, and a talented dude, Larry Robinson, who played guitar. A full-blown band.

"Berry passed by every now and then, saying, 'Sounds good, boys,' and even though we were just having fun, we started to think of ourselves more seriously—'H'm . . . Kerry . . . Motown . . . shoot, let's start something here.' "

The boys named their band Kryptonite, and I couldn't believe it when I heard them play. They'd been doing small gigs for a while, and Kryptonite was dyn-o-mite! They were now rehearsing at the old Kabuki Theatre on Adams and Crenshaw, which my other ex, Ed Singleton (with whom I maintained friendly but distant relations) was remodeling into something along the lines of an Apollo Theater West. Chico had been replaced on drums by a kid named Lenny Greenberg, a.k.a. Lenny Greene. Kerry, a.k.a., little Hitler, was in charge of organization and business. I was practically speechless; Kryptonite had major star potential. "Boys," I said after listening to a few songs, "how'd you guys like to have yourselves a manager?"

I got ready for the blast-off. On the count of ten—I had them rehearse for six months to get them ready for a presentation at Motown.

On nine—Kryptonite went in front of Suzanne DePasse and a Motown attorney, Lee Young, Jr. After the presentation, the boys went up to Suzanne. "Well, what do you think?" All she could say was "You broke my face." They took that to be a compliment.

On eight—Three months later Motown made an offer that included an invitation for me to come into the Creative Division to work with Suzanne, at my old Jobete salary.

On seven—Berry called me. "Suzanne's been telling me about the boys, and I think it's fantastic. I just wanted to congratulate you on your business expertise and to thank you for not bugging me about anything for the last year."

Instead of saying anything, I simply admired his uncanny knack for delivering a compliment and an insult all in one breath.

On six—We threw Kryptonite rehearsals into overdrive. Kerry and Lenny, both electronics buffs, set up an eight-track studio in the warehouse where we had found rental space. We worked day and night, and I was thrilled beyond belief at the kids' dedication. The music was so sensational and their appeal was knock-your-socks-off. My guys, I was positive, were going to be megastars. What's more—it so happened that Berry had put together a group called Switch, which included Bobby DeBarge, that also had great potential. So we had some good old-fashioned competition going. Both bands fell into the teenage bag, with Switch heading in a sophisticated direction and Kryptonite going for bold and dynamic. What more could teen listeners want?

We'll interrupt the countdown briefly to inspect the launching pad—Motown itself. By the late seventies it was moving into an uncertain era. Disco had thrown everyone for a loop. The Jacksons, once Motown's beacon of hope, were long gone. Motown Pictures had been a big flop. The company was relying wholly on only a few superstars, foremost among them Stevie Wonder—who'd already emerged as one of the most successful songwriters in music business history. Coming up in the ranks, showing great potential, were the Commodores. But some important veterans were having problems. Although Marvin Gaye had recently knocked off one of his big hits of the decade with "Got to Give It Up," he was now floundering. Smokey Robinson hadn't cut a hit in so long that he was starting to be a joke among the producers. Diana Ross, after a promising early solo start, couldn't get arrested. Worse yet, the company wasn't developing new talent, and our golden gleaming reputation for being on the cutting edge of the industry was badly tarnished.

That's where Kryptonite came in. The boys were going to fuel-inject the company's creative spirit and put Motown back into a position of leadership and innovation.

On five—The money finally got negotiated. The boys were ecstatic. Each got twenty-five hundred up front, and a hundred-twenty-five-dollars-a-week salary to cover a period of one to seven years—at Motown's option. "C'mon, Cliff," I hollered, "get everybody together. We're going to the bank. And I can deposit my 25 percent commission while we're at it."

Now we were ready to record. After completing most of the backing tracks, I sent a copy of the rough mixes to the great arranger Gene Page for feedback and arrangement assistance. Gene, who had arranged for everybody from Frank Sinatra to Barbra Streisand to Kool and the Gang, and whose arrangement of Barry White's "Love's Theme" was one of my all-time favorites, called me back fast.

"I loved your tape," Gene responded. "But you need one disco tune on it." C'mon guys, I told them, put on your thinking caps. And I put mine on, too.

On four—I heard a groove coming from Kerry's room. "That's it!" I said, feeling it in my bones and skipping into the bedroom with a little disco hustle step. "Now we have to come up with a song for this groove." So I called up Don Fletcher, of "Dancing Machine" notoriety, and got him in on it.

Don took one listen to the beat, and the first words out of his mouth were, "It's your duty to shake your booty." Yeah. It took us only a day to knock off the song, which we call "Krypto Disco."

On count three—Whoops, there was a slowdown due to mechanical difficulties. It turned out that the creators of Superman would not allow the use of the name "Kryptonite," which was unfortunate as the movie Superman was about to be released and the tie-in would have been perfect. At the midnight hour we all agreed on the name "Apollo" and so changed our most recent song title to "Astro Disco," which would be released as Apollo's first single.

On two—Berry attended a live presentation in a small rented studio. He commented to the boys, "Your group is one of the most exciting acts I've seen in ten years." Their wildest dreams were coming true, as Cliff proclaimed, "We've got it made! We've got the man himself here, he loves us, and we're going to be stars!"

Now, before we get to the final launch, there are two important variables to take into consideration. One was me, who at this point had rebounded with cosmic force and was sailing high. I'd found and rented a dreamhouse in Hidden Hills, a community in the San Fernando Valley. Because Berry had a rule that all the kids should be out of his house by age eighteen, Kerry was back living with me. Also at the house were fellow Apollo member Benny Medina, Cliff, and, of course, Eddie and Rya. We were one joyful commune of creativity, living in this beautiful country setting with its swimming pools and tennis courts. Not to mention a happy menagerie of pets—German shepherds, cats, and a couple of Shetland ponies, which had been a dream of mine to own since I was a little girl. It was a paradise and at long, long last, I felt at home. There I was in the living room in Hidden Hills, pep talking my two sons who were about to explode into a major musical success. Looking out the window, I could see Eddie and Rya, each atop a pony. I felt so content.

The house also had an expansive, sunny front porch—where I would sit and talk with my dear friend Marvin Gaye, who lived not far from us. Strengthened by these positive surges, which had transpired in less than nineteen months, I was ready for whatever was going to happen.

The other variable was not so positive. Motown hadn't been putting on a very good show as far as pushing and promoting new acts. Yet we were most encouraged to find that Bob Jones, the PR head at the time, was ready to take the bull by the horns.

And so on the count of one, we let her rip—blast-off. It was March of 1979, just around my forty-second birthday. The album, *Apollo*, with me credited as producer, was released. There was a flurry of activity and hearty acclaim. The company loved the record. Apollo was soon appearing on "The Dinah Shore Show," "Soul Train," and "American Bandstand." The fan mail was tremendous; the Apollo heat wave was rising and rising. They did a Robby Benson movie called *Die Laughing* up in San Francisco and then took off for bookings at all the hottest clubs in Las Vegas. Bob Jones and the editor of *Right On* magazine, Cynthia Horner, got Apollo on the cover of the publication; inside, the guys did a full spread on back-to-school fashions. Showcases, videotape presentations, and highly sophisticated live shows—like an advanced high-tech, space-age Jackson 5. The guys were starting to get mobbed coming in and out of theaters. As '79 rolled along with promise, we began to get ready for a Japanese tour.

"Japan?" Marvin Gaye asked, impressed, back in '78 when the idea was first suggested. It was during one of our afternoon talks over lemonade on the front porch. As the sun set low, we discussed Eastern cultures, speaking little of our personal problems. For my part, I was so buoyant with Apollo's lift-off, that I had shut the lid on old hurts. I knew, though, that Marvin, a man struggling to find himself, was going through hell. His career was in turmoil, as was his relationship with Berry. He and Anna had split a few years before. According to Morris Broadnax, who'd been close to the couple during their last years in Detroit, Marvin had been destructively obsessive about his wife. Morris related one episode in which Marvin had agreed to loan him a hundred dollars and when he arrived to pick up the money, Anna answered the door. Marvin was momentarily out, but Anna went ahead and gave Morris the money. Marvin was livid. No man should have that kind of intimate contact with his wife; she was his, and no person on earth was good enough to touch her, talk to her, or look at her. The marriage was caught in a deep tidepool of Marvin's paranoia, his feuds with Berry, his chaotic finances, and his troubled relationship with his father. All this rage was inflamed by a cocaine addiction.

The marriage was being ripped painfully apart. And, in the summer of 1978, after a protracted legal battle, Marvin recorded his album *Here, My Dear*, the proceeds of which were to be applied, by court injunction, to his divorce settlement with Anna. When it came out that December, it wasn't merely rueful or angry, it was one of the most directly personal statements of resentment ever released in public.

Yet for all the tragedy surrounding his life, during our encounters he was the sweetest, most sensitive man imaginable. That was the paradox of Marvin Gaye. I knew that he was having a drug problem, but he never came to the house high nor did he expose the boys to it. His son, Marvin III, considered a cousin by all the kids, was very close to Eddie. Marvin was a sports fanatic and would invite Kerry and Cliff to his place where he had a gym, a basketball court, and a tennis court.

So Marvin and I never talked about the shadows that fell

across the lawn of the house in Hidden Hills, which included, I feared, his recent second marriage to Janis, which was not starting under the best circumstances.

"Apollo sounds fantastic, Ray," Marvin said. "You're doing your old magic with them."

"Yeah? You really think so?" I refilled our glasses with lemonade.

"Your sons are great," he nodded, staring off somewhere. And then, turning to me, he said, "Don't let anything stand in the way of your working with these kids."

We had another youngster, an ironic yet poignant presence— Kennedy Gordy, Berry's son by Margaret Norton. Berry's dynastic shuffling had never been easy on the children, and for Kennedy it had been very hard. On one hand he had been given a childhood of unimaginable privilege, with servants and paid caretakers answering to his every material need. On the other hand, his own parents were unavailable to give him the most basic of human requirements—love and attention. His father was always working and his mother was unstable, to say the least. Margaret's troubled circumstances included giving birth a year after Kennedy was born to a baby girl who died less than a year after that. I surmised that Berry blamed Margaret on some level for the loss, as well as for much of the ensuing unhappiness.

Though a beautiful girl, Margaret had no direction or skills. From a brief attempt at modeling, she went on, under Berry's sponsorship, to write some songs with his brother George and George's partner, Allen Story. Their efforts yielded "I Promise to Wait My Love" by Martha Reeves and the Vandellas and "I Truly, Truly Believe" by the Temptations.

Though there would remain a controversy over whether Berry and Margaret were actually ever married, I would be one of few to be certain that they hadn't.

"He told me that even though he loved me, because I made those phone calls to you, he could never marry me," Margaret said to me a few years after my breakup with Berry. What was known to all was that once they'd moved to California, they didn't live together anymore. He bought a separate house for her and Kennedy, which was up in the Hollywood Hills, where she would await the moments, then few and far between, when Berry would visit her. Her endless days were spent tranquilized and her nights, drinking in anguish. Berry's numerous conquests of other women were dangled in front of her. The eyes that once held such allure to him slowly became hungry and sick, and over time they'd lost their beauty.

As his mother's condition worsened, Kennedy moved to Bel Air with his dad, and Berry assumed legal custody of him. Margaret was given a settlement, spent some time in mental institutions, and was finally sent back to Detroit.

When Kerry moved to Berry's house in 1973, Kennedy—who'd never forgotten Kerry's Lone Ranger routine in grade school—was soon reintroduced to me. When Apollo headquartered in Hidden Hills, Kennedy often came along with Kerry. Soon he became a member of the family, staying for as long as he could. At his father's house he was so much younger than everyone else, and he was treated as a fourteen-year-old bratty nuisance. At our house, he was older than Rya and Eddie by four and three years. It was the one place in the world where he felt he could just be himself and get all the love and attention the other kids received.

When he spoke of the problems between his parents, in a wounded voice heavy with confusion, I'd just ruffle his hair and say, "It's OK. You're here now. You just stay here and we won't let those problems get us, will we?"

The past, as we know, was forever lurking and interfering, and frequently the phone would ring. "This is Margaret. May I speak with Kennedy, please?" I would call to him where he was happily at play with the other kids, and the summons would erase all joy from his face as though I'd scolded him.

"Well, I can't talk right now," he'd say, with a sad look or a plea that read, "Please don't make me talk to her!"

"Come on, this is your mother." I would hold my hand over the mouthpiece. Then, into the phone, I'd say, "He'll be right there."

On the line, Margaret would pour her sorrows, bitterness, and paranoia into his ear. Kennedy would say very little; would just become more and more upset so that by the time the call ended, he would be morose.

"Hey, kid," I'd say, waylaying him in the kitchen. "What's wrong?"

Kennedy would just shake his head with a weary sigh so inappropriate for a child his age. "I love her, but I can't handle talking to her. I know things aren't right for my mother, but what can I do?"

It was an ongoing cycle. Afterward, when Berry heard of Margaret's phone calls, he would call Kennedy, criticizing Margaret to no end. Naturally, Kennedy would become even more upset, his depression sometimes lasting a week. And so, in my high-flying balloon I would gather up the lost and the disenfranchised, and pray that the air currents would keep us all aloft.

Apollo's takeoff promised a long, happy flight, but in 1979, while we labored to promote the first album and develop material for a second one, a new countdown was in the works.

On ten—Though Berry told me initially that the company was behind Apollo 100 percent, I quickly learned that this was a rather slippery concept. I put in a request in late '78 for funding on group uniforms—space-age, glitzy "Star Trek"-like outfits for publicity and for the album cover. Berry said no.

Nine—I was somewhat surprised. Costumes, after all, were routine expenses. But, being resourceful, I headed over to the art department and described my concept, commissioning the album cover artwork.

Eight—By April of '79 it was clear that the Motown machinery wasn't in sync with us. Bob Jones in PR was working like hell, but the rest of the company closed all valves to dollars for promotion, without which even the best records can take a nosedive.

Seven—By this time, Suzanne DePasse, an Apollo advocate, had left the Creative Division to head up Motown Pictures, and her place was taken by a man named Don Ellis. In the fall of '79, I submitted my budget for the second album to him. It was a courtesy to Don, a formality really, since Suzanne had already OK'd the project. I swiftly received a call from Don: "I don't know if Apollo merits another album."

Six—I was floored. Had Motown completely lost its memory? How many of our greatest superstars took years before hitting? Almost all of them. I refused to let a spiritless mentality infect Apollo's hopes, and I banked on the faith that the company would come to its senses. So I didn't say anything to the kids and immediately went to work on the tracks for the second album.

Five—The gig in Japan came through, a two-month engagement at Club Mugen, the hottest nightspot in Tokyo. It was to start in December. This had the potential to be the shot in the arm that we needed.

Four—Robert L. called me days before we departed, and told me that my salary had been cut by more than half. "What are you all thinking about up there?" I asked him. Berry thinks this group is great, they've got amazing potential. Just let me finish working with them or at least give me a few months."

"No," said Robert. "The company is cutting back, and you are part of the cutback."

Three—I called the guy holding the reins. "Berry, we've just gotten settled in this house. I'm a single parent. I can't afford a salary cutback."

He told me that it was my problem, one I should have thought about before. I asked him what the hell he meant.

"I mean, you've been spending too much time with Apollo and not enough in the office. If you work for the company, you work for everybody."

"Yeah, that's a great thing to say." I tried to use reason. "You know damn well that I can't sit around doing paperwork. What this company needs is to develop new artists. Apollo has the potential to sustain us for years. Think how much time it takes to launch a new act like this. That's exactly what you did for the Jackson 5."

Berry listened to my argument as though I were speaking in Japanese. In California cool he tossed it back, "Well I don't care what I did. You can argue till you're blue in the face. My hands are tied."

We will pause from the countdown to ask an interesting question—who exactly was tying Berry's hands? What powerbrokers could override Berry's decision if he was indeed in favor of a project? Whoever and whatever it was, I was furious at that vague Motown "it"—the penny-pinching, flip entity that had sworn 100 percent backing only to withdraw it before our feet were even on the ground. The idea that "it" was once again Berry himself, playing some heartless, manipulative game to see me fail, was simply too unthinkable. The hopes and dreams of his own son were at stake. To shake off the numbing thought that I was indeed engaged in a struggle with a monster, I tried my damnedest to fathom his point of view. Maybe it was one of those moods in which Berry was feeling used just for money; maybe he was demonstrating to others that he didn't play favorites with ex-wives and with sons. Whatever his reasons were, it was now an even greater task to maintain the enthusiasm of the kids. So I didn't tell Kerry or Cliff or any of Apollo how cold the company was growing toward them and how precarious our financial plight really was.

I did tell them that my salary had been drastically cut and that we'd have to budget expenses. It was my solemn prayer that the Japan trip would generate enough good feedback so that Motown would chalk up enough money for us not to lose the house.

Two—We were sensational stars in Tokyo as Apollo dazzled the audiences four shows a night, six nights a week. It was a magical world in which we pretended that California had fallen into the ocean. I made sure that every moment was filled with happiness, because I knew by now that we were about to return to a financial crunch.

One—We weren't earning much money, especially given the high cost of living in Tokyo. My commission barely covered our expenses. Anticipating the bad weather ahead when we returned to the States, I made a dreaded last resort plea to Berry. In the Christmas spirit he gave us two thousand dollars. I marveled at my chronic inability to second-guess this man. Arriving home a month after that, we were even able to buy Christmas presents, and I had a burst of hope that maybe Berry's testiness had abated. I was three months behind in the rent, which was sixteen hundred dollars a month. Draining all our savings, the pooled amount was enough for only one month.

I was back in my free-fall, plummeting without a net, reaching out in midair with a desperate phone call to Berry. I asked him to either reinstate my salary or advance Apollo enough to work on the second album. "Neither is possible," he said. "There is no company money for Apollo."

I saw my ego splattered below me on the pavement and I was clutching at illusive clouds. "Berry, if you can't help us out with money, could you at least let us use one of your places?" I thought of his several huge houses around town that were usually half empty. I watched them zoom by like rescue helicopters as I continued to plunge. "Berry, isn't Apollo worth at least that to you?" The answer was no. Now I was weeping in front of my sons—something I had never done. Kerry called his father back to request a similar consideration. Berry gave Kerry the same answer. I took that phone from Kerry, a cry choking in my throat. "Look, if you don't want the group, just let us go. Maybe we could do better somewhere else."

"Fine," said the thunder god with a stab of ice. "Your release will be ready tomorrow."

Though we desperately worked on new material and garnered

some interest from other labels, Apollo had an explosive crash landing. Ultimately, the Berry Gordy stigma stymied us—if he wouldn't back his own son then maybe the group wasn't so promising after all, the other A&R heads decided.

Meanwhile, the landlady, who had been bragging that she'd leased a house to the glamorous ex-Mrs. Berry Gordy, had found that after many months of my saying, "Things will get better; give me another thirty days," nothing had improved. Her last call to me had been irate and threatening. I discovered that 1980 was 1964 all over again—New York and the bust and the cold war and then the years of running. I'd been tossed up so high and then with double velocity had been forced down again.

Up in my little office in Hidden Hills, I again paced, as I'd once paced in my bedroom in Detroit when I didn't know where Berry was, as I'd once paced the perimeter of a Manhattan jail. Thrashing around the papers on my desk, I implored the heavens above—what was my crime? The answer resounded in the office— the crime of loving Berry, the crime of having a passion for making music.

In front of me were glaring mementos, contrasts of what was then and what was now. A photograph of Berry, myself, and Kerry on the Hitsville sofa, and a recent clipping Nita had mailed me, a newspaper gossip blurb mentioning that Berry Gordy had just purchased a thoroughbred racehorse for a million dollars. And yellowed score paper, which I now held in my burning palms. It was the song I'd written for Berry after I'd miscarried and he'd stayed with me all those nights in the hospital. "When I Really Need(ed) You" told of a man who had dried the tears of the woman who loved him and who had refused to leave her side when she really needed him there. That was proof of what was then.

I also found the lyrics and melody chart that I'd written in 1976 for "Love Don't Live Here Anymore." I started to read the lyrics, hearing in my mind the hypnotic, plaintive call of the lead vocal. My heart pounded as the words I'd written pierced me to the core. They spoke of abandonment, of a place that was once a loving home now simply a vacancy, of someone asking the un- answerable—why? I threw the page on the floor, unable to read through to the third verse . . . what was now.

There were more scraps and shreds of what remained. A table setting card for a fund raiser Berry and I had attended together only three years before. More photographs of Hitsville: Marvin and Anna, Harvey and Gwen, Smokey and Claudette, Berry and me. The copies of the settlement I'd signed for monies that were now long gone. A haunted picture of me taken not long before I tried to maul Margaret's face with the handle of a gun. It was unbelievable. Berry had recently sent her back to Detroit to a ranch he'd purchased for her. He'd once told me that Margaret was the only woman he'd ever been involved with who had never done *anything* for him, that she was the most selfish person in the world, that he'd done more for her than for anyone else. I'd been one of the main reasons that Berry had amassed his fortune, yet it was Margaret and her son who reaped the monetary rewards of my struggles.

And then I spotted a snapshot of my old mahogany spinet with the mirror. I pressed it to my chest. It was all that I could hold in my heart. The love of my parents and my sisters and brothers— their belief in me. The pride and the dreams of a young girl who loved one thing the most—music. I went downstairs holding the banister, clutching the snapshot, breathing deeply. I was going to make it. I would come out of this storm alive. I had before and I would again.

In the pile of music by our piano I found a copy of *The Motown Story: The First Decade.* I rifled through the pages looking for an old beloved song to play, unable to avoid glancing at the sappy introductions supposedly written by the artists themselves. Here were more pictures—impossibly young faces of people who weren't so young anymore. A strapping, virile Marvin Gaye who now was trying to kill himself, a young Paul Williams who had killed himself. There were the lovely faces of the teenage Supremes. In this picture was a smiling Florence Ballard, now also no longer alive. She'd let herself die, a hopeless case in some welfare dive. Martha Reeves, whom I'd last seen in a straitjacket. I continued to tear through this songbook for some mention of me, my contribution, even an intimation that someone else besides Berry had been there. At last I found the page and covered it with my hand. Please, please let my name appear. Please. This was to be my piece of evidence that my contribution to the past hadn't been erased. It was a photocopy of the now legendary eight-hundred-dollar loan agreement that Berry and I had received from his family. Still not ready to examine it, I thought back to those nights we tried to figure out how we could get that precious amount to produce Marv Johnson's "Come to Me." I lifted my hand to read what appeared on this reprinted document.

I saw the date—January 12, 1959. I read the name of lender—

Ber-Berry Co-op—and the Gordys' old Detroit address. I scanned down the page over the terms of the agreement, until my eyes locked onto what I was looking for. Above the notation of our address, 1719 Gladstone, and our phone number, there were two spaces labeled "Signature of Borrower." One of them contained Berry's familiar signature. The other space was blank.

A few days later, a powerful hammering sounded on our front door. An eviction notice.

I was calm. I'd just signed a new document of my own. A declaration of war.

CHAPTER 16
A&R
1980–1983

I'd never really believed that I could drown. But when I looked for myself in the pages of history and saw that I'd been removed, my last remaining shred of dignity was vanquished. I felt waves of helplessness and humiliation engulf me. The suffocation began in my ears and eyes and spread to my lungs and to my heart. And in the middle of this raging sea, this panic, as I grabbed for passing jagged rocks, the first things that fell into my hands were a pen and a notepad—like a sign from God. I wrote feverishly for many nights, as one possessed. After I finished, I stowed what I had written in a passenger trunk. There in that manuscript, which I thought—for its scathing and incriminating facts—would never see the light of day, I wrote down the truth. And though the text was mildewed by the time I was ready to reopen this Pandora's box, its very presence gave me strength; it validated me. Something else was put into that trunk. My love for Berry. I still owned it, I would love him until my dying day, but I would no longer wear it like a brand that marked me as easy prey. In its place I adorned myself with steel-plated armor, and I began to devise my final strategy. Something extraordinary had happened, and I now owned a secret weapon.

During the Apollo disaster, Berry had inadvertently tipped me off to his greatest weakness: his overwhelming sense of insecurity. It made me his ultimate foe and prohibited him from ever truly loving anyone else but me. These were lessons long in coming, ones that shouldn't have taken me twenty-two years to learn, and ones that would take me another ten years to finally reveal. In the meantime, until I felt ready to take action, I slung the lessons in my little backpack like arrows. I'd forfeited my turn at play under the influence of the heavily seductive promise that we would "work something out." Now three years later it was time again for my move. This time I was going to win.

That steamer trunk and those small arrows, plus an utter disbelief that we would actually be evicted, were nearly all that I had left on the day the city marshall came knocking like a battering ram at my front door. We were given exactly three hours to get our belongings together.

Wearing my new steel-plated armor, I turned from the steel-eyed and steel-voiced city marshall to Kerry, Cliff, and their friend Benny and asked them to move as much furniture as possible to the front yard. The owner had given the marshall a list of things belonging to her, so as we dragged each item of ours out, he checked it against the list.

It was hard enough to decide what we could take and what we would never see again, knowing that I had no money for storage, but the most heartbreaking part was seeing the faces of Eddie and Rya, who arrived home to the specter of that furniture strewn across the front yard. "You better hurry and get your roller skates or whatever you can," I said to them. "We only have two more hours before they lock the doors." I watched as they rushed into the house for the last time. I knew that the worst was yet to come—when they realized that we were going to lose the two ponies.

When our time was up, the marshall closed and padlocked the doors, nailing up a big red sign. We were all out on the front lawn, the kids sitting on their hastily packed suitcases. As the slowing cars of our neighbors and friends passed by us, I lowered my eyes to avoid their appalled faces.

After another hour, Benny spied another member of our extended family driving up. It was the pretty, smart, and supportive Marchella Thompson, Cliff's girlfriend and a senior at Beverly Hills High. She joined Cliff atop a bureau, calling softly over to me, "Don't let this get you down, you just hang in. You're only the most special person in the world."

Finally Cliff spotted our rescuer. "There he is! Ma, look, he's got a moving van and everything." As I raised my eyes to see our redeemer driving up, I shed tears for the first time. In a last-ditch effort, just as the doors were being boarded up, I'd telephoned a very good friend from the past, a man I didn't want to bother, but to whom I knew I could turn. Remarried, with another son by his new wife, Ed Singleton sure was a sight for sore eyes. This was one good guy, who not only helped us pack up the moving van he'd rented but who had also found and paid for a storage space. "Ray, I know you and I know this is only a temporary setback," Ed said as he started up the van's motor. "And besides," he added, "it makes me feel good to be able to help."

We all turned back for one last look at our home in Hidden Hills. Eddie, now thirteen and a half, said, "Don't worry, Mom." At twelve and a half, Rya, with a solemn look, waved good-bye to the ponies. Gazing up at me she said, "Someone will take care of them and then we'll get them back." Kerry, soon to turn twenty, just rubbed his hands together, and threw me one of my old lines—"Next?" Only Cliff, now almost twenty-four, revealed in a subtle flicker of his deep-brown eyes that he knew how serious the situation was. As much as I had shielded him and the others all these years from the circumstances of my relationship with Berry, it had finally dawned on Cliff how dangerous the ongoing game had become.

Marchella gave us a round of hugs, and before she drove off she leaned her head out the car window and said to me, "I've never met anyone as strong as you, Ray." As if she could read my mind, she gave me the high sign. "Go get 'em," said Marchella before flooring the accelerator of her car and peeling out of the driveway. I looked at Cliff and said, "She's a keeper."

And that night after all six of my bunch landed at the two-bedroom apartment belonging to Ed and his wife, Barbara Randolph, I said the same thing to Ed about Barbara. She was a treasure. It had now been ten years since our divorce, and this night was the first night that Ed and I finally got a chance to sit down and talk about what had happened to us: the war at the Donovan Building and my flight from the hold Berry had on me. Now that we were away from Berry's hall of mirrors and now that I was stronger than before, Ed and I were able to reinstate our old friendship that had begun back in New York. Toward the end of a night of laughter and some tears, it was agreed that until the kids and I got back on our feet, Ed would find a place big enough for all of us. And soon we were moving into a nice five-bedroom house that he'd found.

Barbara Randolph quickly became the dearest friend to me and the kids. Her mother, Lillian Randolph, was a renowned actress and drama teacher whose career had spanned forty years all the way up to the late seventies. To my delight, I heard that Lillian had been in one of my all-time favorite movies, *It's a Wonderful Life*, with Jimmy Stewart. Other films included *The Bachelor and the Bobby-Soxer* with Cary Grant and *Hush . . . Hush, Sweet Charlotte* with Bette Davis. Barbara, growing up a child star in Hollywood, had debuted on Art Linkletter's "People Are Funny" and then appeared in such films as *Bright Road, Guess Who's Coming to Dinner?* with Sidney Poitier, and Neil Simon's *Cactus Flower*.

And there was another fluky coincidence, one in a series of many, so it didn't surprise me. When Diana Ross left the Supremes in 1969, Barbara was flown to Detroit to audition for the spot and ended up signing a contract of her own. A couple of singles followed, including H-D-H's "I Got a Feelin'," produced by Hal Davis and Marc Gordon, and her own version of "Can I Get a Witness." After Tammi Terrell died, it was Barbara who toured with Marvin Gaye, singing Tammi's duet parts with him. She also sang briefly with one of the incarnations of the Platters and worked as a DJ for the Armed Forces Radio Network. It was a small world, and somehow, some way, Motown was always the thread, a cord that could never be cut.

As the summer approached, I took one last breather before I undertook the ominous challenges that loomed ahead. I couldn't believe my ears when I received a call from a good friend, Linda Wolfe, who was living in Lake Tahoe. "You heard me," she answered, "I just invited you and your kids up for the summer. I've got a beautiful house here in the mountains. We've got the lake, the recreation center, and the strip for nightlife. I think I can keep you busy."

When one door closes, another door opens, the old saying goes. For me, through the loving support of my family and my friends, many doors had opened. After a summer of sun and mountain air and Linda's marvelous generosity, I packed our bags and turned to Eddie and Rya, who'd become avid water athletes, and asked, "Where would you guys like to live in L.A?"

In unison they replied, "Calabasas Park. On the lake!"

It was entirely out of my price range, a very exclusive area. But I shrugged, smiled, and said "OK, why not?"

Now armed with my secret weapon, the lesson I'd learned from Berry's last attack, I called him and spoke with a steady voice. "Listen, I was the first one on the ship with you. Let me be the last one on the ship when it goes down. And I want the kids on there, too."

"OK," said Berry. Apparently, I'd caught him in a good mood—one of the secrets carried in those strategic arrows I now held. I'd learned that to get a yes from Berry was always a matter of timing. I was ready to go to work, the first steps had been taken. I knew I still had more steps to take, but it was a victory nonetheless.

At the same salary of twenty-five thousand that I'd received three years before at Jobete, I was employed as an assistant to Lee Young, Sr., then head of the Creative Division. The sting of hearing what my pay would be for a job that normally paid approximately seventy thousand was deflected by my many months of toughening. Besides, it was all part of the plan. I immediately hired Cliff for Jobete, and soon I'd have positions opened up for Kerry and Benny, too.

In a few blinks of the eye, and an advance from Berry for a move, I found us a townhouse in Calabasas Park on a sparkling blue man-made lake—in accordance with the kids' wishes. After gathering the gang in our new digs, I was ready to make music.

By 1980, Motown, though solidly established in prosperity and reputation, was no longer at the forefront of creativity. Berry, whose company title was now chairman, was both feared and revered by his underlings. His command post was often for months at a time his home in Bel Air. When he did descend upon the office, it often resembled the spirit of the Spanish Inquisition, as he marched through the halls "restructuring"—"You, you, and you . . . out!—while employees and executives alike quaked in fear. In part, this game of musical chairs was an effort to produce the most efficient team. It was also partly boredom, or that old restlessness, that sent Berry on the rampage. For whatever reason, he was as likely to make a junior member of a division the new chief, having the old chief report to his former inferior, as he was to hire and fire randomly.

When I arrived at my post, I found that, in addition to the constant swirl of changing faces, the actual physical setting at the Sunset Boulevard Motown office was being altered. Workmen were remodeling the entire place. Walls were down, carpet was up, and furniture was scattered about. So I set up a temporary niche in a closetlike room next to Lee Young's office. From this vantage point, I could meet or reacquaint myself with our latest stellar cast of characters.

Nathaniel Montague was simultaneously one of the most interesting and least known figures to ever cut a path through the halls of Motown. Popularly labeled "The Magnificent Montague"—a name inspired by his poetic charm—he was one of the hottest DJs in the country, beginning in Chicago during the early sixties. His favorite tag line, employed every time he played a hot record, was "Burn, baby, burn." Upon migrating to L.A., Montague became the morning DJ for one of the city's biggest black-music stations. Never one to be shy about black pride, he was nonetheless horrified when his trademark tag "burn, baby, burn" came into wide use during the Watts riots of '65, directly intensifying the furor.

Berry hired Montague as a consultant in the mid-seventies to oversee various facets of Motown, a wide-ranging job that brought him closely into contact with top executives. In this position, Montague uncovered numerous scams involving millions of company dollars, and, due in part to his findings, certain well-salaried heads rolled.

After the purge, the would-be hero found that he was resented by the higher echelons as being a spoilsport, even more so than the perpetrators were disliked for trying to rob the company blind. But the straw that broke the camel's back, according to Montague, was that one of the worst transgressors, a top white cohort of Berry's, returned from a prison term and was welcomed back into the fold with open arms. Noting the company's kid-glove treatment of rich, white, sometimes criminal executives and its backhanded dismissal of Motown's black heritage and ex-employees, Montague was outraged. Eventually, he and his lovely wife, Rose, would become disillusioned enough to move on.

And what had become of Barney Ales, otherwise known as Snidely Whiplash? In 1972, when Motown formally left Detroit, Barney stayed in town and managed the careers of a few artists, including post-Temptations David Ruffin, as well as launching the Prodigal record label. After three years, with a minimal cash flow, and missing his exalted status, he came out to Los Angeles to rejoin the ranks.

It had taken Berry a while longer to realize about Barney what I'd always sensed. However, Berry eventually discovered that Barney almost put the company out of business. The whole story of his final parting of the ways with Berry is a matter I would never have enough attorneys to discuss publicly. Fortunately, upon my return to Motown, Barney was there no more.

The company politics, though, had become even more complex than in Barney's heyday. In addition to Berry's chronic and destructive failure to raise the black creative forces up alongside the white controllers, there were now numerous complicated subplots.

Just below Berry on the totem pole was Jay Lasker, president of Motown. An old record-biz pro, Jay had worked at Vee-Jay in Chicago in the early sixties and then at ABC/Dunhill. Jay, like Barney, was a promotion, marketing, and distribution man. A tough character, like Ralph Seltzer before him, Jay had a rep for being unpleasant and abrasive.

Jay Lasker's specialty at Motown was repackaging, taking the existing Jobete catalogue and reissuing it in many different forms—greatest-hits albums and anthologies featuring the most popular Motown songs. According to Berry, Jay's repackaging saved Motown from the near-demise Barney Ales had left behind. Unfortunately, Jay, a shrewd businessman, was not a creative man. And so, with all that repackaging going on, what Motown had to show for itself was a million different albums with "Baby Love" and no new talent.

I was therefore delighted to find that my immediate boss, new A&R director Lee Young, Sr., was a thoroughbred music man—for once, an inspired choice on Berry's part. A veteran musician of many years, Lee was a jazz drummer who had played with many of the greats, including Nat King Cole. His son, Lee Young, Jr., headed Motown's legal department, and his brother, Lester Young, was a renowned tenor saxophonist. He and I were basically of one musical mind, and it looked as if we were going to hit it off just fine.

But first there were tests to pass. The first came when renovations were completed and Lee was assigning offices. As we toured the brightened location of the Creative Division, I was wowed by the front portion. Gorgeous offices were paneled in mahogany, carpeted in plush red or royal blue with matching sofas and padded wet bars, and boasted adjoining bathrooms with monogrammed hand towels. Moving away from the front, rent dropped somewhat, but the offices were still charming. I heard Lee give out the front spaces without a mention of my name. Now to the rear guard he was saying, "Brenda, this is yours" and then "This office is Georgia's." We'd almost reached the end, and only I remained without an office. As we hit the mail room, the whole theme changed—indoor-outdoor carpeting, plaster walls, less space than even the closet I'd had before.

"Uh, this is you," Lee said, cleared his throat, and left.

I was stunned. The office couldn't even accommodate a visitor, and for just me to enter it, I had to turn sideways. To think this was the company I'd helped to form was enough to bring me to tears. But I just let it roll off my back like water. I was the boss's ex-wife, therefore a potential threat; this was a survival move on Lee's part to keep me in a subordinate position. Remembering my overall goal, I swore that from now on there would be no more surprises. I gave myself two years to execute the next steps of my plan.

One important chapter of 1981 began with William "Smokey" Robinson, who had been through quite a long fallow period at Motown. It was in 1972 that he stopped performing with the Miracles, and then, after some time, Smokey quit recording his own music altogether to concentrate on administrative duties. That got old, and for a spell he'd driven Claudette crazy hanging around at home, which eventually spurred him back to recording on his own again. But there were no hits, and he was without direction, especially throughout the late-seventies disco phase. Staff producers saw him as a has-been, claiming, "He has no soul." Smokey had long been seen as a teacher's pet and some of the gloaters weren't sorry to see him out on the ropes.

At one point the company even went into the red with Smokey's albums—something that resulted in Berry finally coming down on Smokey, again to the satisfaction of various onlookers. But, of course, Berry had a short memory when it came to handing out punishment. Shortly after reprimanding Smokey, Berry went to Smokey's house to give him a birthday present of a watch. As Smokey was heaping praise upon the gift, Berry said, "Well, man, I gotta go. Come on outside. There's a car blocking me in your driveway." The two walked out together, Berry poker-faced and Smokey confused. There was a brand-new Rolls-Royce parked alone in the driveway. Berry tossed the keys to Smokey: "It's yours." Through thick and thin, Smokey had passed every test of loyalty, and this was one of his rewards.

His long-term slump, which was tearing away at his ego, had had only a brief respite when he hit with the '79 smash "Cruisin'." Still writing songs, Smokey decided to take a new one to Kim Carnes, whose 1980 version of his song "More Love" had won her much success. Kim Carnes's producer, George Tobin, listened to the song and said, "I want to record this song with you."

"I don't know about that," said Smokey, gun-shy from his recent sales history.

George Tobin, a very shrewd businessman, had the reputation at Motown of a shyster, an ironic viewpoint since there were so many real shysters employed by the company. The owner of a fabulous recording studio, George would later produce and manage teen pop star Tiffany. George and I would work together on many later productions, sometimes also with his skillful production associate, John Duarte. In the late eighties he would hire my daughter, Rya, to be in a Tiffany video, as well as engage my arranging and choreography assistance in a Supremes-styled number called "Radio Romance."

When he saw Smokey's hesitation, and knowing what his own reputation at Motown was, George offered, "Look, tell Motown I'll do the whole album on you for nothing, since you're in the hole there. But I want double the points Motown usually gives," "points" being the percentage points in the profits. The going rate given to producers from Motown was anywhere from two to four points on a record.

Smokey took George's proposal to Lee Young, Jr., top dog at the legal department, and Young laughed. "You mean Tobin's going to put out his money to do this album, and all he's talking about is points? Sure, we'll sign the deal for the eight points." The Motown attorney thought he'd just pulled a fast one—Tobin was assuming all the risk.

George's usual charge to produce an album was around one hundred fifty thousand dollars, though the actual cost to him was less because he owned the recording facility. Still, when he and Smokey went into the studio, Tobin knew he was taking a considerable gamble. The two of them were holding their breath while the company sat back and twiddled its thumbs waiting for the album and the single, both entitled *Being with You,* to die on the vine. As it turned out, 1981 was a good year for Smokey Robinson and George Tobin. Their endeavor was a super smash. The single went double platinum, Smokey was back in the saddle, and Tobin was cleaning up. And the company got mud on its face.

That same year there was a drama starring the all-time diva herself—Diana Ross. By the early days of 1981, her marriage to Bob Silberstein had disintegrated, and she was in a celebrity dating mode with people like Gene Simmons of the group Kiss. But, more than ever, it seemed what she really wanted was to pursue her relationship with Berry Gordy. Her quest to ceremoniously make their union legal was unsuccessful, as Berry made it very clear that nothing could alter the positioning of the seesaw that he and Diana rode.

Financially, Diana hadn't been raising much revenue lately in record sales. She'd been a megastar for years but probably hadn't amassed the fortune that befit her hard work. By 1981 all but one of her movies had fizzled out at the box office, so she may have experienced what other celebs have: with the world bowing down to your glamour and stature, you peek into your bank account and discover the coffers are bare.

So, disappointed in the realms of love and money, Diana went to Berry and lay down all her chips. RCA Records had just made a twenty-five-million-dollar bid to sign her. Since Berry had already nixed her love ultimatum, she may have thought, "Well, look, if there is no romantic relationship here with Berry, then I'm crazy to stay at Motown where I'll never make this kind of money." Out came her second ultimatum: "Business is business, as you say. So, if we're talking business, you either top their offer, or even match it, and I'll stay with Motown. I've been hanging around here because I love you. But now I've got to make some money."

Berry was desperate. He didn't want to marry her, didn't want to lose her, and absolutely couldn't match RCA's offer. The salt on the wound was that he'd barely made a dime off Diana Ross—supporting the lifestyle of a queen had been a costly business. He'd only begun to recoup a portion of his investment. First he leaned toward marrying her. Then he investigated the possibility of selling Jobete to raise the twenty-five mil. In one tiny moment of lucidity he saw that he was about to gamble his entire fortune to secure hers, a risk that could bankrupt the company overnight. So the bottom line to Diana was, "I don't have the money."

Diana walked away from the bargaining table in May and signed with RCA. For Berry it was devastatingly ironic. He'd sacrificed so much, left scads of other careers in the lurch, to realize his dream with Diana Ross. He'd put all his eggs in one basket, and in the end she'd left him anyway.

Some of the other eggs in Berry's basket were starting to scramble off Motown's roster. It was no surprise to anyone when Marvin Gaye, the first and earliest warrior for artistic control, defected to Columbia Records. His personal life before the move had become increasingly complicated. He was a mess—running from the IRS, fighting an unflagging drug addiction, enduring mounting paranoia—and he was unable to finish any of his musical projects. His already strained relationship with Berry simply snapped when the company rejected Marvin's work in progress, seized the uncompleted tracks, edited and overdubbed without his approval, and released the album *In Our Lifetime*. When this transpired in January of 1981, Marvin exiled himself to London with an oath never again to record for Motown. He also threatened to never record again, period, if Berry didn't release him from his contract. Berry thought he knew a lost cause when he saw one and agreed for Marvin to entertain offers from other labels. If Motown could get a good price on Marvin's contract, the artist could be released.

A year or so later Marvin's contract would wind up at CBS Records, while he himself would be in Belgium trying to regroup. Through another ironic handshake of fate, he'd be working again with Harvey Fuqua, his original mentor. Their efforts would produce "Sexual Healing," Marvin Gaye's last great hit. For a time we thought that he was indeed on the mend. Coming to terms with the IRS, he returned to the States for a tour. And for those who knew him and loved him, our fingers were crossed. However, his demons were very real—the scars of youth, the illusive dragon of cocaine that he could never slay, and the resulting paranoia.

By 1982 my life was in a precarious balance. In the year behind me were some overwhelmingly positive strokes. Lee Young's Creative Division, in which I'd played a critical though behind-the-scenes role, had scored some great hits, including one of my favorites, "Let It Whip" by the Dazz Band, produced by Reggie Andrews. There was a certain tactic I was using—the "lay low" technique—which involved maintaining a good relationship with Lee, in spite of my tin can office and the constant threat of trouble. This constant threat was really the ambience of fear bred by Berry's divisive methods, sowed from his seeds of suspicion intended to keep everyone on their toes. Because of this, and because of my history with Berry and with Motown, Lee couldn't fully trust me. I understood this and I worked within these parameters; it helped me to complete another step in my master plan. So far so good.

And with my little arrows and that steel armor protecting my heart, I'd been able to deal with Berry without my old reactions of despair or suspicion. Our relationship during this first year had run the gamut from a total lack of communication, to occasional contact, to begrudging respect, to a fairly familiar ease. In times gone by, this last stage would have been a trap, but I was a lot smarter now. So when Berry dropped by one day, looking for me and found me stuck back in the tin can mail room, I didn't say a thing. As he walked up with that cute, familiar knock-kneed amble, I refused to feel anything. With no room to sit in my office, he plopped down on the edge of the desk, giving me his old tongue-in-cheek stare, and said, "Oh, so this is your office?"

I dodged the dart and only smiled. "What's up?" I asked lightly.

Caught off guard, he took a beat, and then asked me to come to his office so we could have a little more space—a mild under-statement—to discuss an idea. As it turned out, the project he had in mind was right up my alley: the possibility of turning Hitsville into a museum. He had been discussing a plan with his sister Esther and wanted me to go to Detroit, investigate the pros and cons, and return with a report. I accepted at once, thinking it would also be an opportunity to spend some time with my parents. The latest word from home was that Daddy hadn't been feeling very well and Mama was no longer up to taking care of him all by herself.

"I hope I'm not interrupting anything." Skip Miller from the promotion office stuck his head in the door. Looking harried, he said he was there about a new José Feliciano record on Motown called "Everybody Loves Me." Berry was crazy about the song, but none of the pop stations were playing it. Skip said, "We can't get that record played because the DJs say it's too egotistical."

"What the. . . ?" Berry stopped himself, shaking his head. "That's ridiculous. It's not about some cat saying 'Oh everybody loves *me*.' It's 'Everybody loves me, but the one I want to love me is *you*.' Now, how can we get this across and move this record, Skip?"

"Listen," I said to Berry in my new and improved way. "I will get this record played for you in Detroit."

He studied me seriously. "OK. If you get this record played on any of the pop stations, I will definitely see to it that you're rewarded."

"Good," I said. "If I succeed, I want two months' rent paid."

Berry's eyebrows raised, but he agreed. And so I set off for Detroit with a lot on my mind.

Once there, I enlisted the aid of Motown's promotion man in Detroit, Ray Henderson, and together we hit station after station, meeting with incredible opposition—the record wasn't happening elsewhere and *Billboard* hadn't picked it up. But I was a woman with a mission, and at last WJLB's program director, who really loved the song, agreed to put it on the playlist. Berry, very impressed, paid the price the minute I returned.

Before that happened, though, something infinitely more important occurred. On May 25, 1982, Ashby Mayberry died. Daddy was eighty-two years old. Even with a year of cancer, he was still one of the most handsome, proudest men in the world, and continued to stay out of bed until a few days before his death. Here was the man who'd stood on top of our house during the worst of the Detroit riots, putting out the fires with a garden hose. He was invincible; how could he ever die? In our last conversation, I'd asked him, "Daddy, are you afraid?"

"No," he had answered with certainty, "not at all." And, taking my hand, Daddy's words were, "You take care of Mama for me, Raynoma." Until his dying day, he'd never stopped being as in love with his Lucille as he was on the first day they'd met. To honor Daddy's request, I set up a schedule with my brothers and sisters, all seven of them, to each come one day of the week and help Mama after Daddy was gone.

I took courage in knowing what a full life my father had lived, in how much he and I had loved one another, and in remembering how he'd taught me to dream. At the funeral parlor I watched my mother, the strongest person in the world, keeping her head high and straight. I looked around and saw my brothers and sisters, their husbands and wives and children, and thought about the legacy my father and mother had created. And, somewhere very close to me, I could almost hear Daddy's voice evaluating the stately ceremony of his own funeral: "Hey, this is very up-to-date." I knew now, with all the hopes and dreams that still lay before me, Daddy would be with me every step of the way.

Before I left town, I spent an afternoon with my beloved brother Mike Ossman, his wife, Sandy, and their kids, Shelley and Chris. Mike's eyes seemed cloudy and though he was still incredibly attractive, his spirits were low, making him appear much older than his years. "Ray, how's it going—really?" Mike's voice sounded hoarse.

"Mike, it's really great. I'm going to do it this time." I winked at him. "You give me about five years and I'll have you out in L.A. working with me again. Deal?"

"Deal!" He brightened and then asked more seriously, "How are you and Berry getting along?" Mike, more than anyone, knew what I'd been through over the years; he was my soul mate. Even so, I wasn't ready to reveal to anyone what I was really feeling. So I answered, "Berry who?" and got a familiar deep laugh from my brother. And the road I was traveling felt easier, knowing that with each victory that came, I'd be scoring one for Daddy in heaven and another for Mike in Detroit.

"Well, what do you think?" The prospectus for the Hitsville museum that I'd handed to Berry upon my return to Los Angeles was awesome. I'd met with Dr. Fred Cummings, the director of the Detroit Institute of Arts, and his enthusiasm led me to meetings with architects, other curators, and various specialists, all well versed in launching a project of this scope. My report outlined city ordinance requirements and Chamber of Commerce demographics and breakdowns on estimated numbers of visitors to the Hitsville Museum. I envisioned a wax museum within the larger facility, a video auditorium, special revolving exhibits, a collection of Motown-related art commissioned to black artists, and even a tie-in with Disney. Berry was flabbergasted and thrilled at the same time.

But a number of circumstances would soon dictate that the project be put into other hands, and most of my recommendations wouldn't be effected. Which was perhaps a blessing in disguise, since the next series of events would require all my concentration.

The changes began when Berry called Lee Young, Sr., my boss, to a meeting at Berry's home. Berry told Lee he was unhappy with the number of hits that had come out during the past year. In all objectivity, Lee had done everything in his power. His job was a thankless one and, like much of the music business, depended upon capturing the public's whimsical tastes.

"Look, man," said Lee. "I know I'm doing a good job, but if you're not happy with what I'm doing, I'll just quit." Lee should have first asked me about Berry's reaction to ultimatums.

"Oh, you mean you quit?" Berry asked.

"Well, I, uh . . . ." Lee realized his mistake, but it was too late to backpedal.

"I'll tell you what," Berry decided, "you didn't quit, you're fired." Berry never premeditated firing Lee, but he'd been put on the defensive, a position he didn't like very much.

After hearing the buzz about Lee, I received a call from Berry telling me he wanted to see me right away. When I went to his office, his first words to me were, "Listen, I've got something I want you to do, a job. Did you know I just fired Lee?"

Honesty being a good policy, I answered, "Yes."

"I want you to take over the Creative Division."

Feeling a mix of shock, happiness, glory, suspicion, and sympathy for Lee, I stalled for time. "Well," I said, "what happened?"

Almost distracted, Berry said, "Aw, Lee came over and I told . . . well, never mind. You've got the job."

I then used my new strategy. "I don't want the job. It's a horrible job. I know what hell Lee goes through every day. And I like Lee; I don't want him to think I've usurped his position."

"Well," concluded Berry, "whether you want it or not, you've got it. Be here tomorrow morning ready to go."

And thus began my reign as A&R director. My plan was falling into place even sooner than I had thought. With the exception of Jay Lasker, every single employee—from Suzanne DePasse to Lee himself—called to congratulate me and to wish me luck. They all knew that I would need it. Since challenge was my middle name, I was not bothered as much by the demands of the job as by the need of not becoming overly confident in the position. If I was suddenly being made the golden girl, then I knew also that meant a potential trip to the doghouse, at any given mood of Berry's. But damn, it sure was nice to have a decent title again—vice president and operational director of the Creative Division. Having been the first executive vice president of the whole company, it seemed that this was long overdue. The other plum in the deal was that I was moved into Lee's fabulous office with the bathroom and the monogrammed towels. Berry later explained his decision: "First of all I was very impressed with the museum report. But also I picked you for the job just so you could get the big office. I hated that place they stuck you in."

While I was able to handle my feelings about Berry, I still faced the political and dangerous threat of Jay Lasker, who was tight with Lee. The interoffice grapevine told me that Jay was disgusted that I got Lee's job.

As had happened so many times in my various stints back at Motown, a fantastic support team emerged, and this group was rooting for me all the way, warning me about the blunt tactics I might expect from Jay. These longtime Motown veterans—Brenda

Boyce, Georgia Ward, Fay Hale, Miller London—had been valuable cohorts while I'd served as an assistant to Lee and would continue to back me up in the arduous role I'd just taken on.

My first contact and showdown with Jay happened a few days after I'd begun my new post. When the phone rang and a man's voice barked, "Where are this year's projected releases?" I guessed it was Jay and ran into his office with the list I'd fortunately already made. "Very good," he said without further ado. The megastars at the company were still Stevie Wonder, Smokey Robinson, Rick James, the Commodores, and Lionel Richie, who would soon evolve into one of the music industry's all-time greats.

"Oh, wait," he piped up just as I was about to leave. "Who's this group, Kagny and the Dirty Rats?" He was referring to a band I'd just signed, a fantastic group of guys that Benny Medina and Kerry Gordy were producing, which happened to include the talents of a certain Cliff Liles along with the promising artistry of Michael Dunlop and Jerry Thompson. If I could get this passed by Jay, it would be another score in the game plan.

"Oh," I said to Jay, "just some band. They're hot." To which Jay gave me a squint and then waved me off. And such was the fairly innocuous interaction we would maintain for the most part, as I strengthened my vow not to be cut down by politics.

Heading the Creative Division meant handling every detail pertaining to every artist on the Motown roster. Supervising careers, teaming producers with artists, choosing material, setting up sessions, establishing and maintaining budgets, listening to products, coordinating release schedules, keeping track of monies artists received, negotiating deals, arranging travel schedules, and then some. A mind-boggling job with a hundred thousand daily decisions and literally an average of three hundred phone calls a day. And everybody wanting an answer yesterday.

I resurrected my favorite line—"Next?" After wading through the enormous assortment of issues left hanging after Lee's departure, I divided them into two phases. First, it was necessary to firm up the roster—to cut a list of seventy potential artists in half. I took a deep breath and plunged in, making instinctual, straight-from-the-hip decisions on career matters that would have once had me sweating for nights. In a few weeks I was done. It was a trial by fire.

The second phase —actually making music—began. I started putting packages together. I teamed up artists and writers and producers in ways that I knew would work and in ways that I knew would produce new sounds. The old Motown system was long gone, and a serious problem I confronted was the dangerous decrease in the number of in-house producers. To meet the demands of our growing number of artists and to keep in stride with the current marketplace, we needed fresh blood in our producing staff. It was in this pursuit that I unwittingly stepped into a new game, one with many players.

My first move was to get Phil Ramone to come in and produce Smokey. Ramone, a well-respected pro, was on a roll from his work on Billy Joel's "Just the Way You Are" and all its follow-up smashes. Smokey hadn't scored a hit for at least a year, and I knew the two together could work a perfect crossover pop bonanza. On the telephone, I had Phil all psyched to work with Smokey, and I told him I'd be right back with the particulars. But upon seeking an OK from Berry, I got a nice but flat no, with the explanation that it was unnecessary to go outside the company for producers—which was exactly what I knew we needed to do. The silent players in Berry's move were, of course, the money people at the company; Berry's attitude reflected their inability to take creative risks. Undaunted, I would try this play again in a couple of years by proposing that Michael Masser be brought in to work with Smokey; again I would be shot down. And even when Masser had several huge hits with Whitney Houston, I didn't say "I told you so." The only way to win this game was to take nothing personally—and so far it was working.

The next incident had some political undercurrents that I knew nothing about. Willie Hutch, a triple-threat talent—a producer, writer, and musician (and a former Motown artist)—came to me with a song that had that good old I-hear-a-hit feel. "In and Out" was a funky, sexy, tongue-in-cheek, R&B dance number that I danced right over to Berry's house for him to hear. This time Berry gave me a thumbs-up on the song and on signing the artist. So Willie Hutch, an earthy guy with an irrepressible sense of humor, was the first person I signed in my new position. This was the start of an immediate friendship between the two of us. He would become my most valuable collaborator in the coming years and would then go on to become Berry's right-hand music man on numerous projects, including the score to *The Last Dragon*—one of the few Motown movies to make money.

It turned out, though, that Willie and Jay Lasker, from the

ABC/Dunhill days, despised one another. Although I didn't know it at the time, I'd just signed the guy Jay once told, "You'll never work in this town," or some version thereof. When "In and Out" went wild in England but didn't make much noise in the States, I was under the distinct impression that the record was deliberately undersold domestically by Motown's commander of promotion, Jay Lasker. But as I have said before, this time around there weren't going to be any surprises, and I just kept on trucking.

"It's for you, Miss Ray," the receptionist announced one morning. "It's a Reverend Al Sharpton." She and I exchanged shrugs. Later, of course, the Reverend Al would achieve a certain notoriety for his particular brand of gospel, but at this time, he wasn't anybody I knew.

"This is Ray Singleton. What can I do for you?" I said into the phone and heard a formal announcement that the Reverend was representing Mr. James Brown. At the mention of this name my heart began to beat wildly. Wait until I tell Cliff—the representative of his greatest hero was calling me.

"Yes, Mr. Brown is interested in your company. Would you be interested in signing him?"

Gulp. "Well, yes." And then, regrouping, I requested authoritatively that Mr. Brown give me a call. The next thing I knew I was chatting up a storm with the real McCoy—Cliff was going to faint when he heard about it.

"So what do y'all want me to do?" James asked in his Georgia drawl.

"Why don't you come on out and we'll talk about it," I ventured.

"OK," James said. "You send for us and we'll all come. That's me, the Reverend Al Sharpton, and my . . ." and he rattled off four more names of his traveling entourage.

Being much shrewder now than I was in the past, I didn't proceed until I'd received an in-person approval from Jay Lasker. "Jay, would you be interested in signing James Brown?"

Jay looked up from a sales report, nearly dropped his cigar, and wore something that approximated a smile. "Yeah. Sure I'm interested."

Jay's quasi-enthusiasm turned authentic when I told him what else James was offering. "For you, baby, I'll sign for nothing," the very Godfather of Soul had said to me. Artists in his league usually asked for up to the millions for advance money. What a deal! Jay approved, and I called James back to discuss the next steps.

"There's just one thing, though," he said. "Before I sign, I got to talk to Berry Gordy." I went to give James the phone number and he interrupted me. "No, he's got to call me."

Gulp. I was holding my fort in A&R so well, I really wasn't in the mood for an added tussle of egos. However, the coup of signing James Brown would be worth it. "You know, Berry, I'm working with James Brown and he said he'd sign with us for nothing. His only stipulation is that he wants you to call him."

"Me call him? For what?"

"You know, he likes me fine, he knows I'm in charge of A&R, but he wants to deal directly with you. You're the chairman of the board, he's James Brown. I'm great, but I'm not Berry Gordy."

I could have lip-synched Berry's next line, "There's no way I'm calling James Brown."

"Oh, come on, Berry," I said, "I've got him where he's about to sign and he's not asking for any money. And Jay thinks it's great, too."

"I don't care. I'm not calling James Brown. If that's the deal breaker then forget the deal. I've got a lot to do and I don't need to be calling James Brown."

Several sleepless nights later, after more peppy calls from James wanting to know when to expect Berry's call, after numerous beleaguered calls to Berry, and after James finally giving a deadline for Berry's call, I came up with an inspiration. I cooed in the sweetest tone to Berry, one last time, "I understand how ridiculous this is and you know it's really not going to hurt to call him. Just give him a little call. He deserves that kind of respect and he is the Godfather of Soul." And then I doused the last bit with sugar, "I mean, I'm sure he was even your idol in the music business at one time." I knew that calling up Berry's past got one of two very powerful reactions from him—wrath or tenderness. Nothing in between and no way to predict the outcome. I held my breath until Berry responded, "OK, Ray, for you I'll call him."

So Berry called James, James called me back, and shortly after that he was out in California. With his entourage. In their alligator shoes. James played me some of his funky material and I was setting my sights high. But the best part was introducing Cliff to his idol, which then led to some interest on James's part in producing Cliff's band, Kagny and the Dirty Rats.

After James left, though, with the whole company aflutter

about his signing with us, Berry axed the deal. It seemed that a friend of Suzanne DePasse—who had dealt with the Godfather of Soul previously—had suggested to Berry that James Brown was a potential disaster. (Of course, he went on to have some big hit records elsewhere.)

Though I could hardly bring myself to tell the guys in Georgia that the deal was off, I finally did. While there was some reason for Berry to worry about the strange behavior of such an erratic cat as James Brown, I maintained that we could have worked with him. A few years later, Kerry, who was by then working for Berry, decided that he was going to call and get James Brown for the company.

James responded facetiously, "Yeah, Mr. Gordy. I'll sign with Motown."

In a state of elation, Kerry paused to remember that James once offered to sign with me for nothing, and was just about to propose a modest retainer when James added, "But I wants a billion dollars to sign!"

So ended the two tales of James Brown at Motown.

By far the victories were outweighing the losses, and as the months sped by I started thinking about some new projects. One wonderful experience was working with Jean Carn, a sensational vocalist, and Norman Connors, on their album project. Another favorite collaboration was with producer Winston Monseque and a client of his, Bobby Nunn. Not exactly a foreign face at Motown, Winston also managed and produced singer Tata Vega and was now married to Iris Gordy, who'd since broken off with Johnny Bristol. Winston brought in a single for Bobby that I heard right off as having real potential.

"Listen, the song is great," I told Winston, "but the record isn't happening. What you need are some horn licks on it." After several minutes of ranting and raving, Winston calmed down and said that if I could get the money, he'd try. As I expected, the horns transformed "She's Just a Groupie" from a decent record to a smash. Touché. Next there were Teena Marie, Billy Preston, and DeBarge with a knock-your socks-off single entitled "All This Love."

In this positive frame of mind, I geared up for my next project, which would require all my resources. Berry had been bragging to everyone that I could handle anyone in the studio. He may have been already taking bets on how I would pull off the next one. At any rate, he called and asked, "Are you interested in working with David Ruffin?" I answered, "Sure," hoping that David, a phenomenal vocalist, had gotten himself together since his gloomy expulsion from the Temptations.

Jay, on the other hand, was opposed to the project from the outset: "I don't trust David Ruffin. Are you sure you can handle him?" "Absolutely," I answered.

I was basically going in on a dare, as the task was comparable to taming a wild bucking bronco. David Ruffin, known for his horrible temper and for his hardcore addiction to drugs, had a stormy relationship with Berry and the company—including a bitter lawsuit. His post-Tempts solo hits were few and far between—"My Whole World Ended (The Moment You Left Me)" in '69, "Walk Away from Love" in '75—and in '79 he'd left for Arista, where nothing happened either.

As I sized up the situation, it occurred to me that the only time David probably felt like a human being was when he was singing. I'd seen him perform solo once at the Twenty Grand, and before going on he was just sitting backstage, a space case, as stiff and cold as a statue. But all of a sudden, when he was announced, there was this amazing metamorphosis, and he came alive—it was show-time! He tore the house down that night, slaying the women right and left with his begging act, "Oh, baby, baby, please, sweet darling, please don't leave me." And then after the show, he crept back into his shell, completely alone in a theater full of people calling his name. As long as I could keep David in the performing mode, I knew I stood a chance.

Choosing a producer was a critical decision. Everybody was calling me begging to be the one. I finally settled on George Tobin, whose high-tech studio could cost us far less than anyone else's—especially if we had to go into a lot of overtime with David, which was a strong possibility.

After I extracted an OK from Jay on Tobin, I found out that David had an IRS debt of fifty thousand dollars hanging over his head and was about to be thrown in jail any minute. How could he possibly sing with that on his mind, David demanded. I sang my own soothing song, telling him not to worry, that after the album was cut with George we'd pay his taxes.

When David arrived from Detroit, I had accommodations lined up for him in one of L.A.'s finest hotels, handed him a portion of his twenty-five-thousand-dollar advance, and crossed my fingers. George called me after their first day in the studio and was practically crying tears of happiness. "Listen to this," he played the vocal for me over the phone, and it was better than great. David Ruffin was back.

Unfortunately, David Ruffin was back for only two or three sessions over a period of two weeks. The rest of the time he was holed up in his hotel room, all of his advance money gone to the purchase of drugs, we suspected. Most of my time and George's was spent outside that hotel room door. As we pleaded and implored and cajoled, David responded only with threats to kill George Tobin. Then he'd change his mind and go to the studio for another brilliant day. I started to panic: this wasn't just a game; it was a perfect opportunity for a showdown in which Jay could roll my head right along with George's.

In the end we canceled the album, which resulted in more furor from Jay and in a lawsuit by George to procure his full fee on the deal. We sent David back to Detroit, where he was promptly handcuffed and toted off to jail, which we'd warned him about over and over. David's last conversation with me was, "Ray, baby, it's horrible here. I've been in this jail for two days and they ain't even brought me a bar of soap to wash my ass with. Get me out of here."

"David, I did everything. All you had to do was put your vocal on that damn album with Tobin. You wouldn't do it. I almost lost my job messing with you." Within a few months I would be amending my comment to "I lost my job messing with you."

It happened quickly. One morning I received a congratulatory phone call from Berry about what a fabulous job I was doing. He was right; I was. Even though I'd heard rumors that Jay was aiming to replace me, I was placated by Berry's hearty support.

So I trotted over to Jay's office to show him my list of projected releases for the coming year, and before I got a word out he said, "I've hired someone else for your job. His name is Steve Barri. He's coming in tomorrow, so get your things out of the office today."

For a minute I was dumbfounded, but then I remembered my vow—no more surprises—and I stared at him defiantly.

"Oh, uh, Steve is a great producer," Jay said.

"Yeah, I'm a great producer, too, what's that got to do with this job?"

It was the first time I'd seen him hedge. "Look—women

should be in the kitchen. Anyway, you don't have a say in this. Just move into the office next to Steve's." My old closet.

"Wait a minute," I said. "Are you some kind of male chauvinist? Don't you have any respect for a woman's ability?"

"Not really," he said.

"And what about your wife's?"

"Hers neither."

It turned out that Jay had been planning to bring in Steve Barri, his pal from ABC/Dunhill, all along, and was just using me to cover the fort until that time. Berry also had known on the morning of his call to me what Jay had in store. Steve, to his credit, was a genuine music man and seemed embarrassed about what had happened. Also, to my credit, I took the step down as an opportunity to garner an overdue raise. I asked for a hundred thousand dollars to stay on after my demotion. I didn't get that much, of course, but I was now much more proud of my paycheck. That is until one day, three months after the arrival of Steve, for whom I'd spent enormous energy passing on the specifics of the impossibly demanding job. On that day I got a pink slip along with my increased paycheck. I would find out later that Jay Lasker had been so anxious about maintaining control that he'd given Berry an ultimatum: "If you keep her, I quit."

This, it seemed, was one of the few ultimatums Berry accepted. After I received this piece of news I was filled with what seemed to be the buildup of several millenniums worth of anger. With arrow poised, I called him up, and into the telephone I let out a blood-curdling cry, *"Berry!!!"*

"OK," he said, "I know. Don't worry about it. We'll just do something else. How about if I transfer you to my payroll and we start a new production company?"

Squinting my eyes, I lowered my arrow and said, "Yeah? Well . . . great. When do we start?"

"Right away," Berry answered. "Why don't you come over and we'll talk about it?"

Well, what do you know, Berry Gordy and I were partners again. Best of all, I was moving way ahead of my own schedule. In one fell swoop, I had completed more steps of my plan. This one was for Daddy, the next one would be for Mike.

CHAPTER 17
SUPER THREE
1983-1985

It wasn't exactly a full partnership, since the money was Berry's. We were still Motown, but we had an independent budget, which he controlled as chairman of the board, and with which we sought to produce the artists who were the cream of the crop. Also, when he decided it would behoove our venture to bring in Suzee Ikeda, who'd also been booted by Jay Lasker, I was all in favor of the threesome. Suzee had proved her stuff over the years as an aide to Berry, as product manager to the Temptations and Lionel Richie, and right-hand gal to Michael Jackson; she'd even recorded a few sides of her own as a Motown artist. Suzee and I now shared common ground: open animosity toward Jay.

Berry dubbed the triumvirate Super Three, and with a lot of positive energy, we staked out independent turf—our own offices and studio. When the expense of purchasing a new facility became overwhelming, a proposal was brought in by Guy Costa, who would come to play a key role in our venture.

Guy, the technical whiz who'd pioneered the entire Motown studio complex, put in a bid for us to headquarter at the new Hitsville Studios on Romaine Street in Hollywood. Not only would we have two state-of-the-art twenty-four-track studios at our disposal; we could also overhaul a large room that was being used for storage. What a deal!

Ecstatic about regaining so much lost ground, I readied for the move while contemplating Guy Costa. On the plus side, he was technically without peer. As A&R director, I'd always been a proponent of his, having observed him in the studio. At one point I'd even blocked a move of Jay Lasker's to fire Guy. On the minus side, Guy was, to put it bluntly, a schizo, a man whose cheerful accommodating manner alternated with a primal blinding temper. Just forty years old, a bit overweight, around five-foot-ten, Guy had a full head of prematurely white hair and wore horn-rimmed glasses. He was also a frustrated songwriter and the brother of Don Costa, who was a respected musician and arranger before becoming an A&R man at ABC/Paramount. Yes, I thought, anticipating some of his foul-mouthed displays, Guy's was the classic male inferiority complex. I kept this in mind when carving the game plan. Unfortunately, Berry had other ideas.

"You did what?" Unbeknownst to me, Berry had been entertaining a notion to give Guy overall responsibility for Super Three, in effect making Guy our creative director. Once again Berry was confusing technical smarts with artistic vision. Guy Costa could capture anybody else's genius on tape, but he himself couldn't even tap his foot to a beat. I rebelled; this was my new baby at stake.

"Berry, there is no way that this could work. You're putting Super Three in a losing pattern from square one."

He shot back to me, "Nevertheless, I am giving Guy Costa this responsibility."

Later I asked the third partner how she felt about Costa as director. Suzee replied, "There's no way I can work for him." But there we were, the all-knowing Oz had spoken, and all I could do was kick the matter under the rug and continue full-speed ahead, working secretly on the big bang that was going to come at the end of 1983.

That year was one of stepping stones. To launch Super Three, Berry pulled some of the artists from the Motown roster, including Smokey, the latest version of the Temptations, the Four Tops, Charlene, Syreeta, and Gene Van Buren, among others. My old pal Don Fletcher became my administrative assistant. Together we transformed the big storage room at the studio into a glorious office space.

Looking about myself in rapture, I declared, "This is *it!*" A breath of fresh air in warm earth tones, it was a wide and clean space. Instead of a large, dominating desk, we elected to place a small one in a corner, which gave emphasis to the piano, plump sofa, and cozy cocktail table. Of utmost importance, the door was to be permanently left open for artists and producers to come in at any time. In this spirit of the original Hitsville days, it was "all for one and one for all."

Guy, it was clear from the beginning, knew that he was in way over his head. The first telling exchange occurred in the control room one day during a session. Pointing to a studio full of black musicians and singers, he confided, "When we started, I didn't know how I was going to do this job, because I didn't know how I was going to relate to black people." Damn, I thought, how the hell could anyone have gotten this far in the music industry, not to mention the twentieth century, without getting to know black people? So I used the occasion, as I would others, to address Guy's insensitivities and to point out how they undermined his finer qualities. He welcomed the constructive criticism, saying that he was already trying to quell his temper. Often however, he simply wouldn't realize how patronizing he was. We all relied on Diane Martin, an attractive Motown veteran, now Guy's administrative assistant, to keep the peace.

Thank goodness for Don Fletcher, a chivalrous and patient gent if ever there was one. With a perpetually kind expression, the patience of Job, and always a debonair hat, Don had to his credit a backlog of Jackson 5 collaborations—"Dancing Machine," "Get It Together," and "Body Language." He also contributed a wealth of knowledge gained from his having spent the seventies as the right-hand dude to the immensely talented Hal Davis. Everyone involved with Super Three, even Guy Costa, loved Don.

The Motown 25 special, an event I was anticipating with dread, was fast approaching. Despite the fact that I'd just drawn the great artist Junior Walker—Mr. "Shotgun" himself—out of the forgotten regions of Battle Creek, Michigan, and was revving up to close a deal for him with Super Three, I knew that I wouldn't be granted even an honorable mention on the stage that night.

While I was determined not to be surprised anymore, the reality of it cut me to the bone. It was the same feeling all over again of opening up the Motown book to find that my name had been erased, that crippling shock at everyone who could have come forward to be my witness and then did not. Add to that sadness my feelings for the others who'd also written the gospel of Motown and who weren't acknowledged or even invited. Where was Marv Johnson? The Marvelettes? Or Mabel John?

I had a revelation about Berry that came at the climax of the show. I realized that he had an unforgivable inability to be my witness and it altered the tone of the game. This was no longer a passionate love/hate, win/lose, play-for-play, touché battle song. This was my life. And before I would be ready to take up my pen— the mightiest sword of all—there were still two more bridges to cross. I was more determined than ever.

So fortified, I went backstage after the Motown 25 show and found myself, even as a visiting outsider, hugging all the familiar old friends. Brian Holland and Norman Whitfield. The Tempts, Martha Reeves, and Mary Wells. To Junior Walker I said, "Hope you're ready to work tomorrow. I got a go-ahead on the *Blow the House Down* album—you're signed!" Soon I would be orchestrating projects at Super Three for the Temptations, for Norman Whitfield, for the Four Tops, and for a reunion with Holland-Dozier-Holland.

"May I have this dance?" Marvin Gaye asked me at the post-show party, and we whirled on to the dance floor amid a swirl of finery. Our smiles were affectionate as we moved to the music, to a melody that was mixed with both our joys and sorrows. He leaned into my ear, speaking in his whisper voice, "You've just 'out-Gwen-and-Anna'd' Gwen and Anna." I laughed at the compliment—those Gordy sisters were as gorgeous and stylish as ever. Oh, Marvin, I wanted to say, dancing there with him—fight just a little bit harder. For all his demons, he was still one of the most gracious, charming, and sensual men I would ever meet. Although I was aware of the forces tormenting him, I had no way of knowing that this would be our last dance together.

The Junior Walker project wasn't a piece of cake, but with every obstacle that arose I was more tenacious and feisty than ever. Hal Davis had cut two sides on Junior and captured the classic raw, raucous, and country vocalist at his best; on the basis of those two songs we'd swung the album deal. Hal had actually joined the company, along with Marc Gordon, in the early sixties and had produced Brenda Holloway's fabulous song, "Every Little Bit Hurts." In addition to many of the Jackson 5's greatest hits, maestro producer Davis had also produced Michael Jackson's first solo hit, "Got to Be There," Diana Ross's "Love Hangover," Thelma Houston's "Don't Leave Me This Way," and loads more. I knew I'd be at an advantage with Hal on board.

Still, we all had to contend with Junior's bizarre quirks. For one thing, he didn't believe in telephones, or at least he never had one. He was staying in an area called Zuma Beach, way above

Malibu, an hour's drive from the Hitsville studios, and many taxing hours were spent trying to locate him. Racing out there and running through the hills or down to the beach, we'd always manage to find him—"There he is!" Like a kidnapping, we'd throw him in the car. "Come on, Junior, we've got a session."

The album *Blow the House Down* was released in the summer of 1983, in spite of Junior's bad-assed, yet lovable self. Any headaches with him seemed minor, however, compared to the mammoth undertaking that was in the works—dueling recording sessions that heralded the reuniting of the Tempts with Norman Whitfield and the Tops with Holland-Dozier-Holland. As usual, Jay Lasker had been opposed to signing any former Motown artist or, in his words, "has-beens." Nevertheless, I'd jumped that hurdle and had caught up with some old family members whose travels and changes had been as diverse as mine.

The Temptations had ridden down many a road since they'd scored their first hit in 1964. Of the original members only Melvin Franklin and Otis Williams remained. A legal scrimmage with Berry over money and creative-control issues, as well as the 1975 departure of their Midas-touch producer Norman Whitfield, caused the group to leave Motown in 1976. The Tempts were at least able to keep their group's name as a part of their settlement, which was more than could be said of the Jackson 5 or the Marvelettes—whose name was reputed to have been gambled away by Smokey in a card game with manager/promoter Larry Marshak. After the Tempts spent three disappointing years at Atlantic, Smokey helped negotiate a reconciliation, which brought them back to Motown again. With the exception of the return of Eddie Kendricks and David Ruffin for the *Reunion* album, however, nothing much had developed since that time.

The departure of Norman Whitfield in '75 was a "same old song" predicament—the lack of forthcoming money and the need for independence. Norman ended up forming Whitfield Records, which was distributed by Warner Brothers. At first Norman had some big hits with Undisputed Truth and Rose Royce, including their release of the song I'd cowritten, "Love Don't Live Here Anymore." He'd also done well on some movie soundtracks, such as *Car Wash*, but by 1982 his career was chilling and he was broke, the result of business mismanagement at the hands of incompetent advisers and that old devil blood for gambling.

"Norman," I said to him after hearing some of his latest stuff,

"you do it to me every time. You've still got the magic touch, man."
I was always floored by the Whitfield wizardry. Those rhythmic,
pulsating productions drew your attention from the start, so that
by the minute the song hit the first verse, your ass was his. He was
always growing creatively. Norman only grinned at my praise, and
as I grinned back I was also floored by his physical growth. He'd
put on at least a hundred pounds, and a portion of that weight
must have been in his huge head of hair. Having truly come of age
with his work for the Tempts, Norman was the obvious choice for
the comeback album.

By the same token, H-D-H and the Four Tops had always been
a fantastic combination. And the Tops, any way you looked at
them, were an amazing group. Their lineup, Duke Fakir, Obie
Benson, Lawrence Payton, and Levi Stubbs, had signed with Motown in 1964. These four friends had made their first records long
before they were part of the Motown stable, and they had stuck
together like glue, surviving the tours and the label changes and
the career pressures. One story purported that when Berry tried to
lure Levi Stubbs into a solo career, Levi simply wouldn't hear of it.
The fact that the Tops refused to leave Detroit was a reflection to
me of the eternal integrity that was in everything they did.

"Baby I Need Your Loving" was the first release that the Tops
cut at Hitsville, with their first production team, H-D-H, and it
was a smash. Having skipped the regular gestation period that
most artists experienced back then, they continued to hit big for
years. But when H-D-H left in '68, the Tops' pace slackened, and in
'72 they bumped into the same cul-de-sac that had jarred the
Jackson 5 from Motown. Again Berry was unavailable when their
contract came up for renewal, and again Ewart Abner tried to keep
them with such insultingly low renewal terms that they went over
to ABC. There they found, as so many others had, that life outside
Motown just wasn't the same. So the Super Three project was
appealing to all concerned.

Brian and Eddie Holland and Lamont Dozier were names
almost synonymous with major Motown breakthroughs. They were
the secret of the Supremes' success and the composers of innumerable classic Jobete copyrights. Their musical legacy would be
acknowledged in 1988 when they would be inducted into the Rock
and Roll Hall of Fame. I'd last seen them in 1968, when they'd
finally left Motown under unpleasant, drawn-out problems with
Berry. The intervening years bespoke of a similar pattern to Nor-

man's—initial triumph with their labels Hot Wax/Invictus, a cooling-off period, and eventually a nostalgia for times gone by. Even though I'd signed the three to come in as a team, they were no longer one, as Lamont Dozier was already out staking an independent claim as a solo artist. Regardless of everything that had happened over the years, everyone involved with the new projects was immensely positive.

"Next?" Don was helping me go over the list of preparations for the big party I'd planned for the first day of recording. I'd booked coinciding session dates of the twin projects in the two adjoining studios, which were named "Sunrise" and "Sunset."

"Let's see," I looked at my notes. "I've got this great photographer, Irv Antler, coming in. And Berry is bringing Roger Campbell in to videotape it. Oh, and have you heard Willie Hutch's 'The Battle Song'?" Willie, who was already slated to work on the Tops' gig, had written a perfect concept piece for a stupendous show of vocals between Levi Stubbs and the Tempts' Dennis Edwards. Don chuckled at my excitement, adjusting the fancy hat that he'd selected especially for the event.

"Don, where are my shades?"

"They're on your head, Ray," Don said and shook his head. Well, in his words, it was our duty to shake our booty, and it was time to party. And the festivities were enjoyed by one and all. For that one day, time was suspended and the true spirit of Hitsville shone in everyone's eyes. It was great while it lasted, which wasn't long, unfortunately. The problems: timing, money, the old ways versus the new, and the clashing personalities of Jay Lasker, Guy Costa, and Berry Gordy.

At least Guy's troublemaking was cause for some humor. In his blustering fashion he'd dragged me out of the studio one afternoon. "Do you realize what Levi is doing in there?"

"Yeah, he's eating his pork chops." I rolled my eyes at Guy. Levi loved his pork chops, and when a friend cooked him up a batch, he would bring his bag of gold in and pass out tastes of his treats.

"Well, Levi can't eat in there. Go in there right now and tell him and everybody else they can't eat in the studio. If it continues we'll have to shut the session down!" Guy was in a fever.

I sighed a sigh of disbelief. "Look, I tell you what, Guy. You go and tell Levi, OK?" I watched while he huffed and puffed some more and then stormed toward his office. Levi was a nice, down-to-earth guy, but nobody on this planet—not even Berry Gordy himself—would have the damn gall to go in and try to mess with him when he was eating those pork chops.

Jay Lasker's interference was less overt but much more potent. On top of arranging difficult schedules for the two groups, Jay levied ridiculous release dates for the two albums. My appeal to Berry for an extension was met with a no.

And then there was Berry's own interference. Given the existing sensitive relationship between himself and H-D-H, he insensitively and suddenly announced that he wanted half of the publishing from the new songs they'd written for the Tops. Needless to say, the ensuing warfare, which was for Berry just pleasure shooting, dripped new bad blood on the goodwill I was struggling to maintain on the projects.

The outcome of both albums—the Tempts' *Back to Basics* and the Tops' *Back Where I Belong*—released simultaneously in October of '83, was mixed. On one hand neither scored overwhelmingly in sales, perhaps due to the half-hearted promotional campaign headed by Lasker. On the other hand, the two groups were revitalized through the process and took off together on the terrific T 'n' T tour—a big hit with the baby boomers. However, Norman Whitfield took a temporary hiatus from the music business and H-D-H retreated again from Motown. Immediately thereafter Lamont split again from the brothers and began a winning series of collaborations with different songwriters. As far as future Motown recordings of the groups, the Tops would do only one more album for us—the *Magic* LP in 1985—and then would leave for good. But on the positive flip of the coin, the Temptations' next project would follow swiftly at Super Three and it would be a whopping success.

Before that could happen, however, the Tempts had to replace their lead singer, Dennis Edwards, who'd been in and out due to milder forms of the David Ruffin syndrome. Dennis had originally been David's replacement; both carried those strong husky baritones. It was Dennis's vocals that had sailed so beautifully alongside Paul Williams's deep voice on Whitfield's great psychedelic-era Tempts songs such as "Cloud Nine" and "I Can't Get Next to You." After *Back to Basics* was cut, Dennis went back to the basics of the high life and couldn't be found anywhere, so Otis and Melvin were out on a hunt for a substitute.

They struck a double gold mine in the form of two newcomers—Ollie Woodson, whose voice ranged up to a high tenor all the way down to a Ruffin-like soulful baritone, and Ron Tyson, whose clear, gorgeous sound evoked many shades of Eddie Kendricks. "Ray," said Ollie, "I've got this song I want you to hear, baby. I think it's great, but I'd like your comments. Maybe you've got some ideas." Well, did I ever. This was a song with an old-fashioned romantic message about how men should act toward women. I could definitely dig this song and pitched in happily to help structure it. I assigned Suzee to the project, which was right up her alley, for she'd worked with the Tempts for years. And she did a bang-up job on it with producer Al McKay. The song, "Treat Her Like a Lady," and its album, *Truly for You*, both went gold, and the Tempts, one of popular music's most beloved institutions, got their first big success after a long lag.

November 1983 was host to an especially beautiful day for a beautiful occasion: the marriage of Cliff Liles to Marchella Thompson. I was bursting at the seams with pride as the two stood at the altar, while I wished on stars for their future, which I knew would be filled with music. For Cliff, who had been breast-fed in every aspect of the recording business, there really was never any choice.

In the preceding year he'd worked as a writer at Jobete and had cowritten a song with Kerry and Benny called "Very Special Part," which had been recorded by Jermaine Jackson, also a great friend of both my older sons, on his *Let Me Tickle Your Fancy* album. The three ex-Apollo artists had transformed themselves into Kagny and the Dirty Rats—a cross between the Jackson 5 and Led Zeppelin—very eighties hip and very hot. They brought in a sensational lead singer named Sherrick and had a guest appearance by Rick James on "Sundown on Sunset," the funky cut I loved. The album came out in May '83 and the group's local following was tremendous. The guys even invested their own money into making a video that went on to be one of the first black videos shown on MTV. Through my painstaking efforts, the company was an avid supporter of the group and was planning to set up a new label, just for them, to be called Morocco.

Kagny eventually went the way of Apollo, though; at the end there was a sudden cooling, no promotion, no backing. Berry's lethal flips of interest were so horribly unjust. Apollo was brilliant and Kagny just as good. It was so frustrating—my sons were incredibly talented. Even if I did say so myself.

It was inevitable that the children of either or both Berry and Ray Gordy would want to make music. And it was just as inevitable that Berry—not wanting to show favoritism—would abandon them to the fates that all new Motown artists confronted. There was a surprise, however—and one that would be the one landmark hit by a son of a Gordy.

It was in early 1983 when Kennedy, Margaret and Berry's son, came to see me in my office. "Ray, you know that I really want to be a recording artist, but nobody takes me seriously. Like they don't think I have the talent."

"What about your dad?" I asked.

Kennedy shrugged, "Aw, you know . . ."

Since he had been staying on and off with us for years, I'd had the opportunity to hear some samplings of his stuff. "Look," I told him, "I think you're sensational. Let me see if we can do a song of yours together, OK?" I got a big smile out of him.

I ran the idea by Berry, who didn't react one way or the other. Probably thinking that nothing would come of it, he said, "Go ahead."

It wasn't the first time I'd been to Berry on Kennedy's behalf. As a troubled teenager, resenting his father for pushing his mother over the edge—an idea Margaret had placed in his head and emphasized at every opportunity—his behavior in Berry's home had become impulsive and erratic. At the same time, Margaret's psychological imbalance had provoked a lot of anger in Kennedy, leaving him confused about women in general. When times became tense he started drinking heavily, stealing bottles of champagne from Berry's bar every night. Kennedy denied this when Berry confronted him, only to be caught in the act on a video camera that Berry had installed. Booted out of the house, without funds, tearful and distraught, Kennedy came to live with me, bringing with him only a few clothes, a drum machine, and a small keyboard.

After hearing his potential, I'd lobbied successfully to get him a writing job at Jobete, along with my sons and Benny, and Kennedy's spirits rose considerably. Now, a year and a half later, with Super Three newly on the move and Berry's cluck of approval, our next step was to find the right song.

I walked into the apartment one night and became immediately enchanted by a hypnotic bass line coming from Kennedy's synthesizer in the corner of the living room where he camped out.

Dressed all in black, Kennedy was crouched over the keyboard.

Sensing me, he peered over his shoulder, singing a tale of a paranoid, desperate mind. The words and feelings had a powerful and almost repelling effect on me, as I knew that real-life paranoia was being used as a canvas for the work. But it was obviously a brilliant piece and I knew it was the project to record. And so Kennedy Gordy's big hit, "Somebody's Watching Me," was born.

Not wanting the Gordy name to influence the impact of the song itself, Kennedy came up with the name Rockwell to use on the record. When Curtis Nolen showed immense belief in Kennedy's talent, he was hired as the producer on the project. Finally, when we were laying down the lead vocals, Kennedy had a last-minute brainstorm. "I'm going to get Michael Jackson to sing on this song," he stated.

Well, it was a great idea, that being the year of *Thriller*, which had made Michael about the hottest thing on the planet. Kennedy had even already played a demo for Michael, who loved the song— identifying strongly with the paranoid feeling of being trapped in a goldfish bowl, prey to intruding eyes. But getting him out of the house and into the studio was another story altogether. Plus, Michael hadn't sung on a Motown record in eight years or so. "Yeah, getting Michael's a great idea," I said to Kennedy, "but *how* are you going to get him?"

He ran down his game plan and I agreed to give it a shot. It was a highly doubtful proposition but we booked the studio time, assembling at the appointed hour while Kennedy set off in my car on his mission. No one at the studio thought it could be pulled off and I nervously awaited the outcome. We all almost fell into a dead faint when forty-five minutes later Kennedy and Michael Jackson came strolling in the door. Kennedy's plan not to give Michael a second to think about it, just an impromptu "Hey, we're ready to record, come on down to the studio with me" was a triumph. And with the two of them singing together on the chorus of "Somebody's Watching Me," the playback told me that it was destined to be a smash.

As they finished mixing down the record, I could barely wait to rush it over and play it for Berry. "That's pretty good," he began. Then listening hard, his tongue in his cheek as usual, he said, "There's a familiar voice there. Who's that singing with him?"

"Oh, that," I said innocently, "that's Michael Jackson."

Berry's elation almost raised the roof, *"Michael Jackson?"*

When "Somebody's Watching Me" hit number one in a few weeks, Motown happily ate crow—it was the fastest moving single in the country. And I was feeling pretty damn incredible.

Rockwell's album that followed, *Somebody's Watching Me*, was also a smash. Despite a never-ending fight with Guy on every iota of its production and severe stress on the artist, the album went platinum, and Guy was the first to leap forward for credit. Over the first year of its release, Rockwell became—in his father's eyes and in a dramatic reversal—the Winner, gaining an exalted position among the Gordy offspring. With lingering unhappiness from his childhood, though, and later with alcohol and drug problems, Rockwell wavered. His second album, *Captured*, recorded the following year, fell into an odd demographic gap—it sounded too pop for the R&B stations and too R&B for the pop stations. A third and last album, *The Genie*, produced by Kerry, met a similar fate. With Kennedy's failures, Berry's approval was withdrawn. Ultimately, disgusted with the company, and possibly with himself, Kennedy asked to be released from Motown.

Kennedy and I, bonded through the ups and downs, remained friends. Even though his departure from Motown was followed by a period of deep discouragement, by 1989 he once again was bound and determined to start anew with his great talent.

With the victory of *Somebody's Watching Me* behind me, I had almost completed my own game plan. But the tragedy that struck next left me so anguished that I could think of nothing else.

When Cliff called that morning, I immediately heard something strange in his voice. It was a pretty day outside, April 1, 1984. "Marvin Gaye has just been shot and killed." I reeled from shock and disbelief.

Cliff asked, "Where's little Marvin?"

"Oh, no," I said, with a renewed bolt of anguish. "He and Eddie went out to eat." I was heartsick. Marvin III had spent the night at our place and had left a few hours ago with Eddie. Any minute now the news would be blasting on the stereo in Eddie's car, in which they would be driving along, finger-popping, and having a good time. The boys had even talked of dropping by and saying hello to little Marvin's father.

I made my first phone call. "Anna, is what I heard true?"

She sounded solemn, almost sedated, answering, "Yeah, it is."

When I asked her what had happened she said, "They think his father shot him."

In a panic I stood by the apartment window looking into the parking lot where the boys would be returning. For an excruciating hour, I stood at the window, praying that Marvin III would be spared the unspeakable devastation of hearing it on the radio. At last, I held my breath as Eddie's car pulled up. Music was pouring out of the windows, and when the two got out they were dancing and laughing.

I met them at the door. "Marvin, go in the bedroom and call your mother." He didn't look alarmed since my voice was very flat and this wasn't an unusual request from me. I watched him trot off to the phone, and I took Eddie into the other bedroom. On hearing the news, Eddie's knees buckled.

We waited in the living room, Eddie and I, Rya and her boyfriend, Tommy. No one said a word. It was a long time before Marvin emerged from the bedroom, moving very slowly, fighting to hold back his sorrow; only one tear glistened on his cheek. We stood together silently, lending our presence, for no one was able to speak. We were quiet for a long time, and then little Marvin bit his lip and said, "You know, my father told me not to cry."

He looked away and then back at us, continuing, "He told me, when I saw him last week, that if anything happened to him, not to cry. To just go ahead and really do great in school and get ahead in life. 'Just don't cry for me,' he said."

I watched as the silent struggle continued, and Marvin spoke again, first taking in a deep breath. "Today we had planned on having a great time, and so what I'd really like is if everybody just went on like we planned."

So the kids spent the day as it had been planned, playing a video game. They played it for hours and hours, pretending that the world and what had happened in it that morning didn't exist. Inside, I knew, he was dying; he loved his father so much.

Marvin III, at eighteen, was placed in charge of the funeral arrangements. He, with the help of his father's assistant Kitty Sears, picked out the casket, selected clothes for burial—a military type of suit with brass buttons and gold braiding—and even went to the funeral home to dress his father. And he conducted the funeral services. Many people from Motown were there, including Smokey and Stevie Wonder, who delivered a eulogy. Marvin was able to assemble his father's road band, and they played many memorable songs. The most moving was "What's Going On."

The next day, Marvin and Anna took Eddie and a few close friends out on a boat. And there they distributed Marvin Gaye's ashes to the sea, as he had desired.

CHAPTER 18
SHERRICK
1984-1988

I had set ten goals for myself as part of my plan to make it to the other side. What the other side represented to me was freedom. To be liberated, I had to regain what I felt had been robbed from me— my financial security, my sense of accomplishment, my dignity, my heart, and, more than anything, my dreams. I needed to make a dream come true again and stand face to face with Berry, holding it up and claiming it as my own. That was the most important of my goals.

Berry, that thief of dreams, was becoming more unfathomable; it was harder and harder for me to believe he was the man I'd once sworn to love forever, come hell or high water. With every denial, every rejection, every no, his humanity faded away, as did the chains he held on my heart.

In the meantime, I had made it far enough in the Motown political jungle. My instincts had become acutely sensitized, and I was now able both to defend myself from attack and to recognize a hit project that could put me over the top. The funny thing about this jungle was that the perfect prey spotted me first. He was new to Motown, the lead singer of Kagny and the Dirty Rats, and he pointed me out to Kerry, asking, "Who's that lady?" Kerry informed him, "That's my mother."

He'd nodded silently then, only confiding his thoughts to Cliff a few days later, "Man, Kerry's mother sure is fine. I'd love to really rock her world." Obviously, he had no idea that Cliff and Kerry were brothers. "Hey man, chill," Cliff had said indignantly. "She's my mother too!"

I'd noticed this guy's work in Kagny, but it wasn't until the spring of '84 that he came into my office and actually introduced himself.

"Hi, I'm Sherrick. I'm great. I want you to work with me."

Who is this guy?, I thought. A little amused at his nerve, I asked, "Well, why don't you let me hear some of your songs?"

I played it very cool for a long while—if he was serious about a solo career, he'd chase me down. Which he began to do, unflaggingly. Sometimes he'd show up alone, and on a few occasions he would be accompanied by an attractive brown-skinned, emerald-eyed gal named Rita, who worked as an administrative assistant to Lionel Richie.

It would have been hard for anyone to ignore Sherrick. I soon came to know him as an articulate twenty-seven-year-old with an earthy charisma. Six-foot-four with a strong, proud face and a gorgeous physique, he carried himself with a sensual, catlike confidence. At the nape of his neck, from a head of neatly styled dark-brown hair, fell a single braid all the way down to his waist. He had an outstanding voice—a powerful tenor with the silken lines of Luther Vandross and the verve of Jackie Wilson that hinted at his classical training. A true vocal musician. Sherrick was overpoweringly desirable with absolutely all the perfect ingredients for a pop star. He was every woman's dream come true—a fantasy man.

I held him at bay for about six months, waiting for an opportunity to test his mettle, until I finally hired him to do background vocals on Rockwell's *Capture* album. Then, when I casually mentioned that he would be cutting the vocals on "He's a Cobra" the next day, I also dropped this on him: "Oh, and you'll be singing on it with Stevie Wonder." Singing with Stevie was an intimidating prospect, to say the least, and Sherrick appeared to be duly in awe. But when the session began and they were both at the microphone, Sherrick held his own with one of pop music's greatest vocalists. I was most impressed. As the old song said, "the hunter was getting captured by the game."

At the same time, however, I was detecting danger signs from some chronic sources. By early '85 it was clear that, despite everything I'd achieved at Super Three, I would get nothing more from Jay Lasker than a cold shoulder. Time and again our product was pointedly not being pushed by Motown sales reps.

And dealing with Guy had gone from tough to horrible. As Don Fletcher would later say about him, "He was a little boy in a big man's job." He continued to control projects with a clumsy hand and a shrill voice. One would think that Berry would have changed his opinion when he was exposed to a typical Guy-ism during a meeting a few of us had at Berry's house. Willie Hutch and I brought up the subject of Lionel Richie's then-unreleased album, *Can't Slow Down,* and someone commented favorably on the first single on it, "All Night Long." Guy had nothing to contribute to the conversation but plunged in anyway.

"That song's a flop. No one will listen to that record."

Willie, who'd been through it enough times with Guy, said, "Man, you don't know what you're talking about. That song is a smash."

Guy insisted that the public would bear him out, going on and on until he glanced over to the chairman for what he expected would be some kind of salute. All Berry gave him was a trademark look of disgusted incomprehension. Berry lit into Guy: "What the hell are you talking about? Man, I haven't even heard the damn record. But if Lionel Richie did it, as hot as he is, it's got to be a smash."

At the same point that I was deliberating on how to handle Sherrick, Guy came at me one too many times. I had just requested I be given another assistant; Don and I were overloaded, with more than a dozen artists working now at Super Three, and Suzee had been disassociating herself from Guy. My suggestion was to bring in Iris Gordy, Berry's niece. On one hand, dealing with Iris wasn't always a breeze, for me and many others, including her uncle. Berry was often chagrined by Iris for using the family connection to make her way in the world. On the other hand, she was good and I was mainly concerned with making music.

Two weeks went by and Guy finally responded, "Listen, I've taken you up on your suggestion to hire Iris."

"Great, Guy. She's got a terrific ear."

"Yeah," he said. "I hired her. But instead of hiring her as your assistant, I hired her as your boss."

I was ready to roar—two years of slaving to make Super Three really fly, and now this? But I refused to waste any energy on him, or even bother calling Berry. I would need all my wits for the big one.

The following morning I was standing in Guy's office when Iris pranced in with a beret perched on the side of her head. Without so much as a glance to me, she started making calls, the first of which was to Hal Davis. "This is Iris Gordy. I'm now in charge of Super Three. Instead of reporting to Ray, all business will be transacted with me."

On this same day, Iris began redecorating my wonderfully airy, welcoming office into some pink nightmare of kitsch. There was poodle wallpaper and painted porcelain lamp bases that looked like they belonged in a bordello, an ornate massive desk, and—the clincher—a room divider with a secretary stationed in front to keep out the riffraff. Don and I were sequestered to a tiny office in the basement, where we received word that Iris had just fired Suzee Ikeda and that we would probably be next. I had only one thing on my mind—Sherrick. He was going to be my ticket to ride.

I called Sherrick right away to tell him we were going to get a demo together. Thrilled, he asked that I meet him at the Bonaventure Hotel. Over dinner, we established the ground rules: I would manage his career and get him a recording contract at Motown. After dinner, the business meeting adjourned and we proceeded to break some rules.

After our evening at the Bonaventure, I didn't hear from Sherrick for two weeks until at last I got a call from Austin, Texas. Exactly what he was doing there was unclear, but he told me he was flying in the next day and to pick him up at the airport. By now a veteran of complicated artistic personalities, I was not overly surprised to find out, upon our airport rendezvous, that he had no car, no money, no home.

I agreed to put him up in the two-bedroom apartment where I was living with my two younger kids. He had only a few items of clothing and a synthesizer, which he set up in the bedroom. Another humble beginning, I thought. This one had to work.

Just as I did so long ago, I sat down and came up with the bottom line for what it would cost me to finance his demo of four or five original songs. The figure was about ten times as much as the eight hundred dollars Berry and I had needed in that other time gone by. I took the money from a tax refund check, which I'd been saving for a move to a bigger place, and I invested it in my dream. For his part, Sherrick invested every ounce of his energy in the project as I guided him through song structure, melody, lyric, and vocals.

As his mentor, I offered him a way to realize his dream of becoming a recording star; as my protégé, he offered me a way to realize my dream of managing a star. We were a perfect team. Occasional lovers, we were starting to hear the songs that would capture those sensual, sexy rhythms and qualities. On a few occasions, Sherrick made forays into the night, sometimes borrowing my car to buy cigarettes and not returning for two or three days. I decided that whatever restlessness drove him out, I would not fight it. And I was not even startled when he once returned carrying a cute two-year-old girl—his daughter—with a report that he had spent the last night camping out at her mother's house. I didn't lecture or growl, understanding that the intensity of our work together was grounds for these pauses.

I filled my ears with the sounds of what we were building and bolstered myself with that during my daily trials with Iris and Guy at Super Three. For three months, from March to June of '85, Sherrick and I slaved away, until the demo was ready to present to Berry.

It was late on a June afternoon when I was ushered into Berry's impressive office by Edna Anderson, Berry's well-dressed, efficient assistant. The offices were outfitted with a pool table, a fully stocked bar, and an adjoining area with a Jacuzzi and sauna. For an instant, I allowed myself to visit images from another life— the laughter we'd shared, the romance of the dream we'd created together—and then I focused on the man in front of me. Already tired from his day, Berry yawned and stretched out in his throne as I cued up the tape and told him about the artist. And then, as the music played, he perked up, his tongue just rolling in his cheek as he concentrated. As the first song ended, Berry nodded. "Interesting. I like him."

We moved to the second tune, and I was eager to hear his reaction. Knowing that this song, "Just Call," was a natural hit, I was damned proud of the work Sherrick and I had put into it. As the vibes filled the room, Berry was obviously taken with it; its commercial appeal was plain as day. He wore that famous visionary look, as though he were hearing it already pouring out of a car radio or over a dance floor.

As Berry opened his mouth to say something, the door to his office was thrown open.

"Am I interrupting something important?" Not waiting for an answer, Suzanne DePasse strolled right in. I cringed automatically at the sound of her voice, and then at her presence, which at times had the effect of fingernails down a chalkboard. Within seconds, the room was filling with people. My blood boiled as she made introductions of her entourage to Berry, laughing and teasing like a teacher's pet flirting with the laureled professor. This woman was Berry's creation, the ambitious girl he had groomed as his very own brilliant black female executive and spokesperson for Motown. More than ever, the fact that she had become my substitute was inescapable. As she sustained the banter for forty-five minutes, I couldn't help but believe that she had been trained to perceive me as a threat to her hard-earned position with Berry. I gritted my teeth. I had no claims on her territory—I just wanted one of my own.

Finally she left and Berry turned to me, drained, asking if we could postpone the meeting. Given little choice, I agreed, certain that when we next sat down, Berry would be ready to pounce on a deal for us.

Never in my wildest nightmares could I have guessed that this aborted meeting with Berry would be my last as an employee of Motown.

In July 1985, Guy Costa's telephone call came. It was like a dagger to my jugular. "I'm calling to inform you that you are being terminated. Your producer's contract is herewith canceled. You will continue to receive your base salary for the next two years, at which time your termination will be final."

"Guy, this is insane. I'm about to have a meeting with Berry to finish the Sherrick presentation. We're talking about a black Elvis Presley, a potential megastar. Berry liked the songs that he heard. And for God's sake, 'Just Call,' is ready to cut—I know it's a hit."

"No," said Guy, "the chairman told me that Sherrick wasn't that good and the material wasn't strong enough. In August of 1987 your termination will be final."

It hadn't been a test. It wasn't a warning. It was final, and it was the most dire emergency of my entire life. In August of 1987 I would be fifty years old. Almost thirty years had passed since the fateful meeting with Berry, thirty years from the time that I opened my heart and my talents to a raggedy bum who used to scrounge for pocket change. For the past five years, I'd clawed my way up from the bottom of the ocean, triumphed over the devastation of an eviction and the aftermath of having four cars repossessed while continuing to support four children, of having my credit shot to hell, of having dream after dream dangled in front of me and then tossed aside at the last minute. Rage in its purest form filled every cell of my being. But then a new invincible power started to swell from within. I recounted my recent victories. These were the links in the bridge I'd crossed to get to the other side, and so help me God, I had only one more to go before I was securely planted there.

Fortunately, my having played Mama Bear all those years was paying off. One of my cubs, Benny Medina, who'd already worked with Sherrick, had just left a mediocre job at Motown's A&R department to head up the black music division at Warner Brothers Records. Enlisting the excellent talents of producer Michael Stokes, I put the winning package together—artist, material, producer.

The production company formed between Sherrick and myself was named Sheriton Productions; Benny Medina promptly signed us to a long-term agreement with Warner. After all the pain and sweat, and the months of hemming and hawing at Motown, I got a verbal deal from one of the largest record companies in the world in what seemed like a finger snap. I was vindicated.

Sherrick's reaction was a mix of ecstasy, glory, and nerves. Where was the contract? A verbal deal? I explained that contracts sometimes ran up to two hundred pages and could take from three to five months to negotiate. "Relax, Sherrick," I told him. "Our lawyers can handle the contracts. And you and I can celebrate—because this is only the beginning."

"You're right, Ray," Sherrick said, promising to be patient. And as he looked at me, his eyes filled with wonder and excitement. "Yeah!" he sang out.

"Yeah," I purred. It was only the beginning.

Not too many weeks later, I was standing in a hall outside Sherrick's hospital door. He had disappeared again for three days, and I had just received a call from Rita saying that Sherrick had turned up in the hospital and was asking for me to come right away.

She met me in the hall. "Do you know about his problem?" she asked. I shook my head, a knot forming in my stomach. Leading me into the room, Rita said, "I think Sherrick should tell you himself."

When he saw me, Sherrick burst into tears. I fought a tide of dread, sitting down next to him in a chair by the bed. Finally he managed to say, "I have a . . . I'm addicted to cocaine."

Momentarily I lay my head in my hands. There had been occasions when he had returned with cocaine and had asked me to try it with him. Drug and alcohol use, prevalent in this era, was something I had spent years trying to fight. I was never able to understand it. And so, in a vain and foolhardy effort to gain some sense of that hunger for it, I had taken the small glass pipe from Sherrick one night and had drawn in one long puff as he held a torch to the bowl. The feeling had been exhilarating, like nothing I had known before. My curiosity satisfied, I made another blunder by financing a few purchases for Sherrick, thinking that the euphoria it gave him would help him deal with his anxiety waiting for the deal to come through. Twice I was right, but on the third time he underwent a violent physical and psychological reaction. Alarmed, I laid down the law—no more purchases by me and no cocaine in the apartment.

As I sat with him in the hospital room, I blamed myself for having encouraged him even that much, and I took solace in his assurance that the problem could be controlled. "Ray," he said, his eyes focusing tightly on mine, "I'm not going to let anything stand in the way. I'm going to do it." And taking my hand, he added, "We're going to do it."

We both wanted the dream badly, and nothing indicated that it was impossible. Benny and Warner Brothers shared in our enthusiasm and soon the contracts would be ready. In the meantime, Sherrick agreed to check into a twenty-eight-day rehabilitation program at the hospital. I visited him every day, putting everything of myself into his recuperation. During that period I also attended family Cocaine Anonymous meetings to more fully understand and help deal with the disease.

Sherrick made excellent progress, and I was very encouraged. We had nipped the problem in the bud and the contracts were due any day. I could almost see the other side.

"You did what?" Sherrick asked on our drive home from the hospital, noting we were taking an unfamiliar route.

"It's a surprise," I said and smiled. To reward his hard work, and to give him incentive to keep on working, I'd gone ahead and used the rest of my savings to move into a spacious, four-bedroom tri-level townhouse in the San Fernando Valley. The master suite, a splendid space with twenty-foot cathedral ceilings, had been furnished lavishly for him: a solid-oak bedroom set; a king-size four-poster mirrored waterbed made up in off-white satin sheets and pillow cases and matching satin spread; and the pièce de résistance, a forty-eight-inch wide-screen TV. The minute we got to our new home, he dashed upstairs in those long leaps to check the place out. I heard his reaction echo through the townhouse: "Goddamn!" For the rest of the day, we lolled around like lazy cats, watching the TV, laughing and purring, and dreaming of imminent victories, of our success and how it would change our lives, and of the music we were going to make.

That night, when I went down to the kitchen to cook us a couple of steaks, Sherrick quietly took my car keys, slipped out of a side door, and disappeared. His rehabilitation had lasted less than eight hours.

Time slowed down and minutes became lifetimes. The clock on the wall ticked ominously. When I'd worked with David Ruffin, I'd dealt with an artist who had an addiction. I'd seen firsthand that a war with that kind of obsession could be impossible. But with Sherrick my investment was an all-or-nothing gamble. It was either quit now or fight harder and more powerfully than I ever had.

And so, when at four in the morning, he called asking me to come at once and meet him in downtown L.A. with a hundred dollars, I made my choice. I was a fighter. I borrowed Eddie's car and drove through the most nightmarish section of the city, where no one was safe, black or white, anytime, day or night. This was a no-man's-land.

I saw him first. My headlights reflected off a lone, frightened figure, standing disheveled and without shoes, a walking corpse.

"Where's my car?" I demanded.

"Give me the money and wait right here," Sherrick said. Taking the cash, he disappeared down a dark alley.

A few minutes later, I saw my car coasting in my direction, a stranger at the wheel—one of those bloodless entities, fully capable of killing us both on a whim. He got out of my car just as Sherrick shot out of the alley, retrieving the keys from him and jumping into my car. Sherrick pulled away in my car, gesturing for me to follow. The dream had become a nightmare.

It happened again. Only it was a worse neighborhood and he needed two hundred dollars. The same cycle, the same impassioned pledge that nothing could shake his commitment to his career, and then the same demons again. My cycle was despair, anger, hope that he could keep the pledge, and prayer. I'd lost sight of the other side.

When it happened the third time and I met him at the appointed place, an even more hellish hole, I watched him disappear down the alley not to return at all. In a paralyzed state of the purest anger and the purest fear, I'd waited for two hours. I drove home in tears and with fury pounded my hands against the steering wheel, reliving every second of all the other nightmares. Oh, God, I prayed throughout the night, please save him. Please.

The next afternoon Rita called. "Sherrick's in the hospital. He's been shot."

On first sight I thought there had been a mistake. This wasn't Sherrick. Lips swollen twice their normal size. Black and blue bruising all over his face. Five scars gouged into his forehead. Stitches in his eyelids and cheeks. The proud, handsome face had been obliterated. Rita and Lynn, the mother of his daughter, told me he had been shot in the pelvis and beaten with a baseball bat. Fortunately, the bullet bypassed all of his vital organs; because of that he was alive.

Lynn stayed with Sherrick and Rita took me out into the hall. In between sobs she couldn't hold back, Rita said, "I love him. We were supposed to get married. Lionel Richie was going to sing at the wedding. The invitations had gone out, everything was ready, and then, a few days before it, he disappeared." I later found out that the date set for their wedding coincided exactly with the weekend following the night I'd spent with Sherrick at the Bonaventure.

I paced up and down the corridor, looking back over the growing list of the Motown family casualties from dope and drink. Marvin's death headed the list of tragedies. As I paced back and forth over the cold linoleum of the hospital, I recalled James Jamerson telling me about the sessions for *What's Going On*. Marvin and the other musicians stayed in the studio for days, kept up by literally mounds and mounds of cocaine; James himself played the whole session flat on his back. Thousands of dollars were inhaled through noses or burned ritualistically in little pipes. Then there was Paul Williams, who sat in a car and shot himself. And before him, Benny Benjamin, the incredible Hitsville drummer, who suffered a stroke in '69, brought on by inhuman bouts of drinking.

James Jamerson, too, ended up a victim, although his final descent was slower than Benny's. When the company migrated to Los Angeles James still managed to come along and stick it out for a few years. But, eventually, all the decades of abuse caught up with him and he became incapacitated; the producers stopped using him. This great, great musician, such an integral part of the Motown sound, died forgotten and cast aside.

Sherrick was young, and obviously somewhere inside he was in deep pain. But it wasn't too late to heal those wounds, to quiet the beast within. I read him the obituaries of the great heroes of the history of music. "Is that what you want?" I asked him. His answer was a definitive no, his narrow escape from death had changed him. He was ready to save himself.

After Sherrick was released from the hospital, he enrolled in a private, one-year out-patient rehabilitation clinic. It was only two or three days before Benny called saying that the contracts were ready. I was moving back into gear, revving up to win the challenge.

Against all odds, Sherrick stayed clean. He kept all of his rehab appointments and worked from sunup to sundown, for month after month, preparing his debut album. And I'd been swamped with my end of the pursuit, working out the details in conjunction with all the departments at Warner Brothers: budget coordination, recording sessions, wardrobe, bios, press photos, album cover, liner notes, and then development for publicity, marketing, promotion, and videos. I would be eternally grateful to Sherrick's brother and sister-in-law, Richard and Anna Howard, for their constant assistance. A handsome Sherrick look-alike, Richard—also a very talented singer, writer, and producer—came through time and again. His attractive wife, Anna, reminded me a lot of myself, pitching in anywhere and everywhere and always lending a shoulder to cry on.

And I had an absentee force driving me as well. At Christmastime of 1985, I went home to see my family in Detroit. Mama, though without her younger physical strength, was as regal and opinionated as ever. There was, of course, the empty chair where Daddy once sat. But his presence was all around, shining in the faces of his children and grandchildren.

"So you and Warner Brothers, hey?" Mike had asked, just before I played him Sherrick's demo. Looking at my brother, I was heartsick. His health was failing—his eyes bloodshot and his breathing labored. And yet, when I played him the tape, I saw the old Romeo. He smiled brightly and gave me a high sign, "It sounds fantastic. You really are going to do it this time!"

"Look, Mike," I said seriously. "Why don't you come out to L.A. and work with me? We've always been a sensational team, and I know this album is going to be a smash and it would mean more than anything if you were a part of it. What do you say?"

He paused, his face in dark clouds. I knew he wasn't in any shape to make the move. And then, in a voice of conviction, he proposed, "Listen, I'm going to get myself together and come out in the summer. You'll be in the studio by then and I'll be there right by your side. Deal?" I hugged him to acknowledge the deal, yet I didn't think he'd really make it out to L.A.

It was, in fact, the summer during which Mike had promised to come out and work with me that I received the news—on August 27, 1986, Mike Ossman died. It was his heart. My brother, my soul mate, my dearest friend. It devastated me more than any other loss. After his expulsion from the company for which he'd slaved, he had gone into a slide and couldn't raise himself up. The breaking of his spirit had broken his body, and he died alone in his house in Detroit, a ghost town of lost dreams. I could not help but think that Motown had my brother's blood on its hands. In his memory I had to prevail. I had to win.

In August of 1987, *Sherrick* was released. Hearing "Just Call" on the radio for the first time was one of the greatest thrills of my life. I was so proud of myself, and I was so proud of him, for the excruciating struggle he'd won. "And," he said, as we started to hear "Just Call" playing everywhere, "this is only the beginning."

Benny Medina had been a crucial part of the glory, making sure that the album and the single were properly promoted. When the company's initial efforts were merely routine, Benny put his job on the line to make sure the project was pushed. With his work, "Just Call" took off like wildfire, landing in the R&B charts' top five in all the industry publications—*Billboard, Cashbox,* and the *R&R Report*. At one point the R&B radio programmers relayed that it was the number-one most requested R&B record in the country. Sherrick became an overnight sensation. And our impact was even more impressive in England, where the single was number one on the dance charts. At year end the accolades continued to roll in. The English magazine *Blues and Soul* voted "Just Call" Record of the Year; *Impact,* an American publication, touted Sherrick as 1987's Best New Male Vocalist.

Very few people could truly appreciate the sweetness of the victory: after an atrocious ousting from a company to which I'd given birth, my first project out was a smashing success. I could almost feel myself landing on the other side. All we had to do now was sustain the momentum for one more year, and I would be on terra firma again.

In August '87, the month the album was released, my Motown subsistence ran out and my termination was official. I'd been through the revolving door enough times before, but this time I knew it was final. And before I could look back at Motown with love, before I could ultimately go in front of Berry as a separate but equal, I had to make it to the finish line.

My hopes for my protégé were strengthened by the continuing clamor. There were countless interviews with radio stations, newspapers, and magazines. There was an exhausting yet exhilarating promotional tour: New York, Philadelphia, Detroit, Chicago, Cleveland, Atlanta, Birmingham, New Orleans, the Carolinas, Baltimore, and D.C. We then went to London, followed by a ten-day engagement in Tahiti.

Everywhere there was overwhelming adulation for Sherrick, and as I watched him strut magnificently in front of audiences, I was breathless. The possibilities before him were without limit. He had conquered his addiction, having remained straight for a year, and had a great album and popular acclaim as his rewards. And the empowering feeling it gave me was beyond anything I could have imagined.

By the middle of the tour, though, I sensed trouble. There was nothing I could put my finger on, just a warning voice inside. I was therefore quite dismayed when a woman professing to be a psychic, approached me one night and told me that Sherrick had the makings of a legendary superstar. But then, leaning into my ear, she said, "But he won't do it. There is an obstacle. It will be his downfall."

Before I had time to respond, the woman disappeared. And the next night after a show, so did Sherrick. The old patterns showed themselves all over again. The minute we reached a new city he would go off to find a connection. I now lived with the added anxiety that the problem would be revealed to the public or to the record company. Against my better judgment, I had never told Benny the extent of Sherrick's coke problem.

Sherrick and I started having scenes. On certain occasions, he'd find a starstruck young girl to feed his habit, or he'd take off with a rowdy entourage of others who didn't want the party to end. My efforts to take control elicited volcanic displays of rage, with accusations that I was jealous or afraid to live to the fullest, or that I was exploiting him for my own glory. Sherrick was becoming abusive and disrespectful toward everyone.

By this point I knew there was no turning back. I had no choice; I was running too fast. As I ran, my desperation accelerated, my vows multiplied—to protect him from himself, to honor our commitment to Warner Brothers, and to escape the horrible curse that the psychic had whispered in my ear. I managed to pull Sherrick along through three more single releases and videos from the album. Somehow we kept Warner Brothers from seeing the telltale signs. Damn it all, I thought, I would carry him over the finish line if necessary. Hope and doom lived simultaneously within me at every minute. But every time he checked into rehab, I would think, "*This* time he'll beat it for good." But every time I would drive to godforsaken parts of the city to rescue him, or wait in line at the jail to bail him out, I'd know that Sherrick wasn't going to make it.

In January of 1988 Benny contacted me, excited and ready to roll on the next album, wanting to see new material and budgets. I promised him Sherrick would call him in a few more weeks. More time than that slipped by, and Sherrick slid further and further into the gutter. Benny's calls were becoming more and more frustrated. "What the hell's going on? We've got deadlines." By the time Sherrick finally called Benny, it was July and Benny was extremely wary about proceeding. But suddenly Sherrick had a burst of renewed professionalism and determination. Based on this, I promised Benny that the second album would be greater than the first. In September we were given part of the advance to begin recording, and we cut three rhythm tracks with John Barnes, a well-respected synthesizer programmer known for his work with Michael Jackson.

The tracks would remain unfinished. Before the vocals had been completed, Sherrick disappeared with twenty thousand dollars, the majority of the advance money.

Before reaching the finish line, I stopped running. I was crawling really, and in a state of total and pure desolation, living and sleeping a nightmare. Sherrick had been gone for six weeks when I dragged myself into the car one night and drove in utter exhaustion down to the beach in Santa Monica. It was the old spot where I used to walk in my crazy days of going back and forth with Ed. I started out on the pier, and when I got to the end I leaned over the railing and looked into a pitch-black void. I wondered where Sherrick was at that moment, shuddering to think of his private hell. I asked a starless sky how it was possible that cocaine had so completely enraptured his soul. Was it the drug, or did he simply want to die—to disappear into the void? I railed against the heavens for answers. At his core, Sherrick was being devoured by a pain, a terror, and a relentless hurt that only the anesthesia of the drug, the fleeting euphoria, could quell. For that temporary happiness, Sherrick continued to trade his career, his loved ones, and—now probably—his life. I wanted to call to him, to where he was lost out there, to come back and claim that great destiny he had been working so hard to attain.

I wondered, too, where Berry was out there, whether he was so far gone that he could no longer hear the voice of someone who had loved him so well. My question to him was simply—why? He'd forgotten all about the dream—the loyalty and blood and guts and faith and passion that went into molding the miracle. I'd been left unprotected and alone in a cold world, while he slept snugly behind a twenty-four-hour security gate in the lush hills of Bel Air. "Why?" I spoke aloud into the night—and only "why-why-why" echoed back.

I looked down into the dark swirl of the waves and then up again to the sky, and to my surprise I saw stars peeking out from behind filmy clouds. Not many but a few. These were familiar stars, the real stars of my life, twinkling down on me. I named them and thanked them. There was Ed and Barbara Singleton and their son, Daren. Cliff and Marchella Liles. Kerry and his new wife, Karen Gordy. There was Benny Medina. And Eddie and Rya. Stars shone for Alice, Nita, Kathy, Roslyn, Ines, and Tommy—all my sisters and brothers on earth. And I named a constellation apiece for Daddy Ashby and brother Mike—thanking them for watching over me from heaven. When the moon finally came into view, I saw in it my mother's smile and heard her voice telling me to be strong.

I walked back from the pier, got into my car, and drove home. A few weeks later I heard that Sherrick had been found in a hospital and was asking for me. I made him a care package—clothes and shoes and toiletries—and took it to the hospital to wish him well and to say good-bye.

And when I left that hospital, I knew very well that I hadn't finished the big and final race. I hadn't made it to the other side. I had lost.

There was nothing to do but head home, figure out how I was going to make a living, and do some catching up on some long overdue correspondence.

PLEASE MR. POSTMAN
1989

I began this, my long overdue letter, by promising to tell the truth. And so, there is one thing, a lifelong secret, that I should finally confess. When people asked me what kept me going, why I never gave up, I responded in all honesty that it was my undying faith in the U.S. postal service. Now don't laugh, because, as only God knows, it's the damn truth. I'd spent every single day of my adult existence walking to the mailbox. In every house or apartment, in the homes where I was given shelter, and in the places where I made homes for others, I'd wait for the mail to arrive.

There was a song that played in my mind every time I opened up another empty mailbox, a melody and a refrain sung to me by Berry that I'd always believed. It was the lyric that I'd never stopped hearing: "I'll always take care of you."

I cannot even say how strongly I was convinced that one day, somewhere, somehow, that old Mr. Postman was going to come knocking and sing out: "A letter for Miss Ray!" What did I expect to find in that letter? Well, I had a few hopes. A notice of delivery for a Rolls-Royce would have been nice, like the one that Smokey received for his years of loyalty. Or the one that was given to Suzanne DePasse for her hard work. Or a deed to a house, like all those that Margaret had received—the one woman in Berry's life who'd done nothing but cause everyone needless pain. A check, a stock certificate, anything to show me that my efforts hadn't been forgotten. A small piece of the Motown dream returned to me in material form. And I truly believed a letter would also accompany the gesture, a note written in Berry's own handwriting. It would say, "Yes, I remember. You were there."

Well, not to be ungrateful, I should say that I did receive an envelope from Motown one day in 1984. It was a bonus of thirty-

317

five thousand dollars for my work on Rockwell's "Somebody's Watching Me." From that amount, twenty-two thousand dollars had been subtracted by the company accountants, a sum that was explained as monies I supposedly had borrowed over the years. I used what was left to buy one of the kids a car, and I kept hoping, kept believing that another envelope was on its way. Two years later I opened up the mailbox to find a statement from the IRS, advising me that I owed thirty-eight thousand dollars in taxes and penalties on the thirty-five-thousand-dollar bonus I had received in 1984. I still kept the faith, though, skipping or running or walking out to the mailbox every day and humming Berry's tune to myself.

In early 1988, just as the Sherrick expedition headed for its final collision, Motown was sold to MCA for sixty-one million dollars. Meanwhile, my financial straits were becoming so difficult that I would soon move back in with Ed and Barbara Singleton.

"Sixty-one million?" Ed would shake his head. "Hardly seems worth it."

When I first heard the figure I thought it was a princely sum. But when Ed made his remark, it dawned on me that what Motown entailed to me would be nonnegotiable. The sweat and tears, the collective efforts of a family, of everyone whose name began this incredible story. The essence of Motown, its music and its soul, could not have been purchased for a million times what the price tag had been.

And when, later that year, Mr. Postman brought me another delivery, I opened the package with wild anticipation. It was a plaque from Motown with a gold record on it and an inscription to me for my contribution. I looked at it with tears of pride and monstrous pangs of disappointment. Thirty years to the day after I'd met Berry Gordy, I received a plaque. Wow, I wondered, what would happen when Jobete, valued somewhere between a hundred fifty and two hundred million dollars, was sold?

The plaque arrived a few days after Sherrick had simply quit the race and I'd left the side of his hospital bed for the last time. That plaque, that defeat, those tears of pride and disappointment all at the same time, did the most miraculous thing to me. It put me on the other side—I was finally lifted up and over and plunked onto solid ground. I declared myself a winner of a very arduous race and went to that steamer trunk to remove the pages that I'd begun eight years earlier. If the mail wasn't going to bring me what I wanted, I would have to finish writing my own letter. Almost a year later, someone asked when it was that I had stopped going to the mailbox. "I haven't yet," I replied, looking up from the pages I was still writing. "When I do, I'll let you know."

Certain events had come to pass that made telling this story a little easier. In the early eighties a long-running and hugely successful Broadway show, *Dreamgirls*, opened. A thinly disguised history of the Supremes, the musical exposed the tragedy of Florence Ballard and for the first time presented a mixed picture of Berry Gordy, shedding a dimmer light on him than those of the brilliant spots previously reflected. Diana Ross refused to see the show, but Mary Wilson was so moved by it that she wrote her book, *Dreamgirl: My Life as a Supreme*, which gave the facts behind the fictionalized story.

Facts are powerful things. So are feelings, and so are friends and family. I will conclude with some thoughts on all four.

The devastation of my exile from Motown was so powerful that I had never been able to talk about what happened between Berry and myself with any of my old friends or my family. I know others were traumatized as well. Look at Janie Bradford, whose stay of twenty years at Motown was longer than most. The incredible lyricist, the outrageous and rowdy-mouthed woman whose sassy sentiments helped to write "Money," whose creativity had coined line after line—including the title to the song "Love Don't Live Here Anymore"—Janie Bradford now lived outside the house of Motown. Due to a misunderstanding, she'd been released without a pension. As we had never discussed how we each felt about our ending chapters, I picked up the phone and gave her a call.

I found that her sentiments mirrored mine, "It's a feeling of being so distraught," Janie said, "of seeing Motown as a place that I should have always been able to go to—that it was my home and I felt it always would be my home. I never felt that the door would close on me."

She told me about a party, some kind of Motown affair. "When I got there, there was a girl at the door who saw me—she didn't know me, of course—and she put her hand up and blocked the door, and she said that nobody who wasn't a part of the company could come in. And, well . . . you know me . . . I told that bitch, 'You don't know who I am, I'm Janie Bradford. I wrote

"Money" with Berry Gordy, which put Motown on the map, and if it weren't for me your ass wouldn't even be here.' Ray, I went through the whole schpiel!"

Janie and I shared other feelings—an optimism for ourselves, a faith that Motown was still home. Quite active in the industry, Janie owned and managed an exciting, new show-biz publication that she'd launched, the *Entertainment Connection*. I had a sneaking suspicion that she, too, made trips now and then to her mailbox.

Before "Money" there had been "Come to Me" by Marv Johnson. He was another friend with whom I'd maintained contact over time. I called and his words were these: "I'm concerned that my children know about my contribution. I want people to know that I was there. I don't care what the great philosophers try to say about the Motown story, about Berry's genius and all that. It was all of us together, the chemistry we had, that made us special. And we all did a lot of hard work to get to the point where we had a little bit of *money*."

Somehow money had become the inextricable, destructive theme meshed in with those more glorious phrases—the dreams of a small black-owned and -operated company to stake out a claim in the world of music. There is no denying that the early Motown contracts betrayed some of the trust that the naive artists put in someone they saw as their father. It is my belief, however, that this wasn't done intentionally at the beginning. It was done out of our ignorance of the business, really mine and Berry's. The original contracts were just standard form contracts that we followed accordingly. I felt much remorse for the days when I insisted people just sign the contracts without even reading them—as demonstrations of their confidence and faith. By the time I saw the error of those ways, the attorneys and accountants had come in with a level of sophistication that was often at the expense of the artists.

One more friend who I contacted was Beans Bowles, the baritone sax and flute player whose music was an essential ingredient of the Motown sound. His feelings were these: "I think we all believed Motown was something that everyone would share in, so that everyone would have some kind of money. We were absolutely faithful in the beginning. There was nothing that we wouldn't do in the name of Motown. Up until the moment we found ourselves outside, we believed Berry would come through with some kind of profit sharing."

Well, some rewards had been reaped by others—businessmen, lawyers, and accountants, most of them white men. It could be suggested that the head of one of the most successful black companies in history suffered from a black inferiority complex. This was a man who loved to sit down with a dictionary and come up with words he could use to deny the insecurities. Part of this was due to Berry's lack of formal education and his tendency to measure worth by the standards of an educated white-skinned, white-collared corporate world. And he valued other things—a fast-talker, a slick tongue with a knack for abuse, a fox fast on his feet, a calculating mind.

Motown was all black in the beginning, very humbly black. And when Beans Bowles described Berry as having turned his back on the black people, as having betrayed that part of Motown's soul, the comment resonated with the feelings of many other family members.

There were exceptions, of course, most importantly Smokey Robinson. Unique in the pantheon of Motown artists, in his talent and stature, he was likewise unique in his bank account. His situation, however, didn't represent the realities of the countless artists whose loyalties were just as strong and whose ultimate fates found them embattled in endless lawsuits against Motown.

I have talked of witnesses. And more than anyone other than Berry, Smokey had been one. At every peak and valley, he was there. I also had firsthand knowledge of his ups and downs. After those talks in New York, in the early sixties, we had no other opportunities to speak candidly. In our eyes there was always a recognition of that infinite ocean—the triumphs and the heartbreaks—but there was nothing to say. Our last talk took place at my Super Three office. I'd been on the phone and had turned to see him coming in the door. Time was suddenly shifted and all those images of him came rushing back from the past. He smiled that smile I knew so well and waited for me to finish.

As I placed the phone down, I heard Smokey say, "Ray, you look great."

"Thank you," I said, and then waited, studying him.

After a pause, he spoke up. "You know, nothing has changed." Again our eyes flickered with mutual recognition as he repeated, "Nothing has *ever* changed."

"I know," I said then, regretting every word that hadn't been spoken, as well as all the many things that had indeed changed.

There is another, smaller tale within this larger one, which includes many of our main characters, as well as some new ones.

Ian Levine, a kid born in Blackpool, England, in 1953, grew up addicted to Motown, so crazed that by the time he was twelve years old he set out to collect every single Motown record ever released. In 1968, flying with his parents from New York to L.A., he noticed that the guy next to him had an open briefcase full of Motown paraphernalia. The guy turned out to be none other than Mickey Stevenson, and waiting for him at the airport was Mickey's wife, Kim Weston. The two were so impressed with this avid fan that they took him out for the day. A dream came true for young Ian Levine that day.

Ian grew up to be a record producer in England, scoring a smash success with Miguel Brown's "So Many Men, So Little Time," which was number one all over the world. But all along, his deepest ambition had been to work with all the old Motown artists, so he started to pursue introductions like a maniac. Through his agent, Henry Sellers, the opportunity came up to do something with another of Sellers's acts—Kim Weston. Ian practically leapt through the telephone.

After Kim, Ian began meeting others in England—Marv Johnson, the Velvelettes, Jimmy Ruffin, Mary Wells, and Mary Wilson, who was there promoting her book. Ian wrote and recorded a song with Mary called "Don't Get Mad, Get Even." Next, Ian got Brenda Holloway's phone number from Mary, and one contact led to another. He soon launched his own label, Nightmare Records, named after one of the few records released by the Andantes, "(Like a) Nightmare." Soon he reconnected with a fellow in L.A. named Rick Gionatos, another producer/engineer with much experience and similar musical tastes. The two made it their mission to hunt down and record some of the wealth of talent that had, for the most part, been neglected by Motown after the early years.

So, after a bit, it was decided to schedule a recording session in Detroit. Ian wanted to rerecord "Heaven Must Have Sent You" with the Elgins, the original recorders of the song. Rick was all set to go to Detroit to handle the one record, when all of a sudden the project mushroomed. Marv Johnson decided to come in, Kim Weston, the Velvelettes. Everyone had everyone else's phone numbers. Someone said, "Oh, how would you feel if Earl Van Dyke came?" "Earl Van Dyke!" What made it perfect was that most of the original musicians were still in Detroit. The two producers were in seventh heaven—from a simple recording session to a crusade. By the time they arrived in Detroit they had prepared twenty-nine tracks to be sung by nineteen acts. But, as it turned out, there was even more to come.

One of the artists that Ian and Rick most wanted to find and record in L.A. was Barbara Randolph. By phone, Rick started badgering Janie Bradford for phone numbers. He was unsuccessful. He finally got to meet Janie at a Christmas party given by Pete Moore of the Miracles, and they hit it off. Janie coughed up the numbers—including Barbara's. At Barbara's house, Rick was introduced to her husband, Ed Singleton. Excited by the Nightmare project, Ed suggested making it even bigger—every ex-Motown artist available, a worldwide Motortown Revue, the resurrection of the Hitsville sound—the sky's the limit. Ed mentioned that his ex-wife Ray would be just the person to spearhead the invasion.

Rick scratched his head. "Ray Singleton? Where do I know that name?" Then he remembered—the writing credit on an obscure Four Tops song called "Don't Bring Back Memories." It was the same beautiful song Rick had discovered in his New York DJ days and reintroduced to his other DJ pals, making it a dancefloor hit all over town. "That's one of my favorite songs! Your ex-wife wrote that?"

"Yeah, well . . ." Ed explained the story of the song—how he himself had written it but how he had asked me to take the credit back in the war days at the Donovan Building. That led to further details and then to my story. As Ed elaborated—and he is a great yarn-weaver—Rick's jaw dropped lower and lower.

The next thing I knew I was on a plane bound for Detroit.

Thinking back, I know I'll never forget that day. I approached Hitsville driving Dobbs's 1988 Marquis. It was Tuesday, March 14, 1989. Three decades had passed since the day that I'd driven this stretch of West Grand Boulevard and discovered the house with the seductive bay window, which is now a museum—run by Berry's sister, Esther Edwards. From the car I could see a gathering of people getting ready for a reunion photo shoot, but I couldn't make out any faces or familiar stances. My heart was in my mouth while I drove around looking for a parking space.

Finally, three blocks away, I parked and began the long walk home. After all the years of running and running to get home, it seemed that now my steps were almost tentative, as though something inside me didn't want to go back to the past, didn't want to face the remnants of the dream. What if it had been only some sort of illusion, a mirage? Drawing closer to Hitsville, the filmy cloud of faces suggested as much. There was a CBS News truck on the street, and camera crews were set up on the lawn. Come on, Ray, I told myself, you've run enough miles in your life. And suddenly I wanted to drop my bag and run for it, and at just that moment I saw a blur running toward me—"Miss Ray!"

I blinked at the blur and saw that it was Louvain Demps of the Andantes. My first Rayber customer. "Hey," I said, "you never paid me for that last demo. You owe me money."

"You're lying! I paid you all your money!" gushed Louvain. She looked wonderful, and we strolled, arm in arm, laughing, to the front walk. All at once the concrete under my feet turned magically into a red carpet. My name was ringing up and down the sides of it. Marv Johnson was standing close by, smiling. Sammy Ward rushed up to hug me. Bobby Rogers and Ronnie White of the Miracles were calling to me. Halfway up the steps, I turned to inhale the scene—everyone talking at once, laughing, and embracing. Off to the side, Martha Reeves was posing for a photographer and waving to well-wishers; finally she was out from the shadows and the biggest star at the gathering. The funny thing was that I'd heard she was planning to boycott the event; but here she was after all. Over the top of Hitsville was a big sign, WEL-COME MOTOWN ALUMNI, which Esther, who would see to it that the event ran smoothly for all the alumni, had arranged. Also there was Esther's assistant, Doris Holland, a faithful Motown veteran of twenty-eight years.

Standing amid the crowd was Maxine Powell, Motown's first Artist Development person, known for teaching poise and etiquette to young artists such as the Supremes back during the sixties. Maxine, looking as stunning as ever, was also the founder of a charm school and of one of the first black modeling agencies, which at one time had represented Gwen Gordy.

Suddenly, a microphone was put to my mouth, cameras were snapping and popping, questions coming at me right and left. "Uh, Miss Ray, right? OK, Ray Singleton. Uh, what do you think today's turnout means?"

I didn't know what it meant; all I knew was that it was great to be home. Now it was time to make some music.

From the day's impromptu group sing of "The Way You Do

the Things You Do," which was instigated and led by Martha Reeves—much to everyone's surprise—to the climax at 3:30 on Sunday morning, when Levi Stubbs walked in to do the lead on "I Can't Help Myself," it was a dream made real. Rick and Ian were stupendous in the studio, and I, of course, fell easily into my old roles. "Ian, that key is too high for Sammy Ward. Let him come up with a melody that suits him. Come on, Sammy, let's do it. And, oh, can we change the background vocals on this one. . .?"

Going from friend to friend and getting caught up with each one was a book unto itself. Joe Hunter, Mr. Piano Man, with his wide smile, would never leave Detroit, he swore. "It's where I was born and where I'm going to die." And he also said, "All the cats talk about you all the time. There wouldn't have been no Motown without Miss Ray. You did as much for the company as Berry did."

And then there was Crathman Spencer—my boyfriend before Berry and one of the Originals. "When I saw you walking up," he said, "I couldn't believe it. Your being here made it all complete for me." Seeing Crathman made time stand still.

Beans Bowles was another high point of the homecoming. Like most of the guys, Beans was still active, leading or performing in several bands, including one composed of some of the Hitsville musicians and called the Unsung Heroes. The list of talented names on hand was endless—Ivy Jo Hunter, Popcorn Wylie, Dave Hamilton, Choker Campbell, Earl Van Dyke, Clay McMurray, Joe Stubbs, the Elgins, Michael Valvano, Motown's first white recording artist, and more. Sylvia Moy, one of the best and most unsung of the Motown writers, was there with a song she'd composed for one of the sessions. When she recorded it herself, she at long last was finally able to take advantage of her artist's contract.

The most poignant event of the week was the arrival and eventual recording of Wanda Rogers, one of the Marvelettes. Originally Wanda Young, she had sung lead vocal on many songs such as "Don't Mess with Bill" and "My Baby Must Be a Magician," as well as backed Gladys Horton, who usually carried lead, in their first hit, "Please Mr. Postman." Wanda, a pretty, brown-skinned girl with a sweet, soft-spoken personality—much like her singing voice—had married Bobby Rogers of the Miracles, and they had two children. For a while, with both groups among the most popular in the country and with a great marriage and children, Wanda was on top of the world. In the course of events, the Marvelettes fell by the wayside as did everyone else during the Diana

Ross ascent, and the girls were dropped. Bobby was still out touring with the Miracles, and Wanda tried bravely to substitute the life
of a homemaker for the fabulous acclaim and creative fulfillment
she'd known only a few years before.

The story we'd all heard was that one day when Bobby was on
the road, Wanda went to visit her sister, whom she loved dearly.
The two decided to go out shopping and Wanda's sister, just for a
lark, put on a wig that a friend of hers had left behind. In a
horrifying twist of fate, that friend's jilted boyfriend, who had
recently escaped from a mental institution, was waiting across the
street, certain that his ex-lover was in the house and determined to
kill her. When Wanda and her sister emerged, the jilted boyfriend
shot Wanda's sister in the head. She died in Wanda's arms.

And Wanda's spirit collapsed. Bobby began coming back from
the road to find her falling apart, and soon the marriage was in
trouble. Then, several months after her sister died, Wanda's brother
was injured in a near-fatal shooting. He was left an invalid.

Wanda's condition deteriorated rapidly, all her rage turning
on Bobby. When a divorce followed, Bobby was given custody of
the children. Despite all of her friends' efforts to help, Wanda took
her slide all the way down. From the sad reports I'd last heard, she
was a bag lady, a helpless drunk.

Through his tenacity, Ian had reached Wanda to ask her to do
the project. Overcome with emotion, she'd accepted the offer in a
flood of tears. Everyone had warned Ian about her condition but
he'd insisted, "I know I can get a vocal out of her. I know I can."
When she showed up to the dinner he threw a night before the
reunion, everyone was even more shocked. Wanda was a decrepit
mess. Ian was hysterical—how could anyone in her debilitated state
even think about performing?

That night Kim Weston took her in, and in the morning
Wanda was transformed. I was on the porch when I saw the two of
them walking down the street, arm in arm. Kim had dressed
Wanda in a beautiful red suit with a little red straw hat and a veil.
"Oh, Ray," Wanda said softly as they got to the steps, her hand
reaching for mine. She leaned on me slightly. "I'm so happy you're
here. Have you seen my babies?" Wanda hadn't seen them for some
time. Close up I could see the signs of the damage, even through
the veil and the heavy makeup that Kim had applied. What little
hair showed was all white and a few teeth were missing. Yet, after
everyone saying she'd never make it, here she was.

On the night before Wanda's session, Kim, whose heart was made of gold, rehearsed and coached Wanda for hours. But until we started working, we really had no idea how she was going to perform and whether we would be able to get a vocal from her. Ian asked nervously, "Are you ready to sing now?" Kim looked over at Wanda saying, "Well, she's been working on it." And Wanda raised herself up proudly. "I'm ready," she said. Hearing her warm up, we were somewhat encouraged, but when she opened her mouth and started to sing, we almost died. The sound that came out was the Marvelettes. Ian was ready to do handstands, "Oh, God, if I can just get this a line at a time, we can do it." And we pieced Wanda's vocal together like that, phrase by phrase.

I stood there with Wanda, saying "Hey, mama, you're doing it," rooting her on—and seeing that the accomplishment was staggering even to her. When we finished, we all gathered in the control room with Wanda and listened to the playback. She was absolutely astounded. "I did it! I did it!" "You were wonderful," we said to her. "It's the Marvelettes all over again."

"No," Wanda said, "it's the Miraclettes." After that, she sat silently in reflection. Many of us were in tears.

There were obviously many skeletons in the closet, but I tried not to open those doors; nor did anyone linger on bitter notes. Berry, with whom I was no longer in touch, was not on hand, yet he did succeed in making his presence known by sending someone to watch over the proceedings. When that person strolled up, I said to my son, "Kerry? What are you doing here?" With his wife, Karen, taking notes, reminding me of me, Kerry had been flown in to Detroit on official business of the Gordy Company, Berry's newly formed music and film entity, for whom Kerry was employed—as president. Kerry told me with a twinkle and, yes, believe it or not, a recently acquired gesture of rolling his tongue in his cheek, "I'm here to snoop." I guess Smokey was right, at least in this regard, that some things never change. And soon Kerry was hitting it off big-time with Rick and Ian, fully supportive of their great project.

For me it was a completion of so many stories, a culmination of so many years rolled into one glorious and thrilling week. And if nothing else came of the projects, the reunion meant enough in and of itself.

But there was yet so much more to come. The possibilities that sprang from that week and Nightmare Records were limitless. I'd even heard that Robert Bateman was working with Mary Wells, and who knew what opportunities lay in store there. Whole careers could be launched again and in new ways. My old friend Mabel John, for instance, was going to get another shot in the studio. In the meantime she'd done well for herself—owning a publishing company that had produced several hits, managing the careers of Little Willie John's two boys, and working in the ministry. "And look at these," she said, holding up some old photographs taken at a BMI dinner in New York in the early sixties. One was of Mabel, Jackie Wilson, and myself. The other was of the two of us and Berry. "Look at that," Mabel said. "That's how I always pictured Motown in the end, the three of us together."

Fueled by this great renewal of energy and interest, the lead singer of the Marvelettes, Gladys Horton, would soon be putting together her comeback, with extensive concerts and television coverage.

By the spring of 1989, Ian had a total of two hundred tracks, with more in the works. The latest reading of Nightmare's roster was quite impressive: the Andantes, Johnny Bristol, Rose Banks, G. C. Cameron, Choker Campbell, Caston and Majors, Chris Clark, the Contours, Carolyn Crawford, Dennis Edwards, the Elgins, the Fantastic Four, Yvonne Fair, the Fifth Dimension, Frankie Gale, Freddie Gorman, Brenda Holloway, Ivy Jo Hunter, Chuck Jackson, Mabel John, Marv Johnson, Eddie Kendricks, Hattie Littles, the Marvelettes, Ronnie McNeir, the Miracles, Sylvia Moy, the Originals, Gino Parks, Scherrie Payne, Barbara Randolph, Rare Earth, the Rayber Voices, Martha Reeves, Claudette Robinson, David Ruffin, Jimmy Ruffin, Sisters Love, C. P. Spencer, Edwin Starr, Barrett Strong, Joe Stubbs, a late-edition Supremes, Syreeta, Bobby Taylor and the Vancouvers, R. Dean Taylor, Jean Terrell, Undisputed Truth, the Valadiers, Earl Van Dyke, the Vandellas, Tata Vega, the Velvelettes, Junior Walker and the All-Stars, Sammy Ward, Mary Wells, Kim Weston, Blinky Williams, Frank Wilson, Mary Wilson, and Richard "Popcorn" Wylie. Just the thought of reaching all these people, let alone getting them all into the studio, was mind-boggling.

For someone very special, who was at the helm during that week and involved in proposing a "Second Wind" tour, some even more exciting news emerged in late '89. A gold mine was finally struck for forty-year music-business veteran Ed Singleton when it was announced that he would executive-produce the concert "Rap-mania," which would mark the fifteenth anniversary of rap music. It was to be broadcast simultaneously from the Apollo Theater in New York and the Hollywood Palace in Los Angeles on March 9, 1990, with acts that included Tone-Lōc, Kurtis Blow, Run-D.M.C., Kool Moe Dee, Ice-T, Big Daddy Kane, Biz Markie, the Sugarhill Gang, Nefertiti, Afrika Bambatta, and many more. The concert would be taped live for pay-per-view television. Ed's ship had finally come in.

There was another family I got a chance to visit that week. I sat down at Mama's dinner table, and what do you know—everybody started in on me about what I wanted to do when I grew up.

After dinner I came up with an idea to divert them. I piped up, "Hey Tommy, how 'bout one of your famous ghost stories?" As he began, I looked around at my family, hearing the strains of that first music I'd ever heard—his dramatic renderings, our laughter and squeals—and I felt a pride as big as Lake Michigan for all of them. Donald Tommy Ossman, an army veteran, was now retired from thirty years of service with Cadillac Motors. A planner, he'd built a secure and happy life for himself and his wife. And beautiful Juanita Dickerson, always there with shelter and a shoulder, had worked twenty-five years as a nurse at Detroit Grace Community Hospital, and also as an outpatient diagnostic technician and community-relations delegate.

Roslyn Murray, still as shapely and stunning as ever, was now the CEO, as well as the president, owner, and founder, of the very successful Michigan Institute for Child Development. Roslyn also knew what it was to build a dream. And Kathy Bradfield, yet another gorgeous sis, had retired after thirty-eight years of employment in the Detroit public school system. Kathy was also involved in all sorts of cultural activities, including volunteering at the Afro-American Museum.

And Ines Warren, with that subtle, ever-present smile and pretty face, was a principal at the northwest campus of the Michigan Institute. Last but not least, I looked at the youngest of us all, Alice Wilson, remembering our inseparable days when I was that wild, crazy big sister dragging her cute, adorable younger sister into one misadventure after the next. It seemed, however, as though she'd survived my influences. Now she was fabulous-looking—just as ladylike and refined as I always thought she would be. After

graduating from Wayne State University, with a degree as an
educational specialist in administration, she'd gone on to work as
a principal at the main campus of the Michigan Institute, and also
as a reading specialist with the Detroit public school system.

As Tommy's tale came to an end, I could not help but feel a
wash of sorrow at the absence of Mike—the brother I'd kicked
under the table every night and with whom I'd winked in conspir-
acy over everything. I could not lose the regret that he wasn't out
there galloping on some great Jobete horse or that he wasn't on
hand to give me his advice. Nor could I completely get over a
sadness that I hadn't been able to afford to give my parents more,
back when Daddy was alive, and even now when Mama was in her
eighties.

Mike was probably the one person in my family I'd ever told
about going to the mailbox every day, and he'd never questioned it.
In fact, he reminded me of what he'd seen so long ago in our
youth: "Follow your heart. That's all you can do."

In my heart were all the contradictions of more than half a life
with and without Berry Gordy. All contrasting emotions lived
inside of me like a home divided. The love that led me to give all
and the agony of not having that love returned. The gratitude that
I was part of such a profound story and the resentment that it had
been taken from me. My pride in what Motown became and the
humiliation of being given no place in its heritage. It was hard to
know which part of my heart to follow.

Such were my feelings back on a day in May of 1987. This day
stands apart from the other days that had preceded it or that have
followed. And on this day, the wedding day of Kerry Gordy and
Karen Longley, there came a remarkable discovery.

While working at Motown as an assistant to Suzanne DePasse,
Karen had looked up to see Kerry staring at her. A petite, beautiful, and well-bred young creature, she saw that Kerry was quite
smitten. And Kerry noticed that in her green, sparkling eyes,
almost identical to his, there was a great deal of interest.

This was no quick dash to a justice of the peace, like my do-
it-in-a-day marriages. This was a wedding where no expense or
pomp had been spared. The church, decorated spectacularly in
white and off-white, looked like a florist's paradise. When the bride
was ready to walk down the aisle trumpets from both sides of the
balcony played a fanfare for the new Mrs. Gordy.

My day had started many hours earlier. I was determined to look my absolute best, both in honor of my son and in memory of his father, who, though quite alive, I had not seen for a long while. And though I was to see him once or twice following the wedding, this encounter would prove to be our last real connection ever. In preparing to go to the church, I couldn't help but think about the other Berry Gordy offspring. First in the dynastic line, mothered by Thelma Coleman, were Hazel Joy, Berry IV, and Terry. I couldn't believe that it was now twelve years since Terry's marriage to his childhood sweetheart, Desiree. The two married after their graduation from San Diego State—Terry with a degree in accounting and Desiree with one in law—and they both have worked in administration at Motown since then.

After Kerry was born to Berry and me, there was Kennedy, the son of Margaret. Nancy Leiviska, the cute, fun-loving blond who was Berry's girlfriend after Chris Clark, bore a Gordy child in 1976—the now thirteen-year-old Stefan Gordy, whom Berry continues to claim will be the last of his direct lineage. And years after her daughter Rhonda was born, Diana Ross confirmed to Berry that this daughter had been fathered by him.

As always, these thoughts conjured up an overwhelming assortment of mixed feelings. I recalled the early scenes from my life with Berry, when our two families were joined as one, and when I felt so assuredly that no woman but myself could offer him the perfect qualities that so matched his better traits—my passion for music and my strong feeling for family. A lump caught in my throat as I heard the echo of Smokey's statement that nothing has changed. Everything was always changing.

This was confirmed as I entered the church and headed back to the ladies' lounge. I spotted Grace, Berry's current girlfriend. A lovely woman of Japanese-American descent, Grace had an enviable head of ebony hair that reached to her ankles. In her twenties, she was young to take such a prominent place beside a man like Berry, but she seemed to be holding her own—learning to play tennis and backgammon and other pursuits for Berry.

In the small lounge where the ladies were keeping themselves fresh before being called by the photographer, I looked at myself in the mirror. Despite the whirlwind of emotion, I had certainly risen to the occasion, if I didn't say so myself. In my reflection, I saw a soft, flowing, feminine vision in peach chiffon. The dress was a Grecian floor-length gown, cut very low, with peach-colored pearl buttons up the sleeve, peach shoes, and shimmering, peach stockings. My hair and makeup were just perfect. I glanced out the window to the atrium where I saw Berry, handsome and elegant in his black tuxedo, standing alone with his thoughts.

Quickly, I ducked away from the window, not ready for him to see me yet. The makeup artist and hairstylist working with the girls sighed when I asked for just a few more touches. A nip or two of blush, a dab of powder, and a touch of gold to my lips. The mother of the groom was the last to be called out to join the rest of the bridal party. I paused before taking a step and gazed ahead of me. There were Cliff, Kennedy, Chico Ross, Benny Medina, John West—the musical director for the ceremony—and the groom. Then, of course, there was the bride in her exquisite, ivory satin Cinderella gown, along with her bridesmaids in off-white satin. And mingling with the other gentlemen was the father of the groom. I took in a mighty breath and opened the door to the atrium.

At the sight of me gliding into the room, Berry's eyes were wide with awe. I floated over to where the photographer needed me to stand, and when the shots were completed, I turned to find myself looking into those eyes. We were face to face after three decades.

"Hey, little girl." He cocked his head, and rolled that tongue in his cheek. "You want a piece of candy?"

"No," I said, "I don't take candy from dirty old men." After all that had passed, these were the love lyrics we sang.

And then I heard a serenade he had never before sung: "You look incredible."

Following the ceremony, we found ourselves sitting on a wooden bench during the lengthy portrait-taking session. He was attentive and affectionate, and all at once, almost as in a dream, we were as comfortable with one another as if we were an old married couple. Holding hands. Laughing and remembering. Karen's mother, Mrs. Longley, exclaimed, "God, you guys look really great together. You make a great couple."

And then Berry said an extraordinary thing: "Yeah, if she looked like this years ago, I wouldn't have left when she put me out."

I "put him out." That is how Berry has rewritten the history, and how he admits to having lost someone precious. Herein lies the secret that had once served as the ammunition for war. It has to do with memory. Mine is long and clear. Berry's is not. As long as I held on to that memory of who he was, of what exactly had happened in our epics together, he would always have the need to love me and he would always have the power to punish me. And now, more than two years since Kerry's wedding day, as I prepared to lay down my pen, the "Why?" that I'd hollered out into the void echoed back to me. It is finally answered. As long as he has his greed and as long as I have my pride—my inability to beg—and as long as I have memory, we will be necessary opponents, till death do us part. In love and at war.

Over the years Berry has said to me that "when we're ninety years old we'll be together." He has said that I am the greatest mother who has ever lived. He has said, with a degree of self-awareness, "I gained the world but lost my soul." In these phrases are acknowledgments of my importance to him. But these words can't appease the heartbreak of hearing that he would always take care of me but not finding him there when I needed him. In the end, he remains the thief of dreams.

This brings to a close this love letter to everyone who has played such vital roles in my life. To my family and to my Motown family. To Ed, and the final triumphant last reel of a richly deserved success, and to Barbara and Daren. It is especially a love letter to my children. To Cliff and Marchella Liles, supporting themselves in business and television production, respectively, as well as pursuing an inevitable victory with a joint recording project. To Kerry, who is now the president of the K. G. Entertainment Group, which includes his new, futuristic record label, SONG Records (Sound of a New Generation). And to his wife, Karen, vice-president of the organization, who assists Kerry at work, at home, and at every step of the way. To Eddie Singleton, Jr., who is on staff at Warner Brothers Records, working for Benny Medina, vice-president of black product, and to Eddie's dream and capability to become president of the company. To Rya Singleton, college student, actress, singer/songwriter, musician currently being co-produced by computer whiz and musical genius Michael Rochelle with assistance from Los Angeles attorney Raymond C. Reed. Rya is the first female artist to sign with SONG Records. And to the celebration of stardom that awaits a young woman of her extraordinary talents.

These stories are also dedicated to all women who strive for achievement, whatever their fields of endeavor, to everyone who dares to dream dreams, to mothers and fathers who encourage their children to dare. To the joyous existence of music in the world. To the proud and the determined and to every person who has ever loved an undying love and who still believes in the world-wide postal service.

To God and to myself.

P.S. This book, of course, is a long love letter to Berry. But once mailed, it is finally time for me to stop going to the mailbox. See, I don't live at the same place anymore; I've moved on to adventures ahead. And on the envelope that I've mailed, I've written no return address.

AFTERWORD

In writing *Berry, Me, and Motown*, one of the many victories achieved by Raynoma Gordy Singleton was getting an answer to her question, "Can I get a witness?" From several of the leading characters in the Motown story Ray received a resounding yes, and through their contributions of information, interviews, memories, and moral support, she was able to name them—the witnesses who appear on these pages. There were other Motown family members, although unable to endorse her book officially, who sent caring words of encouragement for a story so many wanted told.

By late autumn of 1989, Ray had not seen Berry for almost two years. Seven months earlier, as she was completing her manuscript, she received a series of messages on her answering machine left by either Berry or members of his staff. The messages were left, ostensibly, in Berry's hopes that Ray would assist him in writing his book on Motown. Whether or not this was the case, readers will never know. Ray never returned the phone calls.

UNSUNG HEROES

In life there are many unsung heroes. In addition to those already mentioned in the book, I would like to thank the following creative people:

West Coast musicians:

Keyboards and synthesizer programmers: Greg Philinganes, Joe Sample, Sonny Burke, Russell Ferrante, Eddie "Gip" Noble, John Bokowski, Kevin Bassinson, Richard Rittenberg, Ralph Hawkins, Raymond Crossley, John Duarte, Mike Rochelle, Mike Boddicker, Dave Ervin, John Barnes, William Bryant, Laythan Armour, Dean Gant, Ronnie Foster, Isaiah Sanders, John Hobbs, Leonard Caston, and John West.

    Guitars: Wah-Wah Watson, Paul Jackson, David T. Walker, Charles Ferring, Marv Tarplin, Ray Parker, Jr., George Johnson, Benjamin Bridges, Robben Lee Ford, Carlos Rios, Fred Tackett, T. J. Parker, Ira Ingber, Jeff Silverman, Dan Huff, and W. Dean Parks.

    Bass: Freddie Washington, Nathan East, Louis Johnson, James Jamerson, Jr., Chuck Rainey, Neil Stubenhaus, Carl Sealove, David Cochrane, Nathan Watts, Kenneth Wild, Michael Dunlop, Cliff Liles, Mike Rochelle, Kenny Burke, Tom Hawkins, Joe Chemay, Eddie Watkins, and Gerald Albright (bass and saxophone).

    Drums: James Gadson, Ed Green, Paul Humphrey, Ollie E. Brown, Ricky Lawson, John F. Robinson, Harvey Mason, Leon "Indugo" Chancler, Eddie Watkins, Bobby Forte, Dennis Davis, Carmen Rizzo, Jr., and Michael White.

Percussion: Paulinho DaCosta, King Erickson, Nate Hughes, Everett Bryson, Richard Heath, Bobby Hall, and Eddie "Bongo" Brown.

And thanks to all the great horn and string players.

Background vocalists:

The Rayber Voices, the Andantes, the Love Tones, the Blackberries, Maxine, Oren, and Julia Waters, Merry Clayton, Shirley Matthews, Mona Lisa Young, Terry Young, Oma Drake, Lindy White, Terry De Sario, Mary Lee Whitney Evans, Susaye Greene Brown, Alexandra Brown Evans, Shirley Brewer, Isaiah Sanders, Charlie Collins, Marva King, Pat Henley, and Ivory Stone.

Motown arrangers:

Paul Riser, Gene Page, Wade Marcus, Dave Van de Pitt, James Carmichael, Dave Blumberg, Benjamin F. Wright, Jr., Bruce Miller, Freddie Perren, Dale Warren, Jack Goga, Johnny Allen, Hank Cosby, Gil Askey, Willie Shorter, Maurice King, Choker Campbell, Sonny Sanders, Johnny Pate, H. B. Barnum, Art Wright, Thomas "Beans" Bowles, Lonnie Levister, Willie Hutch, Sam Brown, and Marc Davis.

Recording and mastering engineers:

Lawrence T. Horn, Cal Harris, Art Stewart, Larry Miles, Russ Terrana, Steve Smith, Bob Robitaille, Glen Jordan, Fred Ross, Jane Clark, Tom Flye, Barney Perkins, Reggie Dozier, Bobby Brooks, Fred Law, F. Bryon Clark, Tom Perry, Jack Rouben, Wiley Thompson, Gary Olazabal, Bob Margouless, Malcom Cecil, John Fischbach, Jeremy Smith, Tony Peluso, Brain Holland, Robert Bateman, Phil Walters, Steve McMillan, Ralph Sutton, Kevin Serrells, Michael Johnson, Karen Siegel, Mike Lizzio, Jack Andrews, John Matousek, Ed Barton, Mike Dotson, Tony Atore, Dave Braithwaite, and Tommy Gordy.

Art directors:

Norman Ung, Stewart Daniels, Johnny Lee, and Kav DeLuxe.

And, finally, thanks to all the great DJs all over the world.

INDEX